*Caribbean Crusaders
and the Harlem Renaissance*

Caribbean Crusaders and the Harlem Renaissance

JOYCE MOORE TURNER

with the assistance of W. Burghardt Turner

Introduction by Franklin W. Knight

University of Illinois Press
URBANA AND CHICAGO

"Pushkin" courtesy of the Literary Representative for the Works of Claude McKay, Schomburg Center for Research in Black Culture, the New York Public Library, Astor, Lenox and Tilden Foundations.

©2005 by Joyce Moore Turner and W. Burghardt Turner
All rights reserved
Manufactured in the United States of America

∞ This book is printed on acid-free paper.

1 2 3 4 5 C P 5 4 3 2 1

Library of Congress Cataloging-in-Publication Data

Turner, Joyce Moore, 1920–
Caribbean crusaders and the Harlem Renaissance / Joyce Moore Turner with the assistance of W. Burghardt Turner ; introduction by Franklin W. Knight.
  p. cm.
Includes bibliographical references (p.) and index.
ISBN 0-252-02996-8 (cloth : alk. paper)
ISBN 0-252-07241-3 (pbk. : alk. paper)
1. American literature—Caribbean American authors—History and criticism.
2. American literature—New York (State)—New York—History and criticism.
3. Caribbean Americans—New York (State)—New York—History—20th century.
4. American literature—20th century—History and criticism.
5. Harlem (New York, N.Y.)—Intellectual life—20th century.
6. Caribbean Americans—Intellectual life. 7. Immigrants in literature.
8. Ethnicity in literature. 9. Harlem Renaissance. 10. Race in literature.
I. Turner, W. Burghardt, 1915– II. Title.
PS153.C27T87   2005
810.9'9729—dc22   2005002623

Pushkin
CLAUDE MCKAY

In Moscow, in the old Strastnaia* Square,
I wondered at a frizzly mat of hair,
Gazing upon the image of the man
In whom a nation's flowering began.
The very greatest Russian of his race,
I saw the Negro plainly in his face.

Oh we who rise warm-throated to proclaim,
From pride of race our joy of Pushkin's name!
Have we whose days are dolorous and dim,
Some light-creating thing to learn from him?
This blazing gift of life which we inherit,
Is it not the pure magic of his merit?
The flame white-glowing of that brain and hand
Whose cunning lifted up the Great Bear Land?

The dazzling beauty of that brief career
That scared the Church and made the Sceptre fear?

*Strastnaya. Claude McKay presented this unpublished poem to Richard B. Moore when Moore visited the poet in France after attending the 1927 League against Imperialism Congress in Brussels, Belgium. The autographed manuscript copy is now in the Richard B. Moore Library in Barbados.

The passion of his spirit formidable
That in a Christian world made him a rebel? . . .
Great Russia's Pushkin and the world's and ours.
Oh that his voice could wake our sleeping powers!

Life's a mad carnival for jaded men,
And we who watch it from our ghetto pen,
Yearning for joy, spontaneous, beautiful,
Our warm blood frozen by frost days and dull,
Might find in Pushkin's self some potent magic
To rouse us from our sombre sloth and tragic.
Some drug of Gods to lift us like a star
From this dispairing drift where numbed we are . . .
A man and poet! Fighting he lived and died . . .
Shall we with living death be satisfied?

Contents

Preface   *ix*

Introduction by Franklin W. Knight   *xiii*

List of Abbreviations   *xxi*

Prologue   *1*

1. The Caribbean Comes to Harlem   *3*
2. Uptown and Downtown   *27*
3. "If We Must Die"   *60*
4. Gift of the Tropics   *92*
5. The Radicals and the Renaissance   *123*
6. The Struggle Within   *154*
7. Harlem Goes to Moscow and Paris   *186*
8. Home to Amsterdam   *225*

Epilogue   *249*

Notes   *253*

Selected Bibliography   *273*

Index   *283*

Illustrations follow pages 96 and 224

Preface

It was during the publication of our book *Richard B. Moore, Caribbean Militant in Harlem* that my husband and I became friends with Hermina (Hermie) Dumont Huiswoud. As friends of my father, Richard B. Moore, she and her husband, Otto Huiswoud, had known me as a child but I had no memory of her or her husband despite the familiarity of the name. While conducting research we located her in Amsterdam and sought to visit her. Her initial response was not encouraging. She wrote, "If you insist you are welcome to 'drop' over," and disclaimed having information that we requested. The visit, however, was quickly transformed to a warm encounter when we met in Amsterdam in 1983.

A close relationship developed, and I visited her every year. Her reserve—and perhaps a trace of the caution practiced during the surveillance of her communist years—was apparent on the first visit when she cautioned us not to talk in the apartment and escorted us to Vondelpark. In 1949 she had begun a Dutch life when she joined Otto in Amsterdam. She had built a circle of Dutch and Surinamese friends, including students from Suriname who considered her and Otto their mentors. While she corresponded with former friends and visited a few, including Richard B. Moore on a rare visit to the States, her communist years were behind her and were rarely a topic of conversation. Our relationship was unique, for I was a tie to her past and she was a tie to mine. She felt free to talk about communist experiences with me in a way she dared not share with Dutch contemporaries or historians who sought information from her, but she refused to be interviewed on tape even by me except on her ninetieth birthday. She would say, "Just listen and remember!" When the Soviet Union collapsed she sent for me because she needed to share her grief at the passing of an era in which she and Otto had believed that the

USSR could be an example of a nation free of exploitation. The apparent demise of socialism, which she had embraced for sixty-five years, seemed to herald her own demise.

She was annoyed that Otto was seldom mentioned or inaccurately portrayed in accounts of the Communist Party of the United States, and she revealed her attempt to write a biography. When I pointed out some of the errors in her manuscript and offered to help she indicated collaboration would be possible only if I would spend at least a month in Amsterdam. Plans were never made for an extended stay, and her way of solving the problem was to give me her papers. We never discussed their disposition but we both knew they were intended to help "put the record straight."

Needless to say, this account is not Hermie's story. Only she could have written such a revelation. Her voice and insights have been entwined with documents from other sources in order to initiate a broader and more factually correct account than she might have managed with the few resources available to her. She is referred to in this account as "Hermie" to avoid the confusion with Otto Huiswoud and to lend the warm personal touch she actually represented amid the cold climate often prevalent in communist circles. While it was Otto who led the way to socialism, Hermie made a strong contribution to their personal and political lives. To understand the experiences they and their colleagues had in Harlem it was necessary to explore the motivation that initiated a militant stance on the part of these Caribbean émigrés in New York, their agenda against racism and colonialism and how they tried to implement it in radical political parties in Harlem, and how their journalism and oratory contributed to the Harlem Renaissance. While the Harlem Renaissance is usually associated with literary works, a political aspect fueled and accompanied the creative expressions of the period.

Otto Huiswoud left practically no papers. Hermie's papers are, therefore, the Hermina Dumont Huiswoud Papers, consisting of a few personal items related to Otto and a manuscript, "Negro Slave Revolts in Mexico," that Otto wrote in 1938. (The Hermina Huiswoud Papers will be available at the Tamiment Institute Library at New York University.) Those items were included with Hermie's writings about Otto, brief vignettes about women she had met, her correspondence with Langston Hughes, and her copies of *The Negro Worker*. It was necessary to cast a wide net in order to obtain evidence concerning the Huiswouds' backgrounds in Dutch and British Guiana and their lives and colleagues in New York, Moscow, Paris, and Amsterdam during the Harlem Renaissance.

My husband and I were fortunate to have the encouragement and assistance of a large number of scholars, librarians, and friends as the project turned into a global search for documents. The sharing of documents, ideas, and counsel by Winston James was invaluable. He, along with Robert A. Hill, Theodore Kornweibel Jr., and Mark Solomon, were particularly generous in sharing information critical to piecing together fragmentary evidence. They cannot be thanked enough for the valuable documents and encouragement they provided. We are indebted as well to Truong Buu Lam, Jeffrey B. Perry, and Akito Yamanouchi, who were kind enough to share information that added considerably to our understanding and research efforts. Arnold Rampersad, Floris Barnett Cash, Katherine Sibley, and Scott Taylor were also very helpful. The largest number of primary documents on which this study depends were obtained through the expert research by a Russian historian, Sergey Viktorovich Listikov, who conducted an extensive investigation of records in the Russian State Archive of Social and Political History (RGASPI). Through his assistance we gained access to information on the Communist Party of the United States and the Comintern and Profintern of the USSR that was recently made available to historians outside of Russia. Many of the records are now being acquired by the Library of Congress, but very few were available during the development of this project. We are also indebted to John Earl Haynes, a historian at the Library of Congress, who provided leads to Russian historians and special documents from the Russian State Archive. Without the wealth of assistance this account would not have been enriched and substantiated by so many essential primary sources.

While most of the records from the Russian State Archive were in English, a few of them and some other materials were not. We thank Ingeborg Bauer Knight, Lucia von Wersebe Stephens, Rosemarie Carnarius, Daphne Volle, Alan Yanofsky, Magda Bon Bruno, and Sergey Listikov for translations from German, French, Dutch, and Russian sources.

Research on the socialist, communist, and Harlem Renaissance movements relied heavily on assistance from archives in the United States and the Netherlands. We wish to thank the following individuals who were so responsive: Diana Lachatanere, Schomburg Center for Research and Black Culture; Peter Meyer Filardo, Tamiment Institute Library; Mieke Ijzermans, Internationaal Instituut voor Sociale Geschiedenis (the Netherlands); and Michael Knight, National Archives. Librarians at the New York Public Library, Bellport (New York) Public Library, Tucson (Arizona) Public Library, Frank Melville Jr. Memorial Library at the State University of New York at Stony Brook, the University of Arizona Library, and especially the special collections at Columbia University, Robert W. Woodruff Library at Emory University, and Beinecke Library at Yale University are all due many thanks.

The collection of materials, while fundamental, was just part of the process. Franklin W. Knight provided friendship, inspiration, encouragement, and mentoring that kept the project on track for three years. He read and commented on the manuscript several times and has contributed the introduction that places the Huiswouds and their colleagues historically in a global as well as local context of the African Diaspora. To him I remain eternally grateful. I am also very appreciative of the support by Joan Catapano, associate director and editor-in-chief of the University of Illinois Press, who guided the essential step of transforming the manuscript into a book, and Stephen Barnett, who reviewed the manuscript meticulously as copyeditor.

I would be remiss if I did not acknowledge and gratefully thank family members and friends who also contributed in different ways. Sons Mitchell B. Turner and Richard D. Turner served as editor–research assistant and computer technologist, respectively. Hermie's close friend Magda Bon Bruno was particularly helpful and supportive. Frost Cameron Turner, Ruud Beeldsnijder, Vivian Clark, Margaret Knight, Marilyn Shellabarger, Ruth Utevsky, and John and Christa Fladhammer also rendered valuable assistance. Spencer Peterson and Iris Watahomigie worked wonders with old photographs.

A word about terminology. While I prefer the term "African American," the terms "Negro," "negro," and "Negro Work" have been used in the context in which they occurred at the time of the original documents and activities. The term "African" is used to designate the indigenous peoples of sub-Saharan Africa. In addition, phrases and spelling that are recognizable but conform to the usage of the period and geographic area have been retained in quotations without the benefit of "sic." "Party" refers to the U.S. Communist Party, which had various names during its first decade. In view of the prevalence of multiple names with which communists are identified in the literature, "a.k.a." is used to distinguish between birth names and pseudonyms. The birth name is usually given first, followed by "a.k.a" for the pseudonym, for example, "Otto Huiswoud (a.k.a. Charles Woodson)"; but in cases where a pseudonym appears in a document or is always used by an individual, the given name follows, for example, "George Padmore (Malcolm Nurse)." Questions have been raised regarding the pronunciation of the name "Huiswoud." The final syllable rhymes with "loud."

Researching and telling the story of the radicals of the Harlem Renaissance has proven to be a challenge and a rich learning experience. It was only through extensive research and the assistance of so many librarians and scholars, especially my husband and collaborator W. Burghardt Turner, that some of the thinking and experiences of a small group of Caribbean crusaders could be revealed. Responsibility for this rendition, however, is mine. I hope that this endeavor, inspired by Hermie's friendship, trust, and invaluable information, will do justice to the story of Otto and Hermina Huiswoud.

Introduction

FRANKLIN W. KNIGHT

The biographies of Otto Huiswoud and Hermina Dumont Huiswoud, as well as those of many other Caribbean immigrants to the United States during the early part of the twentieth century, clearly illustrate the pronounced degree to which the peoples of the Caribbean have been unusually peripatetic.[1] This condition was not merely a late-colonial or postcolonial phenomenon. It constituted instead an essential and inescapable dimension of the entire history of the Caribbean peoples. The pre-Hispanic populations of the islands of the Caribbean—the Caribs and Arawaks—were relatively recent arrivals when their lives were shattered by the unexpected appearance of Christopher Columbus and the profound trauma that ensued.[2] Since 1492 a succession of migrant waves has poured across the region from many places, and a continuous intra-Caribbean movement of unprecedented proportions accompanied this immigration.[3] These movements of populations have had extensive repercussions on local societies and cultures and over the long term have affected the psyche of the peoples of the region.

Although migration may be considered a localized phenomenon, especially when islands lay in such close proximity as they do in the Caribbean, social and economic factors played an important role in expanding it. Caribbean populations have long reflected the broad and consistent input of peoples from all over the world. The first European colonial settlements attempted to recreate in tropical microcosm the familiar—or sometimes imagined—towns and villages of the settlers' homelands. Between 1518 and 1870 several million Africans arrived, mostly through the vigorous transatlantic slave trade, laying the foundation for the lucrative plantation agriculture that catalyzed European trade and commerce.[4] With the gradual abolition of the slave trade and slavery in the Caribbean during the nineteenth century, tens of thousands of Indians and Chinese arrived from the Asian subcontinent as a form of supplemental labor for the declining or former slave labor systems.[5] At the beginning of the twentieth century a steady trickle of economic migrants arrived largely from the Mediterranean areas of the disintegrating Turkish Empire—Syrians, Lebanese, and Turks, along with a few Jews and a new wave of Chinese.

In the same way that people moved into the Caribbean, they also moved across the Caribbean. Some of this movement derived from the erratic nature of competitive colonialism. As the Europeans competed overseas for political hegemony within Europe, various colonies changed hands during or after the periodical wars, moving fluidly between Spanish, French, and English spheres of political administration. In 1655 the English captured Jamaica from the Spanish, who had colonized it for 145 years, forcing many of the Spanish residents to flee to nearby Cuba with their African slaves. Following the Seven Years War (1756–63) between the French and English, as well as after later conflicts between those two countries, St. Lucia, Grenada, St. Vincent, and Tobago were incorporated into the English sphere. In 1797, the English captured Trinidad, held by the Spanish since Columbus's arrival in 1498. As a result of the Napoleonic Wars, the English acquired three mainland South American colonies from the Dutch, Essequibo, Berbice, and Demerara, forming them into the single colony of British Guiana (now Guyana).

Colonial wars, however, provided only one impetus for the continual movement of subject peoples. The stabilization of colonial boundaries did not diminish the impetus to move about within and outside the Caribbean region. Caribbean peoples also relocated for economic reasons, especially after the abolition of the coercive system of slavery in the region.

As the basis of the local economies changed from predominantly plantation production for export to a combination of internal and external commerce, people migrated within the Caribbean, seeking to improve their economic circumstances. The roots of this economic migration lay in the transformation of the colonial economies from yeoman agriculture to intensive capitalist plantation enterprises during the middle years of the seventeenth century. The change to plantation agriculture, usually for the production of sugar, unsettled several local island societies, especially among the early English settlement colonies such as St. Christopher, Nevis, Antigua, and Barbados, causing many families to move to Jamaica or to the mainland British North American colonies. Indeed, many of the founding families of Virginia and the Carolinas originated in this migration from Barbados or other small islands of the eastern Caribbean.[6] Changes in the intensity of plantation agriculture led to the redeployment of labor both during and after the slave trade. With the technological change in sugar production in the later nineteenth century, central factories required enormous quantities of sugar cane to maintain optimal productive efficiency, and the manpower needs at the harvesting stage often far exceeded local labor supplies.

Perceived economic opportunities at the beginning of the twentieth century provided a powerful catalyst for movement, and temporary labor immigration was the response. Cane cutters traveled long distances from island to island or to the mainland if wages were attractive enough. British West Indians moved from one small island to another, attracted by better wages or sometimes just the opportunity to get a job. Jamaicans, Barbadians, and Haitians constituted significant sectors of the rapidly expanding agricultural workforce in Cuba and the Dominican Republic in the first decades of the twentieth century, as they did in the construction crews of the Panama Canal and the expanding banana plantations of Costa Rica, Nicaragua, and Honduras. For several decades Antiguans, Barbudans, and Virgin Islanders provided seasonal labor for the sugar plantations of the Dominican Republic, leaving a heritage of Anglo-Saxon names among several sugar villages, especially in the southeastern part of the country. Trinidad and the Guianas attracted large numbers of Barbadians, Grenadians, and St. Lucians.[7]

The most consistent magnet for Caribbean migration before 1924 was, however, the United States of America. Before the immigration law of that year, which was intended to control the free entry of individuals from all over the globe, the Caribbean exported a large number of citizens seeking economic amelioration in that perceived northern land of opportunity. They came from every part of the Caribbean: Cuba, Jamaica, Haiti, the Dominican Republic, Puerto Rico, Nevis, Barbados, St. Lucia, Trinidad, and the Guianas. They were skilled and semiskilled, with the semiskilled predominating as the immigrants increased in numbers. As Winston James points out, the numbers of arrivals from the Caribbean increased dramatically from a few hundred in 1899 to more than 12,000 in 1924. They eventually constituted a significant proportion of the 140,000 non-white immigrants in 1930. Indeed, by 1930 Caribbean migrants accounted for about one-quarter of the population of Harlem.[8] The Huiswouds, the subjects of the present study, formed a part of that large early twentieth-century exodus.

The history, economy, culture, and social organization of the Caribbean peoples help explain the local centrifugal forces at work in the Caribbean at the beginning of the twentieth century. Except for a few isolated places such as Cuba, Trinidad, and the Guianas, local economies were in dismal shape.[9] The export sector of these territories was in a perilous decline. Metropolitan governments and their colonial supporters had placed an unbounded faith in sugar production and a few other plantation staples as the foundation of a self-sustaining colonial economy. But free trade had battered the Caribbean economies, especially those of the British sphere, after the middle of the nineteenth century. Caribbean sugar was not doing well on the world market, largely as a result of the increasing competition from beet sugar producers in Europe and the United States. Still, Caribbean producers continued to place their faith in hopes that the price of cane sugar would continue to increase, and sugar-based incomes remained for too long the principal barometer for the overall economic conditions of the region.

Increased productivity, especially in Jamaica, Barbados, Trinidad, and British Guiana, could not disguise the long-term negative trends and the insoluble problems of unstable prices and unreliable markets. Until about 1884 the British market still supported a large number of small sugar exporters. But the increased dumping of European-produced beet sugar, especially from German producers, forced down the prices on the London sugar market. The doleful repercussions were felt around the sugar-producing world.[10] In a single year British Guiana sugar, considered the best on the market, fell from twenty-six shillings per hundredweight of 112 pounds to fifteen shillings, and general muscovado (the basic raw sugar) fell from twenty shillings per hundredweight to thirteen shillings. The impact across the Caribbean was devastating. A number of small producers abandoned production. Middling and large producers adopted a number of drastic measures in order to survive. Some consolidated their holdings, forming large central factories to replace multiple producing units. Others leased out their cane holdings or separated the agricultural and industrial aspects of production, leaving the cane-growing to a number of small farmers who then bore the brunt of the risk and suffered the most from the erratic pricing structure in the sugar market. Almost everywhere producers reduced costs by lowering wages or altering the formula for calculating the value of everything from independently produced sugar cane to finished sugar manufactured in their mills. The adjustments were not easy for any sector.

In Grenada, sugar production fell by about sixty percent between 1883 and 1884. By 1886 St. Vincent cane growers abandoned more than two-thirds of their cane fields, and the incidence of bankruptcy increased sharply. In Jamaica a number of estates closed down, while others improved productivity and overall efficiency. By 1900 the top producers had installed better sugar mills, increasing the proportion of cane juice extracted and employing the technical innovation of the centrifuge to improve crystallization and the overall quality of the sugar. Nevertheless, technical improvements were slow and piecemeal, with the most common measure for improving manufacturer profits being the arbitrary reduction of seasonal wages. Sugar production still employed the largest sector of the working population, but as more and more small islands abandoned sugar production altogether, their populations were driven to subsistence agriculture or emigration.[11]

The predictable decline of sugar opened up opportunities for peasant agriculture, and over time peasant production would help restore some measure of economic stability and well-being not only to the plantations but also to whole territories. But the problems of the Caribbean were severe and could not be addressed by mere agricultural diversification and controlled land distribution. Caribbean people wanted better wages, but they also wanted to improve the general quality of their lives. This was especially true of the more educated among the working classes. Migration simultaneously satisfied several goals.

In the case of Otto and Hermina Huiswoud, it is clear from this study that they were unusual individuals, even in an age that produced an abundance of outstanding types. What set them apart from many of their fellow migrants whose record remains undiscovered was their unrelenting political activism over a long period. They were not alone, however. They were part of a band of distinguished activist émigrés from the Caribbean—Cyril Briggs, C. L. R. James, Arthur Schomburg, Marcus Garvey, Hubert H. Harrison, Claude McKay, W. A. Domingo, Richard B. Moore, George Padmore, J. A. Rogers—whose extraordinary political self-consciousness propelled Caribbean and black causes onto the world stage. Their Caribbean background provides only a part of the insight into these interesting lives.

Yet it is probably accurate to state that the Huiswouds acquired, in Suriname and British Guiana before their individual departures, the self-confidence, flexibility, intellectual curiosity, and ample view of the world that allowed them to adjust easily in the bustling clamor of a complex and vibrant city like New York, where they found a large community of expatriates who fearlessly shared their views and tirelessly looked for ways to change their world. Migration and Diaspora communities create unexpected circumstances that force individuals to rise to occasions for which they were generally unprepared. While the immigrants were desperate for jobs, they were reluctant to surrender the sense of personal dignity and self-worth that they brought with them.

A modestly educated Caribbean individual had few opportunities for upward mobility in their home territories. While colonial governments might have provided a good elementary education for all, they signally failed to provide adequate jobs for qualified nonwhites. Discrimination of all sorts inhibited the upward occupational and economic opportunities of local nonwhites. Indeed, the colonies were still regarded as a sort of dumping ground for the marginally able from the metropolis, whose major preferential qualification depended on the place of their birth and the color of their skin. Debilitating colonial racism radicalized a number of the West Indian expatriates, although, by her own admission, Hermina Huiswoud does not fall into the category of the overtly politicized. A surprising number of the early Caribbean migrants, however, were politicized before they arrived in the United States. Some, like W. A. Domingo and Marcus Garvey, had been involved in fledgling trade unions, and some, like Samuel Haynes of Belize, had served in the British war effort and been disillusioned by the experience. Others, like Claude McKay of Jamaica and Charles Petioni of Trinidad, had been influenced by the British Fabians and espoused an equalizing socialism. The political and social climate of New York and Harlem in the 1920s would intensively radicalize many of the immigrants, including Otto Huiswoud. As Winston James points out, "Caribbean migrants came to America with a long and distinguished tradition of resistance with few parallels in the New World. They therefore entered the United States with a sense of self-confidence and pride that would have predisposed at least some of them to radical activity, as the harsh racism battered their self-esteem."[12]

The story of the Huiswouds and their immigrant and peripatetic peers broadly expands our understanding of the history of the Caribbean in the formative years from the end of the nineteenth century through the middle of the twentieth century. But it does much more. It provides a probing window into a period of world history that links the changing experiences of several societies. This study is therefore extremely valuable for several interrelated area histories of the Caribbean, the United States, Western Europe, Japan, and the early Soviet Union. Nor is that all: the migratory experiences of Otto and Hermina Huiswoud enormously enrich our understanding of the complicated processes of migration.

Yet Harlem was more than the nexus of immigrant streams. *Caribbean Crusaders and the Harlem Renaissance* makes a significant contribution to our understanding not only of the world of Harlem but also of the important role that this mixed collection of individuals played in the Harlem Renaissance during the first part of the twentieth century. The distinctive world of Harlem entered its own during those decades, boosted in large measure by the massive exodus from the South of the persecuted black population. This was accompanied by a rapid relocation of much of the mid-Manhattan social activity northwards, as Jervis Anderson described in his enthralling study *This Was Harlem: A Cultural Portrait, 1900–1950*.[13] Harlem became a powerful magnet that irresistibly attracted a diverse population from all over the world, especially people of African descent. It quickly established a powerful international reputation as the centripetal Mecca of the entire African Diaspora. Most of the early West Indians who arrived in New York went to Harlem, and a great proportion have made Harlem their home since. Harlem was a newly constructed, architecturally attractive, socially dynamic division of a rapidly expanding city, a place that no one then could have visualized as the crime-ridden, drug-infested ghetto that would become its hallmark later in the century. In the 1920s Harlem was not a ghetto and nothing about it was substandard. It was, for a decade or so, the magnificent reified hope of political integrationists.

As this book makes abundantly clear, Harlem was much more than a mere geographical location on the island of Manhattan. It was also a state of mind. The author details in this work how Harlem provided the conduits that facilitated the crosscutting of the fundamental American social cleavages of race, color, class, and condition. Harlem represented the place where individuals encountered opportunities that changed their lives forever. It was that indelible combination of physical state and state of mind that gave Harlem its qualitative distinctiveness. Many other American cities, such as Philadelphia, Baltimore, Chicago, St. Louis, Cincinnati, and Durham, all had predominantly black sections with throbbing clubs that vended music and other cultural activities that attracted large numbers of whites. Yet no one spoke of a "Durham Renaissance" or a "Chicago Renaissance" the way that blacks in Harlem in the 1920s and 1930s self-consciously spoke of the Harlem Renaissance.[14] Harlem represented more than entertaining clubs and crassly commodified culture. It brought together artists, entertainers, playwrights, journalists, novelists, poets, thinkers, politicians, evangelists, charlatans, and utopians of all races and colors. Not only did they meet on an equal plain, but they also reciprocally catalyzed one another. Moreover, Harlem manifested a fleeting cosmopolitan ambience that gave it and the Harlem Renaissance its incomparable vitality. That was the special chemistry that permeated life in Harlem in the 1920s and 1930s.

Nostalgic historians reconstructing this dramatic episode of the American past did not invidiously impose the term Harlem Renaissance on this period. The term was common currency in the popular contemporary discourse of the participants, of people like Alain Locke, Langston Hughes, James Weldon Johnson, Cyril Briggs, and Richard B. Moore. Briggs wrote in 1918 that his new magazine, the *Crusader,* would be dedicated to a "renaissance of Negro power and culture throughout the world," and Locke titled part one of his book the *New Negro* "The Negro Renaissance." Obviously the term was widely used by this group of self-conscious advocates of a new, aggressive attitude of intellectual race reconstruction.

The characters who move through the pages of *Caribbean Crusaders,* as well many who are not included, exhibited a boundless confidence and a spontaneous enthusiasm that they could construct a radically new world in which all groups would have equal access and equal respect. Even before the Great Depression of the 1930s deferred their hopes and shattered their dreams, many of them realized that the ideas and visions they articulated would never be achieved in their lifetime. Harlem was merely the prologue to the play.

Abbreviations

ABB	African Blood Brotherhood
AFL	American Federation of Labor
AFTU	African Federation of Trade Unions (South Africa)
Agitprop	Department of Agitation and Propaganda (USSR)
ANC	African National Congress (South Africa)
ANLC	American Negro Labor Congress
CEC	Central Executive Committee (CPUSA)
CCNY	City College of New York
CDRN	Comité de Défense de la Race Nègre (France)
CI	Communist International (Third International, or Comintern)
CID	Criminal Investigation Department (Great Britain)
CGTU	Confedération Général du Travail (France)
CP, CPUSA	Communist Party, USA
DEC	District Executive Committee (CPUSA)
DW	*Daily Worker*
ECCI	Executive Committee Communist International
FBI	Federal Bureau of Investigation
ILD	International Labor Defense
ILS	International Lenin School or University (Moscow)
ILGWU	International Ladies Garment Workers Union
Inprecorr	*International Press Correspondence* (CI)
ISH	International Seamen and Harbour Workers
ITUC-NW	International Trade Union Committee of Negro Workers
IWW	Industrial Workers of the World
KKK	Ku Klux Klan
KUTV	University of the Toilers of the East (Moscow)
LAI	League against Imperialism and for National Independence

LC	Library of Congress, Washington, D.C.
LDRN	Ligue de Défense de la Race Nègre (France)
LSNR	League of Struggle for Negro Rights
MOPR	International Association for Aid to Revolutionary Fighters
NA	National Archives, Washington, D.C.
NAACP	National Association for the Advancement of Colored People
NKVD	People's Commissariat of Internal Affairs (USSR)
NTWIU	Needle Trades Workers Industrial Union
NWA	Negro Welfare Association (Great Britain)
NYPL	New York Public Library
PCF	Parti Communiste Français (French Communist Party)
Polcom	Political Committee (CPUSA)
Politburo	Political Bureau (Russian CP)
RILU	Red International of Labor Unions (Profintern)
RGO	Revolutionary Trade Union Opposition (Germany)
RA	Russian State Archive of Social and Political History (RGASPI), Moscow
S&HWU	Seamen and Harbour Workers Union (South Africa)
TUEL	Trade Union Educational League
TUUL	Trade Union Unity League
UNIA	Universal Negro Improvement Association
UWU	Unemployed Workers' Union (South Africa)
USSR	Union of Soviet Socialist Republics
YCI	Young Communist International
YCL	Young Communist League

*Caribbean Crusaders
and the Harlem Renaissance*

Prologue

Wittenberg

Silence. At 11 A.M. quiet permeates the building as if no one were there. At the far end of the corridor there appears a portrait of the head and upper torso of a man. At closer range it becomes clear that the erect form is alive but perfectly still, framed in the center of a window, looking straight ahead. A glass door to the left of the window presents additional immobile forms—fifteen gray-haired Dutch women seated in green armchairs around three tables. Their eyes may be closed or open, and it is apparent that they share solitude rather than past experiences or current complaints. A faint ray of March sun peeks through the ubiquitous mist of the Netherlands, but to the residents it does not seem to matter whether the day is rainy or sunny. All thoughts are turned inward.

One frail woman stands out not only because of the tan tint in her complexion but also because she is of smaller build and English is her primary tongue. Partly blind, she drifts between slumber and apparent sleep without missing any of the activity around her. The silence is broken when her visitors kiss her and she comments, "Oh, you came back. What are we going to do today?" Someone suggests that they might go downstairs to the cafeteria or down the hall to her room to talk a while. She quickly replies, "I have no room." When reminded that she does have a room, the retort is even more swift and emphatic: "I have one-quarter of a room!" To Hermie Huiswoud, the shared room at the Wittenberg nursing home is not "her" place.

In the lunchroom the conversation turns to the ocean voyage from Guyana to New York when she was fourteen years old. "It was a medium-sized ship.

The crew was very kind to us. The food was ordinary, but good. What did we know? We ate it. The ship stopped at every island, or so it seemed—Trinidad, Barbados, St. Lucia, St. Kitts, St. Croix and St. Thomas, which were Danish ports of call at the time. All the saints! The trip took fourteen days. When we finally arrived in New York we did not go to Ellis Island but right in to a dock where my mother's sister, husband, and daughter and maybe some others met us. We took the subway uptown." Later she talks about Langston Hughes. "It all started when he stepped on my foot. We were in some production down in the basement of a building, probably the auditorium of the 135th Street Library, and he came around from the side and stepped on my foot. He was just Langston. He was older than I; we were both still young. It was much later that he was Langston Hughes, the poet. We became good friends." She explains that they spent six months together in Moscow and also once traveled on the same ship from Europe to New York.

All her companions at Wittenberg Verpleeghuis in March 1997 have a story to tell from their long lives, but at ninety-two, Hermina Dumont Huiswoud[1] may have one of the more unique yet untold stories to reveal. The raconteur of yesterday can only recount bits and pieces of her life as she realizes that her memory is fading. She explains, "I have been assigned to be here the rest of my life. I try not to rock the boat; one goes along to survive."

Other sources must be tapped to discover why this nursing home resident and her husband, Otto Eduard Huiswoud, traveled so far from the Caribbean to Amsterdam via New York, Moscow, and Paris, for the rebel in Wittenberg has now been silenced.

1. The Caribbean Comes to Harlem

The long trip from British Guiana (now Guyana) to New York undertaken by Hermina Alicia Dumont with her mother in 1919 was typical of many residents of the Caribbean who chose to leave their homeland for a better life in the North. For centuries the peoples of Africa had been dragged to the West, but the beginning of the twentieth century marked a change not only in direction but in determination. History has stressed the idea that the original mass transatlantic shift in population from Africa was associated with the slave trade conducted by European powers. But the nuances of the African Diaspora have not always been equally clear. It is easy to forget how fate held different futures for the thousands of Africans widely distributed in the seventeenth century around the Atlantic rim in every port a European ship could reach, from Canada to Argentina. The practice of slavery in parts of the Caribbean and the United States during the eighteenth century was particularly harsh. After 1800 states within the United States established discriminatory legal barriers that codified the "peculiar institution" and prevented African absorption into the population of European settlers. The concentration of Africans and the restrictions placed upon their movements by chattel slavery greatly intensified the number and subjugated condition of African Americans and African Caribbeans in the United States and the Caribbean.

Escape to northern states and Canada from the slaveholding South was the main avenue of African American movement during the early part of the nineteenth century. Emancipation created the critical opportunity for change because it theoretically carried the right of mobility, but it could only be taken advantage of in limited ways. The implementation of Black Codes, "Jim Crow," and other forms of discrimination continued to impoverish and restrict movement of African Americans from the rural South to the industrializing North. Back-to-Africa movements and schemes for migration to Mexico had little impact on population shifts. Although some former slaves and free African Americans moved westward during the latter part of the century, the opportunities for African Americans to exercise the right to migrate within the United States were extremely limited. In the Caribbean, however, the Diaspora began to spread to Central America, especially to Panama during the building of the railroads and canal, and to England, Canada, and the northern United States. Despite colonial restrictions and the geographic isolation of the small Caribbean islands, African Caribbeans were more mobile than most African Americans. According to Winston James, African Caribbeans had already established by the end of the nineteenth century a complex web of institutions adapted to a continuous large-scale and long-distance migration from their homelands. These peripatetic people perceived the sea as an avenue of exploration and escape.[1]

By the twentieth century two streams of migration marshaled momentum, and both had a historic impact on New York. During World War I, recruitment of workers for industry encouraged African Americans living in the South to seek work in the North. African Americans who served in the armed forces were far more mobile when they returned from Europe and also helped swell the population in cities like New York. The railroads set the pattern of movement from south to north. African Americans residing in the eastern states such as North Carolina found their way to the terminal in New York; those farther west in states such as Kentucky and Alabama ended up in Chicago. According to Charles S. Johnson, by 1925 the New York City population included 25,000 African Americans from Virginia, 20,000 from North and South Carolina, and 10,000 from Georgia.[2] The second significant migration was spurred by economic problems in the Caribbean and the development of shipping line routes that coincided with demands of the U.S. labor market. It has been estimated that during the teens, 45,000 African Caribbeans moved to the United States. Of the 102,000 who entered the United States between 1901 and 1924, when immigration was curtailed, the great majority were from the British Caribbean, and many of them settled in New York.[3] Johnson estimates the diverse population mix of New York in the twenties to be one part native New Yorkers, three parts southerners, and one part Caribbean immigrants.[4]

Hermie Dumont was one of the thousands of immigrants traveling from distant tropical colonies under British rule. As the stream intensified a family member, friend, or friend of a friend was usually a contact who could provide newcomers an initial place to stay and suggestions for employment.

Hermie and her mother relied on Edith Tucker, Hermie's mother's sister who had earlier settled in the Bronx. But why had they left their native British Guiana? The decision to go north was not arrived at easily. Following the death of her husband, Hermie's mother had managed to earn money by sewing and operating a small hotel in New Amsterdam, but a fire changed their lives. Not only had flames and smoke caused the two of them to jump from a back second-story window into an adjacent stream and flee cross a series of back yards, the damage made it impossible to continue in business. Rumors circulated that the next-door neighbor had set a fire in his business to cover his losses, and the fire had spread to the small hotel. But proof of this was not easily established, and the loss was borne by the residents of the affected building.

The destruction of her possessions and business was the second serious loss for Alice Jannette Dumont. The first had been the death of her husband, Hermann R. C. V. Dumont, who had a fatal accident on July 17, 1908, while prospecting far away in Guatemala. Hermie had been born October 8, 1905, and named Hermina for her father and Alicia for her mother. It is not clear when "Hermina" became "Hermie," but it probably was an early transition. She preferred the shortened form and used Hermie throughout her adulthood, except on official documents. A son, born a year earlier, had died in infancy, and Hermie was the apple of her parents' eyes. Even though she was not quite three years old when news was received of her father's death, she always remembered the father she was never really to know. As a forest ranger and gold prospector he was away for long periods and would bring back samples of plants and fruits that he planted around the house. He always brought some special gift for her when he returned. She remembers climbing on his lap, affixing her little body to his tall, handsome frame, and becoming his shadow whenever he was home.

Hermie and her mother continued to live in New Amsterdam after the death of her father, but her childhood seemed catapulted into adulthood. Except for attendance at school she was always in the company of adults: her mother, grandmother, mother's sister, and a blind uncle who relied on her for assistance. She fetched things and assisted him in other ways, and she carried throughout her life a fear of blindness. She always hoped that loss of vision would never be her fate. By 1919 her grandmother had died and her aunt had gone to America. The abrupt change in Alice Dumont's economic situation following the fire forced her to consider moving to New York. Arrangements were made for Hermie and her mother to depart on the SS *Korona* from Georgetown on October 22, 1919.

To a fourteen-year-old girl, crossing the Caribbean Sea from island to island and sailing the Atlantic Ocean was a fascinating adventure, and the anticipation of what she might find in New York escalated the excitement. For thirteen days she watched the scene gradually change from glorious green to drab gray as the ship steamed from the coast of South America to the coast of North America. Starting at the most distant port they traversed the length of the stream of migration. Each stop brought more travelers aboard seeking to change their lives by trading the sun-bathed tropics for cold, crowded cities. They landed in New York City on November 15.

New York was unlike any port the travelers had experienced along the way. Buildings that pierced the sky crowded out the pale sun, and the enormity of the city defied imagination. Long, narrow asphalt streets traversed the city in both directions for block after block. Trains rattled along noisily in dark tunnels underground. Hermie and her mother found some relief when they finally arrived at her aunt's two-story family house in the Bronx, which was unlike the tall and forbidding concrete structures they saw on disembarkation. The warm welcome did not last long, however, as Hermie began to perceive an irritation at their presence. The problem of color reared its ugly head—the aunt was lighter in complexion than Hermie's mother, and her second husband was white. According to Hermie, the poor lady twisted and squirmed trying to convince people that she, too, was white. It became apparent that she was not eager to share her home with her browner relatives, and they planned to find other quarters. Soon a stranger arrived to inquire about the school-age immigrant. The family had been remiss in not registering Hermie promptly for school according to the law, and she was enrolled in the business program at Theodore Roosevelt High School. Hermie enjoyed school and participated in the Accounting and Social Problems Clubs. She graduated in January 1923 from the three-year course and one year later from the four-year course. Hermie looked forward to applying her secretarial skills because she was determined to help supplement her mother's income.

Her mother was able to find work as a dressmaker and in time developed a private clientele. These relationships not only provided income but were a source of odd experiences for Hermie. She often told of one delivery she made for her mother:

> There was a movie actress, Lorna Deck, who played hair-raising stunt parts [and who was] engaged to the then Vice President of Brazil, and she gave her trousseau sewing to my Mother. Whenever mother was finished with a batch she would send me with it to Miss Deck. Then on a certain hot Sunday in June mother sent me with a set of pyjamas made from airplane cloth for the lady's intended husband . . .

The movie actress lived very simply, occupying an apartment . . . with no elevator . . . A scorching sun beat down on my bare head so I hurried into the house and up to the top floor, five flights up. Exhausted, I pressed the doorbell, at the same time leaning on the door. To my surprise, the door went open almost simultaneously as I leaned on it. The opening was so abrupt that I fell into the arms of—Charlie Chaplin . . . When I was a girl, I wore my hair in curls. Charlie tugged at the two front curls, as one would milk a cow, exclaiming, "The milkman is here!"[5]

Hermie did not wait until graduation to start working. Not far from where she and her mother had relocated on 141st Street in Harlem, she found a position at an employment agency for twelve dollars a week during the summer months and on Saturdays when school was in session. The owner of the agency, Ioanthe Sidney, was well known in Harlem and catered to many of the new arrivees from the South and the Caribbean seeking jobs. She also hired Hermie occasionally to serve friends she entertained. While working in the office Hermie met a man engaged in real estate, and he offered her a job in his downtown office. The day after graduation on January 30, 1924, Hermie was ushered into a suite of offices on the corner of Broadway and Wall Street. It was not long before this first full-time job was to teach an unexpected lesson instead of launching her on a career in the financial district. To the naive employee the realization was slow in dawning that the African American employer was fronting for a white realty company engaged in shady deals. Hermie was having to sign documents as "secretary" of the firm. As the date approached for a tax department inspection of the manipulated books, Hermie realized it was best to resign. During this period she was also attending Hunter College and City College of the City of New York at night, and she decided not to seek another job immediately. When classes were over she obtained a part-time job through Sidney's employment agency "tidying up" a ten-room apartment on Central Park West.

Hermie really needed full-time employment. The only job that seemed available was in a dress factory. Before she was due to start work at the factory, however, she received word that the National Association for the Advancement of Colored People (NAACP) was seeking a clerical assistant, and she reported there instead. She was delighted with the job as Robert Bagnall's secretary, but after three weeks a complication developed. A friend of the executive secretary had a daughter in need of a job and Hermie was let go. Hermie's career became a series of jobs that utilized her organizational and secretarial skills and widened her experiences as well. She learned much from her association with Ms. Sidney, who treated her as a protégée. In time the association was to lead to a marriage and a life that she could not then have foreseen. Harlem provided Hermie entry into a career of secretarial work; Harlem set her on a course that would reach far beyond British Guiana and New York.

Hermie considered Harlem a beautiful part of the city. In 1920 African Americans lived in a relatively small area, roughly three blocks wide by sixteen short blocks long, extending from 129th Street to 145th Street. The main arteries were all broad: Lenox Avenue, a continuation of Sixth Avenue north of Central Park, was an unpretentious street considered Harlem's Bowery because of its dirt and noise, "its buildings ill-used, and made shaky by the subway underneath."[6] Noisy tracks on which elevated trains rattled overhead cast a deep shadow on Eighth Avenue, with its push carts and small, seedy shops. But Seventh Avenue was a glorious boulevard with trees planted down the center of the street and along the curbs of the wide sidewalks. Many of the attractive, well-constructed apartment houses were no higher than five stories, providing an opening to the sky. Several streets had magnificent churches and beautiful brownstone town homes that had been designed by outstanding architects such as Stanford White. Seventh Avenue became the Champs Elysees to stroll along on Sunday afternoons, the venue for spectacular parades, the Hyde Park for soapbox orators with burning political or religious messages—the heart of the community.

Families were still in the process of moving from less-desirable areas of the city such as the Tenderloin, where housing available to African Americans was scattered between 20th and 53rd Streets on the west side, and the San Juan Hill section between 60th and 64th Streets and Sixth and Ninth Avenues. Harlem had become available as a potential community for African Americans in 1903. An African American real estate agent, Philip Payton, was able to take advantage of an economic slump and convince the landlord of an empty house on 134th Street that he could supply African American tenants. In 1904 he founded the Afro-American Realty Company, which bought and leased houses, and he purchased a Victorian Gothic brownstone at 13 West 131st Street for his own family.[7] Early settlers of the island of Manhattan had clustered at the southern tip, leaving the northern area as remote farmland for many decades. Gradually it changed from an autonomous village, Nieuw Haarlem, established in 1658 by Dutch farmers, to an area inhabited by wealthy homeowners who escaped the city heat during the sweltering summers. Some areas were also changed by Irish squatters who erected shantytowns when the farms became unprofitable during the mid-eighteen-hundreds. The pressure of the growing population in lower Manhattan ultimately led to the development of urban townhouses and "new law" tenements with elevators in the northern part of the city. Access for lower- and middle-class working people was created by the extension of the subway system: the elevated train up Eighth Avenue during the 1880s and the subway up Lenox Avenue to 145th Street in 1904. The northern end of Manhattan was transformed into an African American domain after Payton established the beachhead on 134th Street. The expansion proceeded house by house and block by block on the heels of white flight. African American Harlem gradually adjusted its boundaries and became a center of cultural activity as well as a residential community.

There was a price, however, for that growth. The movement from other areas of the city along with the pressure from newcomers arriving daily from the South and the Caribbean created an imbalance in the housing situation. The demand for housing always far exceeded the space available to African Americans. Discrimination and segregation played into rent gouging by owners as each apartment became available. In order to increase living quarters, apartments and brownstones were subdivided, rent parties were held to cover the high rent, and renting a room became a way of life for many residents. A constant game of musical chairs was played to get into houses as they were vacated by white residents. The Dumonts were typical of Harlem residents: starting in another part of the city, renting a room in Harlem, finding an apartment in which rooms might be rented to someone else, and watching for new openings with improved facilities.

Hermie's description of one such move portrays the tense aspiration of Harlem residents:

> Every morning upon awaking, I would look up towards the hill that was separated from my dwelling in Harlem by a public park.
>
> The houses on the hill were newer than those in my neighborhood. Although the house I was then occupying had been renovated . . . the former large apartments were converted into smaller units . . .
>
> Every morning, especially on sunny days, I would vow that one day I would live in one of those houses on the hill. I suppose I was so preoccupied with the subject that one night I dreamt that I had moved there. The next morning, when I looked out of my window, I saw a large sign-board affixed to the top floor of an apartment complex with words large enough to read with the naked eye. It announced that apartments in that group of houses were offered to "respectable colored tenants."
>
> Counting ourselves as respectable, but above all, feeling that we were entitled to live wherever we could afford to, we dressed hurriedly and almost ran up the hill to investigate. There, a black representative of the Jewish landlord showed us the only vacant apartment that was available. The number of rooms and the rental suited us, although we suspected that we were being charged more rent than the former occupant. Later on, we were proven correct in our

surmise. We were charged $67 a month whereas white tenants paid only $60 for the same accommodation.⁸

The population explosion required adjustments in living arrangements, but housing in Harlem was considered an improvement over the old tenements south of Harlem and the sharecropper shacks south of the Mason Dixon line. More importantly, the emerging community took on the spirit and excitement of a new age. Harlem became the crossroads of different cultures and the venue of new experiences. Ultimately this new movement required new characterizations: artists and activists considered themselves "New Negroes," and the literary and musical outpourings became known as the "Harlem Renaissance."

Even though Hermie was at the hub of activities at Ioanthe Sidney's employment office located on Seventh Avenue between 134th and 135th Streets, she heard nothing of a "Harlem Renaissance." Along with her friends or her mother she would stop in the evening as a crowd gathered on a corner in front of a soapbox or ladder to listen to orators. By far the most electric and best informed was Hubert Henry Harrison, who could lecture persuasively on any topic with clarity and logic. They made a special effort to catch his lectures. She also attended plays and programs at the YMCA on 135th Street, the YWCA on 137th Street, and the public library near Lenox Avenue on 135th Street. The plays and musicals at the Lafayette Theater, the blues and jazz heard on records or played at home from sheet music, and the books, paintings, and sculptures by African American writers and artists did not seem unusual or novel. It was simply part of the fun of growing up in Harlem. To Hermie the term "Renaissance" referred to the popular Renaissance Casino constructed on the corner of Seventh Avenue and 138th Street in 1923, where she and her friends spent many Sunday evenings watching basketball games that were often followed by a dance. One of the referees was an attractive "Dutchman" from Dutch Guiana (now Suriname), Chris Huiswoud. "Dutch," as he was called, was the first African American to be licensed as a referee from the Amateur Athletic Union of the United States and to serve as an official basketball referee for the Intercollegiate League. His presence on the court added to the excitement of the game.

In 1923 Hermie was to meet a different "Dutchman" who happened to be an older brother of Christopher Huiswoud. Otto Huiswoud was a frequent visitor to the employment agency. Following one of his visits Ms. Sydney remarked that he had recently been to the Soviet Union. Hermie found that interesting but she was not terribly impressed and did not inquire further about his trip. A second encounter occurred at one of Sydney's dinners, where

Hermie was decked in a maid's white cap and apron to help serve the guests. Otto's arrival an hour early provided time to talk. He continued to drop by the office, and she learned that his migration to New York had been quite atypical. He had not followed the usual migration pattern from Dutch Guiana: instead of island hopping as a passenger he had worked as a cabin boy on a freighter bound for the Netherlands.

Otto Eduard Gerardus Majella Huiswoud, born October 28, 1893, in Paramaribo, Dutch Guiana, was the fifth child of eight of Rudolf Francis Huiswoud and Jacquelina Henrietta Bernard (born November 18, 1858). Otto's father had been born a slave on August 30, 1852. After slavery was abolished in Dutch Guiana on July 1, 1863, he was apprenticed to a tailor at the age of eleven. He worked in that trade until his death in 1920. While Otto was still young his father apprenticed him to a cabinetmaker, where he learned inlay work in the afternoons. Upon completion of the school year, when he was thirteen years old, his father apprenticed him to a printer. Working in the trade for three years inspired a great interest in books, and the few he acquired were lent to his friends on a businesslike basis. Reading opened new vistas and he began to dream of travel to far lands. His oldest brother, Egbert, had already left home to serve in the Dutch colonial army in Indonesia.

Shortly after Otto's sixteenth birthday, in October 1909, a captain of a Dutch ship in port visited his father, and Otto became inspired to become a seaman. He was able to persuade his father to permit him to travel to Amsterdam. The captain agreed to take Otto to Amsterdam and see to it that he was entered in the seaman's school. Otto eagerly left his family in Paramaribo and set sail for what he thought would be Amsterdam. But the captain who was so mild-mannered and charming when he talked to Otto's father changed disposition as soon as the receding harbor disappeared. Rum turned him into a tyrant. He made Otto his cabin boy and cursed him incessantly despite the fact that during part of the rough voyage he had to rely on Otto, even to take the wheel once, because only the two of them escaped being seasick. More importantly, the ship proceeded to different ports depending on the cargo that was taken on and never seemed to turn in the direction of Holland. When they arrived in frigid New York on January 17, 1910, and still were not headed toward Otto's destination, he decided he had experienced enough training on that ship. He confided in two Surinamese young men who worked in the galley that he planned to leave the ship, and they decided to disembark with him. They skipped ship with what they were wearing and wandered around Brooklyn and lower Manhattan until it began to get dark. Since Otto had originated the plan to jump ship and had learned some English from an older sister who taught the language, it fell to him to seek a haven. Unexpectedly, at the age of sixteen he was really on his own in a strange city whose Dutch-speaking settlers had disappeared eons ago, over three thousand miles from home where he knew not one soul.

The never-to-be-forgotten story of his introduction to New York was unknown to Hermie until many years later. She recounted it, however, as Otto must have told it:

> Otto had no travel documents, only a birth certificate and a letter of recommendation from his parish priest. None of the boys had any money between them and only tropical clothing. Nevertheless, when they got shore leave, Otto and the others headed over the Williamsburg Bridge for Manhattan arriving at the Bowery, almost frozen and covered by snow. Soon, night was enclosing and just when they were losing hope, a black man was approaching from the opposite direction. Accosting the man, Otto, in his best schoolbook English asked him if he could recommend some lodgings for the three of them. It turned out that the man lived over one of the many saloons the Bowery was rich in. He invited them to ascend with him, introduced them to his Irish wife and little son . . . Upstairs they were ushered into what normally was the parlor, but it had been converted into a bedroom with two beds, washstand, two chairs and a potbellied, unlighted heating stove. Soon they were called to the kitchen where a steaming meal of Mulligan stew was served after the landlord had returned from the saloon below with a bucket of foamy beer. Dinner eaten, he proceeded to question the boys—Otto acting as spokesman—about their intentions to look for work. Learning that Otto had learned two trades, one being printing, he said that Otto should be ready to leave with him the next morning. In the loft building where the man worked as janitor, there was a small printing shop run by a German-Jewish owner. He said he felt he could place Otto there and that he had a trump card for he had done many a favor for the printer and this was a good time to ask for some repayment. Next morning . . . [Otto] left with his host, dressed in the man's heavy sweater, muffler and cap.
>
> The slippery snow-covered streets took up his attention as they rode uptown to 22nd Street near Madison Square. After negotiation, Otto was taken on for a day's trial. His boss spoke to him in German, hearing his name was Otto, then in Yiddish and then in broken English. . . . The first day's work so pleased his employer that he was taken on permanently. Less than 24 hours after arrival, Otto had been drawn into the American labor market. His benefactor told him he knew hardship for he had come up from the south where he knew only agriculture [sic] work and had to make it in the industrial north.
>
> Otto worked for the printer for approximately three years but modern print methods and machines soon pushed Otto's boss who was operating on a shoestring out of business with the consequent unemployment for Otto. He remained with the Brown family as star boarder and was considered part of that family.[9]

The awe that struck Otto when the ship glided by the Statue of Liberty, the towers of Manhattan, and the Brooklyn Bridge to enter a Brooklyn pier was soon diminished by the squalid sights of the Bowery where the boys came to rest. Entering one of the older sections of south Manhattan was not to encounter a city of beauty. Ernest H. Gruening has described how the lack of space in New York City constricted the soul: "Throughout their childhood and through their lives millions are denied horizontal vision. Their outlook is eternally on stone or brick walls. Even the sky is circumscribed, shrouded in dust, its vault gouged by great cornices. There is limitation not only for the eye, but for every sense. Nowhere has constriction been carried further. In the poorest sections the population reaches a density not approached elsewhere on earth."[10]

The concrete environment, so dismal and stifling compared to Paramaribo, was a minor concern for Otto on that January morning. It did not take long before the more crushing reality struck, revealing the dichotomy between a cosmopolitan city that boasted of welcoming immigrants from all over the world and the practice of severe discrimination against people of color. Gruening credits the Dutch with establishing a tolerant city that was a refuge for exiles from other colonies, with some eighteen languages spoken in New Amsterdam in 1650. He claims that "the most inherently American doctrines of religious toleration, or personal freedom are our Netherlandish, our New Amsterdam, our Manhattan heritage."[11] While Otto had been most fortunate in coming across a kind person who befriended him and was able to introduce him to someone in the trade in which he had been trained, he soon learned that the Dutch tradition of tolerance did not extend to the Dutch of African descent. Finding work and a place to live were severely restricted for people of color. He was barred from becoming an accredited printer because the union did not accept African Americans in the trade. When he lost his job in the printing house he was forced to work in a variety of menial temporary jobs. He and his younger brother, Christopher, who had joined him in 1912, tried a job at the Algonquin Hotel as "gravy cooks" even though they knew nothing about cooking. Otto also tried serving as assistant cook at a boardinghouse for male European immigrant workers in Tarrytown, New York. He worked as a waiter, dishwasher, janitor, house painter, and elevator operator. He even shipped out as a seaman on the British ship *Newcastle*, but his service was terminated when World War I erupted in 1914. Years later he worked with his friend, Wilfred A. Domingo, who established a tropical produce business.

Otto had brought to New York the Caribbean culture that was to be part of him all his life, but metropolitan forces were to transform the lad who envisioned becoming a seaman to a man who would become a revolutionary. He sought to improve his English by reading newspapers and listening to orators at lunchtime in Madison Square Park at Madison Avenue and 23rd Street or Union Square at 14th Street. He confirmed that not only was there lack of opportunity and justice for African Americans, there were bestial attacks upon them in the South. The specter of lynching was unthinkable and appalling. The problems facing American society were laid bare, and all manner of solutions were offered by soapbox orators near his first workplace with the printer. The speaker that fascinated him the most was distinctive in many ways: broad in his knowledge of history, articulate and clear in his analysis of colonialism, firm in his conviction that socialism could solve the evils visited upon workers by their employers, and passionate in his denunciation of the unjust laws and treatment accorded the African American. Strikingly, he was of brown complexion—a learned man also from the Caribbean. At the time Otto came across Hubert Henry Harrison the soapbox orator was imbued with the solution that socialism offered to combat inequality and injustice. Otto's introduction to socialist politics began with the election campaigns with which Harrison was involved. Not only was Harrison engaged in spreading propaganda in support of the Socialist Party of America he had joined in 1909, he was carefully studying Marxism, economics, science, anthropology, and history—particularly African and African American history—and developing his own philosophical argument. He was exploring the relationship between the African American worker's plight in the United States and the positions of the Socialist Party that had been virtually silent on the issue, constructing his thesis that would appear in several publications. Otto followed his line of reasoning carefully and sought to learn more about this informed, logical orator.

Harrison was ten years older than Otto, having been born in the rural area of Estate Concordia in St. Croix on April 27, 1883. He reported that his parents, William Adolphus Harrison and Cecilia Elizabeth Haines, from Barbados, were "well off as West Indian families go." But his friend, J. A. Rogers, viewing Harrison's life forty-four years later, put it differently. With a touch reminiscent of Countee Cullen's marveling at making a poet black and bidding him sing, Rogers wrote that poverty was Harrison's life-long enemy: "Destiny sent him into this world very poor. And as if this were not enough, she gave him a critical mind, a candid tongue, a family to support; a passion for knowledge; on top of all that, a black skin, and sent him to America." Rogers considered this combination "a most formidable string of handicaps."[12] Rogers was keenly aware that Harrison had been a star pupil in the various schools he attended in the Virgin Islands and had an insatiable thirst for knowledge. But the loss of his father in 1898 followed by confiscation of the family property by the Danish crown and the death of his mother in January 1899 dealt him a cruel blow. As an orphan thrust into poverty he was forced to interrupt his education and support himself.

On September 15, 1900, Harrison sailed from St. Croix to New York and joined his older sister, Mary, who worked as a domestic and lived at 220 West 62nd Street in the San Juan Hill area. He worked a series of jobs as an elevator operator, bellhop, messenger, and even as a stock clerk in a Japanese fan company, but managed to attend night school despite sometimes working two nights a week in addition to full time in the day. He won an award for oratory for which he was acclaimed a "genius" in a major daily newspaper, uniquely achieved grades of 100 percent, and graduated from DeWitt Clinton High School. His high achievement in a civil service examination resulted in an appointment on July 1, 1907, as clerk in the United States Post Office at six hundred dollars per year. Working in the post office was well above the usual jobs available to African Americans, and Harrison could now consider marriage. On April 17, 1909, he married Irene Louise Horton. In time their family grew to five children.

Harrison had not been content solely to support himself and complete high school. When he arrived in the United States at the age of seventeen, ten years ahead of Otto, he too had been struck by the emasculating prejudice so rampant in his new country. With no opportunity to attend college, he instituted his self-instructed "university" in order to better understand conditions in the wider world as well as in the United States. He was organized, methodical, and disciplined. He delved into a wide-ranging in-depth study of various fields. He established a modus operandi that he followed throughout his life. Night after night he read, taking notes, organizing files, maintaining annotated scrapbooks of newspaper clippings, practically devouring books by taking out sections to be marked, commented on, and remembered. The painstaking organization was preparation—he never used notes during his speeches. He honed his oratorical skills at two lyceums conducted at neighborhood African American churches on 53rd Street, St. Benedict the Moor Roman Catholic Church and St. Mark's Methodist Episcopal Church, where debates were held regularly. He also began writing letters to editors of newspapers, then moved on to writing reviews of books and articles that appeared in leading socialist and other publications. Along the way he embraced socialism.[13]

It should not be forgotten that the period when Harrison entered the New York scene was a devastating one for African Americans—the nadir of the backlash following Reconstruction. By 1900 Jim Crow laws had been instituted and lynching was an accepted practice in the South; economic and social injustice prevailed throughout the land. A militant response was beginning to simmer, and parallel conditions in the broader community were seeking redress. Portia James has focused on some of the issues facing workers in the early 1900s that would attract young militants like Harrison to the Socialist Party: "New York City was very turbulent then; and labor unrest in the form of militant strikes swept the immigrant communities on the East side of the city. The socialist party was particularly visible, having sustained a long period of activity among the immigrant textile workers there. In 1909 thousands of textile workers went on strike; in 1910 sixty thousand cloakmakers went out and as a result won a collective bargaining agreement. The militancy and subsequent victories of these workers, primarily Jewish immigrant women, must have made a lasting impact on the city's Black community."[14]

Harrison, no armchair socialist, was in the fray. The price was his job. His pursuit of socialism and his outspoken lectures and writings on various aspects of economics and society, including attacks on certain African American leaders, resulted in Booker T. Washington exerting pressure to have him dismissed from the post office. On September 23, 1911, after four years' service with a good work record, he was out of a job and forced to rely on speaking and teaching to feed his family. He was convinced that the Socialist Party needed to correct its position that race problems would be solved by addressing the class issue and should direct propaganda to African Americans, who represented a large segment of the working class. He was keen on developing a program to be implemented among residents of the emerging African American community in Harlem.

Shortly after Harrison's dismissal from the post office, Samuel M. Romansky, an officer of Branch 5, to which Harrison belonged, wrote on behalf of the branch to Julius Gerber, executive secretary of Local New York, proposing that Comrade Harrison be made "a paid speaker and organizer for Local New York for special work in negro districts." Philip Foner marks Romansky's recommendation as the first time special attention to the "Negro Question" and a special campaign among African Americans had been called for by a branch since the formation of the Socialist Party in 1901. On October 18, 1911, the local's executive committee engaged Harrison, and he threw himself into the election campaign. The socialist vote among African American voters was increased and the committee announced plans on November 28 for a new branch in Harlem. Harrison enthusiastically worked on plans for a "Colored Socialist Club" and a series of lectures on African American history.[15]

Harrison had not confined his expositions to the soapbox. One of his major essays appeared in the *Call* on November 28, 1911, as "The Negro and

Socialism" and in the *International Socialist Review* in July 1912 as "Socialism and the Negro." Harrison's thesis employed a deliberate and logical development, appealing to reason rather than to sympathy. The opening described the economic status of the ten million African Americans as "a group that is more essentially proletarian than any other American group" and linked the fact that they were brought here as chattels to their continuous and fixed low social status. He continued, "Inasmuch, then, as the Negro was at one period the most thoroughly exploited of the American proletariat, he was the most thoroughly despised. That group which exploited and despised him, being the most powerful section of the ruling class, was able to diffuse its own necessary contempt of the Negro first among all other classes of Americans ... Race prejudice, then, is the fruit of economic subjection and a fixed inferior economic status ... The Negro problem is essentially an economic problem with its roots in slavery past and present."[16]

Harrison went on to point out that special socialist propaganda was preached to Poles, Slovaks, Finns, Hungarians, and Lithuanians, while African Americans were left to become a great menace utilized as scabs by the capitalists. He considered the time ripe for socialists—indeed, it was their duty—to take a stand against the disfranchisement of the Negro, which violated the provisions of the Constitution, and suggested that the Socialist Party would "not be guilty of proposing anything worse than asking the government to enforce its own 'law and order.'" He asked, "If the Negroes, or any other section of the working class in America, is to be deprived of the ballot, how can they participate with us in the class struggle? How can we pretend to be a political party if we fail to see the significance of this fact?" His questions boldly challenged the party to face its reluctance to deal with the racist attitudes that prevailed within it: "Southernism or Socialism—which? Is it to be the white half of the working class against the black half, or all the working class? Can we hope to triumph over capitalism with one-half of the working class against us?"[17]

On February 23, 1912, the committee abandoned the project for the Colored Socialist Club. Objections to a segregated branch had been raised by W. E. B. Du Bois and other African American leaders. Du Bois's concerns went beyond the implications of a segregated branch. His own experience with the Socialist Party had led him to conclude that "there is a kind of fatalistic attitude on the part of certain transcendental Socialists, which often assumes that the whole battle of Socialism is coming by a kind of evolution in which active individual effort on their part is hardly necessary."[18] In a 1913 article he charged that "No recent convention of Socialists has dared to face fairly the Negro problem and make a straightforward declaration that they regard Negroes as men in the same sense that other persons are." He raised questions similar to

Harrison's: "Can the problem of any group of 10,000,000 be properly considered as 'aside' from any program of Socialism? Can the objects of Socialism be achieved so long as the Negro is neglected? Can any great human problem 'wait'? . . . what is anti-Negro socialism doing but handing to its enemies the powerful weapon of 4,500,000 men who will find it not simply to their interest, but a sacred duty, to underbid the labor market, vote against labor legislation, and fight to keep their fellow laborers down?" Du Bois doubted that the average modern socialist could grasp the extent of the hatred against African Americans in the South, "which violently opposes any program of any kind of reform that recognizes the Negro as a man." To Du Bois the "Negro Problem" was "the great test of the American Socialist." He concluded by asking if the socialists paid the price the South demanded, "will the result be Socialism?"[19]

The objection raised by Du Bois and others to a Colored Socialist Club was not the only reason the socialists had second thoughts about the project. Harrison had committed two sins. More and more he was voicing support for the Industrial Workers of the World (IWW), which had shown strong support for the inclusion of African American workers in their organization. Perhaps most damaging was his espousal of sabotage as a tool available to workers engaged in union activities. The New York Socialist leadership strongly opposed the use of sabotage, but Harrison sided with Bill Haywood of the IWW on this issue and lost favor with the more conservative New York party leaders. As Harrison persisted in his increasingly radical positions, party leadership attempted to rein him in. The struggle became nastier in 1913 when he signed the "Resolution of Protest" attacking the removal of Haywood from the national executive committee of the Socialist Party and assumed an active role along with Haywood and Elizabeth Gurley Flynn in the silk workers' strike in Paterson, New Jersey. Ironically, the leadership of the Socialist Party responded like Booker T. Washington to silence Harrison's pronouncements. The executive committee of Local New York put the final touch on the relationship when they notified him on May 18, 1914, that he was suspended—but Harrison had already gone his way. While he continued to pursue and promote socialism he persisted in developing his own philosophy and program. By the time of his death in 1927 he had become one of the most prolific African American writers on socialism. His biographer, Jeffrey Babcock Perry, has identified approximately seven hundred writings, including printed articles and book reviews in socialist and other publications, in the *Negro World,* which he edited in 1920, and in local newspapers.[20] Winston James has characterized it succinctly: "American socialism did not keep faith with Hubert Harrison, Harrison kept faith with socialism."[21]

While it is not known exactly when Otto Huiswoud became acquainted with Harrison it is clear that contact was established while Harrison was stumping on behalf of the Socialist Party. Huiswoud discovered Harrison in the same manner as Richard B. Moore, who used his lunch hour to listen to the orators in Madison Square Park. In time they would also encounter Harrison's writings. To Huiswoud and Moore in those early years Harrison was the model militant. Harrison was not the first or only African American espousing socialism, but at the time there was no informed, logical, articulate, courageous voice like his. Describing himself as a "Radical Internationalist," he inspired in his young listeners an appreciation of socialism as the rational, scientific alternative to the unfair and unjust system of capitalism and colonialism. They took him seriously—they bought and borrowed books, studied independently and later together, practiced their debating skills, and in time mounted the mighty soapbox themselves. Harrison became one of Huiswoud's and Moore's earliest mentors and played a key role in introducing them to socialist ideas.

Years later, Moore, while recognizing that Harrison was a prolific writer, stated that Harrison's major influence stemmed from his street orations during the lunch hour on Wall Street or Madison Square Park and especially in the evenings, first at West 96th Street off Broadway and later on Lenox Avenue. "His ability to make complex subjects clear and simple, and the power of his logic and presentation gained him a hearing in some very difficult situations."[22] Moore described Harrison as "a pioneer in nonconformist thought" and gave some insight into his demeanor on the soapbox: "Of dark hue and medium height . . . Harrison was not prepossessing but quite impressive. His sparse hair covered his head lightly and his high forehead seemed to make his head taller and add to his stature. His keen black eyes could almost transfix an opponent; when they opened slightly and his lips pulled up somewhat, then a withering blast was on its way. Although generally amiable and never pompous, he bore a reserved but pleasant mien, always bearing himself with conscious dignity."[23]

Huiswoud found other mentors not far from his workplace. At first he was attracted to the courses on English and speaking offered at the Rand School of Social Science located near Union Square on East 19th Street at that time. It was a unique educational institution founded in 1906 on a model that was developed in Europe and was quite successful in Brussels at the turn of the century. The focus, however, was not on English for immigrants; the school specialized in courses on "socialist theory, economics, economic history, American history, and literature" taught by leaders of the socialist movement, distinguished academicians, and trade union leaders.[24] In this milieu he was to meet Sen Katayama, a Japanese revolutionary in exile, and S. J. Rutgers, a Dutch engineer who was promoting the Socialist Propaganda League.

Huiswoud formed a close relationship with Katayama (1860–1933), who began his long, arduous journey to Moscow with the name Sugataro on December 7, 1860, in Hadeki, a rural village in Japan. During his childhood in the Yabuki family he felt lonely and rejected as the second son born to parents who were disappointed that he was not a girl. He felt keenly the loss of his father due to a family dispute when he was three or four years old. Despite the poverty experienced following his father's departure his mother managed to arrange education for him in the Buddhist temple schools. He assumed the name Sen Katayama at the age of nineteen when he was legally adopted by a friend of the family.[25] Against extreme odds he sought education and the ascent out of poverty in 1881 in Tokyo as an apprentice and assistant in a printing establishment. He became associated with a group studying Christian socialism that was concerned with the conditions of the workers during that period of Japanese industrialization. On November 26, 1884, at the age of 24, he set out for the United States, arriving in San Francisco with sixty cents. He worked at any job he could find, struggled to learn English, and between 1888 and 1895 attended Maryville College in Tennessee, Grinnell College in Iowa, Andover Theological Seminary in Massachusetts, and Yale School of Divinity. Over the next two decades his vision of socialism would evolve from being closely associated with Christianity to more revolutionary ideas associated with the Left.

Katayama returned to Japan in January 1896 and felt pressed to help organize trade unions. He established a socialist study club and the first successful labor newspaper there. In 1901 he and Shusui Kotoku founded the Japanese Social Democratic Party, and on December 29, 1903, he traveled to the United States to attend the national convention of the American Socialist Party in Chicago. His main destination, however, was the Sixth Congress of the Second International scheduled for August 1904 in Amsterdam, where he was warmly received as a representative of the Japanese Socialists. Katayama's biographer, Hyman Kublin, credits the Sixth Congress as the event that transfigured Sen "Joe" Katayama "by the socialists of the Occident into a solitary symbol of proletarian struggle against tyranny and oppression in remote Asia."[26] His return to Japan in 1904 was marked by heightened political agitation, including involvement in strikes in the iron industry, against the backdrop of war with Russia. The strikes led to surveillance and the internment of socialists by the Japanese government. In 1912 he was sentenced to prison for his political activities. Upon his release in 1914 he went into exile in the United States, where he became closely associated with the Left Wing of the Socialist Party in New York and later organized a small group of Japanese socialists living there. He saw his role as an interpreter of the workers' struggle in Japan. He wrote *The Labor Movement in Japan* and many articles on Japan, including those appearing in the Rand School publication *American Labor Year Book* and in the *International Socialist Review*. Over the years his literary output was to exceed forty books and monographs and five hundred articles.[27]

Sebald Justinus Rutgers (1879–1961) began his life on the opposite side of the world from Katayama, in Leiden, the Netherlands, on January 25, 1879. He came to New York City via China and Japan from Indonesia, which he left in March 1915 after working as a director and chief engineer for the Netherlands East Indies. He had joined the Dutch Social Democratic Workers' Party in 1899 but was expelled for his Left Wing agitation as expressed in their organ, *De Tribune*. He helped form the "Tribune Group," or the Social Democratic Party, in 1909, which later became the Communist Party in the Netherlands. While in Indonesia he had developed a concern for peoples under colonial rule and became a strong opponent of colonialism. Rutgers met Katayama at the Amsterdam Congress in 1904 and extended an invitation to Katayama in 1916, who was in San Francisco at that time, to join him in New York City and live with the Rutgers family in Brooklyn. During that stay, Rutgers introduced Katayama to Marxist leaders from Europe and the United States. Although Katayama was nineteen years Rutgers' senior, Hyman Kublin considers Rutgers to be Katayama's mentor because of the shift toward the Left following Katayama's experiences in New York.[28] It was in New York that the strong friendship and collaboration was forged between the two men from far distant points halfway around the globe.

While working in New York during World War I as a purchasing agent for the Deli Railway Company and the Netherlands-India Railway Company, Rutgers was also a key organizer and fundraiser for the Socialist Propaganda League, which was responsible for assisting in the establishment of a succession of radical newspapers: the *Internationalist,* the *New International,* and the *Revolutionary Age*.[29] He was very influential in promoting the concept of mass action. He recognized the lack of political influence of the working class in the United States and pointed out that "far more than one-third of the workers do not even have a vote: Negroes in the South, immigrants in the North, and men who must keep moving in pursuit of jobs."[30] He helped shape the leftist positions of American socialists who later established the Communist Party and served as a strong link between European and American socialists. Akito Yamanouchi has pointed out that his more than twenty articles in the *International Socialist Review* provided American readers with news of European left-wing developments, and his approximately thirty reports in *De Tribune* provided Dutch socialists with important information on American problems and activities.[31] His influence extended to Huiswoud not only because of his interest in colonial peoples but because both spoke Dutch and Rutgers could clarify Marxist ideas for the young student of socialism. Huiswoud's contact with Rutgers in New York ended in 1918. Rutgers left the United States when he realized he was under police surveillance for his socialist activities and because the companies for which he worked as an engineer were suspected of German connections. He decided he could no longer be productive in the United States and proceeded to Moscow via Japan, where he made contact with some of Katayama's socialist colleagues. He arrived in Moscow in time to attend the founding congress of the Comintern as a delegate representing the Dutch Social Democratic Party (Communist Party) and as an official spokesperson of the Socialist Propaganda League. He also delivered the Japanese socialist leaders' expression of sympathy with the Russian Revolution.[32]

Within three years Katayama, feeling the heat of the Palmer Raids, also left the United States. He first attended the Second Congress of the Comintern, convened July 17, 1920, in Petrograd, and on his return in November stopped in New York with Louis C. Fraina (a.k.a. Lewis Corey), an American delegate and former editor of a series of leftist publications, "for a goodwill mission to U. S. Communist leaders to promote party unity."[33] In March 1921 he and Fraina went to Mexico City and joined Manuel Gomez (Charles Phillips), who was at the time functioning in the Mexican Communist Party, where they spent almost eight months working on a Comintern assignment to establish the organizing center of the Red International of Labor Unions for Latin America.[34] Katayama then proceeded to Moscow, arriving in December 1921 at the age of sixty-one.

It was not the Dutch engineer but the Japanese revolutionary with whom Huiswoud built a lasting friendship. Katayama could easily have seen himself in young Otto. The similarities in their introduction to American culture were striking: both were motivated to seek opportunities in a more cosmopolitan location than their birthplace could provide; both were thrust on the shores of the United States alone and penniless; both had to learn a new language; both were trained as printers but forced to work in temporary menial jobs to make ends meet; both had unexpectedly entered a culture steeped in race hatred and experienced discrimination; and both were challenged by an economic and social system that promoted oppression of workers, colonialism, and imperialism. Ultimately both were driven to seek ways in which the lives of the kinsmen they had left behind could be improved.

It was in New York that the young student of socialism from the distant Caribbean colony was privileged to learn about Marxism directly from three pioneers in the radical movement, none of whom had been born in the United States: Harrison, the "Father of Harlem Radicalism;" Katayama, the "Father of Japanese Socialism" and the "Father of Asian Communism"; and Rutgers, a founder of the Dutch Tribunists, which would become the core of the Dutch Communist Party. While Otto's personal contact with the three key socialists might have been limited, their influence was extended through their writings. They were theoreticians as well as organizers and all published articles in the *International Socialist Review.* The *Review* and other socialist journals did not have wide circulation in the African American community, but Otto was exposed to contemporary socialist literature during his association with the Rand School. This remarkable confluence of influences at a critical time left its mark on the young man who was to become the sole African American charter member of the Communist Party in the United States. New York was indeed a major crossroads of radical intellectual development. The paths of Huiswoud and Harrison would continue to meet in Harlem during the next decade; the paths of Huiswoud, Katayama, and Rutgers were all to cross in later years in Moscow. Interestingly, by 1922 all three had found their way to the emerging Union of Soviet Socialist Republics.

The mid-teens was a difficult period for the Huiswoud brothers. Problems associated with finding adequate work and the encouragement from his mentors convinced Huiswoud that he should pursue additional education. Hubert Harrison in particular stressed the value of education. In 1917 Huiswoud managed to attend the College of Agriculture at Cornell University, where he took courses related to farm crops and animals, farm management, and a basic course in chemistry. While he was at Cornell the Russian Revolution was in progress, and he followed the news of it along with socialist fellow students. It is a mystery how he selected Cornell University, located in upstate New York, instead of the City College of New York like other Caribbean immigrants and why he chose to study agriculture. A turning point emerged in the summer of 1918, when Huiswoud worked for the Fall River Line, which operated pleasure boats between Boston and Maine. Working conditions were extremely poor, and the African American crew had no redress because they were not served by the union. Huiswoud organized a grievance committee but the company was adamant that it would not consider any changes. When they were preparing to sail again from Boston, the home port, the men stood on the pier with folded arms and the passengers were forced to handle their own luggage. Huiswoud acted as spokesman for the crew and the negotiations resulted in more pay and improved working conditions, including better food. During this time he had been grappling with the contradictions and seeking answers to questions about American society; he decided to take advantage of a scholarship offered by the Rand School in its new People's House at 7 East 15th Street in New York and did not return to Cornell for the fall semester. The negotiations with the Fall River Line had stimulated his interest in the trade union movement. At the age of twenty he now knew that Cornell could not prepare him for the work he wished to pursue.

The full-time six-month Workers' Training Course he entered in November 1918 was designed to "train and equip the students for efficient service in the Socialist and Labor Movement, whether as regular officers or employees of the party, the unions, and related bodies, or as volunteer workers in their respective localities and organizations." The *Rand School News* reported that the 1918–19 class of twenty-seven students could "lay claim to the true spirit of Internationalism" and that "Otto E. Huiswoud claims the honor of being the Socialist representative from Dutch Guiana." In vast contrast to the program at Cornell, the curriculum included courses on socialism, economics, political science, the socioeconomic history of the United States, the history of the working class movement, American civics and politics, criminology, natural science, statistics, public speaking, and English. Students were assigned to directed field and office work. They were also expected to make regular use of the gymnasium "to avoid the ill effects likely to result from too sedentary a life."[35]

Evidently Huiswoud had already joined the Socialist Party; activity in the Party was one of the criteria considered in awarding scholarships. The date he joined is unknown but Hermie has indicated that he became acquainted with the Socialists while working with the printer and that he followed the campaign of Eugene Debs in 1912. He entered the Rand program committed to socialist ideas, and he left in the spirit expressed in the valedictory address—determined to "help educate the workers of America so that their slogan, 'a fair day's wage for a fair day's work' [would] be replaced by the revolutionary slogan, 'abolition of the wages system.'" In September the *Alumni Notes* reported that he was doing a "great deal to aid in the emancipation of his race" and that he was connected with the *Messenger*.[36]

All was not Marx and Engels, however, for Huiswoud; a romantic comradeship developed with another member of the class, Anna Leve, who was from Philadelphia. Following graduation she was reported to be working in the small towns of Pennsylvania, organizing the shirtmakers' union. She found her way back to New York and they lived together for several years, during which time they attended the meeting of the Left Wing faction when it split from the Socialist Party and established the Communist Party in 1919.

During that decade he, like many other African Americans, changed his residence from downtown to uptown. The other young men who had left the ship with Huiswoud went their ways, and only he continued to live with the family that had rescued them. He moved with the Brown family from the Bowery to West 53rd Street and by 1916 was established in Harlem.[37] Subsequently he roomed with the mothers of close friends Grace Campbell, Cyril Briggs, and Hermie Dumont. Within nine years, Huiswoud matured from an adolescent Caribbean immigrant wandering lower Manhattan in search of shelter to a socialist organizer poised to deliver the gospel of Marx in Harlem.

As the friendship with Hermie developed he introduced her to the small coterie of friends he had developed in Harlem. His closest friends were W. A. Domingo from Jamaica, Richard B. Moore from Barbados, and Cyril V. Briggs from St. Kitts–Nevis. He took her to forums and debates, including programs at the Harlem Community Church, where E. Ethelred Brown from Jamaica was the minister, as well as to basketball games and social gatherings. One gathering place they frequented was the home of Grace P. Campbell, as described by Hermie:

> Grace Campbell, a very quiet-spoken lady was in her mid-forties, I think, when we became friends although she was twice my age . . .
>
> I remember her with greying hair and jet-black beady eyes that glistened and twinkled as if she were perpetually enjoying something amusing. No wonder that her home was always full of visitors. She kept a permanent open house, offering food and shelter to whomever knocked on her door.
>
> Saturday evenings, she received guests; blacks of various levels of education and political plumage, congregated in her living room to discuss burning issues affecting the Negro people specifically on matters of international import, particularly regarding the working class.
>
> Men like Hubert Harrison, a walking encyclopedia, from the Virgin Islands, Rev. Ethelred Brown, a Socialist and Unitarian clergyman, J. A. Rogers, the writer of Jamaican origin and his country-man, the poet Claude McKay, Richard B. Moore, whose oratory charmed and convinced listeners. Dick had the capacity to speak as eloquently to an audience of two as two thousand. Otto was also a frequent visitor and when I became friendly with him, he took me along to those weekly sessions. It was one of the best periods in the history of Harlem.[38]

It was impossible for Hermie to foresee how these social and cultural good times would merge with political activism. She could not imagine that the friendship developing with Otto Huiswoud and his associates would bring a life shaped largely by the political perspectives of the emerging American Left and the Soviet Union's Communist International (Comintern). The struggle led by Huiswoud and his comrades for the equality of African Americans in the United States would be joined with the effort to end colonialism in the Caribbean and Africa and further entwined with producing a socialist state in Eastern Europe. Her life with Otto was to be played out on an international stage that would take them even farther from their homelands in the Guianas.

2. Uptown and Downtown

There was much about Otto Huiswoud that Hermie never knew. He was by nature quiet, modest, and reserved—referred to by some friends as "The Sphinx." His demeanor was well suited for his chosen work. Hermie respected his reserve for two reasons: she too was a very private person and she accepted that the nature of his work was best not treated as public information. In fact, she learned not to ask certain questions. When they first met Otto was a known communist, but in 1923 that had little significance to a seventeen-year-old girl in Harlem. Knowledge of his involvement with the communist movement was confined to a few comrades in the Workers Party. Later she realized that it was only in New York that his conversion could have taken place. Radical thinking was by no means emerging only in one city; it was part of an international movement. But the radicalization of African Caribbeans in New York was forged by a particular combination of circumstances, and Huiswoud stands as a prime example of that metamorphosis. Life in Harlem seemed pregnant with promise, yet many Caribbean immigrants experienced disappointment, disillusionment, and dismay. Although answers to many questions about this metamorphosis will remain shrouded in mystery, it is important to probe some of the complex factors contributing to their adoption of a radical political perspective. To discover the route by which these émigrés turned despair into protest and propaganda it is necessary to examine the impact of the relationship between uptown and downtown upon their radicalization.

The Harlem that Hermie Dumont and Otto Huiswoud sought and with which they identified was not the enclave frequently presented in descriptions of the Harlem Renaissance. There were two Harlems: one of the day and one of the night. Accounts abound of the journey taken under the cover of night to seek exotic entertainment in dark Harlem. White New Yorkers who lived in downtown Manhattan streamed uptown to the Harlem theme park of the 1920s. There they hopped from cabaret to cabaret, listening to the blues and dancing to the jazz of African American musicians who had blown their horns up the Mississippi from New Orleans, Memphis, and Kansas City to Chicago and New York. As the main character in Wallace Thurman's *Infants of the Spring* explained: "There are a quarter million Negroes here, and it is fashionable only to take notice of a bare thousand . . . the cabaret entertainers, the actors, the musicians, the artists, and the colorful minority who drift from rent party to speakeasy to side-street dives. The rest are ignored. They're not interesting."[1] Entertainment was the principal industry that engaged African American workers in Harlem.

The literature contains little about the African American professional and business men and women who resided and worked in Harlem and even less regarding the exchange of labor that occurred in the light of morning. Harlem residents who were not already working on the railroads and steamships as porters abandoned uptown early in the day for work downtown as elevator operators, seamstresses in the garment industry, domestics and nannies in the homes of white families, and other types of menial jobs. From downtown came the store owners and clerks, public school teachers, policemen, doctors for Harlem Hospital, movie house operators, landlords to collect rent, insurance policy writers, agents with supplies for women who made lampshades and artificial flowers at home, restauranteurs, push cart vendors to line up fresh produce on Eighth Avenue, itinerant salesmen with bundles of blankets or other linens for sale, peddlers with ice or equipment to sharpen knives, and truck drivers with coal that slid into basements to keep the steam heat fired. Harlem was a walking market, a place where white entrepreneurs sought consumers even if credit had to be extended. Harlem was the workplace for white professionals because African Americans were denied employment even in Harlem no matter how qualified they might be. Many European Americans who made their living in Harlem showed a friendly side and in some cases a dedication to the people they served. They felt safe during the day and after hours they could retire to their homes in other neighborhoods and not be a part of the Harlem community. Landlords were never seen in a positive light, regardless of their color, but there were examples of positive encounters, especially in the public schools. Kenneth Clark has pointed out that "Children attending Harlem schools in the 1920s and 1930s had average academic achievement close to, if not equal to, the white norms."[2] This is a testament not only to the parents' quest for education but also to the commitment of the many white teachers working in Harlem schools during that period. It was not strange, therefore, to see white faces in Harlem. Besides, the boundary between African American Harlem and other neighborhoods was never farther than a few blocks away.

For Americans of African descent the urbanization process in New York was similar to that taking place in other large cities. Typically, they experienced a stranglehold on their employment that limited opportunities to low-paying jobs; crowding and high rents in restricted neighborhoods; and social lines that were carefully maintained. Harlem, however, offered an excitement that was distinct from the mood in well-established African American neighborhoods in Boston, Baltimore, Chicago, Philadelphia, and Washington, D.C. Gone were the old family and community controls, ties, and traditions. Anonymity prevailed. Many of those attracted to Harlem were young—the stage of life most given to revolt and most open to new or different ideas. They did not have to contend with former teachers or ministers with their reminders of great expectations, nosy neighbors who checked on bedtime, or grandmothers intent upon trying to protect sons and grandsons from the lynchers. Despite the negative aspects of large-scale urban life, Harlem beckoned as a light to help free the soul of the cancer of racism. In its newness and favorable locale in Manhattan, it offered release from some of the pent-up pressures through the arts and the pen. One might dare to say in New York what one might hesitate to express back home. There was encouragement in numbers as well as in the stimulating exchange among writers and artists. It was not necessary to join a political party or civil rights organization to consider, flirt with, or adopt a radical position. The intense exchange of ideas within and outside Harlem set young aspiring writers free to explore unconventional ideas and modes of expression.

Like Hermie, the writer Arthur P. Davis found beauty upon arriving in Harlem in the mid-twenties:

> Harlem in the 1920s was a delightful place, particularly so to a youngster reared in a small Southern town. With its broad avenues uncluttered then by excess traffic, with its clean streets and its well-kept apartment houses; with its favored residential sections like Strivers Row . . . and its swank apartment dwellings on Sugar Hill . . . there were thousands of other migrants like me who felt the charm of the black ghetto. Harlem was then still a relatively new settlement for Negroes, and the grime and the deterioration that came with the subsequent years of poverty and job-discrimination and frustration had not blighted the black city . . .
>
> But this enjoyment was not the phony exotic primitivism which the white folks came uptown nightly to find in cabarets and other hot spots. Our enjoy-

ment was in part the pride of having a city of our very own—a city of black intellectuals and artists, of peasants just up from the South, of West Indians and Africans, of Negroes of all kinds and classes.[3]

Davis's view of Harlem mirrors James Weldon Johnson's earlier description in *Black Manhattan* in which he claimed that Harlem covered "one of the most beautiful and healthful sites in the whole city. It is not a fringe, it is not a slum, nor is it a 'quarter' consisting of dilapidated tenements. It is a section of new-law apartment houses and handsome dwellings, with streets as well paved, as well lighted, and as well kept as in any other part of the city."[4] Both descriptions paint a portrait of Harlem in its external attractiveness and the feeling of pride that accompanies identification with a place and its residents. But Harlem did not wait until the Great Depression to experience poverty, crowded housing, rent gouging, the rebuff of the downtown workplace, and the denial of service at certain uptown cabarets and restaurants such as Childs and Frank's on 125th Street. Getting to Harlem was only one giant step toward facing the reality of the American experience.

As Huiswoud and his serious colleagues from the Caribbean added to the swell of African Americans and African Caribbeans moving from downtown to Harlem during the teens, they groped their way from menial job to menial job—washing dishes, running elevators, stocking shelves, shining shoes. They appreciated the improved physical surroundings but they pondered not only their individual fates but the sharp economic differences and privileges between folks who lived uptown and those who lived downtown. They perceived that the apple, so rosy and shiny on the outside, was rotten at the core. It was not long before they began to discern the dependence of uptown upon downtown and question how that relationship could be altered. Many writers have set the flowering of literary and artistic development characterized as the Harlem Renaissance as the 1920s. But that ignores the frustration that earlier arrivees in New York experienced, their search for redress and the establishment of a climate that would encourage budding writers and foster expressions of protest. Urbanization was far from smooth and had its radicalizing aspect.

As early as 1903 W. E. Burghardt Du Bois (1868–1963) described the deep frustration of discrimination and the defenses available to African American youth:

> To-day the young Negro of the South who would succeed cannot be frank and outspoken, honest and self-assertive, but rather he is daily tempted to be silent and wary, politic and sly; he must flatter and be pleasant, endure petty insults with a smile, shut his eyes to wrong; in too many cases he sees positive person-

al advantage in deception and lying. His real thoughts, his real aspirations must be guarded in whispers; he must not criticise, he must not complain. Patience, humility, and adroitness must, in these growing black youth, replace impulse, manliness, and courage . . .

On the other hand, in the North the tendency is to emphasize the radicalism of the Negro. Driven from his birthright in the South by a situation at which every fibre of his more outspoken and assertive nature revolts, he finds himself in a land where he can scarcely earn a decent living amid the harsh competition and the color discrimination. At the same time, through schools and periodicals, discussions and lectures, he is intellectually quickened and awakened. The soul, long pent up and dwarfed, suddenly expands in new-found freedom. What wonder that every tendency is to excess,—radical complaint, radical remedies, bitter denunciation or angry silence.[5]

Despite his seeming reservation about the tendencies to excess in the North, Du Bois's book *The Souls of Black Folk* should be viewed as a watershed marking the transition toward widespread expressions of protest and creating a literary home in New York for many writers of African descent. As one born in 1868 and a scholar of history and sociology, Dr. Du Bois was well aware that the promise of emancipation and reconstruction had been thwarted by legal restrictions and segregation, inferior education, political duplicity and chicanery, peonage and sharecropping, and especially the unchecked violent attacks on persons and property. The nineteenth century had ended with the status of the African American at its nadir and an incipient genocide gripping the South. At the dawn of the twentieth century Du Bois provided an eloquent description of "the struggles of the massed millions of the black peasantry" and set the stage for the protest that had to be mounted. His collection of essays was lyrical yet political, examined the past yet forecast the future, and exposed the horrors of lynching yet extolled the harmonies of the spirituals, conveyed the despair of one father's loss of his first-born yet revealed the sense of "twoness" experienced by all Americans of African heritage. His most prophetic line still haunts us: "The problem of the twentieth century is the problem of the color-line."[6]

In less than a decade Du Bois came to view organization and propaganda as significant and necessary strategies to address racism in America. In 1910 he traded academia at Atlanta University for the National Association for the Advancement of Colored People (NAACP), a mass organization that was being established in New York City. He relinquished editorship of the annual Atlanta University studies on the Negro in America for the NAACP's organ, the *Crisis,* intended for mass distribution. From the heart of downtown New York he was to lead the polemicists in a national campaign to combat discrimination. He would pursue socialism and continually analyze the status of the peoples of African descent. In 1910, at the age of forty-two, the scholar was ready for a more radical approach in the North.

Many writers and artists have indicated how indebted they were to Du Bois. From his excellent model of writing and analysis of race relations they realized their creative talents and found that they could use the pen to express their frustration and confront the rampant negative stereotypes in the media by depicting a more affirmative view of life in African American communities. It is important to recognize, however, that fiction like Jean Toomer's *Cane* or verse like Langston Hughes's "The Weary Blues" were preceded by the prose of protest mounted during the first two decades. The Harlem Renaissance did not develop simply as an answer to problems faced by African American writers who had not been able to have their works published. Their attraction to Harlem, their inspiration, encouragement, self-realization, race consciousness, and audacity were often derived from or stimulated and affirmed by nationally distributed articles published by civil rights and political organizations that served as catalysts. The tone was set by the explosion of agitation released by publications such as the *Crisis* in 1910, followed by the *Voice* in 1917, the *Messenger* in 1917, the *Crusader* in 1919, the *Challenge,* and others. The movement was also aided by African American newspapers, particularly the *Amsterdam News* and the *Negro World* in New York and others such as the *Chicago Defender* and the *Baltimore Afro-American.* Protest was far from new to Africans in the Diaspora; it had consumed them from the time they were snatched from Africa. But the heightened racism prevailing at the end of the nineteenth century and the response of the accommodationists demanded outspoken, courageous men and women and a revised literary expression. Robert Hill has commented on the journals that articulated the New Negro mood: "This outpouring of political and social commentary far exceeded anything seen or heard since the days of the proliferation of black anti-slavery newspapers."[7] Out of the milieu of the teens the "New Negro" envisioned by Hubert Harrison emerged with renewed self-confidence, and the Harlem Renaissance asserted itself into American literature.

Although it is true that New York was a magnet for writers during the 1920s, Otto Huiswoud, Cyril Briggs, W. A. Domingo, and Richard B. Moore had not left their homes in the Caribbean in search of a publisher for their manuscripts. They had arrived in New York at a young age about a decade earlier without the financial support of a father and were pressed to find employment. Both of Otto's parents were alive when he left Suriname, but his decision to abandon ship had left him on his own at the age of sixteen. The departure and arrival were somewhat different for the three others. Regardless, their struggles with the economic and social barriers and their outcry placed them among the vanguard of the emerging Harlem Renaissance. As they engaged in comprehending the American experience during the teens they became polemicists of the period. Huiswoud, Moore, and Domingo sought answers in the political arena and were to become significant players in the new socialist movement in Harlem.

Richard Benjamin Moore (1893–1978), born August 8, 1893, in Barbados, the same year as Otto, arrived in New York on July 4, 1909, just one-half year earlier than Otto. His father, Richard Henry Moore, was a builder of custom homes in addition to homes on land he purchased that he would then sell. He also operated a bakery and grocery. The family, living in their own home in Hastings in the parish of Christ Church, would have been considered relatively well off by Barbadians. The two daughters and three-year-old son, however, suffered the loss of their mother in 1896 and their father five years later. Their father had remarried so the children had a stepmother to care for them. As in the case of Hubert Harrison, the death of the male breadwinner signaled a serious loss of income. A merchant who had extended credit to Moore for building materials seized the family home and other assets. Fortunately, the property owned by their stepmother combined with the property willed earlier to the children by their natural mother helped maintain them for a few years. Young Richard was able to continue his education at Lynch's Middle Class School in fulfillment of an agreement his father had made earlier to educate his son in payment for repairs Moore had made on Lynch's house. Richard was sent to live in Bridgetown with an uncle in order to attend Lynch's school. After his graduation in April 1905 he obtained employment as a junior clerk in a department store and remained in the city. His father had been a lay preacher of a small sect, The Brethren, that had congregations in Bridgetown as well as Oistins, but Richard came under the influence of white missionaries from Tennessee and was converted to the Christian Mission sect. He and seven young converts went about the city preaching their new-found religion. When his stepmother realized that their dwindling income would not sustain the family much longer and decided that it was best to join her sister in New York, Richard was eager to seek better employment and a wider religious experience in the new land of opportunity.

Even though only fifteen years of age when he landed in New York, Moore considered himself the man of the family and set out to find employment with the help of his stepmother's nephew. Despite his clerical skills, including shorthand, he was able to find work only as an office boy and subsequently an elevator operator. His attempt to increase his skills in a typing and shorthand class given at the midtown YMCA met with rejection by the school, and his visit to the Christian Missionary Alliance one Sunday was met with curt instructions to sit in the gallery that served as the segregated area for African Americans. This lesson on racial barriers was swift and cutting. While his demeanor remained cool his blood ran hot, and he questioned that such rebuffs entitled the YMCA and the church to have "Christian" in their names. The turning point in his views of religion and America had begun. During his lunch hour on the various jobs he held downtown he would rummage through books at the used book stores on Lexington Avenue at 23rd and 25th Streets and listen to the orators on socialism. Madison Square Park was the venue where he first observed Hubert Harrison. It was an encounter he would never forget and one that eventually changed the direction of his life.[8] It is quite possible that Moore met Huiswoud in that setting but there is no evidence regarding when they met or when Moore joined the Socialist Party. In 1919 he married Kathleen Ursula James, a seamstress, who had migrated from Jamaica in 1914. They settled in Harlem and had a daughter, Joyce.

It is not known how early Huiswoud and Moore met Wilfred Adolfus Domingo (1889–1968), who came to New York in 1912. Domingo had come to Boston in 1910 when his uncle, Adolphus Grant, helped finance his voyage from Jamaica to pursue a career in medicine. He had been born on November 26, 1889, in Kingston, Jamaica, the youngest child of Francisco and Alice Domingo. His father owned and operated a fleet of hansom cabs, but both parents died while Wilfred was quite young and he was raised by his mother's brother, who lived in St. Ann's Bay. He attended Calabar School, which was conducted by Baptists, and Kingston Board School. After graduation he worked as an apprentice tailor in Kingston. He joined S.A.G. Cox's National Club—the first local organization to agitate for self-government—and frequently submitted articles to the local press under various nom de plumes. It was in the National Club that he became friendly with Marcus Garvey: Domingo served as first assistant secretary of the organization and Garvey as second. In 1910 he collaborated with Garvey in writing a pamphlet, *The Struggling Mass,* describing the political struggle in Jamaica.

In August 1910 he joined his older sister, who operated a boarding house for Jamaicans in Boston. In preparation for entry into a program in medicine he attended night school but also became involved with organizing a Jamaica Club. His interest in pursuing medicine diminished while the lure of New York City increased. In two years he moved to New York and within a year began agitating for a democratic constitution for Jamaica that would provide for universal suffrage, free labor unions, civil service reforms, and self-government.[9] He worked with an English importer of foods from the Caribbean, an experience that would prove very valuable later when he decided to develop his own wholesale importing business. Meanwhile his interest in political self-government for Jamaica was broadening, and he was becoming increasingly involved with friends who were also questioning power relationships in international affairs and exploring socialism. Even though he helped organize the British Jamaican Benevolent Association in July 1917, his interests were not confined to that one island. As political organizations and organs emerged such as those sponsored by Hubert Harrison, socialists A. Philip Randolph and Chandler Owen, Marcus Garvey and Cyril Briggs, Domingo could be counted on for assistance. His keen, analytical mind, acerbic writing style, and gregarious manner soon placed him at the center of radical thinking among Caribbean immigrants settling in Harlem. He was often the kinsman to be contacted when new arrivees made their way from Jamaica to New York. In 1918 he married Eulalie Manhertz, also from Jamaica, a talented pianist who had won scholarships for two years to study music in England, where she earned a diploma from the Royal Academy of Music. She played for musical programs on a New York radio station but lost her job when she insisted on being identified as an African American instead of their "charming Spanish pianist." She continued to give private piano lessons. They had two children, a son who was named Karl Marx Domingo in keeping with the socialist enthusiasm of the day, and a daughter, Yolanda. The family became close friends of Richard B. Moore and his wife.

While Huiswoud, Moore, and Domingo were pondering their way into the Socialist Party they established relationships with other members of the African American community. A friendship that would endure for many years was forged with Cyril Valentine Briggs (1888–1966), who arrived in New York on July 4, 1905, on the vessel *Trinidad*. Slightly older than Domingo, he was actually the first of the quartet to experience the metropolis. He was born in St. Kitts–Nevis on May 28, 1888. His mother, Marian Huggins, was of African heritage and his father, Louis E. Briggs, was a white Trinidadian overseer of a sugar plantation and a bookkeeper. His mother's wages helped support the family, which consisted of her only child, Cyril, her father, her sister, and her sister's two children. It would seem that Briggs had little relationship with his father, who was not married to his mother. Throughout his life Cyril sought to compensate for the fact that he had inherited his father's appearance and had a severe stutter. It was as if nature had played a cruel hoax: it gave him a white countenance with a black consciousness, it bade him speak yet tied his tongue. In Communist Party records he stated that he attended public school and graduated at the age of fourteen. There is evidence, however, in notes he prepared for an autobiography that all the schools were parochial at that time and he attended schools conducted by Baptist, Anglican, and Wesleyan Methodist denominations for children of African heritage: the Baptist primary school at Brown Pasture, the Church of England school at St. John's, and Ebenezer Wesleyan grade school on St. Kitts. His fascination with works by Robert Ingersoll and books on imperialism that he discovered while working in the library of the Baptist minister and a report that he declined a scholarship indicate his high intellect and curiosity. He considered that the education he was getting was intended to turn out Black Anglo-Saxons, glorify whites, and denigrate Africans. It provided, nonetheless, an education that armed him with the linguistic tools he could use to counteract false stereotypes. He began work at the age of fifteen as an apprentice in a tailor shop, then worked as a printer's devil in a newspaper office and later at a job printing plant of the Express Publishing Company in Basseterre, St. Kitts, for two years. During his final year in St. Kitts he worked as a cub reporter for the *St. Kitts Daily Express* and the *St. Christopher Advertiser*. In 1905 he joined his mother, who had migrated to New York in 1903, and worked in a factory as a presser and in laundries.[10]

Briggs worked as an elevator operator until he found a job with the *Amsterdam News,* which had been founded by James H. Anderson in 1909. Briggs has written that he joined the staff of the *Amsterdam News* in 1912, worked as a leg man for some months, was promoted to sports and theatrical editor, and by 1914 was writing the paper's editorials under the title of associate editor. He stated, "For some months I also worked as City Editor (actually Managing Editor). For several years up to my resignation from the paper I was editor in all but name."[11] On another occasion he explained that he resigned in 1918 "in protest against the publishers' attempt to censor my editorials, following their intimidation by government agencies." His editorials had opposed World War I as an imperialist war and criticized President Wilson's slogan regarding making the world safe for democracy as a "sham and fraud" in view of lynchings in the United States and poor treatment of American soldiers in France.[12]

Briggs actually resigned from the *Amsterdam News* twice. He left in 1915 to found the *Colored American Review: A Magazine of Inspiration* for the Harlem business community. The magazine did not last long. In an editorial, Briggs encouraged African Americans to patronize Negro enterprises and lambasted white Harlem businesses for gouging Harlem residents. Hubert Harrison responded with an enthusiastic commendation for the editorial. The publisher of the review was E. Touissant Welcome, an African American real estate broker engaged in developing a market for African American homeowners in Jamaica—a suburb in the borough of Queens. Most real estate brokers were considered suspect in their relationship with renters and potential homeowners; Briggs's attack might have struck too close to home. At any rate he was able to return to the *Amsterdam News,* where he continued working until June 1919. As a journalist he covered all aspects of life in Harlem. He enjoyed drama, musical productions, and sporting events, particularly basketball, as well as observing meetings of various organizations. His editorials revealed his radical interests, and he has been cited frequently for his bold proposal in the *Amsterdam News* of May 15, 1918, that following the Armistice, African Americans should "claim and take a tenth part of the territory of the United States, seeing that they form a tenth part of the population."[13] He never joined the Socialist Party along with his friends, yet he frequented their public meetings and engaged in the exchange of ideas critical to the formulation of a "New Negro."

During his association with the *Amsterdam News* Briggs married Bertha Florence Johnson of Talcott, West Virginia, on January 7, 1914, and they made their home in Harlem.[14] He applied for citizenship on February 24, 1916, and was issued a certificate of naturalization on August 6, 1918.[15] In September 1918 he launched his own magazine, the *Crusader,* "dedicated to the honorable solution to the 'Negro Problem' and to a renaissance of Negro power and culture throughout the world."[16] His wife became a staff member of the magazine in July 1919 and assumed responsibilities as business manager with the August issue. Typically most wives were unknown in the movement regardless of the extent of their assistance with clerical chores or financial support of their husbands. He stated that he left her a year after joining the Communist Party because of her hostility to his political involvement and that he had a daughter in 1931 with a woman in Trinidad.[17]

Despite the lack of evidence as to when and whether Huiswoud, Moore, Domingo, and Briggs met in socialist or Caribbean social circles, there is no doubt that their friendships were cemented during the teens and provided a powerful base for implementing their militancy. The insularity that normally prevailed in each colony was easily overcome in New York, and the fact that they were from four different areas of the Caribbean enhanced their international perspective. They had in common a seriousness imposed by the responsibility to support themselves, a sense of loss through separation or the death of one or both parents, a keen intellectual ability that sought answers to questions posed by society, a sensitivity to injustice, and a thirst for knowledge that was stimulated but severely unquenched by a grade school education. Individually and together they pondered the dichotomy of uptown versus downtown. As adolescents in a new land their task was to identify who they were. Although poverty and prejudice were not confined to Caribbean immigrants, American culture had established a rigid standard for manhood: simply put, regardless of intelligence, abilities, training, or proficiency in English, to be white was to be a man, and to be Black was to be considered less than a man. African Americans who had relocated from the South had been conditioned to Jim Crowism because their lives depended upon acquiescence. They found New York to be a relief from the terror of the lynch mob. On the other hand, the newly arrived Caribbeans, despite their second-class status as subjects of colonial empires, could not accept the racial inferiority and self-hatred that had been imposed by the southern psyche. They discovered, as Ira Reid has noted, that "the foreign-born Negro brings into the American occupational picture skills and experiences for which little or no opportunity is provided for Negroes in the United States save in the limited occupational field of racial service . . . The label of democracy is found to be fictional. Accustomed to class lines that he has learned to respect even though he may hate them, he can find little of immediate solace in a system that brands him as inferior even before he is known."[18] The decision to pull up one's roots and invest everything in a foreign land had required serious thought, preparation and courage. One could not go home again. The best option seemed to be to question and protest the unjust system.

At the core of the uptown-downtown relationship, so symbolic of the country's race problem, was the question of identity. As they were transformed by the act of migration, Caribbean immigrants faced a dilemma: Were they Barbadians and Jamaicans or West Indians? British and Dutch subjects or American citizens? Were they "colored," "Negro," or "Afro-American"? Were they "New Negroes" or Washingtonians? Republicans or Socialists? Were they only hewers of wood and drawers of water or professionals, artisans, and leaders? Most significantly, were they men or beasts, humans or subhumans? The four men from the Caribbean spent hours discussing, debating, and discoursing these questions that had been sharpened by the American negation of their very being. They were in basic agreement that their manhood demanded vigorous assertion and protest. In time they came to appreciate that collaboration with others would be needed to create an organized base of action and a revised historical record closer to the true accomplishments of Africans, African Caribbeans, and African Americans. Their aspirations extended to striking a blow for all peoples of African descent. All four men lacked the university education and degrees common among leaders of the existing civil rights organizations, but their excellent basic education provided in accordance with British and Dutch standards was superior to instruction in most of the segregated schools of the United States. Educational policy differed among European colonial powers, where the objective was to train a workforce in remote colonies that included civil servants. According to Ira Reid, 98.6 percent of

Negro immigrants admitted in 1923, for example, could read and write.[19] In marked contrast, the United States considered educating African Americans "dangerous" and established programs to produce industrial, farm, and domestic workers. Ironically, for the Caribbean Americans, the imposed study of the history of colonial empires and world geography took them far beyond the boundaries and experiences of the tiny islands where they were born and ultimately aided their analysis of imperialism. They understood the relationship between the colonies and the so-called mother countries better than their peers educated in the United States.

Beyond the contrast in basic education there existed a difference in self-image both as individuals and as members of a "racial" group. Moore often mentioned that his stepmother impressed upon him that he was a person of worth, a luxury that families in the South could scarcely afford when faced with the necessity of inculcating a demeanor that might save sons from lynchers. Caribbean Americans' previous experience was in a setting where people of African descent constituted a majority even though their power was very limited, where color distinctions were not legally institutionalized, and where lynching was unknown. Their educational and community forms of expression had included an appreciation of the written and spoken word. The populations of many areas were quite literate and fostered the development of literary interests as well as debate and logical argument. The propensity for the art of argument that the Caribbean radicals exhibited might have been honed on socialism in the United States but was forged in the Caribbean.

Winston James has pointed out that Caribbean migrants came with a "long and distinguished tradition of resistance with few parallels in the New World." A sense of self-confidence and pride predisposed some of them to "radical activity, as the harsh racism battered their self-esteem."[20] Domingo had been a member with Garvey in S. A. G. Cox's National Club in Jamaica, but Briggs, Huiswoud, and Moore had not been involved with political organizations prior to migrating to New York; and all four certainly were free of any traditional tie to the Republican Party of Abraham Lincoln. But their seeming apolitical background should be considered in view of their age at the time of migration. Political discourse was considered a normal activity in their homelands. As A. A. Thorne of Guyana has pointed out, African Caribbeans took a keen interest in politics.[21] It is not surprising that these angry young men should consider political activity a strategy for change. They might not have been any more frustrated, resentful, or angry than their American peers but they were emboldened to be heard in their cry for justice. James has cogently summarized the main factors that disposed Caribbean immigrants toward radical politics: "This included their majority consciousness; their prior political and organizational experience; their extensive prior experience of travel and migration; a politically protected status in the United States (at least for those from the British Caribbean) as subjects of the British Crown; a somewhat lesser attachment to the Christian faith and Christian churches; and educational and occupational attainments generally beyond the reach of Afro-Americans."[22]

In New York the relationship between uptown and downtown went much deeper than the exchange of the lopsided economic gain received by each group. New York was a center of radical thought, and the ideas rampant at the time analyzing wage inequalities and enunciating theories of class conflict could not be confined to downtown circles. Socialist street orators, literature, forums, and educational centers such as the Rand School promoted ideas that were noted by many and taken seriously by some African Americans. The main downtown thoroughfare that they passed as they went to work or shopped on 14th Street screamed with radical phrases that were difficult to ignore. In explaining why Katayama might prefer New York to San Francisco, Kublin described the scene:

> For the rebel, the crusader, and the nonconformist in general, opportunities for the expression of pet social schemes and political platforms were, as nowhere else in the United States, available at every hand and turn. In the city's numerous auditoriums, where overflowing audiences regularly gathered to listen to earnest lectures and heated debates, native-born reformers, restive over the many failures of the American dream, rubbed shoulders with immigrants whose political faiths summarized the hopes and disappointments of a century of Old World millenarianism. Union Square in Manhattan had long since become world famous as an arena for nightly political jousts alfresco and in hundreds of kiosks scattered about town newspapers and journals collectively presented the rich spectrum of unorthodox social theory.[23]

It should be noted that not only were unorthodox ideas put forth, African Americans were welcome to associate and enter into discussions with white proponents. This was unthinkable in most of the country, and it made New York unique as a place to participate in the dialogue on class struggle and race beyond those efforts established in New York in 1909 by the NAACP (with prominent Socialists as founding members) and the Urban League in 1910. It was no accident that both of those organizations established their bases and maintained their national offices in downtown New York, and it was no accident that the militant voices of Caribbean immigrants were also to be sounded in New York. Had their journey from the Caribbean to the United States followed one of the earlier routes of their kinsmen trapped in the slave trade, they might have landed in Charleston, South Carolina, and faced a very different environment.

For the most part it was not the established white residents of New York who created the climate of radical thinking and some acceptance of people of color. Rather, the milieu was shaped largely by the immigrant population that had not been steeped in the racism of the American South and had been exposed to socialism in Europe. Socialism was not simply a turn-of-the-century European importation. The rise of the merchant class and the industrial revolution during the nineteenth century in the United States had created terrible working conditions and urban congestion that cried out for reform. The response included the development of labor unions, socialist groups, political third parties, experimental utopian communes, and cooperatives as an integral part of nineteenth-century America. From 1848 on conditions in Europe pressed citizens of various nations to seek a new life in the United States. It has been commented that "the entire world seemed to be reassembling itself on the streets of Manhattan." The "City of Nations" was to become by 1907 "the largest Jewish city in the world, the largest Irish city, one of the largest German cities . . . [housing] more than 700,000 Russians . . . [and] more Italians than Rome."[24] The migration crescendo reached enormous proportions, with almost twelve million arriving in New York between 1892 and 1924, creating crushing pressures for jobs and housing along with an outspoken press. At the beginning of the twentieth century New York was the fastest growing city in the world.

Theodore Draper, in describing "this inflammable social climate" mentioned that "employers fought labor organizations by every possible means. Strikes were ruthlessly crushed by armed guards, police, sheriffs, militia, and federal troops. Court injunctions tied the hands of unions on the mere threat of a strike. Working conditions often ranged from the primitive to the abominable."[25] Immigrants drew upon their knowledge and experience with socialism in their native lands in order to combat the unexpected adverse conditions they found in their new country. While they did not face the racism experienced by native-born African Americans and immigrant African Caribbeans, many did encounter discrimination. It has been observed that among the "German, Italian and Swedish, the mood of the radical press—at home and among immigrants—changed from admiration to criticism, indignation and denunciation. By the close of the century, the myth of America as a land of freedom was being subjected to systematic critique."[26] Draper has pointed out that "the American Socialist movement was peculiarly indebted to the immigrants" and described the first convention of the Socialist Labor Party in 1877 as "composed of representatives of seventeen German sections, seven English, three Bohemian, one French, and a general women's section."[27]

Draper concludes, however, that the immigrant character of the organization did not mean that it was "un-American":

> America was a land of immigrants and the American working class was largely immigrant in character. The disproportion of newly arrived immigrants in the Left Wing resulted as much from the rejection of these immigrants by the dominant political institutions as from the rejection by the immigrants of the dominant political institutions. The major political parties neglected them or permitted them to become pawns of corrupt political machines. For many immigrants the dream of American equality came true in the Left Wing where they were received without prejudice and given a means of political expression. Moreover, a large proportion of Socialists were immigrants, but a small proportion of immigrants were Socialists.[28]

There is no question that the character of the socialist movement in the United States was tempered by the socialist experience of European immigrants. There is also no question that the above description applied to Caribbean immigrants whose experience was tempered by the American version of socialism.

While the first- and second-generation immigrant population from Europe clung to their ethnic neighborhoods and language cohorts, learned the value placed on "whiteness" in United States society, and accepted many of the discriminatory barriers established in the city, some were open to positive dialogues with members of the African American community. When referring to the International Ladies Garment Workers Union (ILGWU) and the Amalgamated Clothing Workers of America in New York City, Domingo noted the difference in attitudes: "Negroes are not refused admittance into these unions which are mostly officered by and composed of foreigners. Discrimination is oftenest met in unions whose membership is largely made up of English-speaking and native born white workers."[29] It is possible to conjecture that had racism not been so prevalent the immigrants from the Caribbean attracted to socialism would have constituted an ethnic enclave of radicals similar to the Finnish, Hungarian, and Italian units that had arisen among immigrant nationalities as branches or clubs of the Socialist Party around 1910 and later continued in the communist parties. Harrison's proposed Colored Socialist Club would not have been viewed negatively as a segregated unit but simply as one of many ethnic chapters. Discrimination forced Caribbean immigrants to share the fate assigned to African Americans. While transformed from "Jamaicans" or "Barbadians" to "West Indians," they were classified as "Negroes" rather than Caribbean immigrants. Their protest, therefore, merged with citizens born in the United States and became the voice of African Americans rather than the voice of Caribbean Americans.

The fact remains that African Caribbeans did not arrive in New York with a socialist orientation and a desire to form ethnic political alliances. It was the racism experienced following their settlement in New York that was in large part responsible for pressing them to look at the socialist ideas being promulgated downtown. They were not citizens and were not entitled to vote, yet they recognized the power that political activity carried for change. When Hubert Harrison or candidates for office like Eugene Debs exhorted their listeners during the teens to make themselves heard politically the course seemed very rational to Huiswoud and his colleagues. The tall, kindly, modest, charismatic Debs, who drew listeners from miles around, peppered his sentences with inspired calls for political action: "The united vote of those who toil and have not, will vanquish those who have and toil not, and solve forever the problems of democracy."[30]

In 1901 Debs had helped negotiate a merger of several dissident groups, including factions abandoning the Socialist Labor Party that had been founded in 1877, the American Railway Union, and Social Democracy of America, into a new political party. The Socialist Party of America propounded a popular vision of socialism that appealed to Americans who were wary of the monopolistic directions of the big corporations. Within ten years the party had reached the pinnacle of its power and influence. The rhetoric was often avant-garde, but the issues the local parties emphasized and their entry into regular politics moved the Socialist Party to a position closer to the mainstream. A biographer of Debs has reported that by 1912 "the Socialist Party had a following in every state in the union. Socialist mayors and municipal officers were no longer rarities, particularly in industrial areas. Socialist newspapers were plentiful. There were 13 daily, 298 weekly and 21 monthly publications."[31] This description of the Socialist Party's rise to prominence is further illustrated in *Schooling for "Good Rebels"*: "In 1912 alone, about 1,200 socialists were elected to public office throughout the United States in 340 municipalities, including 79 mayors in 24 states. The Party could boast of the election of two U.S. Congressmen, Victor Berger of Milwaukee in 1910 . . . and Meyer London of Manhattan in 1914 . . . Two local daily newspapers, the *Milwaukee Leader* and the *New York Call,* had circulations of 35,000 and 22,200 respectively during the same year."[32]

The extent of public communication by the socialists cannot be measured, however, by statistical data on newspapers and journals printed or estimates of readership. The major arena for agitation was the street, where public rallies and soapbox speakers drew upon successful strategies of earlier American activists in support of abolition of slavery, woman suffrage, temperance, and other populist causes. At the millennium it is impossible to appreciate the intensity of the major media of the day during the first decades of the twentieth century. "Talking heads" on television sets in living rooms and thirty-second sound bites have replaced the one-half to two-hour extemporaneous speeches given by soapbox orators on the corner. In fact, mounting the soapbox was considered such a significant strategy that articles and courses were designed to assist those who dared face a street audience. They were reminded, for example, that the soapbox orator must be able to speak extemporaneously, come to the point quickly, be accurate and thus "distinguishable from the politicians and reformers," make the contented "wage slave" see that things are not all right, have a plan of action for immediate use, have wit, and use humor and ridicule. They were warned that "the street crowd is the most critical gathering in the world" and includes listeners who are quick to voice disapproval and will move on within two minutes unless their interest has been engaged. Soapboxing was considered a "precarious as well as a laborious existence, making a very great demand upon one's mental and physical resources."[33] Debs was considered one of the foremost orators, as was Harrison. Huiswoud, Domingo, and Moore dared to imagine projecting their protests against racism from the soapbox. They drew upon Caribbean and African American models of oratory in addition to socialist guidance. They employed humor, sarcasm, and logic, and incorporated techniques ranging from an engaging, slow-paced, low-key, modest, apologetic tone to a high-decibel, rapid, passionate crescendo to stir the audience to agreement. They castigated the oppressors, quoted data on disparities in the economic system, portrayed images of Ku Klux Klan lynchers in their sheets terrorizing African American communities in the night, and related historic events and acts of courage and defiance.

Socialists did not confine their activities to political campaigns, propaganda through the press and the soapbox, or involvement with unions. The slogan "Agitation, Education, Organization" was implemented by a wide range of educational and cultural programs. The Rand School became noted as an outstanding adult education program and served as a model. Some of the instructors were regular faculty members of universities such as Columbia. The program was extended through correspondence and extension courses to other areas of the city and adjacent New Jersey. The full-time curriculum, established in 1911, was not only for intensive training but also for students living outside New York City who could enroll for six months, then return home. The school was particularly attractive to immigrant workers who had problems with the new language or would not have felt comfortable in the local high school or college. Algernon Lee, educational director of the Rand School, also considered the lectures and debates that the locals conducted part of the broader educational program. He recollected that "Every branch was a little school of Social Science, much more than it was a political club."[34]

Seldom mentioned is the educational network the socialists developed for their children. Sunday schools were organized to supplement public school education and provide an alternative political and social vision for working-class children. It has been estimated that approximately one hundred English-speaking Sunday schools affiliated with the Socialist party were founded in sixty-four cities and towns in twenty states and the District of Columbia during the first two decades of the twentieth century. The emphasis on educational programs for all age groups indicates not only the socialists' appreciation of education but their concern that some aspects of American culture undermined their vision of society. To offset the tension that political activity imposed on families and to enhance recruitment opportunities, local branches sponsored a wide variety of cultural activities: festivals, concerts, bazaars, carnivals, picnics, encampments, dancing bands, singing societies, theater groups, debating clubs, literary societies, and athletic groups. The street became a major cultural arena, with parades and marches where "songs were sung loudly, slogans chanted defiantly, banners and flags and placards were carried proudly, and the radical spirit in general was publicly and vibrantly displayed . . . One New York City parade in November 1912 reportedly drew 40,000 participants and 150,000 onlookers."[35]

It would have been difficult to miss the socialist message in New York. The newcomer Huiswoud followed socialist activities very carefully, especially Debs's fourth campaign for president of the United States in 1912. This interest in socialism formed his perception of American politics and taught him much about the United States. For example, unlike other highly industrialized countries, the United States had no social insurance for its workers; no state provided insurance against old age and unemployment, and few states had workers' compensation laws. Debs and the Party advocated a system of social insurance for workers, public ownership of the trusts, woman suffrage, abolition of child labor, legislation for an eight-hour workday, and other reforms.[36] The ideas made a favorable impression on Otto, and in the 1916 election he participated in the campaign for socialist candidates. It was not necessary, however, to go downtown to experience the campaign; it came uptown to support Socialist candidates in Harlem.

The tragic 1911 fire in the Triangle Shirtwaist Factory in Greenwich Village that resulted in the death of 146 garment workers ignited a deep sense of anger and grief. Unionization became more urgent, and a rapid expansion of trade union activity was accompanied by a parallel involvement in the socialist movement by "predominantly Jewish or German sections of the painters, carpenters, brewery workers, bakers, ornamental iron workers, carriage and wagon makers, piano makers, typographers, machinists and cigar makers unions . . . all inspired by the garment workers." A succession of strikes mobilized workers, many of whom had not been organized previously, and they picketed and marched incessantly. In October 1916, street, subway, and elevated carmen involved in a tense strike joined a "torchlight parade of twelve thousand persons that wound through the streets of Harlem." During the final week of the campaign party members reported fifteen rallies a night in Harlem and Brownsville.[37] While the Socialists ostensibly brought socialism into the neighborhoods, it is not likely that the description of marchers "of all nationalities and races" included many African American workers, who were still banned from trade unions. As observers rather than participants they could sense nonetheless the socialist presence. This militant socialist milieu proved to be quite attractive to Huiswoud, Domingo, and Moore and promised to be a force within which they could pursue their own agenda for liberation.

Among the many issues that the Socialist Party had to confront were two of particular interest to the Caribbean immigrants. Developing a position on U.S. immigration policy continually plagued the Party. Members were torn between opposing principles. According to David A. Shannon the question was "Should American Socialists, then, adhere to the idea of the international solidarity of labor and welcome immigrants, or should they cooperate with the trade unions in attempting to pressure through legislation restricting immigration?"[38] Ironically, a party of immigrants had difficulty opening the door to other immigrants. The bitter debates also revealed that some Socialists who favored open immigration confined their approval to immigration from Europe and were vehemently opposed to immigration from Asia. The compromise position offered by Morris Hillquit favored "legislative measures tending to prevent the immigration of strike-breakers and contract laborers, and the mass importation of workers from foreign countries . . . for the purpose of weakening the organization of American workers" and opposing the exclusion of any immigrants on account of their race or nationality."[39] The Caribbean immigrants favored an open policy and opposed exclusion based on race or nationality but recognized the prejudice camouflaged by the code words of the resolution and the freely expressed references to the "Mongolian hordes" and the "yellow peril."

At issue also was the position of the Party that Hubert Harrison had confronted. Debs's reply in 1908 when queried by an African American regarding his stand on the Negro question kept echoing through the teens: "The people of your race are entitled to all the rights and opportunities that other races are entitled to, but they have never had them, nor will they ever have them under the administration of either the Republican or Democratic Parties . . . [This] is not a race question but a class question, and when the Negroes . . . understand their true economic and political interests, they will join and support the Socialist Party."[40] Another example of the attitude displayed toward the condition of African Americans was the experience of Benjamin Gitlow, one of the leaders of the Communist Party who joined the Socialist Party in 1909. He related that his first fight in the Socialist Party was over the Negro question. An African American member of the party who was a cigar maker refused to join a strike called by the Cigar Makers International Union and was suspended by the New York local of the Party. His defense was based on the ground that the union discriminated against African Americans by barring them from the union. When Gitlow supported him, arguing that the union's action deserved censure and that the worker had registered censure in the way he believed would be most effective, Gitlow was threatened with expulsion.[41] After reviewing reports from branches in both North and South and stands by members who urged a more sympathetic understanding and action by the Party, David A. Shannon concluded, "How many Negroes there were in the prewar Socialist Party and exactly what role they played in the organization cannot be ascertained. But some things are certain: they were not important in the party, the party made no special effort to attract Negro members, and the party was generally disinterested in, if not actually hostile to, the effort of Negroes to improve their position in American capitalist society."[42] Huiswoud and his African American fellow socialists, especially Domingo, tried to change the position of the Party but were forced to the same conclusion by the early twenties.

Two interconnected international events shattered the rise of the Socialist Party as a viable third party: World War I and the Russian Revolution. The entry of the United States into the war touched all Americans, and opinions were divided regarding involvement in the war. For socialists this was not a personal matter but one of principle. In an emergency convention on April 7, 1917, in St. Louis the Socialist Party formulated their policy regarding the war. Opposition to the war was supported by an overwhelming majority of the delegates on the basis that it was a capitalist war that would crush democracy. Their plan of action included propaganda opposed to the war, conscription, military training, and restrictions on freedom of speech and the press.[43] African American members had their own perspective. They were forced to consider not only the impact of the war on their lives and "brothers and sisters" still under colonial domination but the increasing intensity in the domestic war against African Americans. They could not ignore the forty-five reported lynchings in 1917 that would bring the total of known cases to 2,472 men and 50 women lynched between 1889 and 1918.[44]

The year 1917 marked the period in which Harlem had become sufficiently established as an African American community and the pressures on African Americans throughout the nation had become so volatile that Harlem radicals moved to mobilize their own resources to organize and protest. Hubert Harrison had forsaken the Socialist Party but not socialism. He had rephrased his argument to parry the Socialist position of "class first" with a call for "race first." Capitalism in the United States had taken a virulent form of oppression of African Americans, and racism pervaded the entire system. Tales of terror against African Americans evoked the desire for self-protection and retaliation. Harrison keenly felt that his emphasis and priority should be shifted to protecting the race. According to Jeffrey Perry, Harrison reasoned that the protective reaction on the part of African Americans was "race consciousness" that responded to several factors, including "the white-race-first approach of the Socialists and the organized labor movement and the America-first attitude that was encouraged as the World War flared in Europe," and "the World War being fought in the name of democracy while the most basic democratic rights were denied to Afro-Americans in the United States." Harrison also argued that it was the task of white revolutionists to "show their sincerity by first breaking down the exclusion walls of white working men before they ask us to demolish our own defensive structures of racial self-protection."[45]

By 1917 Harrison was ready to launch his own organization uptown. It was conceived as a New Negro Manhood Movement among Negroes. He provided a description of the initial meeting on June 12 of his Liberty League of Negro Americans: "Two years ago Mr. Harrison withdrew from an international political organization, and, a little more than a year ago, gave up lecturing to white people, to devote himself to lecturing exclusively among his own people . . . The most striking passages of his speech were those in which he demanded that Congress make lynching a Federal crime and take the Negro's life under national protection, and declared that since lynching was murder and a violation of Federal and State laws, it was incumbent upon the Negroes themselves to maintain the majesty of the law and put down the lawbreakers by organizing all over the South to defend their own lives whenever their right to live was invaded by mobs which the local authorities were too weak or unwilling to suppress."[46]

The inaugural issue of the *Voice: A Newspaper for the New Negro* on July 4, 1917, was indeed a voice of the New Negro. It included an article, "The East St. Louis Horror," calling for armed self-defense, and a reprint from the June 1917 *Crisis* that revealed European desires for African riches as a principal cause of the war in Europe. Subsequent issues initiated a series on police brutality and developed a case for independent political action. Despite advertisements for Socialist Party meetings and activities Harrison wrote on the "drift" toward an independent, race-first political position demanding "what the Irish and the Jewish voter get: nominations on the party's ticket in our own districts." He threatened: "And if we don't get this we will smash the party that refuses to give it . . . For we are not Republicans, Democrats or Socialists any longer. We are Negroes first . . . We demand, not 'recognition,' but representation, and we are out to throw our votes to *any* party which gives us this, and withhold them from any party which refuses to give it."[47] Huiswoud, Briggs, Domingo, and Moore all held Harrison in high regard and witnessed the launching of the Liberty League, but they did not seem ready to become deeply involved. Even though Domingo served as assistant secretary it is quite plausible that Harrison's philosophical race-first arguments were not considered completely compatible with those being pursued by Huiswoud, Domingo, and Moore, who were budding socialists at the time.

In contrast to Harrison's organized efforts to disassociate African American protest from the political interests of the Socialist Party and to promote an exclusive African American political base, sentiment was developing for a socialist base in Harlem. The establishment of the magazine the *Messenger* by Asa Philip Randolph (1889–1979) and Chandler Owen (1889–1967?) in November marked the second critical event of 1917 in the political and cultural development of Harlem. The magazine burst on the scene the same year the United States entered World War I, boldly proclaiming that it was "The Only Radical Negro Magazine in America." Not only did the journal present radical ideas hitherto not published in African American circles, it also encouraged African Americans from both southern and Caribbean migrant streams to work together, offered an opportunity for African American writers to find their voice, stimulated the formation of an organized group of African American socialists that in turn created a base for African American candidates to run for office, provided a cadre for courses on the African American experience at the Rand School and other venues, and cemented a tie between African American socialists uptown and white socialists downtown. It proved to be a significant stimulus in the radicalization process taking place in Harlem and a force to shift the balance in the relationship between socialist uptown and downtown. Harlem was no longer just a recipient of "socialist truth"; it was a contributor to socialist thought.

Randolph had come to New York from Florida in 1911 after graduating from the high school at Cookman Institute in Jacksonville. He combined work in a succession of odd jobs with evening courses in political science, history, economics, and philosophy at City College of New York (CCNY), where he encountered socialism. A job on the Fall River Line as a waiter lasted only one trip because he was discovered organizing waiters and hallmen to protest the horrendous conditions in which they lived on the boat.[48] Evidently Huiswoud was more successful later in leading a similar protest in 1918. Like Huiswoud, Randolph was a "student" of the open-air streetcorner classes and became an admirer of Eugene Debs and Hubert Harrison. In 1916 he joined the Socialist Party along with Chandler Owen, a native of Warrenton, North Carolina. Owen had graduated in 1913 from the Baptist-sponsored Virginia Union University in Richmond, Virginia, and come to New York as a National Urban League fellow. His studies included sociology, political science, and law at the New York School of Philanthropy and at Columbia University.[49] Randolph and Owen were interested in promoting the trade union movement and projected plans at different times to organize African American workers who were barred from existing unions either because of prejudice or the nature of their work. When they decided to launch a publication they received some financial and moral support from various socialist groups, but the ideas they expressed represented African American radical thought. They defined radicals as those who had the courage of their convictions and who sought to get at the root of social problems.[50] Randolph and Owen favored the Party's official position on the war and considered themselves conscientious objectors. It is not surprising that the articles during the first year were strongly antiwar. Philip S. Foner has judged that "in its militancy the *Messenger* was far in advance of anything up to that point in the history of black radicalism. In fact, it was even in advance of the very Socialist party to which it advised its readers to turn."[51]

Sally Miller has pointed out that while the editors followed the usual socialist critique they inserted an African American twist:

> It was emphasized that colonial rivalries and the exploitation of colored peoples was the real issue of the World War. The magazine proposed the establishment of an International Council on the Conditions of the Darker Races to administer, educate, and insure the self-determination of the oppressed. The League of Nations was dismissed with a reflection on white capitalist associations of governments. The editors stressed that democracy and self-determi-

nation of peoples must become a reality within the United States. Since these conditions were absent, it was clear that Negroes had no taste for the war. When Du Bois advised the closing of ranks behind the national war effort, the *Messenger* attacked him and compared his "disgraceful" position with the Atlanta Exposition philosophy of accomodation [*sic*]. It argued that no "subject race" ever improved its position by participating in the oppressors' wars.[52]

This summary reveals a strong critique of colonialization by socialists from the Caribbean and an early application of the concept of self-determination to the oppressed of both the colonies and the United States.

The *Messenger* took a partisan stand during election campaigns and supported Morris Hillquit for mayor of New York in 1917. By 1918 Randolph and Owen were candidates of the Socialist Party for the New York Assembly from the Nineteenth and Twentieth Assembly Election Districts, respectively, and in 1920 Randolph was a candidate for state comptroller of New York and in 1922 for secretary of state of New York. The magazine greatly aided his campaigns as well as those of other candidates. Randolph was on the road to national leadership. In later years he was to explain that "one of the fundamental forces that shaped his life was his study and reading in Socialist philosophy and literature and his participation in the Socialist movement [to which] he owed his understanding of social forces, his awareness of the mission of the working class, and his world perspective."[53]

There was a significant step, however, between the launching of the *Messenger* and placing African Americans on the Socialist Party ticket. In July 1918, eight months after its initial issue, the magazine carried an announcement that African Americans were organizing in the Socialist Party and that the branch had grown to about one hundred members in two weeks: "The new Negro is awakening. After having been the political Rip Van Winkle of America for fifty years, sleeping in the cesspools of Republican reaction, he has at last opened his eyes. In New York City, in the very heart of the Negro settlement, there has been organized the Twenty-first Assembly District Socialist Branch which includes all white and colored Socialists in the district." Readers were urged to join a worker's party, that is, the Socialist Party, and were also reminded how both Republican and Democratic Parties stabbed African Americans in the back through laws and court decisions promoting and enforcing Jim Crowism, segregation, lynching, disfranchisement, and discrimination.[54]

The Socialist Propaganda League printed a similar announcement in its publication the *New International* in February 1918: "A Harlem Branch of the Socialist Propaganda League has been organized in New York City with more than forty new members."[55] There is evidence that Randolph and Owen initiated the Harlem branch in the Twenty-first Assembly District. They attended a meeting of the executive committee of Local New York on October 10, 1917, and stated that their Independent Political League of Harlem was anxious to work for the Socialist Party during the next campaign. On February 27, 1918, Randolph informed the committee that a number of African Americans were anxious to join the Socialist Party and establish a branch in the colored section of the nineteenth district. The committee donated fifteen dollars per month for two months to help establish the branch. The May 1, 1918, committee minutes indicate that thirty-four applicants had joined the newly organized branch in the twenty-first district. On September 4 Randolph was officially appointed as organizer.[56] The Socialist Propaganda League moved out of Harlem and located its headquarters south of 110th Street.

During the formative stage of the branch, Huiswoud was attending Cornell University, but other African American socialists were being trained by the Rand School to work in socialist endeavors. Frank R. Crosswaith from the Virgin Islands and Louis Laurent from British Guiana were enrolled in evening classes and Lovett Fort-Whiteman from Dallas, Texas, was enrolled in the 1917–18 full-time program.[57] Fort-Whiteman, purported to have joined the Socialist Party in 1915 while living in Mexico, had also been involved in the 1917 Hillquit campaign and was concurrently engaged as the drama editor of the *Messenger*. Subsequently Crosswaith was granted a Forward Scholarship in the part-time course in 1918. Domingo was listed as a lecturer of the Rand School Lecture Bureau, established in 1918, and Randolph and Owen taught courses entitled "The Economics and Sociology of the Negro Problem" in 1919 and "Internationalism and the Negro Problem" in 1920.[58] The cadre was strengthened in May 1919 when Huiswoud graduated from the Rand full-time program and was assigned to the Twenty-first district branch. He must have considered his involvement with the branch personally significant; one of the few mementoes he retained throughout his life was a 15–cent ticket for "A Benefit For a Sick Comrade Given by 21st A.D. Socialist Branch At 116 West 133rd Street Friday Evening, September 26, 1919."[59] The *Rand School News* reported in September that Huiswoud was "now connected with the *Messenger*." It is not known what that connection entailed, but his article "Dutch Guiana: A Study in Colonial Exploitation" appeared in the December 1919 issue.

By the time the Twenty-first district branch was organized Harlem militants had come to the same conclusion as Du Bois. Organization and propaganda were essential. Even though Du Bois had embraced socialism earlier, the young upstarts rejected the road he had taken as too conciliatory, too "old guard." Of course they rejected the entrenched conservative forces in Harlem that wielded sufficient influence to threaten jobs such as Harrison's with the post office and Briggs's with the *Amsterdam News*. African Americans were entering politics in the Republican and Democrat parties, and the conservative press such as Fred R. Moore's *New York Age* released a constant tirade against radical ideas from its office on 135th Street. During an election campaign in 1918, for example, the newspaper warned that a vote for African American Socialist candidates would be a vote for the "reign of terror, the arson, the rape and pillage of Bolshevism."[60] African American socialists perceived themselves as "New Negroes" and took a road to the Left. Their propaganda was to be militant. This can be observed in articles in the *Messenger* and government surveillance reports on the People's Educational Forum. In typical socialist manner they formed a study group that met on Sunday mornings to read, evaluate, and discuss theoretical works on socialism. In the afternoon they conducted the People's Educational Forum, organized by members including Huiswoud, Domingo, Moore, and Grace Campbell and held in a room at the Lafayette Hall on Seventh Avenue and 131st Street. Speakers such as David Berenberg of the Rand School, Franz Boas, W. E. B. Du Bois, William Ferris, Elizabeth Gurley Flynn, Hubert H. Harrison, Fenton Johnson, and Walter White were presented. A period of questions and discussion followed the presentation, with an opportunity for the speaker to summarize. Moore characterized the sessions as an "intellectual battleground."

Not much is known about African American members of the Socialist Party. Moore has identified members who were regular street speakers. Included, in addition to Crosswaith, Domingo, Huiswoud, and Moore, were Victor C. Gaspar, A. Elizabeth Hendrickson, Anna Jones, John Patterson, Frank Poree, Thomas Potter, J. Ramsay, Rudolph Smith, and Herman S. Whaley.[61] There were also the candidates for office other than Randolph and Owen, namely Grace P. Campbell, Rev. George Frazier Miller, and William B. Williams, as well as other speakers who stumped for candidates, including Rev. E. Ethelred Brown, Clarence Carpenter, H. Leadett, and Alexander Rawming. Martin Luther Campbell, in whose tailor shop at 127 West 135th Street Domingo, Moore, and others gathered in the evening, should also be included. Such a roster underscores that although the organization was male-dominated, women also played a role. While several men and women joined the Socialist Party or attended the Rand School, it was not until Harlem became their community and the Twenty-first district branch formed that they could participate collectively in a neighborhood unit. Thus the development of Harlem provided the opportunity for African Caribbeans to join with African Americans to help forge a cohesive organizing arm that would extend in a more structured way from uptown to downtown. It was not a struggle for power as much as a skirmish of ideas. The Twenty-first district Socialist Party branch can be considered a later development of Harrison's efforts and a contributor to the Harlem Renaissance. The combination of the *Messenger,* the branch, the study group, and the People's Educational Forum gave understanding and expression to radical thought intended to bring together solutions to the problems associated with economic deprivation and racial bigotry as well as seeking to influence leaders of the political Left downtown.

Ironically, the ascent of socialism in Harlem occurred as the descent of socialism was being choreographed downtown and in Chicago. With the advent of the Russian Revolution a fork in the road suddenly appeared, and downtown socialists were faced with having to choose between the familiar road of American socialism and the unchartered left road of Russian-inspired communism. In contrast, uptown socialists and nonsocialists were facing a blockade and were forced to cope with postwar problems. James Weldon Johnson has explained their concerns:

> With the close of the war went most of the illusions and high hopes American Negroes had felt would be realized when it was seen that they were doing to the utmost their bit at home and in the field. Eight months after the armistice, with black men back fresh from the front, there broke the Red Summer of 1919, and the mingled emotions of the race were bitterness, despair, and anger. There developed an attitude of cynicism that was a characteristic foreign to the Negro. There developed also a spirit of defiance born of desperation. These sentiments and reactions found varying degrees of expression in the Negro publications throughout the country; but Harlem became the centre where they were formulated and voiced to the Negroes of America and the world. Radicalism in Harlem, which had declined as the war approached, burst out anew. But it was something different from the formal radicalism of pre-war days; it was radicalism motivated by a fierce race consciousness.[62]

Many socialists watched with fascination and glee the fireworks that gave birth to the Union of Soviet Socialist Republics. Instead, African Americans watched with horror and indignation the raging fires of the Red Summer of 1919 that were destroying their communities in the United States. Violence against African Americans erupted across the nation, including Charleston, South Carolina; Longview, Texas; Washington, D.C.; Chicago; Knoxville; Omaha; Phillips County, Arkansas; and Bogalusa, Louisiana. It has been estimated that there might have been as many as twenty-five "disturbances" or "riots" or "pogroms," varying from brief clashes to major attacks resulting in the loss of life and property. Fighting back in self-defense was applauded, and even Du Bois was quoted as threatening, "When the mob moves, we propose to meet it with bricks and clubs and guns."[63] In Harlem the radical rhetoric escalated, more radical journals emerged, and organizations like the African Blood Brotherhood (ABB) were conceived. As Harrison's Liberty League and *Voice* began to falter in 1918–19, Briggs stepped into the void with the *Crusader* in September 1918 and a new organization, the African Blood Brotherhood for African Liberation and Redemption (ABB), in 1919.

The *Messenger,* from its inception in November 1917, was forthrightly a magazine devoted to socialist philosophy and politics. The *Crusader,* like Harrison's *Voice,* proclaimed in its inaugural issue that "while it is neither pro-Socialist, pro-Republican nor least of all, pro-Democratic, it is distinctly Pro-Negro!" Within the same paragraph, however, there was a caveat: "And when the Socialiist [sic] Party, as now, shows a disposition of cooperating with and rewarding its Negro members, the Socialist Party we will support." The article went on to support Miller, Randolph, and Owen, who were candidates on the Socialist Party's ticket.[64] Of greater interest is the lead article, "Africa for the Africans," which reinforced the mottoes on the masthead, "Onward for Democracy" and "Upward with the Race," by discussing President Wilson's remark that "No peace can last which does not recognize and accept the principle that governments derive all their just powers from the consent of the governed." The first issue also listed five aims of the *Crusader.* Briefly, they included spreading the Eternal Truths regarding equal rights to life, liberty and the pursuit of happiness; supplying necessary historical background to eradicate the evils of an "alien education"; supporting African kinsmen in the propagation and enforcement of the doctrine of Africa for the Africans; awakening African Americans to the strategic position of the race in South American and West Indian republics and the possibilities for trade, nation-building, and liberty; and carrying on an uncompromising fight for an equitable solution of the race problem. The "Race Catechism" restated these aims in a question-answer format.[65]

Not to be overlooked was an article Briggs reprinted from the *Amsterdam News* recommending naturalization by Caribbean settlers in the United States: "The American Negro and the West Indian Negro are one in blood, one in achievement, and one in the aspirations for equal rights and opportunities. They are both of the seed of Africa . . . Unfortunately, however, he [the West Indian] has not the same stimulus for becoming a citizen that is given to the white Slav or Teuton . . . He still ignores or has not yet seen that his duty as a Negro lies in Naturalizing as an American citizen and so politically allying himself with the most important group of the Race in the New World: and aiding at the polls the devoted band of American Negroes who seek remedy for their ills through this means."[66]

Historians have given close attention to Briggs's opening statements as a reflection of the radical thinking of the day. Indeed, they were typical of sentiments expressed by Harrison and other militants. They provide a standard by which to compare subsequent articles and thereby trace the evolution of the movement toward an acceptance of communist philosophy while uniquely welding socialism and Black liberation. Subsequent editorials tied the cause of the African American to the interest of labor and the demand for self-determination. In the July 1919 editorial "Make Their Cause Your Own," Briggs praised the socialists for the *New York Call*'s concern and comments on wrongs against African Americans and their party's antilynching plank in the national platform, demand for self-determination for African peoples, and the end of disfranchisement in the southern states. He declared, "With no race are the interests of Labor so clearly identified with racial interests as in the case of the Negro race. No race woul [*sic*] be more greatly benefited by the triumph of Labor and the destruction of parasitic Capital Civilization with its imperialism incubus that is squeezing the life-blood out of millions of our race in Africa and the islands of the sea." He concluded, "We need not fight alone."[67] But Briggs did not mean African Americans should not form their own organizations.

The first announcement of the Brotherhood appeared in the September 1919 issue of the *Crusader*. It is not known what meetings might have taken place prior to printing that issue or who Briggs invited to join initially. In 1924 Briggs indicated that the African Blood Brotherhood had been organized in the spring of 1919.[68] Moore was quite definite in crediting Briggs as conceiving and organizing the Brotherhood and stated that he was invited to join by Briggs after it had been formed.[69] Briggs referred to Moore, however, as a charter member. Unfortunately, he did not reveal who else he considered charter members, other than Theophilus Burrell.[70] Briggs used the fraternal order, a model well known in the African American community, combined with an image of the military. In June 1920 he described the organization as "probably the first Negro *secret* organization to be effected in the Western world, having as its sole purpose the liberation of Africa and the redemption of the Negro race." Secrecy was stressed to provide protection for members as well as prevent disclosures to the "enemy." The structure included a supreme council, or war college, of five who were responsible for the appointment and tenure of commanders of various posts and for formulating policies and directing activities. Membership was restricted to persons of African blood. Briggs explained in 1958 that "The Brotherhood never attained the proportions of a real mass organization. Its initial membership was less than a score, and all in Harlem. At its peak it had less than three thousand members."[71] Among colleagues known to hold positions on the supreme executive council and referred to as international officers during 1923 were Briggs as executive head, Theophilus Burrell as secretary, Huiswoud as national organizer, Moore as educational director, Benjamin E. Burrell as director of historical research, Grace P. Campbell as director of consumers' cooperatives, Domingo as director of publicity and propaganda, and William H. Jones as physical director. The New York post was named Post Menelik, and some of its officers were also national officers, with the exception of Post Commander Reed. Rev. E. Ethelred Brown served as chaplain.

The aims of the Brotherhood were not stated at the time of its announcement, but guidance was offered such as affiliating with liberal, radical, and labor movements; patronizing and investing in race enterprises; learning a trade; waging war against the alien education taught in the white man's schools; organizing literary clubs for the discussion and study of Negro history; and encouraging the Universal Negro Improvement Association movement. In June 1921 the *Crusader* became the "Organ of the African Blood Brotherhood" according to the statement on the masthead but the constitution printed in that issue and revised in December was silent on the relationship of the magazine to the organization. The name of the organization was simplified to African Blood Brotherhood, the aims made similar to those initially stated for the magazine, and the titles of officers of local units and territorial councils greatly expanded. The grand plans projected in the December issue for an elaborate international organization sponsoring its First International Congress on July 16, 1922, were followed by silence. The January–February 1922 issue was the last but not quite the finale of the Brotherhood. The *Crusader* and the activities of the Brotherhood testify to Briggs's drive to tie strands of socialism to the Black ethos. The years 1919 to 1922 were critical in formulating alternatives and determining whether racism in America could be best attacked through membership in a political party or an Afrocentric organization. Briggs tried to fashion an alternative model to Marcus Garvey's Universal Negro Improvement Association that embraced radical politics. While sharp with the pen, his severe speech problem robbed him of the opportunity to command the platform with the charismatic eloquence expected of African American leaders. But his handicap was only one of many determining factors limiting the success of the Brotherhood and the magazine. While Briggs never joined the Socialist Party, he was on a personal journey to Marxism. Domingo, Moore, and later Huiswoud joined him in the Brotherhood to combat hatred and violence against African Americans.

Otto Huiswoud had a very different orientation to socialism than his fellow radicals from the Caribbean. Through the Rand School he was indoctrinated in Marxist philosophy and strategies and trained to be an organizer. His closest companions arrived at their militant posture via individual routes—through personal reading and study and small group dialogues and argument. Moore has stressed that they were constantly searching—seeking to understand the basis for the racism so rampant not only in the United States but other places in the world, seeking strategies to combat discrimination, and most importantly, seeking forces that could be combined to overcome colonialism. Together the four seized the link between uptown and downtown and inserted in the socialist movement a particular strength and audacity derived from Caribbean sources. Their relationship was initiated and strengthened by their deep concern for the inhumane conditions that Africans and their descendants in the New World faced at the turn of the century. They did not always see eye to eye nor march in lockstep. They had strong personalities, and each was driven to act upon his own convictions. Their differences are manifested in the fact that Briggs never joined the Socialist Party, Huiswoud was not a member of the African Blood Brotherhood during its formative stage, and Domingo was not to join the Communist Party. The cohesive element was their ultimate goal of liberation and the stimulation provided by bouncing ideas from one to another. Their discussions, whether personal or within organizations, were often harsh and combative but always in the African Caribbean spirit of "good palaver." Their friendship was a comforting and creative force. Huiswoud, Briggs, Domingo, and Moore became an awesome foursome who established countless organizations and poured forth pronouncements and invectives with pen and voice. With the exception of Briggs, who had a severe stutter, they mounted the platform regularly to deliver inspired speeches or engage in fiery debates. The election campaigns of Randolph and Owen in 1918 motivated them to develop their soapbox oratory skills. They now had African American candidates from their own neighborhood to stump for as well as the escalating violence of hate to overcome.

Hermie's rating of the Harlem soapbox orators always commenced by placing Hubert Harrison as the number one model without a peer. She observed that he usually had the largest audience, and when he occupied the platform, "it was not long before the crowd swelled to several dozens and even children ceased romping, keeping quiet as he developed his subject. His audience was always spell-bound and attentive as his address was so simply presented that his listeners had no difficulty understanding the subject and were also amused at the subtle humor he injected from time to time. He stimulated his serious listeners to join the public library in order to borrow books that he usually mentioned in the course of his lectures. He repeatedly urged them to READ, READ, READ." Hermie rated Moore second and characterized him as a spell-binder. In the early years he "larded his speeches with biblical references and quotations. One word picture he drew often was 'hewers of wood and drawers of water' which his listeners understood through personal experience, since it applied to their lot. Moore decried the lot of the Black man who the world over was relegated to the station of a draft animal suggesting that it was time that a change in this status be realized. One could hear many an 'Amen' echoing from the audience who were tired of supplying only brawn and muscle." She explained that Huiswoud and Domingo "used their oratory to convince their listeners that socialism was the correct path. Then after 1919 Huiswoud spoke on the developing course that the Russian Revolution had influenced and the need to examine what the newly founded Communist Party of the USA had to offer the workers of both races. There were always in such crowds detractors and even paid provocateurs who tried disrupting the speakers. However, at that early stage the reactionary elements were few and usually made impotent by the solidarity of the public."[72] Domingo was rated third. She felt that Otto did a creditable job but added that she preferred for him not to be in that role because of his heavy Dutch accent.

Unfortunately orations were not recorded and therefore escape present or future analysis. A good representation of the writings of the foursome, however, is still available, and it provides a window to the topics and tone enunciated even though the passion could not be fully preserved. Over two decades they edited and wrote for a series of radical magazines and newspapers: Domingo and Huiswoud for the *Messenger;* Briggs for the *Crusader;* Domingo for the *Negro World;* Domingo and Moore for the *Emancipator;* Briggs, Moore, and Huiswoud for the *Daily Worker, Negro Champion,* and its successor, the *Liberator;* and Huiswoud for the *Negro Worker.* Hermie also assisted with Briggs's Crusader News Service, contributed articles for the *Liberator,* and helped edit and write for the *Negro Worker.* Their writings are not generally treated as part of the literature of the Harlem Renaissance, but their trenchant essays and thunderous orations had a direct influence on readers and listeners, including many acknowledged Harlem Renaissance writers. They made a contribution to the fight against racism and colonialism both uptown and downtown.

3. "If We Must Die"

Hermie Dumont's introduction to Harlem was through the eyes of a teenager. Her small group of girlfriends did not wander far from home, and the main entertainment beyond their parlors was either the silent movies, local basketball games, or strolling the avenue. Walking along broad Seventh or Lenox Avenues they expected to encounter other young people, a sparkling parade, or a series of speakers mounted on short stepladders trying to capture a crowd's attention. As she described it, "Not only serious speakers but jackleg preachers as well as out-right charlatans competed for the passersby attention. The serious speaker commanded attention by mounting the 'platform,' a soapbox or orange crate, usually enhanced by an American flag, and began addressing the first few curious who halted nearby."[1] One evening as Hermie and some friends ventured along 138th Street, they discovered a meeting in progress in a large hall. The message that rang out in Jamaican cadence sounded to them like other speakers on the avenue rather than a church sermon. Hermie noted that when the leader shook her hand, not only was he of dark hue and short stature, as often described, but had soft, small hands. The girls did not dare linger through the long program, but the pageantry and the excitement they sensed in the crowd intrigued them. Marcus Garvey's Universal Negro Improvement Association (UNIA) was in session.

Malcus Mosiah Garvey Jr. (1887–1940), known as Marcus Garvey, entered the Harlem scene in March 1916 determined to organize the UNIA after having failed earlier in Jamaica, the country of his birth. His travels to Central America, England, and Europe in addition to his experience as a printer and activist in Jamaica had underscored the universal plight of peoples colonized by Europeans. Garvey considered African Americans "the best organized and the most conscious of all the Negroes in the world . . . They live in very close contact with organized racial prejudice, and this very prejudice forces them to a rare consciousness that they would not have had otherwise."² According to Robert Hill, "Garvey's assessment was that in 1916, Jamaicans 'were not sufficiently racially conscious to appreciate a racial movement because they lived under a common system of sociological hypocrisy that deprived them of that very racial consciousness.' Conversely, he felt that the American Negro would respond to his calls to racial action."³

The establishment of his base in Harlem was greatly facilitated by W. A. Domingo, with whom Garvey had been associated in Jamaica. Garvey wrote Domingo in 1915 of his plans to visit the United States, and upon his arrival in New York Domingo introduced him to prominent African Americans in the city as well as close friends. Among those he met was Domingo's socialist colleague, A. Philip Randolph, who later explained how he had introduced Garvey to the stepladder circuit in 1916 on the corner of 135th Street and Lenox Avenue: "I was on a soapbox speaking on socialism, when someone pulled my coat and said, 'There's a young man here from Jamaica who wants to be presented to this group.' . . . After I'd spoken a few more minutes I told the people I had a surprise for them . . . Garvey got up on the platform, and you could hear him from 135th to 125th Street."⁴ In a relatively short time Garvey was spreading his message at meetings and street corners. He rented desk space in the office of the Cosmo-Advocate Publishing Company, in which Moore was involved with several associates, two of whom Moore later identified as Isaac Newton Braithwaite, a court stenographer, and Orlando M. Thompson, an accountant. Moore has stated that Garvey often discussed with them his project of forming an international race organization. Moore has also pointed out that Garvey's first attempt to organize a mass meeting was a failure.⁵ It was Hubert Harrison, however, who was most responsible for providing the platform from which Garvey was able to gain a foothold for his UNIA organization. Harrison's report on the launching of the Liberty League related that he introduced Marcus Garvey, who spoke "in enthusiastic approval of the new movement and pledged it his hearty support."⁶

James Weldon Johnson, a columnist for the *New York Age* at the time, later gave a more complete picture of Garvey's presentation to "some two thousand people":

> Mr. Harrison introduced him to the audience and asked him to say a few words. This was Harlem's first real sight of Garvey, and his first real chance at Harlem. The man spoke, and his magnetic personality, torrential eloquence, and intuitive knowledge of crowd psychology were all brought into play. He swept the audience along with him. He made his speech an endorsement of the new

movement and a pledge of his hearty support of it; but Garvey was not of the kidney to support anybody's movement. He had seen the United States and he had seen Harlem. He had doubtless been the keenest observer at the Liberty League organization meeting.[7]

The event encouraged Garvey to proceed with his own plans for an organization at precisely the time he had become disillusioned and was considering returning to Jamaica. Within two years Garvey's initial setbacks were reversed, and the UNIA had eclipsed the Liberty League. The brutal attacks on African American residents in East St. Louis, Illinois, and soldiers in Houston, Texas, provided large audiences for Harrison, but he found it impossible to travel the country to solicit memberships in the League and publish a newspaper regularly on the minuscule income he could raise. The *Voice* that had begun as Harrison's vision of the first African American publication to express the New Negro consciousness floundered for lack of financial resources and folded in 1919. Garvey was also disturbed by the terrorism perpetrated against African Americans and seized the opportunity to escalate his appeals and attract members. Harrison had inadvertently passed the leadership baton to Garvey.

Garvey was astute. He adopted some of Harrison's ideas but was careful to eschew the political orientation Harrison had so passionately enunciated. Garvey packaged an appealing program fashioned on Booker T. Washington's self-help principles, the historic interest in Africa as a homeland, the strength of African American churches, and a recognition of the need for the psyche to experience a psychological boost, and added his own colorful pizzazz. Like Harrison he was articulate enough to reveal and relate to the oppression and discrimination experienced by the masses and bold enough to verbally attack the oppressors. But he captured other forces in a manner unrivaled at the time. He was clever enough to create economic ventures to provide jobs and income; wise enough to provide religious sentiment and ritual while maintaining a nondenominational base; flamboyant enough to create a world of fantasy—a royal court where the individual's self-esteem was elevated; insightful enough to appreciate the nature of the Diaspora—the global plight of those of African descent and the disastrous effect of colonialism; and visionary enough to paint a picture of a glorious past and future.

Marcus Garvey became more than a household name in Harlem. Even though Domingo never joined the UNIA he continued to help when Garvey established the UNIA and its organ, *Negro World*, in 1918. Domingo introduced him to the printer, Henry Rogowski, who produced the Socialist Party's newspaper and who was willing to extend credit so that Garvey's newspaper could get started.⁸ Domingo served as its first editor, and over a period of four years Garvey convinced skillful writers such as John E. Bruce (Grit), William H. Ferris, T. Thomas Fortune, Hodge Kirnon, Duse Mohamed, William Pickens, Eric Walrond, and even Hubert Harrison to serve as editors or columnists.⁹ He was successful in developing a newspaper with sections in Spanish and French that circulated to readers throughout the Diaspora and attracted thousands of members to the UNIA. He expanded his organization to 835 branches in the United States and 286 branches in 41 other countries.¹⁰ In time it became clear that he was a force that Huiswoud and his friends could neither ignore nor join. They were to spend many hours contending with this brand of Caribbean militancy and trying to "bay the tiger."

Garvey's initial decision to come to the United States had been motivated by his interest in Booker T. Washington's success at Tuskegee Institute. The school's fame had spread to Jamaica and had also influenced another Jamaican who was to add spice to the Harlem literary pepper pot. Festus Claudius McKay (1889–1948), known as Claude McKay, left home four years prior to Garvey to pursue education at Tuskegee Institute.¹¹ Arriving in Charleston, South Carolina, in 1912 instead of New York, he observed racism in its most blatant form:

> It was the first time I had ever come face to face with such manifest, implacable hate of my race, and my feelings were indescribable . . .
>
> The whites at home constitute about 14% of the population only and they generally conform to the standard of English respectability . . . The government is tolerant, somewhat benevolent, based on the principle of equal justice to all. I had heard of prejudice in America but never dreamed of it being so intensely bitter; for at home there is also prejudice of the English sort, subtle and dignified, rooted in class distinction—color and race being hardly taken into account . . .
>
> In the South daily murders of a nature most hideous and revolting, in the North silent acquiescence, deep hate half-hidden under a puritan respectability, oft flaming up into an occasional lynching—this ugly raw sore in the body of a great nation. At first I was horrified, my spirit revolted against the ignoble cruelty and blindness of it all. Then I soon found myself hating in return but this feeling couldn't last long for to hate is to be miserable.¹²

After a disappointing six-month stay at Tuskegee, McKay enrolled in a two-year course in agronomy at Kansas State College. In 1914 he concluded, as Huiswoud did, that agriculture was not to be his life work. He had experienced some success as a young writer in Jamaica and wished to advance his craft as well as escape the expectation that his verse should be in dialect. He affirmed, "I desired to achieve something new, something in the spirit and accent of America. Against its mighty throbbing force, its grand energy and power and bigness, its bitterness burning in my black body, I would raise my voice to make a canticle of my reaction."[13] New York City was the logical place to go. McKay could speak about the burning bitterness because he did not enter New York harbor naively with his back to the Caribbean as the others had done. He came to Harlem through the back door—after two years in the South. His description of Manhattan on his return from England in 1921 not only extolled the "pyramids of New York in their Egyptian majesty" with "clean, vertical heaven-challenging lines" but accentuated the loss of innocence he and his fellow radicals from the Caribbean experienced: "Oh, that I should never draw nearer to descend into its precipitous gorges, where visions are broken and shattered and one becomes one of a million, average, ordinary, insignificant."[14]

Following a succession of typical menial jobs, McKay succeeded in obtaining what was considered a coveted job as a dining-car waiter on the Pennsylvania Railroad. During this time he not only became acquainted with members of the African American community in Harlem but learned about the New York publishing business and was able to penetrate the heart of the radical press in Greenwich Village. Some of his poems were published in *Pearson's Magazine* and the *Liberator*. The sonnet that evoked the most acclaim and electrified readers well beyond Harlem was "If We Must Die," printed in the July 1919 issue of the *Liberator*. The attacks on African Americans during the "Red Summer" of 1919 touched him deeply, and he explained that the poem exploded out of him: "Our Negro newspapers were morbid, full of details of clashes between colored and white, murderous shootings and hangings. Traveling from city to city and unable to gauge the attitude and temper of each one, we Negro railroad men were nervous. We were less lighthearted. We did not separate from one another gaily to spend ourselves in speakeasies and gambling joints. We stuck together, some of us armed, going from the railroad station to our quarters. We stayed in our quarters all through the dreary ominous nights, for we never knew what was going to happen."[15]

The poem was reprinted in September issues of both the *Messenger* and the *Crusader*. W. A. Domingo was inspired to dash off an editorial, "If We Must Die," for the *Messenger* in which he incorporated the poem as the finale of his essay. In part he charged:

> No longer are Negroes willing to be shot down or hunted from place to place like wild beasts; no longer will they flee from their homes and leave their property to the tender mercies of the howling and cowardly mob. They have changed, and now they intend to give men's account of themselves. If death is to be their

portion, New Negroes are determined to make their dying a costly investment for all concerned . . .

The New Negro has arrived with stiffened backbone, dauntless manhood, defiant eye, steady hand and a will of iron. His creed is admirably summed up in the poem of Claude McKay, the black Jamaican poet, who is carving out for himself a niche in the Hall of Fame:

IF WE MUST DIE

If we must die, let it not be like hogs
    Hunted and penned in an inglorious spot,
While round us bark the mad and hungry dogs,
    Making their mock at our accursed lot.
If we must die, oh, let us nobly die,
    So that our precious blood may not be shed
In vain; then even the monsters we defy
    Shall be constrained to honor us, though dead!

Oh, kinsmen! We must meet the common foe;
    Though far outnumbered, let us still be brave,
And for their thousand blows deal one death-blow!
    What though before us lies the open grave?
Like men we'll face the murderous, cowardly pack,
    Pressed to the wall, dying, but—fighting back![16]

McKay was not the first or last to put his poetic life on the line fighting the "tyrant's torch or gun." The year before, for example, William Pickens had written an "Afro-American Hymn" to the tune of "The Marseillaise" that declared, "We will be free if die we must!"[17] Du Bois had expressed his deep aggravation in prose in 1911: "We have crawled and pleaded for justice and we have been cheerfully spit upon and murdered and burned. We will not endure it forever. If we are to die, in God's name let us perish like men and not like bales of hay."[18] But McKay's poem rolled trippingly and forcefully off the tongue at the precise moment of heightened community anguish. It was powerful and needed no interpretation or clarification. Domingo's editorial, however, helped to place it directly before the Harlem community and tie it to the New Negro movement. Understandably it became a classic of the Harlem Renaissance cited in most literary anthologies. The poem is credited, for example, in *Dark Symphony* as marking the beginning of the "full flowering of the Negro Awakening"[19] and the editors of *Cavalcade* considered that "perhaps no expression of the new spirit had such impact as a poem entitled "If We Must Die."[20] Certainly it captured the spirit and mood of the times.

McKay and Garvey might have entered the United States with visions of Booker T. Washington and Tuskegee and both experienced disillusionment by the racism they discovered, but their view of themselves was vastly different. Garvey saw himself as a great leader marshaling massive numbers of Black troops in the vanguard of freedom for all peoples of African lineage. He needed a mass movement to carry out his objectives. McKay's perspective, on the other hand, was that of a writer observing the human condition and pursuing change through the impact of the written word. In his autobiography, *A Long Way from Home,* there are many detailed accounts of the downtown liberals and radicals with whom he became acquainted. Some uptown friends, such as Hubert Harrison and Grace Campbell, are mentioned, but descriptions of his involvement with the core of socialist and communist comrades in Harlem are tantalizingly omitted. McKay was very much at home in Harlem, not just Greenwich Village. Close friendships were established, for example, with Domingo and Moore. Both of their wives were from Jamaica and he was often a guest in their homes. The two friends frequently met at meetings in McKay's quarters along with Huiswoud and Briggs. Even though he sought relationships with individuals both downtown and uptown he savored his independence and solitude, for in the end the act of producing great literature is a solo endeavor.

Joel Augustus Rogers (1880?–1966), another Jamaican who sought opportunity in the United States, not only differed in stature and complexion from Garvey and McKay but arrived in New York in 1906 with an entirely different outlook. No messianic messenger bent on changing society—he was introspective and placid and intent on becoming an artist. He settled in Chicago so he could combine attending art school and supporting himself by working as a Pullman porter. His introduction to American prejudice produced the typical shock. W. Burghardt Turner has explained, "Like many of the light complexioned immigrants from the West Indies, he learned with bitterness of the color prejudice which existed in the United States. He had suffered little in Jamaica from prejudice directed against him. There is the likelihood that he had not thought of himself in terms of color but rather of class." Turner pointed out that Rogers had been told that the Africans had never accomplished anything in all of history and now realized that this applied to him. "It was from this background that Rogers was launched into the study of the achievement of persons of African descent."[21]

Rogers substituted the pen for the artists' brush. Like painting, writing was a solitary activity but more likely to reach and provide people of color a higher self-esteem and a new understanding of history. His first book, *From "Superman" to Man,* which he had printed in 1917, drew on his experience as a Pullman porter to present a fictionalized account of an ongoing dialogue on a Los Angeles–bound train between a southern senator and a porter whose education at Yale had been interrupted by the war. The stupidity of racism was revealed as the porter presented argument after argument to counter the legislator's southern attitude and misinformation regarding African Americans. It was a best seller in Harlem. Harrison reviewed the book and considered it "the greatest little book on the Negro that we remember to have read." He concluded his review, "This conversational device gives the author an opportunity to present all the conflicting views of both sides of the Color Line, and the result is a wealth of information which makes this book a necessity on the bookshelf of everyone, Negro or Caucasian, who has some use for knowledge on the subject of the Negro."[22]

When Rogers returned to New York in 1922 he lived with the Moore family and at another time with the Harrisons. He was attracted to the Baha'i faith and considered himself a nonjoiner of political organizations. Over the years the various editions of *From "Superman" to Man* reveal his opinion of socialists and communists. For example, in early editions he wrote, "The Socialists appear to stand for unqualified fair play to the Negro, as witness articles in their papers," yet noted that "when it comes to employment of the Negro, they maintain the same attitude as the rest of the whites." He agreed with a professor who claimed, "As long as the Socialists worship at the shrine of racial antipathy they will so long continue to be an unreliable factor in the progress of civilization!"[23] In the 1957 edition of the book the question of the senator had turned to the porter's opinion of the communists and the Negro. The porter's reply was much longer than in earlier editions and said in part, "The Communists . . . did a splendid social service not only for Negroes, but whites as well, between say 1920 and 1936. They were the principal ferrets of injustice against the working people and the most outspoken. America would certainly have been worse off but for their activities. Nevertheless, I do not like their tactics. They are opportunistic to the last degree, and are quite as nasty in their way as the vested interests, whom they condemn, are in theirs."[24]

Rogers's encounter with a "radical economic group" to which he belonged in Chicago about 1912 evidently colored his estimate of socialism and socialists: "When during a discussion at one meeting I mentioned great Negroes and how I had been collecting their names, there was a general howl of disapproval from the whites and most of the Negroes. They called me a 'chauvinist' and said that I was suffering from an inferiority complex." Rogers was accused of being a "capitalist hero-worshipper" and informed that such a pursuit "would be useless when 'the industrial revolution' came and color differences mattered no more." After giving much thought to the value of such a study he concluded that a past is as necessary to man as roots to a tree and that biography "will ever be the highest and most civilizing form of literature."[25] That became his life's work, and he eschewed joining any political party. Despite his personal opinions he continued to have positive relations with those who had chosen political action. Moore has commented that "Rogers had the capacity to get along with people even when he saw things from the opposite point of view."[26]

Rogers's dedication to revealing positive contributions by people of African heritage and the extent to which sexual interaction between the races had occurred was a significant strategy during this period of agitation. The sins of omission and commission of European and American historians were viewed as responsible in part for the prejudice against people of color, and history was considered an essential tool in counteracting racism. His writings were labeled "revolutionary" not because they espoused revolutionary politics but because they broke with traditional scholarship in presenting topics on race and sex that were taboo, cited events that European and American historians ignored or misrepresented, and popularized historical accounts. He had to publish his works privately because he was not the typical academician with a degree from a recognized university. His early articles in the *Messenger,* his later books, and regular newspapers columns that included brief historic facts were followed by a large audience. Thus he contributed to the outpouring of essays that spawned the Harlem Renaissance.

The fourth Jamaican to arrive who became involved with the militant scene in Harlem was Rev. Egbert Ethelred Brown (1875–1956). Like Garvey he came with a plan for an organization. Far less grandiose and complex in scope than Garvey's design, Brown envisioned establishing a liberal church in Harlem. He stated, "I sailed from the Island of Jamaica determined to establish a Unitarian Church in Harlem, and all that mattered to me in March 1920 was that the venture should be launched without delay. And it was."[27] Brown might have been unaware that there had been a Unitarian church in Harlem. Moore had been married at the Lenox Unitarian Church on Lenox Avenue and 121st Street in 1919, but the church was sold that year to a Jewish congregation. Brown's intent was to minister to a congregation in what he referred to as the "Negro Mecca of the world." Later he indicated, "I am informed that Dr. Harrison attempted to organize a church to be named 'The Liberal Church of Harlem' but for one reason or other the attempt proved abortive. And so when I came here there was no movement of religious liberalism and there was presented to me a fertile field in which to plant the seeds of a reasonable faith."[28]

This was not Brown's first trip to the United States. Against great odds he had been ordained at the Meadville Theological School in Meadville, Pennsylvania, as a Unitarian minister on June 4, 1912. He struggled to develop congregations first in Montego Bay and then in Kingston. Like Garvey he too failed in his attempt to gain followers in Jamaica. In eight years he was not able to attract sufficient local financial support for a Unitarian church, and when the American Unitarian Association (AUA) withdrew its grant Brown was "forced to surrender and pull down the flag of Unitarianism" in Jamaica. He decided that African Americans in cosmopolitan Harlem might be ready for the Unitarian message and left Kingston on February 21, 1920. Brown had been a featured speaker at an UNIA forum in Jamaica in 1916, but it was Domingo, not Garvey, who introduced the newcomer to the community.

The timing of the organizational meeting of the church and the names of those who responded indicate the haste with which the church was launched. Brown landed in New York on February 27 and the organizing meeting was held on March 7. According to Brown:

> The historical fact is that eight days after my arrival in New York I called a meeting to consider the advisability and feasibility of organizing a Unitarian Church in Harlem. That meeting was held in a room of the Lafayette Hall, 131st Street and Seventh Avenue, New York City, on Sunday evening, March 7, 1920. The question was carefully discussed and it was then and there decided to organize such a church. The following nine persons signed the roll as Charter Members, namely, Martin Luther Campbell, Grace P. Campbell, Hayward Shovington, Ella Matilda Brown, Wilfred A. Domingo, Frank A. Crosswaith, Thomas A. Potter, Richard B. Moore and Lucille E. Ward. The church was named "The Harlem Community Church" primarily in recognition of the marked interest shown at that early stage of the venture by the Reverend Dr. John Haynes Holmes, Minister of the Community Church of New York.[29]

Examination of the names of charter members reveals that at least six of the nine persons were fellow socialist associates of Domingo, and one was Brown's wife. In a short time Brown was engaged in socialist activities, including actively campaigning for Socialist Party candidates in the Nineteenth and Twenty-first Assembly Districts in 1921. He also served as chaplain of the African Blood Brotherhood. There is no indication, however, that Domingo was Brown's mentor; the city provided the environment to expand Brown's socialist interests and activism. Brown and his biographer wrote that "he was discovered by the Socialist party late in 1925," but it should be noted that Brown discovered the Socialists in 1920.[30] Brown was hired by the Socialist Party after he had worked as an elevator operator for years to support his family, but the forty-five-year-old Brown was on his socialist road when he arrived in New York.

Later Brown raised the question, "What relation if any did the fact that the foundation members of the church were Socialists bear to the early trials of the movement?"³¹ He made no attempt to propose an answer. It is interesting that in linking the name of the church with the downtown Unitarian Church, Brown not only revealed a tie between uptown and downtown but also that the main Unitarian minister to support Brown's efforts, Rev. John Haynes Holmes, was a founder of the NAACP and an active socialist. It was Rev. Holmes who had decried in 1912 that the church "is an institution dominated very largely by that section of society which is responsible for the social injustice of the present age" and pointed out that "When the slaveholder sat in the pew, there was no abolitionist in the pulpit."³² Seven years after the Harlem church was established, there was an effort to remove Brown's name from the list of Unitarian ministers in the American Unitarian Association year book. Brown objected and stated his rationale for a Unitarian church in Harlem: "Harlem needs a liberal church—needs it first as a neutralising influence staying the poisonous spread of superstition, ignorance and fanaticism—and needs it also as a means of getting together those who have intellectually and ethically outgrown the fundamental doctrines of the older churches, to make of them the living apostles of a rational and practical religion."³³ He vowed to continue to work. And he did for thirty-six years.

Brown's article "Labor Conditions in Jamaica Prior to 1917,"which appeared in the *Journal of Negro History,* actually preceded his migration to Harlem. His thesis was that the laboring population in Jamaica was no better off economically in 1916 than the period immediately following British emancipation in 1838.³⁴ His voice was not heard in journals as much as in organizations and from the pulpit, where he was to endure despite his tragic family and financial problems and the continuing antagonism of the American Unitarian Association. His presence in Harlem created a different type of religious experience that combined religion with the seething debate on class and race and involved the broader community in issues relevant to both Harlem and the Caribbean. Brown's little church was in great contrast to the grand edifices that many African American congregations relocating from downtown erected or acquired from fleeing white congregations. The church met for years in the same brownstone house at 149 West 136th Street, also the meeting place for the African Blood Brotherhood. It provided a unique "Temple and a Forum," as he called it. Domingo, Moore, Frank Crosswaith, and their families, including Mrs. Domingo as pianist, continued as members during the twenties. On occasion other activists including Otto and Hermie Huiswoud attended services of the small congregation even though they never became members.

These four outspoken Jamaicans—Garvey, McKay, Rogers, and Brown—who hailed from different sections of the island serve only as examples of critics of the American system of racism. Criticism and agitation were not confined to them or to those of Caribbean background. In focusing on the role of Otto Huiswoud, however, it is important to examine his relationships with peers and the evolution of their thinking. Harlem was teeming with diagnosticians and therapists focused on the race question. Huiswoud and his colleagues examined and exchanged ideas with all who would engage in the debate. There is no question that Garvey, McKay, Rogers, and Brown contributed to that debate. Their accounts also helped reveal that while the wider circle of militants from different areas of the Caribbean shared common elements in their analysis of the issues, there were also stark differences in their solutions. Their homelands were marked by diversity, as were their opinions and activities in Harlem.

When considering the political development of Caribbean immigrants who helped shape the direction of expression in Harlem during the first two decades of the twentieth century, the date of arrival and the origin of the immigrants does not seem as significant as their age upon arrival. Harrison, Briggs, Moore, Huiswoud, and Domingo arrived between 1900 and 1912, and their ages spanned fifteen to twenty-one years, whereas Rogers, McKay, Garvey, and Brown arrived between 1906 and 1920, and their ages spanned twenty-four to forty-five years upon arrival. The older men were not only more mature but their visions were in sharper focus. The younger men were still discovering who they were and what career might be of interest or, as they learned, open to them. They were in the process of searching for answers to conditions they observed and seemed readier to embrace a radical form of politics. They found no contradiction in joining a socialist or communist party, the race-oriented African Blood Brotherhood and the Unitarian Church. All nine, however, shared a common background and social concern for the plight of the victims of colonialism, and each threw himself into the fray at different positions on the barricades. Like highly energized meteorites that interacted and occasionally collided, they spread their efforts from the political international Left of Marxism to the separatist Black Nationalism of Garveyism. As the second decade drew to a close there seemed to be agreement among the African American and Caribbean militants of the need for pressure on the government to protect individuals from lynching and other violent attacks; changes in the unfavorable working and living conditions experienced by people of color in the United States; exposure of the negative aspects of colonialism; and publication of balanced histories of Africans and their descendants in the Americas. There was far less agreement, however, on establishing a political base that incorporated the plight of the African American, seeking an alliance with the trade union movement, and asserting the right to self-defense when government failed to protect citizens against attack.

The year 1919 proved to be quite significant, especially for Huiswoud. The shots of the 1917 October Revolution in Russia had reverberated around the world. The success of a feudal society overthrowing a tyrannical monarchy was not according to predictions laid down by Marx and Engels, but socialists everywhere were elated with the prospect of the establishment of a model socialist state. The impact on socialist parties, however, proved to be far greater than anticipated: they were now forced to choose the mode of operation for each national party. Did they support a reformist or revolutionary stance? Furthermore, did they seek a revolution of international proportions or would the establishment of one significant model serve their ultimate purpose? The basic question was not new. In fact, it had created divisions within the Socialist Party in the United States for years. Factionalism assumed a more volatile and virulent character after the Russian Revolution and led to the split that created a communist party, seriously diminishing the membership and effectiveness the Socialist Party had gained during the first two decades of the century.

In 1919, when organizational steps were taken to form a communist party in the United States, Otto was present to witness the momentous event. The party was born out of factionalism, and factionalism was to be its nemesis. Opposition elements were already present in the Socialist Party when the Russian Revolution occurred. S. J. Rutgers was involved in helping advance a Left Wing, and his description, written years later, of his report to Lenin in 1918 on developments in the Socialist Party in America in 1915 was very revealing: "I contacted through the Dutch group, 'The Tribune,' F. Rosin, secretary of the Latvian group no. 1 in Boston. We decided to form in Boston a new oppositional group based on Bolshevist principles, the so-called Socialist Propaganda League . . . A few issues of the newspaper 'Internationalist' as organ of the Socialist Propaganda League appeared in Boston. Then the center of this group and its organ were transferred to New York and the name of the newspaper was changed to 'The New International.'" Rutgers revealed that members of the League were recruited mostly from groups of workers of foreign extraction, who were fought stubbornly by the American Socialist Party. They expected a break would come.[35]

Indeed, the anticipated break did occur after Rutgers left the country in 1918. A description of the meeting with a few Russians and the impending split was provided by Sen Katayama, described by Rutgers in his report as "one of the most devoted co-workers and propagandists of the League":

> A meeting of Left Wingers was held early in the winter of 1917, in Brooklyn. There were some seventeen or twenty comrades present: Comrades Leon Trotsky, A. Kollontay, N. Bukharin, S. J. Rutgers, L. Lore, L. C. Fraina, L. B. Boudin, myself, and others . . .
>
> We intended to organize the Left Wing under the direction of Comrade Trotsky, and Madam Kolontay [sic], who was going to Europe, was to establish a link between the European and American Left Wing movements. But soon the Russian revolution flamed in action. Comrade Trotsky left for Russia and later Bukharin. America entered the war against Germany, then came the St. Louis Convention which engrossed the attention of the American Comrades.
>
> But with the Bolshevik revolution the physical as well as the spiritual relation between the American Left Wing movement and the Russian Bolshevik Party was firmly established.[36]

The series of Left-oriented publications edited by Louis C. Fraina continued to present the Left Wing perspective and helped expand the number of adherents of the Left.

The Socialist Propaganda League was the first organization to attempt to rally socialists in support of the principles of the Bolshevik Revolution. The problem was how the Left would gain control and transform the Socialist Party. The Left Wing was organized in Boston and Chicago by the end of 1918, but New York was not well organized because of strong opposition by New York leaders such as Julius Gerber and Morris Hillquit. The Left Wing Section of the Greater New York Locals of the Socialist Party was formed on February 15, 1919, at an all-day conference in New York City. The fireworks began in May 1919 when seven foreign federations comprising approximately two-thirds of the membership were expelled by the Socialist Party's national executive committee. The Left Wing responded by calling a National Left Wing Conference in New York starting on June 21, 1919. The conference was in session for four days and attended by ninety-four delegates from twenty states. The most important issue was whether they should immediately abandon the Socialist Party and form a communist party or wage a struggle within the Socialist Party.[37]

The Left Wing was not successful in prevailing at the emergency convention of the Socialist Party and the result was the establishment of two communist parties: the Communist Labor Party on August 31 and the Communist Party on September 1. In May 1920 the two groups combined to form the United Communist Party, but that was not the end of the factionalism. New entities, alliances, and realignments continued to emerge. The major structures that evolved were the Workers Party of America in December 1921, and later the Workers (Communist) Party in 1925 and the Communist Party in 1930. Not only was the Party in disarray because of the bitter internecine warfare that continued unabated, but all factions were subject to raids, harassment, imprisonment, and deportation by the government. From 1919 to April 7, 1923, groups were forced underground, and communist activity assumed the characteristics of an undercover operation. It has been estimated that the price was the loss of some five-eighths of the initial adherents, in addition to the serious loss in membership of the Socialist Party.[38] Factionalism not only resulted in handicapping the operation of the communist movement, it had a severe impact on the relationship among the leaders of the Communist Party in the United States and between the Party and the leaders in Moscow.

While Huiswoud was a participant in the founding of the Party in 1919, he was not privy to the inner circle planning in which Rutgers, Katayama, and others were engaged. But he was exposed to their Left Wing ideology and was a delegate, along with Anna Leve, to the June 21, 1919, National Left Wing Convention. The June 21 meeting gained significance in the history of the Communist Party even though the September 1 meeting is recorded as the day the party was born. Anna Leve has written, "He joined the C. P. Sept. 1, 1919. Went to founding Convention, was charter member and he worked in (Black) West Harlem."[39] A subsequent letter confirmed this: "When the CP was organized in 1919 we were both charter members. We belonged to the same unit in Harlem." It is not known what branch of the Socialist Party he first joined and whether he became involved with the Socialist Propaganda League while attending the training program at the Rand School. He was involved with the Twenty-first district branch of the Socialist Party when he became a charter member of the Communist Party, but it is not clear how his role changed when the split occurred. He must have been aware that the Communist Labor Party made no mention of the Negro question in their platform, but that the Communist Party stated in the program adopted in September 1919 that "the Negro problem is a political and economic problem . . . The Communist Party will carry on agitation among the Negro workers to unite them with all class conscious workers."[40]

Huiswoud's presence at the meeting in New York in June not only established him as a founding member at the age of twenty-six but committed him to the life of a communist revolutionary. He has been identified as a "functionary" in the early years of the Communist Party by others in addition to Anna Leve. Benjamin Gitlow referred to him as "a paid Party official almost from the organization of the Party in 1919,"[41] but the records are silent on how that role was assumed. While the socialist Domingo loudly extolled Bolshevism, the communist Huiswoud was "The Sphinx." Other early members were Arthur Hendriks, at one time a roommate of Huiswoud, and Lovett Fort-Whiteman, who had been trained at the Rand School the year prior to Huiswoud. Hendriks has been identified as a theology student from British Guiana who suffered from tuberculosis. He was one of the "pioneer members" of Brown's Unitarian church in 1920 and became a member of the African Blood Brotherhood along with Huiswoud in 1922. Brown indicated on a church membership roll and in a 1929 history of the church that Hendriks had left the city.[42] It was assumed by some colleagues who lost contact with him that he died from tuberculosis. Fort-Whiteman left New York on an assignment as an itinerant organizer after completing the course at the Rand School in 1918. In 1919 he traveled to Philadelphia, Pittsburgh, Braddock, and New Castle, Pennsylvania, as well as Youngstown, Cleveland, Toledo, and St. Louis, where he spoke to various socialist and African American audiences. He joined the Industrial Workers of the World and was arrested in St. Louis for helping organize a local unit. Shortly afterward he joined one of the communist factions and the ABB following his return to New York.[43] A brief article in the March 13, 1920, *Emancipator* indicated that Fort-Whiteman was arrested with eleven white members of the Communist Labor Party, suggesting that Fort-Whiteman first joined that faction of the Communist Party.

Socialists like Domingo, Randolph, Owen, and Moore were not involved in the internal factionalism that transpired in the Socialist Party after the Russian Revolution but they reacted to press reports and commented on the significance of the Revolution. Articles appearing in the *Messenger* like Domingo's "Did Bolshevism Stop Race Riots in Russia?" and "Will Bolshevism Free America?" reflected the interest expressed in Harlem. Domingo raised the question: "Will Bolshevism accomplish the full freedom of Africa, colonies in which Negroes are in the Majority, and promote human tolerance and happiness in the United States by the eradication of the causes of such disgraceful occurrences as the Washington and Chicago race riots?" His answer portrayed a view of Soviet Russia as a country in which "dozens of racial and lingual types have settled their many differences . . . which no longer oppresses colonies . . . from which the lynch rope is banished and in which racial tolerance and peace now exist."[44] He declared that "Bolshevism—Socialism—is the only weapon that can be used by Negroes effectively to clip the claws of the British lion and the talons of the American eagle in Africa, the British West Indies, Haiti, the Southern States and at the same time reach the monsters' heart . . . in London, Paris, New York, Tokio and Warsaw."[45] He optimistically wrote of the impact the Revolution would have on African peoples throughout the world: "Every oppressed group of the world is today turning from

Clemenceau, Lloyd George and Wilson to the citadel of Socialism, Moscow . . . It is the revolutionary Socialist, Lenin, who . . . sent out the proclamation: 'Slaves of the colonies in Africa and Asia! The hour of proletarian dictatorship in Europe will be the hour of your release!'" He lamented that other peoples of color were "in advance of Western Negroes with the exception of little groups in the United States and a relatively well-organized group in the Island of Trinidad."[46]

Domingo's advocacy of Bolshevism reflects the rationale that he and his colleagues were deriving from their experiences in the Caribbean and the United States and their close study of Marxist literature and worldwide current events. Similar editorials appeared by A. Philip Randolph, "A New Crowd—A New Negro" in the May–June 1919 *Messenger,* and by Cyril Briggs, "Bolshevism's Menace: To Whom and To What?" in the February 1920 *Crusader.* The articles explain the attractiveness of the Soviet model to socialists trying to fight racism and colonialism at that time. Linking colonialism and imperialism to the fate of minorities in the United States and advocating the concept of self-determination became a prominent part of their agenda, but the Socialist Party was not ready to make that leap. The activities of the socialists in Harlem were still focused on creating a socialist message that applied to the African American experience—one that bridged "straight socialism" and the particular problems of the African American worker. Moore has related that they asked themselves before mounting the soapbox, "Shall it be propagate straight socialism or shall we talk Negro-ology?" They had two separate messages because the Socialist Party had not come to grips with the "Negro Question."[47]

W. A. Domingo decided to bridge the gap with a direct approach to the Socialist Party. He submitted a draft to leaders at the Rand School for a leaflet obviously intended for white members entitled "Socialism Imperiled, or the Negro—A Potential Menace to American Radicalism." He considered that at a time "when sparks of proletarian unrest" were passing from Russia to other countries, it behooved those agitating along radical lines to understand how African Americans develop negative attitudes toward white workers and radical organizations. He argued that African American media and educational institutions expressing Negro thought functioned in the interest of capital and that the majority of African Americans were deprived of the stimulating influence of advanced political thought. He described two scenarios in which the Left or the Right might emerge from the struggle within the party. Regardless of which side gained power, they still had to recognize that "failure to make Negroes class conscious is the greatest potential menace to the establishment of Socialism in America whether by means of the ballot or through a dictatorship of the proletariat."

Domingo listed seven actions American radicals should take to attract African Americans, including condemning all forms of injustice against African Americans, gaining admission in unions on terms of equality, preparing special propaganda, supporting radical African American publications, and reaching audiences with competent white and African American speakers. His final admonition that "upon white radicals devolves the duty, out of consideration for their own self-preservation and the success of their cause, to aid to the limit of their greater ability to enlighten this most benighted section of the American proletariat . . . If America with her boundless resources remains non-Socialist, she will be a menace to world Socialism and America can remain non-Socialist if 12,000,000 negroes so will it." He then threw down the gauntlet: "But perhaps this attitude on the part of American radicals is because of the fact that they are Americans and share the typical white American psychology towards negroes. If this is so, then their radicalism is not genuine and is deservedly doomed to failure." This Harrisonian appeal for support of specially designed programs for African Americans was seized with files and publications when the New York State Joint Legislative Committee Investigating Seditious Activities, referred to as the Lusk Committee, raided the Rand School on June 21, 1919—the same day the Left Wing Conference began. Instead of being circulated by the Rand School the full text was published in the proceedings of the Lusk Report and characterized as "perhaps the best statement of the reasons for carrying on Socialist propaganda among the negroes."[48] Interestingly, some of the same ideas were presented in a considerably shorter editorial aimed at readers of the *Messenger* in the May–June 1919 issue.

The Harlem socialists were also committed to election campaigns of African Americans who were running for office on the Socialist Party ticket, particularly their friend and colleague, Grace P. Campbell (1882–1943), who was a candidate for the State Assembly in the Twenty-first District in 1919 and the Nineteenth District in 1920. The *Messenger* boasted that she was "the first colored woman to be named for a public office on a regular party ticket in the United States of America."[49] Campbell had moved to New York from Washington, D.C., in 1905 but was originally from Georgia, the daughter of a Jamaican father and an African American mother. She operated the Empire Friendly Shelter for young women and their babies and was also a civil service worker for New York City, where she progressed from probation officer to parole officer to court attendant for the courts of sessions.[50] She was not only active in the Socialist Party, serving as secretary of the 21st Assembly District Club, but has been referred to as the sole woman member of the African Blood Brotherhood. She was known for her warm, caring, generous nature. Somewhat older than her comrades, she has been described as a "mother hen," attending to secretarial details, collecting dues, arranging for meetings, offering her home at 206 West 133rd Street as a venue for meetings, holding open house on Saturday evenings, and assisting friends whenever called upon. Hermie has remarked that the men did not involve "their women kin in their activities, adhering to the theory that the women's place was in the home. Nevertheless, they accepted Grace Campbell as their mentor."[51] Campbell contributed militant opinions in her quiet way as well as other resources in meetings and campaigns. She did not write but made long public speeches that Hermie considered well delivered in a sincere manner. The important characteristic to note was her unwavering dedication to the socialist cause.

The concerns of the militants went far beyond the Socialist Party. They were part of a broader rising tide created by the return of African American soldiers from World War I, local problems associated with restricted job opportunities and housing, reports of lynchings and riots in numerous cities, and continued news of poor living conditions of the peoples of the Caribbean. W. A. Domingo and Richard B. Moore decided that there was need for a weekly newspaper and established the *Emancipator* published by the New Negro Publishing Company with the assistance of socialists Frank Crosswaith and Thomas Potter. Domingo was listed as editor-in-chief and Chandler Owen, A. Philip Randolph, Cyril V. Briggs, Anselmo Jackson, and Moore as contributing editors. The first issue of the four-page "Paper with Principle and Purpose" appeared on March 13, 1920. The editors explained that the purpose of the *Emancipator* was "to free the human family, white, brown, yellow and black, from the bonds of ignorance, race prejudice and wage slavery, to bring to the Negro race in particular an emancipation more complete, more genuine, than that for which our fathers fought and died fifty years ago." These lofty aims were also stated in narrower socialist terms, including championing "the cause of the oppressed of all lands; the right of workers everywhere to secure the full social value of the products of their toil; the prescriptive right of native Africans to their ancestral domains."[52] The news included articles on labor conditions and conflicts in South Africa, Jamaica, Panama, Trinidad, Cuba, and other Caribbean islands as well as in the United States. Later issues carried a series of articles on reports presented to the 66th Congress by the Department of Justice attacking the radical African American press. It was straight socialism tempered by the African American experience. There were no articles featuring cultural or sports events; no pages directed to women or children. Social and sports events were undoubtedly planned for future editions; government agent "WW" reported that he had been asked to work on social and athletic writing for the paper.[53] The initial format and serious tone would have appealed only to a relatively small audience. It lasted for ten issues and might not have survived historic note had it not appeared at the time the government was trying to prove seditious acts on the part of African American militants.

The *Emancipator*'s value, however, is not solely its additional voice at the apex of radical journalism in Harlem but its wonderful snapshot of the vortex of Harlem socialism in 1920. In its few pages can be discerned the cooperative efforts and writings of leading African American socialists. In addition to articles by Domingo and contributing editors, there was news of Rev. E. Ethelred Brown's arrival in New York and the inauguration of his church, Claude McKay's departure for England, Lovett Fort-Whiteman's release on bond from arrest in St. Louis, and Cyril Briggs's disclosure of malevolent business schemes. There were also descriptions of programs sponsored by the People's Educational Forum, where speakers included Chandler Owen on "Destruction, the Advance Guard of Progress," Rev. Brown on "Religious Liberalism and the Negro," and Otto Huiswoud, who joined others speaking on behalf of amnesty for Eugene Debs and other radicals who were in jail. One of the editorials of the first issue written by Moore was a tribute to four white members of the carpenters' union who were gunned down on November 22, 1919, in Bogalusa, Louisiana, while protecting the life of an African American fellow worker alleged to have been "stirring up members of his own race."

Advertisements in the paper for the *Messenger,* the *Crusader,* and the *Challenge* reveal close collaboration among the editors of those journals. One advertisement, however, was intended to convey an adverse message. Domingo was successful in obtaining an advertisement from Marcus Garvey's tailor, who was white, and he used it to demonstrate that Garvey did not always practice what he preached. By 1920 the schism between Garvey and the socialists had widened, and the newspaper was a vehicle for attacks on Garvey. Considerable harmony had existed during the New Negro formative years while militant individuals and organizations were discovering and defining who they were. It might have been expected that the "Red Summer" would foster closing ranks, but the twenties brought conflict.

The UNIA under Garvey's leadership had gathered incredible strength and embarked on several business enterprises. The boldest and most controversial undertaking was the launching of a steamship line. Domingo announced his departure as editor of the *Negro World* in the September 1919 issue of the *Messenger.* Reportedly the break was provoked by Garvey's displeasure at inclusion of socialist ideas in the editorials, Domingo's questions regarding the financial dealing associated with the steamship line, or Domingo's insistence on being paid on time. Perhaps it was a case of all of the above. Regardless, questions continued to be raised by a host of observers regarding Garvey's management of UNIA funds, and considerable enmity was aroused. Garvey claimed the *Emancipator* "caused him and his company thousands of dollars, and Domingo was the most spiteful man he had ever met." One FBI agent reported that Garvey followers were so bitter they swore to kill Domingo at the first opportunity.[54] Domingo later reported that following the publication of his article "Black Star Line Exposed" he had to stay home for weeks. A Garvey follower did stab him in the back but an overcoat protected him from a serious wound.[55]

The rift was not confined to bitterness between the two former colleagues from Jamaica. Rev. Brown was also slashed in the pulpit of his church because of his criticism of Garvey's leadership.[56] As a result of Briggs's critical articles in the *Crusader* Garvey accused him of being a white man "claiming to be a Negro for convenience." Briggs's sense of identity was not based on his complexion but on his self-concept; he proudly acknowledged and asserted his African heritage in spite of his blond appearance. Garvey's charge wounded Briggs, as intended, and he sued Garvey for criminal libel. The court hearing on November 11, 1921, resulted in Garvey retracting his statement and publishing an apology.[57] Physical attacks and the continual jostling and harassment that ensued during street meetings indicated the intense animosity that developed within the community. The UNIA, ABB, and socialist and communist parties were all attempting to attack discrimination and colonialism, but their members' passions and philosophical perspectives unfortunately drove them into conflict among themselves. Reactions to the "Red Summer" did not foster unity among the various forces. The Harlem Renaissance trumpeted sounds of dissonance as well as dissent.

The conflict within the community was a reflection of the enormous pressure experienced by African Americans at that time. A wide array of local organizations as well as national organizations like the NAACP and the Urban League with branches in Harlem were actively engaged in trying to promote change for African Americans. It is amazing the degree to which a community the size of Harlem could mount organizations and promulgate written and verbal appeals. The intensity of the relatively small number of militants is described in *Richard B. Moore, Caribbean Militant in Harlem:* "Harlem was in ferment. The Socialist Club was only one example of organized radical reaction. The sense of frustration . . . is evident from the number of organizations and publications emerging from such a tiny enclave. It was a matter of steps between the offices of Randolph and Owen's *Messenger* at 2305 Seventh Avenue, William Bridges's *Challenge* at 2305 Seventh Avenue, Cyril V. Briggs's *Crusader* at 2299 Seventh Avenue and Marcus Garvey's *Negro World* at 56 West 135th Street, and no more than a few blocks to homes, soapboxer corners, and meeting halls of the African Blood Brotherhood, Universal Negro Improvement Association, the Liberty League, and other militant organizations."[58] The extent of their pamphleteering was revealed in the Lusk Committee report, issued April 24, 1920, that claimed the circulation of radical Harlem publications was as follows:

The Challenge	Weekly	6,000
The Crusader	Monthly	4,000
The Emancipator	Weekly	10,000
The Messenger	Monthly	33,000
The Negro World	Daily	30,000

That represented over eighty thousand copies of radical print pouring out of a couple of Harlem blocks each month, in addition to the circulation of the *Crisis,* estimated in the report at 104,000 copies per month.[59]

The nuances of the diverse messages enunciated by each organization were missed, however, by government agencies responsible for the "security of the nation." The rhetoric of the small enclave of militant African American polemicists heralded not only the political aspect of the Harlem Renaissance but also the surveillance of their literature and organizations by the federal government. Agencies that had been organized for the purpose of gathering intelligence and pursuing those suspected of sedition or sabotage as a wartime measure during World War I gained permanent status in 1919 even though the war was over. As Theodore Kornweibel Jr. has so well chronicled, the Justice Department and its Bureau of Investigation, the Post Office Department, the Military Intelligence Division (MID), and the Office of Naval Intelligence (ONI) became institutionalized from 1919 to 1921 and formed a network to respond to the unrest generated during the "Red Scare." He points out that the MID, "like the Justice Department, was active both in fostering the Red Scare and suppressing those who were its targets. MID weekly bulletins—intended for the president, cabinet secretaries, the army command structure, and intelligence executives in other departments—were by the second half of 1919 'unusually hysterical about the Bolsheviks, the IWW, the Rand School, strikers, pacifists, Negro subversion,' and other targets."[60]

All of the federal agencies and some state sedition agencies like the New York State Legislature Lusk Committee tracked, reported, and sought punishment for anyone suspected of "Negro Agitation." Huiswoud was the only individual identified as "Radical-Negro" in a Bureau of Investigation report listing 150 radicals in New York City compiled by investigators of the Lusk Committee.[61] The British Intelligence Services also became involved because of their concern over the growing radicalism in their Caribbean colonies. They were suspicious that the ferment in the colonies might be connected with agitation in New York and fomented through the distribution of Garvey's *Negro World* and Briggs's *Crusader*. The initial warning from the British called attention to the *Crusader* as a "very extreme magazine" because of its "abuse of the white man" and articles opposing imperialism and favoring Bolshevism.[62]

Practically no distinction was made between the various perspectives of these publications and organizations, and certainly none was made between the causes for complaint and the nature of the rhetoric. One agent warned that "if any International disturbances occur among the Colored People you may be sure that [Briggs, Domingo, and other West Indian radicals] will be the instigators."[63] Another singled out Moore as "the most rabid of the Negro radicals."[64] Briggs was referred to as a radical of the worst sort, the ABB as the worst of the radical groups,[65] the People's Educational Forum as "the greatest school and the most effective spot for the spreading of and the teaching of Bolshevism among Negroes in general."[66] Randolph was branded as "the most dangerous Negro in America" and the *Messenger* as "the most able and the most dangerous of all the negro publications," representing the "fullest flower of negro sedition and flagrant disloyalty."[67] When Rep. James F. Byrnes of South Carolina and J. Edgar Hoover, who was head of the Bureau of Investigation's General Intelligence Division at the time, were pressing for prosecution of the *Messenger* and its editors, U.S. Attorney Francis G. Caffey in New York conceded that it was legal for African Americans to arm themselves to prevent lynching and to organize for the purpose of striking and that he did not see any direct evidence in the *Messenger* of a conspiracy to overthrow the government or oppose the authority of the United States or delay the execution of the law. But he was quick to add, "There can be no excuse for its publication."[68] There was a constant disconnect between the government and the African American perspective on lynching. Citizens of African descent were not supposed to protest lynching, and certainly the government was not to be expected to accept responsibility for protecting their right to life and liberty by investigating and punishing perpetrators of that horrible crime. At the time, editors of the *Pittsburg Courier* made an interesting observation on the nation's reaction to World War I veterans' change in attitude: "We never heard of a Negro Bolshevist as long as the Negro remained quiet . . . As long as the Negro submits to lynchings, burnings and oppressions—and says nothing, he is a loyal American citizen. But when he decides that lynchings and burnings shall cease even at the cost of some human bloodshed in America, then he is a Bolshevist."[69]

Instead of gaining redress for crimes committed against people of color, the bold rhetoric attracted a bevy of federal agents and informants, swelling the audiences at meetings and even assisting in the distribution of the so-called incendiary magazines. While the notes they took and the daily reports they made have added to the documents of the period, their bias and exaggerations must be viewed as revelations of the hysteria of the period. They saw "reds" under every bed, mayhem fostered in magazines, sexual misconduct encouraged in integrated meetings, antiwhite sentiments expressed in collections of African and African American history, and Bolshevik manipulation in organizational efforts and labor disputes. Attorney General A. Mitchell Palmer's report to the Senate in 1919 stated that "practically all of the radical organizations in the country have looked upon the Negroes as particularly fertile ground for the spreading of their doctrines. These radical organizations have endeavored to enlist Negroes on their side, and in many respects have been successful . . . the Negro is 'seeing red.'" J. Edgar Hoover gave priority to investigation of the *Messenger,* "stated to be the Russian organ of the Bolsheviki in the United States and to be the headquarters of revolutionary thought." Even President Wilson worried that African American veterans of World War I would be "our greatest medium in conveying bolshevism to America."[70] Some government officials recognized that African Americans might be susceptible to the lure of radical organizations but were eager to deny that they had legitimate problems created by society, the capacity to analyze their condition, and the ability to protest on their own.

This mischaracterization of the intent of the "pamphleteers" fueled their radicalization. Editors of the *Messenger* had their own definition of radicalism: "Radicals are hunted, outlawed and jailed for propagating . . . 'dangerous thoughts.' Whoever seeks to find out the root-cause of social diseases is a radical . . . all radicals are opposed to the status quo; they desire change: but not mere change, but progressive change."[71] Despite the fact that activists from the Caribbean were at greater risk because as noncitizens they were subject to be deported, they dared to taunt the federal agents. At one meeting of the People's Educational Forum, Chandler Owen and others denounced Department of Justice agents who were observed taking notes as "snooping spies and suggested that they had worked overtime and should join the bookkeepers' and stenographers' union." Moore called them a "bunch of skunks, who always left an unpleasant odor behind," at which point the three agents departed.[72] Domingo then expressed sorrow at their departure and asserted they were looking for him.[73] In the November 1919 *Crusader* Briggs attacked the suppression by government agencies "at the first grim evidence of the Negro's new-found determination to fight back in *self-defence.*" He wrote: "Both the

Lusk Committee and the Southern Congressional 'investigators' of Negro unrest are motivated . . . not by the slightest interest in locating the real causes underlying Negro (or other) unrest or by desire to remove or ameliorate these causes, but *principally and primarily by the malicious desire to remove or suppress the radical leaders of the race.*" He warned that suppression of radical magazines and jailing African American radicals would "only increase the possibilities of a gigantic conflagration."[74] The Lusk Committee report revealed awareness of "elements of our population that have a just cause of complaint with the treatment they have received in this country" yet the committee's solution was encouragement of "all loyal and thoughtful negroes in this State to organize to oppose the activities of such radicals."[75]

The second decade ended with the combination of increased violence unleashed against African Americans across the North as well as the South, and surveillance of the outspoken leaders and writers who objected to the attacks. The "Red Summer" of 1919, which earned its designation "red" among African Americans from the flow of their blood during riots rather than from socialism or communism, was accompanied by the "Red Scare." To African Americans fighting racism the "Red Scare" twisted the perpetrators of violence into heroes and the victims into the enemy. The government's attempt to suppress dissent drove the radical movement from the streets to the underground. No longer could socialists wave their banners so freely or combine their cultural and political events so openly. The pattern of federal surveillance and suppression of African Americans established at that time was to last for decades. In time Garvey, McKay, Rogers, and Brown were placed under investigation, in addition to Harrison, Huiswoud, Domingo, Briggs, and Moore. Even Rogers, who refrained from joining any political organization, was described by a Department of State special agent as a "negro of West Indian extraction, who cuts quite a figure in not only the colored salons of Harlem, but among the Pink Tea Radicals of the aristocratic sections of this city." He commented on Rogers's plans for a trip to Devonshire and Cornwall, England, to secure local color for a novel: "In view of Mr. ROGERS's peculiar conviction concerning race equality, there is hardly any doubt that the novel . . . will demonstrate that the heart of a Devonshire dairymaid or Cornish lass can beat just as truly for a 'cullud gemman' as for a British Jack Tar . . . He is a bad egg and worth while watching." Indeed Rogers was watched, and when he realized he was being shadowed from New York to England he enhanced his bad-egg reputation. He reported, "When he [the detective] finally brought up the subject of Communism one evening as we paced the deck . . . I was ready for him and shot him a full dose of the usual line of Communist chatter. I thought that if he was a 'dick' I'd not let him take all that long trip for nothing."[76]

As a result of the "Red Scare" Huiswoud felt it necessary to be circumspect regarding his new affiliation yet maintain the friendships he respected and needed personally and politically. He was caught in a dilemma between being a member of the Workers Party and associating with Socialist Party and ABB friends. His friends who had shared his concerns and goals were also comrades he hoped would ultimately join him in his new organization. He did not have long to wait before dissatisfaction with the Socialist Party's attitude toward the Negro question created a crisis. The Harlem socialists decided to invite Algernon Lee, director of the Rand School, to their People's Educational Forum as a guest speaker. Moore's version of the outcome is important in making the distinction between the split of the Left Wing, in which Huiswoud participated, to create a communist party in 1919 and the split that occurred between the Socialist Party and some of the prominent Harlem socialists in May 1921:

> Seeking to discover whether the Socialist Party would furnish any significant force for the organization of their victimized people, the Afro-American socialists asked the Euro-socialist leader Algernon Lee at a session of their Harlem Forum: "What program does the Socialist Party have for organizing the Afro-Americans, especially in the South?" Algernon Lee answered that the Socialist Party was the party of the proletariat, that by proletariat Marx meant the workers in industry, that the Socialist Party did not have enough forces to carry through this primary task and therefore had no forces to organize the Negroes. Though such organization was needed, said Lee, it would have to be done by some other bodies or by the Negroes themselves.
>
> Algernon Lee was therefore soundly condemned for his doctrinaire position by the militant Afro-American socialists. The disciplinary attempt which followed by the Socialist Party District Committee further served to convince most of the Afro-American activists in the Harlem branch that the Socialist Party, as then controlled, had little or nothing to contribute to the solution of the situation of racist oppression in America, and accordingly, these withdrew from the Socialist Party.

Moore added that "before the curtain thus came down on this activity under the aegis of the Socialist Party, the Afro-American militants had played a not inconsiderable role. They had thus gained the attention of the *Crisis* magazine . . . which in an article of March, 1920, noted: 'For the first time in the Negro's history, he has a Left Wing or Radical Group.'"[77] The "Left Wing" in Harlem developed in response to the issue of democracy at home rather than communism abroad. This opened the way, however, to actively recruit members for the communist cause among the Harlem socialists.

On June 13, 1922, Huiswoud achieved his goal of establishing a West Side Harlem Branch of the Workers Party. Subsequently an announcement was made that the provisional officers were Huiswoud as organizer, Briggs as recording and financial secretary, Comrade Pierre as delegate to the City Central Committee, Comrade Silverman as Literature Agent, and Moore, Campbell, and McKay as the Propaganda and Educational Committee. It was stated that while the branch would work mostly among Negro workers of Westside Harlem there would be white workers who transferred from Harlem (Eastside) English and Negro workers who were formerly affiliated with Yorkville English.[78] The report of the meeting failed to reveal how many members were in the branch, nor is it known when the various members joined the Workers Party. It has been speculated that it was during Huiswoud's campaign to organize a Harlem branch that Grace Campbell joined the Workers Party. She had campaigned as a candidate for the Socialist Party in 1920 but was on the Workers Party's ticket in 1922. She was probably the first African American woman nominated to run for office by the Socialist Party or the Communist Party. It is noteworthy that Domingo's name is missing in the announcement regarding the new branch. By that time he had decided that editing radical newspapers and magazines did not support a family and redirected his energy and acumen into a wholesale business importing Caribbean produce. The Department of Justice was eager to establish the date Moore joined so that deportation action could be instituted, but they could only estimate that it was following his naturalization in 1924. He was careful not to reveal the date at any time, but he wrote on a Workers (Communist) Party of America Sixth National Convention form dated March 1929 that he joined in 1922.[79] That would be a logical date considering his involvement with the Socialists until 1921, his stated hesitation due to his experience with the Socialist Party, and the announcement of June 1922.

Evidence is more confusing regarding the date Briggs joined. In the June 1920 issue of the *Crusader* he identified himself as a "Socialist." It has been confirmed by Briggs and others that he never joined the Socialist Party. Obviously he was embracing socialist philosophy, but that did not mean membership in either the Socialist Party or the Communist Party at the time. The 1929 Workers Party questionnaire and brief "Autobiography" dated April 16, 1932, written by Briggs stated he joined in 1919, a year he also tried to pinpoint when corresponding with Theodore Draper in 1958. That correspondence reveals that he was struggling to remember the year by associating his initial membership with certain events. In 1932 he stated that at the time he established the *Crusader* (September 1918) he "had no connection with the revolutionary movement, and only a vague knowledge of Socialism," then confirmed in 1952 that the ABB was "already in existence when I had my first contact with the Communists through the visits of Rose [Rose Pastor Stokes] and Bob [Robert Minor] to my office."[80] The significant point Briggs was establishing in various interviews was that the African Blood Brotherhood was founded in 1919 independently of the Communist Party and that his association with the Party began later.

With the internal machinations of various factions in the party competing for power and attempting to structure the party in addition to contending with government surveillance, it is highly unlikely that the Party had established a policy or modus operandi for the inclusion of African Americans or that white members Stokes and Minor would have been recruiting in Harlem in 1919. There is evidence that Briggs was in contact with Stokes and Minor through the efforts of McKay in 1921 following McKay's return from London earlier that year. When interviewed by Wayne F. Cooper in July 1965 Briggs confirmed that "McKay had been a member of his African Blood Brotherhood and had become a party member, along with himself and others in the group."[81] Strong evidence of a date later than 1919 is McKay's letter of December 23, 1922, in which he states that he introduced Briggs to the Communist Party and that the *Crusader* "died a few months after its editor joined the party."[82] The last issue of the magazine was January–February 1922. Briggs's statement that he "held office of sub-district organizer for 9 or 10 months in underground just prior to organization of Workers Party,"[83] his reference to Stokes, Minor, and McKay, along with McKay's claim in 1922, point to a strong possibility that Briggs more likely joined the underground Communist Party in 1920 or early 1921 and attended the meeting of the Workers Party as a representative of the ABB along with Huiswoud in December 1921. Moore has stated that Briggs joined before he did and that the sequence was Huiswoud as the African American charter member followed by Arthur Hendriks, Fort-Whiteman, Briggs, and himself.[84] It is clear that Briggs was one of the early members and that his writings at the end of the decade reflected his strong interest in the communist movement. It is also clear that membership in the Communist Party was entirely different for African Americans and their white counterparts from 1919 to 1922. Mark Naison has pointed out that "Communism followed a very different trajectory in Harlem than it did in ethnic communities . . . where it could draw upon a longstanding socialist tradition. In those communities, especially ones inhabited by Russian immigrants, thousands of left-wing Socialist Party members joined the Communist party en masse . . . Such a development could not occur in Harlem: there were socialist intellectuals, but no socialist subculture that permeated daily life." He concluded, "It was the anticolonialism of the Bolshevik Revolution which commanded their attention, not the organizational accomplishments of American Communists."[85]

McKay became active in the West Side Harlem Branch when it was formed. He had spent a year and a half in London working as field reporter and associate editor with Sylvia Pankhurst, editor of *Workers' Dreadnought.* In 1920 he joined the Workers' Socialist Federation, a Marxist faction that later became part of the Communist Party of Great Britain.[86] His New York friends were delighted to welcome him back into the fold in 1921. In the fall a Department of Justice agent who gained his confidence reported that McKay stated he was a member of the Communist Party of America.[87] McKay confirmed his membership while in the Soviet Union in 1922, when he wrote to Comrade Wallungus on November 28 requesting that his credentials from the Workers Party be returned.[88] He also declared in a newspaper article of December 3, 1922, reprinted in his book *The Negroes in America,* that he was a communist and had previously requested that his membership be transferred from the illegal party to the legal one in the United States.[89] Determining the actual dates Briggs, Campbell, McKay, and Moore joined the Communist Party, however, is not as important as understanding the experiences that drove them to take such a giant step and the activities they promoted to influence other members of the community toward the Left.

While Huiswoud was one important link between uptown and downtown communists, McKay, as assistant editor of the *Liberator,* was also helpful in arranging meetings. In mid-1921 at the suggestion of Harrison he invited Huiswoud, Campbell, Domingo, Briggs, Moore, Joseph P. Fanning, and Harrison to a meeting with Robert Minor in the office of the magazine. McKay identified the purpose as a discussion on the possibility of making the Garvey movement more class-conscious.[90] Perhaps McKay envisioned influencing the direction he had expressed regarding the Garvey movement in the article on socialism: "Although an international Socialist, I am supporting the movement for I believe that, for subject peoples, at least, Nationalism is the open door to Communism."[91] Around the same time Edgar M. Grey also reported to a government agent that he had been invited to a supper hosted by Rose Pastor Stokes that included Harrison, Domingo, Briggs, and McKay. He claimed that Stokes tried to convince Harrison to utilize the Liberty League to help spread communism among African Americans. Harrison was not interested but the government set out to determine whether money was being channeled to the ABB and urged Grey to join the Brotherhood.[92]

It has been suggested that securing members for the Workers Party was Huiswoud's motivation for joining the Brotherhood. He became a member of the supreme council and was named national organizer for the Brotherhood, a position that created an excellent opportunity to develop and promote the emerging communist perspective of the ABB. As the conflict sharpened between Garvey and Briggs and between Garvey and the socialists, the philosophical stance of the UNIA and the ABB distilled into two divergent movements with the UNIA finding common cause with the Ku Klux Klan and the ABB finding common cause with the Workers Party. Briggs had not originally conceived of the ABB as a front organization of the Workers Party; the Workers Party did not even exist when the ABB was formed. The Brotherhood was transformed as some of its key leaders became members of the Workers Party. As the road to justice and equality worsened and the new socialist state in Eastern Europe presented alternative solutions, a merger of the ABB and the Harlem Branch of the Worker's Party seemed mutually attractive. At a meeting of the ABB chaired by Huiswoud on November 23, 1923, at the home of Grace Campbell, Briggs announced that the supreme council and the Harlem Branch of the Workers Party had joined together for the purpose of securing an office to serve as headquarters and venue for a forum.[93] The affiliation did not produce the desired results, and the Brotherhood ran out of steam.

Life for Huiswoud was still one of economic constraint. He was living with Anna Leve, working at whatever job he could find, and developing his skills as an organizer in the new party. Membership in the Communist Party was not for the lighthearted or carefree; it was for the serious, dedicated, and disciplined. One did not simply carry a card. It was expected that members would attend meetings, demonstrations, and campaigns; study socialist doctrine and party pronouncements; sell the *Daily Worker* and other publications; and protect the identity of comrades. To be a functionary was in effect to take a vow of poverty. Remuneration from the Party for work and expenses was small and irregular. Expenses for tours were expected to be met through contributions solicited at meetings and provision of lodging and meals by comrades in the host city. Sometimes it was necessary to thumb a ride from one location to another. It helped to have some employment, not only to provide limited income but to give the appearance of a normal work routine and to be in a position to influence fellow workers if employed in an industry to be unionized. The Party sought to cultivate members who committed themselves fully to the work of the party and were not dependent upon capitalism and attracted to the trappings of the bourgeoisie. Missionary zeal was the motivation, not monetary remuneration.

Occasionally there might be a different type of reward. In 1922 Huiswoud was selected as a delegate to the Fourth Congress of the Communist International in Moscow. To the small cadre of the Harlem Branch of the Workers Party this was a definite sign that communism offered an exciting opportunity not only to theorize on the predicament of workers but to provide an international force to overcome the plight of African Americans along with other peoples who suffered under colonization. With the encouragement of Brotherhood members and Max Eastman, who was planning to go to Russia, McKay decided to attend as a representative of the ABB. McKay later recalled his motivation to join the delegates: "Russia signaled. A vast upheaval and a grand experiment. What could I understand there? What could I learn for my life, for my work? Go and see, was the command."[94] No doubt Huiswoud shared a portion of this sentiment but surely not McKay's urge to "escape from the pit of sex and poverty, from domestic death, from the cul-de-sac of self-pity, from the hot syncopated fascination of Harlem, from the suffocating ghetto of color consciousness." To Huiswoud the voyage from the "Negro Mecca of the world" to the mecca of international communism was the next step toward enabling him and others to raise color consciousness and strike a blow against discrimination and oppression of the darker peoples of the world. He was the first of his race to be selected for such an assignment and he was intent on carrying the mantle with honor.

For McKay the lack of official status meant getting to Moscow on his own. There was a flurry of activity to help finance his trip. McKay sold autographed copies of his book of poetry, *Harlem Shadows*, and in August Grace Campbell and Moore mounted a fund raising campaign. In one of the letters to solicit assistance directed to Arthur Schomburg, Moore wrote, "This trip of his should mean a great deal to our race. First of all, he will investigate at first hand the actual condition of the Jews and other minority groups to determine just what advantages or disadvantages have accrued to them under the new regime. Then he will be able to ferret out what opportunities may exist for the race in the South of Russia where the climate is favourable, and where social conditions may conduce to that welfare which is our age-old quest." Moore added that McKay should be able to detect also the pulse of that political movement as it related to subject peoples.[95] Thus in the fall of 1922 the printer turned politician from Suriname and the "vagabond" poet from the hills of Jamaica set out independently for Moscow. Travel to and from Russia was arranged either through Mexico across the border of Texas, Cuba via Florida, Canada via Montreal, or the port of New York. Huiswoud's secret itinerary devised by the Comintern was probably by ship from New York; McKay shipped out as a stoker on a slow freighter to Liverpool. The sole African American visionary who had helped charter the Communist Party of the United States and the bold writer who had heralded the Harlem Renaissance embarked on their internationalist journey, leaving in their wake the Statue of Liberty in order to search for liberty and equality for all.

McKay remained in Europe for almost twelve years, but his poem "If We Must Die" continued to reverberate in Harlem. The Justice Department considered that it was "calculated" to arouse racial hatred.[96] Harlem recognized it, however, as a response to racial hatred. Charles S. Johnson, a promoter and participant of the Harlem Renaissance, reported that the poem was written "at the most acute point of the industrialization of Negroes when sudden mass contact in the Northern states was flaming into riots" and it voiced for Negroes a mood of "stubborn defiance." He credited McKay with sounding "the first startlingly authentic note" of the social and economic forces "moving beneath the new mind of Negroes, which burst forth with freshness and vigor in an artistic 'awakening.'"[97] The poem was taken up as the clarion call—recited by ministers, soapbox orators, organization leaders, and students. It could be heard in church pulpits, African American schools, lodge halls, meeting places, and was a favorite on street corners. Why on the eve of a Renaissance to be marked by the creative outpouring of lyrics, stories, jazz, painting, and sculpture should the threat of death be so symbolic? Who were the kinsmen McKay was addressing? Fellow Jamaicans? Immigrants from the Caribbean? African Americans of his newly adopted country? It struck a responsive chord in all the oppressed of African heritage because the rising resentment and rage required resistance and revenge.

Hermie and her friends did not participate in or even comprehend the agitation swirling in their midst as the twenties began. For her, the legacy of the period was swept into the years of the Harlem Renaissance by McKay's poem. Even though she never knew McKay as Otto did, the poem assumed major significance. Throughout the twenties she would hear it recited over and over in meetings as the symbol of the New Negro. In the sixties she was to remind her friend Langston Hughes, regarding his omission of W. E. B. Du Bois and Paul Robeson in two of his books, that he had enjoyed enough prestige and reputation to be independent and must always bear in mind Claude McKay's poem. She added, "Only I'd say if we want to live let us not live on an inglorious spot."[98] She could never forget the impact of the call that proclaimed the Harlem Renaissance and resounded over the decades. The kinsmen, pressed to the wall, were fighting back!

4. Gift of the Tropics

References to the twenties evoke visions of "flappers" in short skirts bouncing to the beat of hot jazz. That stereotype belies the contradictions and diversity that New York produced during the first two decades of the twentieth century. The designation "Jazz Age" correctly reflects the characteristic sound, intensity, and pace of the period but fails to convey the lack of respect exhibited toward the people whose history and culture gave birth to jazz. Harlem was alive with jazz but rich improvisations and innovative interpretations were not confined to that form of expression. In spite of, or perhaps because of, continued oppression and discrimination, Harlem became a center for creativity in art, literature, theater, and dance, as well as in the blues and other forms of music. The twenties has been heralded also as the prime decade of the Harlem Renaissance.

Young Hermie Dumont flung her legs with abandon to the beat of the Charleston. Guyana was receding into faint memories and Moscow merely a dot on the world map in her classroom. Only Harlem was on her mind. She was barely aware of the upsurge of literary expression and the explosion of militancy that marked the Harlem Renaissance and communist movements. The two streams were to flow along parallel banks with occasional converging and mingling of currents. The dawn of the twenties would bring maturity and decisions to set her on a path that commingled both streams. In time the star rising far in the East would embrace her, as it was to claim Otto Huiswoud and Claude McKay in 1922. McKay's compass had already pointed to the East in his 1919 poem "Exhortation: Summer, 1919." The last line bids his brothers: "Wake from sleeping: to the East turn, turn your eyes!"[1] These lines not only expressed the hope McKay placed in the new experiment in Russia but also was a reminder of events that motivated the journey he and Huiswoud were to undertake. The "Red Summer" and the "Red Scare" drove the young radicals to an even higher intensity of activity and more vituperative forms of expression.

Unfortunately the "Red Summer" was not the end of violence against African Americans. On May 31, 1921, the blight hit Tulsa, Oklahoma. It was an attack that Huiswoud and McKay would not forget. According to the commander of the Tulsa Post of the African Blood Brotherhood, the incident that started the riot was the arrest of an African American man, Dick Rowland, who had accidentally tripped when getting in an elevator and allegedly stepped on or fell against the white female elevator operator. An exchange of gunfire ensued between African American men who attempted to protect the prisoner held at the courthouse and the white mob that looted hardware stores and pawnshops for weapons and ammunition to carry out threats against the prisoner and his defenders. The police sided with the white mob by swearing in white deputies, calling out the white militia, and directing attacks upon the African American community. Reports circulated that the attempt to burn down the African American district was aided by dropping incendiary bombs from airplanes.[2] The *New York Call* reported that one hundred seventy five people had been killed, with seven thousand Negroes left homeless, and also stated that the main cause of the massacre was the Negro wealth in Oklahoma.[3] While the number of deaths remained uncertain, later studies indicated that 1,256 homes were destroyed "along with virtually every other structure—including churches, schools, businesses, even a hospital and library" in the African American community.[4]

It was not unusual for blame to be placed upon African Americans but this time the accusation was that the local ABB had "fomented" the riot. This elevated the Brotherhood and Tulsa to the front pages of newspapers across the country. The NAACP sent Walter F. White to investigate and report. James Weldon Johnson, executive secretary of the NAACP, prepared an analysis of the underlying causes of the mayhem:

> An event of tremendous importance and one indicative of the growing tension between the races because of the Negro's increasing racial and economic solidarity was the Tulsa riots of May 31–June 1, 1921. The Negro in Oklahoma, and especially in Tulsa, has achieved greater unity than in almost any other section of America. Many of them have gained economic independence through the discovery of oil. Others have had great success in business and agricultural pursuits. In Oklahoma there are a number of whites who bitterly resent economic progress on the part of colored people. These white workers have been carefully manipulated and forced to believe that their interests have no com-

mon basis with those of colored workers. Combined with this resentment was a vicious newspaper propaganda against the Negro as well as a rotten political and police situation. These factors combined, resulted in the Tulsa riots which cost the lives of ten or more white people; between 150 and 200 colored men, women and children; and the destruction of 44 square blocks of Negro residential and business property valued at more than $1,500,000.[5]

Cyril Briggs alerted ABB posts and members to the tragedy in Tulsa and distributed to the press a denial that the Brotherhood bore any responsibility for the occurrence. The New York Post Menelik organized three mass meetings—June 12 at Palace Casino addressed by Moore, aided by Domingo and Joseph P. Fanning; June 19 at St. Mark's Hall addressed by Domingo; and June 29 at Lafayette Hall with Moore, Domingo, and Grace Campbell as speakers. The attack on the community and the accusations against the organization gave the ABB a boost in membership as well as renewed vigor to stress self-protection. Briggs was careful in his written statements to deny that the ABB organized for aggression and fomented and directed the Tulsa riot, but he was quick to establish that the Brotherhood was "organized for protection of otherwise defenceless Negroes."[6] Evidently neither state nor federal government officials were convinced that they had a case against the ABB. On June 8, 1921, a State Department report referred to a Military Intelligence Division survey that indicated that the information available "hardly warrants the conclusion reached in some quarters that the 'African Blood Brotherhood,' or for that matter, any other negro organization, 'fomented' the affair. It is undoubtedly true, however, that practically all negro organizations have been preaching the doctrine of resistance and that the race has to some extent absorbed it."[7] A report of the same agency on July 9, 1921, revealed that the "Grand Jury which investigated the Tulsa race riots of May 31st and June 1st held that the negroes were responsible inasmuch as they were the aggressors. The negroes who first assembled, it found, were armed, whereas the whites were not."[8]

Unlike the millions of Europeans who had sought escape from discrimination and deprivation in their homelands and found at least hope for improving their lives in the "land of opportunity," African Americans were finding that they had exchanged the noose of the lynch rope in the South for pogroms in the North. Tulsa crystallized the fact that half a century after Emancipation they were still trapped in the cage of racism. The ABB was certainly not alone in trying to discern the best tactic to release the chain of the all-encompassing discriminatory social structure that bound them. In an interview ten days before the eruption in Tulsa, Briggs was reported to have given credit to Marcus Garvey and the UNIA and to the NAACP for "tending to make the colored people here and elsewhere take stock of themselves and ask themselves why they should submit tamely to the bondage and slavery in which the white people desire to keep them." He had pointed out that the African American now realized "that he can get his rights, if not by talking and preaching, and from the courts, at least by his ability to fight and defend himself. The Negroes all over the country are purchasing arms and ammunition."[9]

Briggs appeared to throw caution to the wind when confiding in government informer P-138 (Herbert S. Boulin) in August 1921. The Department of Justice report claimed that Briggs showed the agent a catalogue picture of a Thompson submachine gun that had been ordered for distribution to ABB members across the country. Ostensibly the order for three hundred guns had been placed on the pretense that they were intended for Ireland.[10] Briggs's expectation that the Workers Party would help finance purchases of small shipments of arms from Mexico was echoed by Huiswoud, according to a State Department report of a Comintern committee meeting held in Moscow on December 22, 1922.[11] Huiswoud's statement made more than a year later suggested plans for the future rather than past purchases. There is no evidence that the ABB had the financial resources or the capability to organize a national armed defense despite Briggs's optimism that Rose Pastor Stokes and the Communist Party were willing to help "financially and morally." Briggs was acting on the conviction he had expressed in November 1918: "*Organized force* is the only language intelligible to *all* the world (the only language that Europeans understand in dealing with Colored races) and the foundation upon which all white civilisation is in reality based."[12] Tulsa was additional proof to him and his colleagues that the African American was indeed "pressed to the wall" and desperate enough to fight back.

The Tulsa authorities gave the impression that white Tulsa would make reparations and rebuild the burned area, but in reality they made attempts to prevent African Americans from rebuilding their community in the same location. It has been estimated that almost one thousand African Americans spent the winter of 1921–1922 in tents and in the end rebuilt their homes and businesses themselves with some assistance from outside sources. John Hope Franklin, who grew up in the area, has written about the self-esteem that was generated following the attacks: "The self-confidence of Tulsa's Negroes soared, their businesses prospered, their institutions flourished, and they simply had no fear of whites."[13] The violent attack left a scar in the community that had not healed by the end of the century and has generated several recent studies, publications, history conference deliberations, and a play entitled "If We Must Die." Alfred L. Brophy, who studied the case recently from a legal standpoint, considered that it "offers one of the most searing examples of racial violence in American history and chilling evidence of government complicity in the destruction." He confirmed, "The riot was not caused by black radicals; it was caused by lawless whites who wanted to keep blacks in their subordinate status."[14] On February 4, 2000, a commission appointed by the Oklahoma state legislature recommended that reparations be made to the eighty known survivors and victims' descendants.[15] The report of the commission cited acts against African American citizens including pogroms in at least ten other towns; disfranchisement of the African American electorate through constitutional amendment; segregation of public schools, transportation, and neighborhoods through municipal ordinances; and the lynching of twenty-three African Americans during ten years leading to 1921. It acknowledged that in some cases government participated and performed the deed; in none did government prevent the acts or punish the perpetrators.[16] Fearing that the state would continue to ignore the commission's findings and recommendations, a team of eighteen tort and civil rights lawyers filed a suit in 2003 against the state and the city of Tulsa and its police department seeking damages for survivors. Oklahoma is still trying to come to grips with acts of terrorism by whites against African American citizens in 1921.

By the time Huiswoud and McKay were ready to sail for Moscow in the fall of 1922 Domingo and Moore had severed their ties to the Socialist Party; Tulsa still burned in their memories; McKay had widened his international socialist experience in England; Huiswoud had established the Harlem communist base; Randolph, Owen, and Crosswaith had begun an anticommunist phase; and Garvey had been indicted for mail fraud. The philosophical gap had widened and some friendships had been torn asunder. Leaders of the African Blood Brotherhood had turned their eyes to the new dawn breaking beyond the boundaries of Harlem as they pondered what role an international body might play in counteracting racism and colonialism. Huiswoud and McKay were optimistic that their "pilgrimage" would help them discover a balm in the East.

The sponsor of the congress that would provide a place in history for both men was the Communist International, or Comintern, established by the Russian Communist Party in 1919 to coordinate the activities of communist parties in various countries. The leaders of the Russian Party had concluded that a new international body was required to distinguish between the emerging revolutionary parties and the reformist elements that had been allied in the Second International. On January 21, 1919, a call was issued for the First Congress of the "New revolutionary International" in Moscow. Lenin's pro-

The main cross street between Seventh and Lenox Avenues, 135th Street, Harlem, circa 1915. The Harlem Branch of the New York Public Library on the right was a venue for meetings and debates, and the nearby corner at Lenox Avenue was the site of soapbox orations and protest demonstrations. (Courtesy of Photographs and Prints Division, Schomburg Center for Research in Black Culture, the New York Public Library, Astor, Lenox and Tilden Foundation.)

Typical Harlem street merchant scene in the 1930s: "Watermelon Seller" from *Harlem Document* by photographer Aaron Siskind. (Courtesy of Museum of Fine Arts, St. Petersburg, Florida. Gift of Dr. Robert and Chitranee Drapkin.)

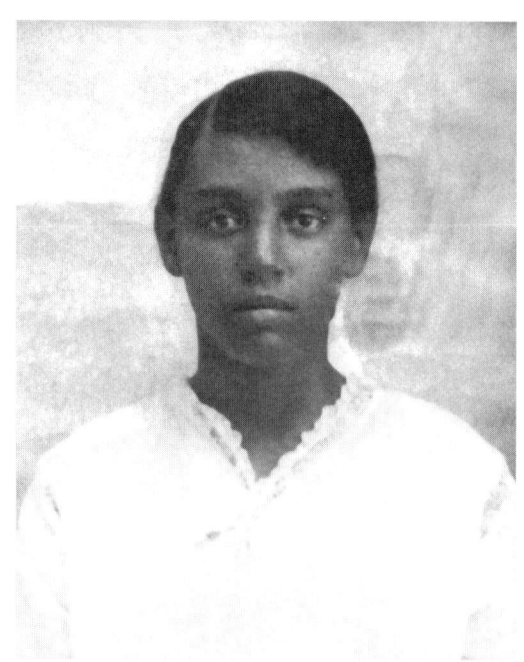

Hermina (Hermie) Alicia Dumont, circa 1919. (H. Huiswoud Papers.)

Hermie's maternal grandmother, Emily Adcock (1844–1916). (H. Huiswoud Papers.)

Hermie's father, Herman Robert Claudius Vlier Dumont (1864–1908). (H. Huiswoud Papers.)

Hermie's mother, Alice Jennette Dumont (1867–1947). (H. Huiswoud Papers.)

Otto Huiswoud's parents and siblings, circa 1913. *Left to right, seated:* Antoinette (Netje), Rudolph Francis Huiswoud (1852–1920), Jacquelina Henrietta Bernard Huiswoud (b. 1858), Netje's husband, Albert Chateau. *Standing:* Hilda, Lucien, Louise, Christopher, Lise. (Dutch Guiana) Otto and older brother, Egbert, had left home before the picture was taken. (H. Huiswoud Papers.)

Otto Eduard Gerardus Majella Huiswoud (New York). (H. Huiswoud Papers.)

Egbert Huiswoud, in the Dutch colonial military service in Indonesia, with his wife. (H. Huiswoud Papers.)

Hubert Henry Harrison. (Courtesy of Jeffrey R. Perry, Wesleyan University Press, and Charles Richardson.)

Sen Katayama. (From *The Labor Movement in Japan* by Sen Katayama, 1918.)

Sebald Justinus Rutgers. (Courtesy of International Instituut voor Sociale Geschiedenis, Amsterdam, the Netherlands.)

Grace P. Campbell. Campbell gave Hermina Huiswoud this photo of a painting of Campbell. Artist unknown. (H. Huiswoud Papers.)

Otto Huiswoud with Hermina Dumont, circa 1925. (H. Huiswoud Papers.)

Richard B. Moore, circa 1935. (Author's possession.)

Wilfred Adolphus Domingo. (Author's possession.)

Cyril Valentine Briggs, 1960, from FBI files. (Courtesy of Robert Hill.)

posed criteria included inviting only those "who are *for* a socialist revolution *now* and *for* the dictatorship of the proletariat" and "who are *in principle* for 'Soviet power,'" a type of government "*higher* and *closer* to *socialism*."[17] Deliberations were hampered by the difficulties of getting invitations to potential parties and problems experienced by representatives trying to get to Moscow. Asian delegates, including representatives from the old Tsarist empire, were present but none from the peoples in Africa and Latin America. It was S. J. Rutgers who called for the congress to "adopt practical resolutions on the struggle we have to wage in the colonies hand in hand with the brown and yellow proletarians," but no resolution was presented for action.[18] On March 6 the congress established the Communist International and thereby created the instrument by which the ideals and accomplishments of the Russian Revolution could be expanded globally as well as providing an international forum to consider mutual problems and chart potential solutions from a communist perspective. For many peoples throughout the world the Comintern was to become the agency that transformed the way they thought they might find relief from poverty and oppression.

W. A. Domingo and other African American socialists called for participation by the Socialist Party of America in the Comintern in 1919, but the only delegate from the United States granted official credentials by the congress was Boris Reinstein, a member of the Socialist Labor Party who happened to be in Russia at the time. Both socialist parties refused to be associated with the Comintern. The Left faction of the Socialist Party was intent on qualifying for membership and contributed to the split that resulted in two communist parties: the Communist Party and the Communist Labor Party. Both parties sent representatives to the Second Congress in July 1920 but the Comintern advised them to unite and made it clear that only one party was acceptable. In response to Lenin's Draft Theses on the National and Colonial Question, John Reed, delegate of the Communist Labor Party, spoke in favor of starting organizational work among African Americans, particularly in the South. Lenin's theses parenthetically mentioned African Americans: "All Communist parties should render direct aid to the revolutionary movement among the dependent and under-privileged nations (for example, Ireland, the American Blacks, etc) and in the colonies."[19] Reed expanded on the critical conditions of the Negro and concluded his long speech by affirming that the best and quickest way to destroy race prejudice and develop class solidarity was to unite the Negro and white laborer in common labor unions. He warned: "The Communists must not, however, stand aloof from the Negro movement for social and political equality, which is developing so rapidly at the present time among the Negro masses."[20]

Thus the Negro question was posed as part of the Theses on the National and Colonial Question at the outset and would remain in that context. Hélène Carrère d'Encausse's study on nationalities and the Bolshevik state distinguished "Western Marxists" who remained "obstinately attached to the exclusive importance of the class struggle" from the "Eastern Marxists" (Soviet) who "recognized the growing significance and potential of nationalist aspiration." The Bolsheviks had inherited a national problem when they assumed power in 1917. The large number of dissatisfied multinational groups conquered and absorbed into the Russian Empire between the sixteenth and nineteenth centuries constituted a non-Russian population that slightly outnumbered the ethnic Russians. They varied greatly in language, history, religion, and ways of life, and in their relationship to the Tsar. During and following the Revolution pragmatism prevailed in order to gain the support of the various national groups and give attention to their aspirations. D'Encausse maintained that World War I was instrumental in shifting the national question in Russia from a "domestic conundrum" to international politics, and it was at that time that "the idea of seeking international protection for minority rights began to take root." She posed the question Bolsheviks had to face following the Revolution: "How were they to reconcile the belief, nestled in every Bolshevik's heart, that a proletarian revolution would surpass and erase all national borders, with their earlier promise to national minorities that the proletarian revolution would work to the benefit of their emancipation?"[21] Unlike American socialists who insisted that the defeat of capitalism would take care of the race problem, the Bolsheviks were forced to adjust former theoretical pronouncements and develop a "temporary" policy to maintain loyalty of non-Russian territories. While the agenda of the Comintern was intended to examine and propose policies that would create change in the relationship of proletarians to the state in other parts of the world, Russian leaders were influenced by the internal struggle regarding national groups as well as considerations of the revolutionary role of peoples who were under the domination of European empires. It was necessary to take into account the championing of self-determination by President Woodrow Wilson and the League of Nations and to expose the nature of imperialism. The concern for nationality groups in the former Russian empire, the recognition of the potential of nationalist aspirations, and the championing of self-determination by the Soviets were the key concepts that attracted Briggs and some other members of the ABB to the communist movement.

In 1921 Kremlin leaders faced the reality that revolution was developing at a much slower rate in other countries than the First Congress had assumed, and the program of the Third Congress, from June 22 to July 12, was set to strengthen the Comintern. The 509 delegates from forty-eight countries far exceeded those attending the previous two congresses. They focused on the structure of the Comintern, the organization and tactics of national parties, and their relationship to the Comintern. No special programs for the colonial peoples or African Americans were adopted until the final session on July 12, when the South African delegation proposed that the executive committee should consider the Negro question.[22] A U.S. government report dated July 16, 1921, on the Unity Convention of the communist parties stated: "One member announced that he had been instructed by radiogram from Moscow in methods of appeal and approach to the negroes, as 'Moscow deemed this matter to be very important.'"[23] Lenin's keen interest, messages from the Comintern, articles in the U.S. communist press, and pressure by the African American radicals helped set the stage for consideration of the Negro question at the launching of the Workers Party in December 1921 and the Fourth Congress of the Comintern in 1922. The program and constitution of the Workers Party pledged that it would "support the Negroes in their struggle for Liberation, and will help them in their fight for economic, political and social equality . . . Its task will be to destroy altogether the barrier of race prejudice that has been used to keep apart the Black and white workers."[24] The Fourth Congress had much more to say.

To a small group like the ABB the Fourth Congress was a rare opportunity to present to a world body the grievances of a subjugated people that were not acknowledged and addressed at home. It was to be a realization of Briggs's seemingly far-fetched statement in the October 1921 issue of the *Crusader* that the ABB planned to establish contact with the Communist International. Hopefully Huiswoud, who was assigned delegate status on the delegation of the Communist Party as a member of the Brotherhood, and McKay, the Brotherhood's unofficial representative, would be able to gain support for oppressed peoples in Africa, the Caribbean, and the United States. Having learned of Lenin's argument linking the national problem to imperialism and stressing the struggle for the rights of oppressed peoples, Huiswoud anticipated that the opportunity was at hand to press the Negro and colonial questions beyond the meager attention received at previous congresses and in his own party. He was prepared to advance his agenda on behalf of his people while serving as a reliable representative of his party. McKay was in basic agreement with Huiswoud on the case that needed to be made. McKay underscored the necessity for "all struggling minorities of the United States to organize extensively for the world wide propagation of their grievances . . . And the Negro, as the most suppressed and persecuted minority, should use this period of ferment in international affairs to lift his cause out of his national obscurity and force it forward as a prime international issue."²⁵ There were many indicators that a warm, sympathetic response could be expected at the Moscow congress. The two comrades left New York in harmony, but an unrelated factional dispute raging in the Party was to sever their friendship.

Just getting to Moscow was an adventure. McKay "discovered the way" by working his way to England in front of a fiery furnace on a freighter, then traveling to Berlin, where a friend arranged for a visa in order to proceed to Stettin, Petrograd, and Moscow.²⁶ Huiswoud's itinerary through Europe was similar to McKay's. There is evidence he traveled via Berlin and not Shanghai as the American Legation in Riga, Latvia, claimed. After arrangements were made for a visa he was also sent to Stettin, where he took a boat to Petrograd and a train to Moscow. Gerard J. M. van het Reve has described his own efforts as editor of *De Tribune* to get from the Netherlands to the Fourth Congress despite being advised by David Wijnkoop (leader of the Communistische Partij Holland) that the delegates from Holland were already chosen. He contacted communists in Germany, who indicated they would help if he came to Berlin. There he rendezvoused with Genosse Franke of the daily newspaper of the German party:

> I went to the House of the Trades-union, where I met comrade Franke . . . who seemed to be very embarrassed . . . He evidently was not able to make himself understood as he faced two exceptional figures, the one being a Negro and the other, as I supposed, a Turk, because of his red headgear, a fez . . . They asked me: "Do you speak English?" . . . Comrade Franke . . . confessed to me that he only spoke German . . . Comrade Franke noted our names, our origin, the numbers of our passports and the rest and when I revealed that I came from Amsterdam, the Negro suddenly spoke Dutch fluently. He seemed to be a delegate of the C.P. of the United States and in that capacity his name was comrade Billings, but his own name, which stood on his Dutch passport, was Otto Huiswoud. He explained to me that he grew up in Suriname and worked in the U.S.A. for years. Suddenly our problems were solved . . . The Turk was an Egyptian . . . Comrade Franke did not comprehend any more than our Egyptian comrade did how fortunately everybody could understand each other through the unknown language [Dutch] that was familiar to the American Negro as well as to me . . . We three formed a nice picturesque little group, for I looked rather strange. Because I did not possess a proper overcoat, Mrs. Wijnkoop lent me a long, rough woolen pelerine, in which I, as Otto Huiswoud wittily remarked, nearly looked like a real monk.²⁷

Moscow was ablaze with red flags and streamers to celebrate the fifth anniversary of the Russian Revolution and to extend a festive welcome to the 408 (343 voting) delegates. Huiswoud was exhilarated by the warmth of the

Russian people and the challenge of sharing deliberations in the heart of world communism with comrades from fifty-eight countries. He moved among the delegates comfortably, speaking Dutch with delegates from the Netherlands and a bit of German learned while working with the printer in New York. He was delighted to be united again with his friend Sen Katayama, now a resident of Russia, and with the prospect of their working together in some of the sessions. The thrill of arriving in the impressive city crowned with brilliant, multicolored onion-shaped domes was soon muted by McKay's attempt to obtain permission to attend the Fourth Congress. As early as September 1921 McKay had revealed to a Federal Bureau of Investigation informant that he was a close friend of Rose Pastor Stokes and that while he agreed with her principles of communism he was "opposed to ideas of the Party functioning underground because he believes that in order to arouse the masses it is necessary to carry on as a legal organization."[28] McKay's description of his encounter with Stokes in November 1922 is somewhat disingenuous: She "casually asked if I did not think that an illegal Communist party was the best suited for America. I answered no, emphatically . . . So now in Moscow, before I was fixed in place as an unofficial observer . . . Stokes had got it from me that I was opposed to the majority of the American delegation, and that was bad."[29]

Throughout McKay's voyage from England to Petrograd he had been warned by European comrades that he needed the endorsement of his national party, but for some unknown reason he had prepared to register with only his letter from the unofficial obscure ABB and "credentials" indicating membership in the Workers Party of America. The red carpet was not rolled out when he arrived. According to McKay, the chairperson of the American delegation, Ludwig E. Katterfeld (a.k.a. John Carr), who had been in Moscow from 1921 serving on the executive committee of the Communist International (ECCI), refused to endorse McKay. McKay's anger at the difficulty he experienced obtaining credentials as a guest was directed primarily at Stokes in a letter addressed to Comrade Wallunyus on November 28, 1922. He complained that Stokes knew of his work more than anyone else, knew that he had returned from England with the proper credentials, and knew that he was responsible for getting the best Negro group in New York in touch with the Communist Party. He went on to say, "Her only objection to me now is because I feel that the American comrades have neglected the work among Negroes . . . If I speak out boldly and seem in conflict with the American comrades, it is because I know they have spent all their time in petty squabbles while the big work of reaching the American Labour movement & the Negroes is left undone."[30] Insult was added to injury when he was downgraded from a comfortable room at the Lux Hotel to a cold bare room with a cot—a fate shared by the American leader of the minority and chairman of the Workers Party, James P. Cannon, who was also shifted from the Lux to improvised quarters for overflow delegates.[31] No doubt the cool reception McKay received was related to what would have been viewed as an alignment with the minority's position on legalizing the party plus the fact that he had not sought the party's endorsement prior to his departure. This seriously compromised his relationship with Huiswoud, who was a member of the majority faction and committed along with Stokes to maintaining the illegal party.

The credential problem was settled by the intervention of Sen Katayama, who had made McKay's acquaintance in New York. McKay was granted guest status. It was a rare privilege for a nondelegate, and McKay thoroughly enjoyed the special status and attention. He was invited to participate in the deliberations of the auspicious commission on the Negro Question. Georgii I. Safarov (representing eastern countries) presided, and Otto Wilhelm Kuusinen served as secretary. Kuusinen of the Presidium, Secretariat, and Executive Committee; Nikolai I. Bukharin of the Presidium and Executive Committee; and Katayama and Safarov of the Executive Committee served, along with U.S. delegates Huiswoud (a.k.a. J. Billings) and Stokes (a.k.a. Sasha); Sidney P. Bunting, representing South Africa; and five others identified by Stokes as representing Belgium, France, England, Java, and Holland. It is not clear how the Theses on the Negro Question were generated. The minutes of the session held on November 28 indicate that statements had already been made to the congress by Huiswoud and McKay but suggest that this was the first meeting of the commission. The agenda was basically a report by Huiswoud.

Bukharin opened the session with a statement on the task of assisting the liberation of the "whole race which is in slavery . . . by the white people in America and Africa." He predicted a "bright future when the word 'negro' will not be a synonym for slave," and pledged the support of the international proletariat." Following a brief statement by McKay, Huiswoud was called upon to report on "the prospects of the negro movement in North America." Huiswoud identified three types of organizations, UNIA, NAACP and ABB, and stated that only the ABB could be counted on to overthrow the bourgeoisie by methods of revolutionary struggle. He stated, "We are not in favor of an immediate armed uprising but that an armed fight will come we have no doubt." He then described a plan for establishing a Committee of Action in one of the southern cities to revolutionize the masses of Negroes. Fighting organizations would be developed for self-defense with arms shipped from Mexico. Finances would be derived from dues, contributions, and the Negro section of the American

Communist Party to increase propaganda and agitation.[32] Huiswoud had undoubtedly done his homework; his test balloon was more calculated than daring. He was drawing upon previous statements by Lenin and the Comintern as well as the resolution adopted by the Third Congress regarding a communist party's antimilitarist agitation: "Intensive agitation must be directed not against the military training of the youth and the workers but against the military order and the autocracy of the officers. Every opportunity of getting weapons into the hands of the proletariat must be vigorously exploited."[33] Katayama proposed that the general scheme concerning the establishment of the Committee of Action be approved. According to Stokes's account the way had been led by John Reed at the Second Congress and a comprehensive report that was submitted to the Comintern executive committee during 1921. She reported that credit was due to America for introducing the question of a Negro Commission to the Presidium, which had voted unanimously to create the Negro Commission.[34] Huiswoud was elected permanent chairman at the first meeting and introduced and presented the theses recommended by the commission to the congress on November 30.

Huiswoud's introductory remarks included a complaint that the important colonial question adopted at the Second Congress was being treated as a stepchild and warned that the Negro question must begin in the proper direction. He pointed out that although the Negro problem was fundamentally an economic problem, there was a psychological aspect aggravated and intensified by friction between the races. He described the exploitation of Negroes in America, the West Indies, and Africa, the cruel brutality of the U.S. South, how the bourgeois ideology was cultivated in the minds of African Americans, the conflict created between workers, and the attitude of the unions against African American workers. In explaining the types of organizations and press developed by African Americans to counteract the violence against them he pointed to Tulsa, where a courageous fight had been waged. In addition to the Theses on the Negro Question, the Negro Commission had prepared definite proposals for implementing work among Negroes throughout the world, including the establishment of a Negro Bureau as part of the ECCI. Huiswoud then read the Theses on the Negro Question. Karl Radek made a motion that the document be returned for "clarification and amplification" because it was "too Marxian in its phraseology." The report was returned to a small subcommittee of the commission for editing. McKay followed Huiswoud with a statement in support of the work that needed to be conducted, especially in the South. He identified his race as the "most oppressed, exploited, and suppressed section of the working class of the world." In describing how the capitalists set the races against each other he dealt with the use of Negroes in the military of America and Europe—forced not only to fight against the soldiers' own interest but also against organized labor. He charged that the situation was so ugly that few were willing to face the problem, including socialists and communists. He identified prejudice as the greatest difficulty the communists of America had to overcome: "They first have got to emancipate themselves from the ideas they entertain towards the negroes before they can be able to reach the Negroes with any kind of radical propaganda." He cited Karl Marx's fight against chattel slavery and the work that had to be done against wage slavery and the suppression of opinion in the South.[35]

Rose Pastor Stokes read the final version of the theses. Briefly it claimed that World War I, the Russian Revolution, and a movement of revolt against imperialism among colonial peoples had "roused the consciousness of millions of the Negro race whom capitalism has oppressed and degraded beyond all others for hundreds of years, not only in Africa, but perhaps even more in America." Secondly, it proclaimed that the rich history of revolts and disturbances qualified Negroes to play "an important role in the liberation struggle of the entire African race . . . The post-war industrialisation of the Negro in the North and the spirit of revolt engendered by post-war persecutions and brutalities has roused a spirit which although suppressed, flames into action when a Tulsa or other inhuman outrage cries aloud for protest and places the American Negro, especially of the North, in the vanguard of the African struggle against oppression." The theses also linked the enemy of the Negro workers' race, capitalism and imperialism, with that of the white worker and the oppressed of the world who are striving for "political, industrial and social liberation and equality."

The theses concluded with the following statements:

> The Fourth Congress accordingly declares it to be the special duty of Communists to apply the "Theses on Colonial Questions" to the Negro problem. 1. The Fourth Congress recognises the necessity of supporting every form of Negro movement which tends to undermine or weaken Capitalism or Imperialism or to impede its further penetration. 2. The Communist International will fight for race equality of the Negro with the white people, for equal wages and political and social rights. 3. The Communist International will use every instrument within its control to compel the trade unions to admit Negro workers to membership or, where the nominal right to join exists, to agitate for a special campaign to draw them into the unions; failing in this, it well [sic] organize the Negroes into unions of their own and specially apply the United Front tactic, to compel admission. 4. The Communist International will take immediate steps to hold a general Negro Conference or Congress in Moscow.

Stokes's concluding remarks regarding the status of the unions stressed that "our chief work lies in getting the industrial Negroes into the unions where they can fight equally with the white workers for their equal emancipation."[36]

A rare opportunity for Huiswoud to assume a leadership role was presented on December 5 when Katterfeld passed his mantle as leader of the United States delegation to Huiswoud. For some unknown reason Katterfeld expected to be "cooped up and unable to report at all" and sent a letter to Huiswoud with instructions regarding the care and disposition of important documents and supplies, travel arrangements to the United States for some delegates, and reports that were to be made every week to the CEC. He wrote, "I am writing the Secretariat that you & Sullivan are in Enlarged Exec [of ECCI] and you take my place as Party representative until other arrives." He warned that "If Cook [Cannon] & Co make trouble in the delegation remind them of the Party decisions that those that represent majority viewpoint of CEC (now yourself and Pullman) have two thirds vote within Delegation. That was one of the conditions on which we consented to send Marshall [Max Bedacht]."[37] Stokes also sent a letter to Huiswoud on the same date cautioning him that the Americans had been warned in the American Commission to display a little more humility. "When we strut about, puffed up with self-importance, we must seem doubly ridiculously small to the men who have a background of experience that we cannot hope to acquire during the rest of our natural lives—unless we pass thru a couple of real revolutions . . . like themselves." Obviously Stokes was aware of Katterfeld's instructions to Huiswoud and added her "earnest advice." She reminded him, "You happen to remain in a job that requires *somebody*. Take the job and do it in a *humble spirit,* with Communist understanding of course, and with a determination to grow and get out of the experience all that you can for Communism."[38]

Huiswoud informed McKay that the Comintern was planning to subsidize a newspaper directed to African Americans. On December 23 McKay wrote to Vasil Kolarov, general secretary of the ECCI, and Katayama that he considered such a plan a mistake before the American situation was determined because there "is a group of us in New York that is convinced that the pushing of propaganda work among Negroes within the next few years depends on our concentrating on open work . . . Billings [Huiswoud] and Briggs are not of this group even though we are all a unit on the purely Negro problem. Furthermore, as I have told Billings, Briggs is not a capable editor." McKay went on to compare the various African American radical publications and recommend the young men who published the *Emancipator*.[39] Clearly he had Domingo in mind, whose article he quoted at length in his subsequent book,

The Negroes in America, published in Russia. Neither the Negro Congress nor the subsidy for a publication were forthcoming.

In the end the issue regarding the power of the legal party that had divided the American delegation so vehemently was settled in favor of the side McKay had supported. James P. Cannon (a.k.a. Cook) had arrived in Moscow the first of June as the American delegate to the Plenum of the ECCI and served as a member of the Presidium. He pursued arguments in favor of legalizing the American Party in personal discussions with key members of the ECCI. Max Eastman, who was attending as a nondelegate and who favored legalizing the American Party, arranged a meeting with Trotsky, who indicated that he would support legalization and expected that Lenin and other Russian leaders would do the same. After listening to arguments by delegates representing both sides, the American Commission unanimously recommended that the party be legalized, advocate for the construction of a labor party based on the trade unions, and appeal to seceding members to return to the party.[40] The decision of the American Commission was an interesting shift considering that the ECCI had pressed the American Party in August to construct the new legal party to be under the complete control of the underground Communist Party. The notice signed by Bukharin, Radek, and Kuusinen stressed that the underground organization "must not be liquidated . . . It must guide and control the legal revolutionary Party thru its members." The American Party was scolded for not "having satisfactory connection with the masses," and the Negro mass movement for racial betterment was cited as an example of strategies that should be undertaken to lead the working masses. The Workers Party had already been established in December 1921, so the real question was not whether there should be a legal or an illegal party. At stake was control. The minority resented the domination of the foreign federations, and the final warning of the ECCI reveals the underlying problem: "It is foolish and harmful . . . if fractional opposition accuses the Party Executive of oppressing the foreign language organization. You must make an end of such accusations, comrades."[41] The decision at the Fourth Congress was instrumental in changing the structure of the American Party.

A report of the American delegation's continued internal conflict during the congress cited an example of disunity during the nominations of representatives to the ECCI. When Damon's name was placed in nomination as an alternate, Huiswoud reportedly objected and claimed that the American delegation had selected him.[42] It seems out of character for the freshman delegate to challenge the election of Charles E. Ruthenberg (a.k.a. David Damon), the national secretary of the Workers Party who had been released from jail earlier in the spring. The contention probably was based on Katterfeld's instructions in early December that he was notifying the Secretariat that Huiswoud was to be in the enlarged executive of the ECCI. It would have been logical for Huiswoud to assume that "take my place as Party representative until other arrives," meant that his functions would temporarily include Katterfeld's role as member of the ECCI. Damon (Ruthenberg) was elected in absentia in the list of nominees endorsed by the Presidium and voted upon unanimously en bloc.

The monthlong series of ponderous sessions were interspersed with lighter cultural programs and personal exchanges such as the festive trip to Petrograd, grand performances at the Bolshoi Theatre, and a private dinner for Huiswoud and McKay with Karl Radek's family. The Dutch editor van het Reve was successful in rejoining the Egyptian (Hosni) and Huiswoud in Moscow, and again the trio was conspicuous as they joined the throngs in Red Square to observe the parade of soldiers and demonstration of the people celebrating the fifth anniversary of the Revolution. On November 7 the three attended a big dinner party at the Kremlin that van het Reve described: "Hosni, Otto and I came into a mighty hall with arches and many dining areas. The tables were covered with heavy silver cutlery with an eagle! After dinner we wandered through the Kremlin palace full of marble and gold. Later on there was a big feast and people danced."[43] Huiswoud and McKay were made honorary members of the Moscow Soviet. McKay and Stokes were interviewed, and articles appeared in the Soviet press featuring the plight of African Americans. The crowning event for Huiswoud was the personal meeting with Lenin. The sad note of the congress was Lenin's absence, except for one appearance on November 13 to deliver an address. Lenin monitored the congress from his sickbed and sent for Huiswoud to query him on the condition of the African American people in the United States. Huiswoud was proud and pleased to confer with Lenin, and while he mentioned the meeting subsequently the details are unknown. McKay reported that he tried to see Lenin but was not successful.[44]

The Fourth Congress assumed a significant milestone in the development of the American Party. The leaders of the Comintern certainly gave attention to the problems of the American Party and the grievances of African Americans. Not only did the congress resolve the problem of the structure of the American Party, it shifted the focus from a heavy European perspective to the important task to "systematically and willingly assist American-born workers . . . [to] play a leading part in the movement." It was pointed out that "the Communist immigrants have brought many virtues with them to America . . . however, their greatest weakness lies in the fact that they desire to apply the experience they have acquired in the various countries of Europe, mechanically to American conditions."⁴⁵ The Theses on the National and Colonial Question committed the Comintern to press national parties with populations of color to fight for their liberation and acceptance in labor unions. In effect it tied the functioning of American workers to the Party's involvement with African American workers. It is ironic that the Russians should have had to remind, in fact direct, American Communists how to function in America.

Huiswoud left Moscow inspired to vigorously renew his work as an organizer but the road home was not direct. Travel to and from the Soviet Union often involved "getting lost" to avoid or reduce problems with U.S. immigration officers. The U.S. legation in Riga indicated that the Americans were expected to travel via Shanghai, but Huiswoud simply spent a month in Germany and then time in the Netherlands, where he was a citizen. It had been a twelve-year circuitous journey from Suriname to his original destination, but now that he was finally in Holland he was eager to resume revolutionary work in America. He embarked on the Dutch ship *Ryndam* and landed in New York on March 1, 1923. This was his first legal entry into the United States.

McKay remained in Moscow for six months to take advantage of an offer to write articles for and about the Soviet Union. He stressed in his autobiography that he "was not received in Russia as a politician, but primarily as a Negro poet." The government and the people bestowed upon McKay the adoration and respect they had for writers, especially for their beloved Alexander Pushkin, of African lineage, regarded as the founder of modern Russian literature. The Soviets seized the opportunity to employ an American writer who could share the African American experience with Russians and other peoples and who might generate works informing the American people of the Soviet experiment. The red carpet was rolled out for the acclaimed poet. Access to various sites of interest and comfortable accommodations were provided, and according to him, he was "magnificently" paid. His major work, *The Negroes in America,* was printed in Russian in 1923 but was not available in English until 1979. The book articulated many of the ideas he, Domingo, Briggs, Huiswoud, and Moore had previously hammered out during their nocturnal deliberations in Harlem. His approach was from a class point of view; his stated aim was to let his Russian comrades "know the truth about the American Negro, his place in the workers' movement, and his relationship to that movement; about his place in American society, and about the relationship of organized labor and American society to him."⁴⁶ Even though a project to write about the Russian Revolution for an American audience was still pending, the "vagabond" was ready to move on by June. The prospect of returning to New York and resuming responsibility for his wife, who had shown up in New York after years of separation just prior to his departure to Russia was not in keeping with his temperament. So now Berlin and Paris beckoned. He left Russia, traveled to Germany, and "settled" in France, where he was to roam and write for ten years.

On February 1, 1934, McKay finally returned to New York; he had distanced himself both geographically and philosophically from Moscow. Two years later, eleven years after his Russian sojourn, he completed his autobiography, *A Long Way from Home*. Unfortunately there is no autobiography by Huiswoud, and McKay's writings have become a major source for discerning their relationship. It is difficult to see Huiswoud through McKay's pen, and even McKay is elusive. Nonetheless the dim light cast from various sources reveals a striking contrast between the two men of the Caribbean, not simply in physical appearance but in personality and persuasion. McKay was flamboyant, gregarious, boisterous, fun-loving, outspoken, impetuous, and independent. Huiswoud was taciturn, reticent, quiet, serious, cautious, calculating, and committed. McKay boldly proclaimed his name; Huiswoud used an assumed name, like others of the American delegation. McKay took to the streets to take the pulse of the Russian people; Huiswoud worked the congress to take the pulse of the Kremlin and the delegates. McKay the freelancer was on a lark; Huiswoud the party man was on business. Huiswoud's comment to McKay during the congress is illustrative: "Say, fellow, you're all right for propaganda. It's a pity you'll never make a disciplined party member."[47] To some extent these differences were complementary and eliminated the potential for an image to be drawn of "the typical Negro." Together they created a strong presence; their two vigorous voices contributed to one message.

It was unfortunate that McKay's personal account of their contributions and success at putting the African American's plight before a world body was marred by his retaliation at the rejection he perceived at the beginning of the congress. He honored Huiswoud's preference to remain anonymous at the congress but could not resist striking a blow, Caribbean to Caribbean, where it was bound to hurt. Referring to Huiswoud as "the mulatto delegate," like Garvey calling Briggs a white man in disguise, was intended to demean. The depth of his feeling was conveyed in the poem "Mulatto," where he expressed the searing hate within his soul for the white man who put "his bastard birthmark on my face." In the last three lines he professed: "When falls the hour I shall not hesitate / Into my father's heart to plunge the knife / To gain the utmost freedom that is life."[48] McKay could articulate how imperialists used color to create and maintain class and caste distinctions but failed to recognize that he was still a victim of that colonial strategy. Several of McKay's friends took exception to what he said about them in the autobiography; Huiswoud ignored the attack. They were not to meet again. Huiswoud was back in Moscow by the time McKay returned to Harlem in 1934.

As soon as Huiswoud returned to New York in 1923 he embarked on plans to organize African Americans. Huiswoud had gone to Moscow holding the trump card of having organized the first branch of the Workers Party in an African American community; he had returned armed with a mandate from an international body that had committed its members to fight for the rights of African peoples throughout the Diaspora and to open the workplace and unions to African Americans. To Huiswoud's colleagues the theses represented the culmination of questions and demands presented during the previous decade to the socialists by Du Bois, Harrison, Domingo, and a host of lesser-known African American radicals like Thomas Potter, who had complained in 1911 that the socialists "were as silent as a clam on every question that affects the negro."[49] The African American cadre knew that implementation would be difficult, but they were determined to continue their agitation. They welcomed Huiswoud home greatly encouraged by the resolutions acclaimed at the congress.

On February 23, 1923, the Comintern followed up on the theses in a letter signed by Kuusinen to the central committee of the Workers Party stating that the Presidium felt that the proposed "negro-world congress [was] too unprepared" and would be considering the matter in April. "It was further decided by the Presidium to request your party provisionally to take care of the propaganda for the development of the negro-movement, and also in general to prepare the ground for the coming negro-congress."[50] Thus the Comintern placed the implementation of the theses directly in the hands of the communists of the United States. Interestingly, on March 21 the American legation in Riga, Latvia, reported that among the effects carried by Sen Katayama that were examined by Latvian secret service agents when he was returning to Russia were pictures, including one of Katayama with Huiswoud, McKay, and Stokes; a draft of a manifesto by the ECCI addressed to the "oppressed negro peoples of the world" that included reference to "the Negro Conference"; a document entitled "Draft Proposal for the Organization of the Negro Bureau (for Africa and America) Within the Executive Committee of the Communist International in Moscow" with a staff of five; an "unfinished memorandum concerning the international organization of negroes" stating that "New York City is at present the political center of the negro peoples of the world;" instructions from the Comintern outlining a plan of action concerning propaganda work among Negroes; and an estimation of the cost of operating a weekly paper.⁵¹ It is clear that someone was preparing for the implementation of the theses other than leaders of the American Party. Typically, the wording of the theses became another arena for dispute among the leaders of the Workers Party, and they notified the Comintern in March 1923 that the "Party does not agree with the thesis adopted by the Fourth Congress on the Negro Problem. It is collecting material to be submitted to the Comintern. The problem consists in developing the social phases: the tenant farmer in the south and the industrial workers in the north."⁵² Evidently Katayama was aware of the reluctance of the American Party because he stated in a paper calling for action on the theses that the entire American delegation except Huiswoud and Stokes had been against the Negro resolution in the American section meeting.⁵³

The Fourth Congress had not gone unnoticed by the African American press. Briggs's Crusader News Service sent out news releases in which Huiswoud was identified only as a Negro delegate while McKay's name was included. One account indicated that "President Kolaroff [Kolarov] had proposed that detailed reports on the Negro be submitted for the purpose of clarifying the subject for European members who are unfamiliar with the problem in other countries," but the work ahead entailed clarifying the subject for the American comrades.⁵⁴ The article by Huiswoud in the *Worker* on April 28, 1923, did not mention the Fourth Congress or the Comintern. It asserted that the "Negro Problem was one of the most important problems facing the Workers Party;" that it demanded "special attention and careful study"; and that it was "the duty of the Workers Party to attract this section of the American Working Class." It is not clear why the Workers Party was having problems with the Theses on the Negro Question or whether Huiswoud was aware of the February 23 letter from the ECCI.

As the year progressed the small cadre became a beehive of activity. Briggs and Huiswoud worked together preparing and distributing Crusader News Service releases and other propaganda materials. In the role of National Organizer of the ABB, Huiswoud went on various tours, including Pittsburgh, Chicago, Jersey City and other New Jersey cities, Philadelphia, and Washington. On the last two he was accompanied by Domingo. Huiswoud sought the cooperation of Canadian union groups through the Workers' Party of Canada and worked closely with the eastern organizer of the Trade Union Educational League. A memorandum from the Department of State indicated that one of the chief activities of the Brotherhood was organizing African Americans into unions and seeking assistance of trade unionists "in breaking down the prejudice against the blacks." The writer concluded: "The point worthy of note is that the Negro revolutionists and the American communists are cooperating by means of the *most innocent yet most effective* Communist machinery on the North American continent, the Trade Union Educational League."[55]

The bold headline in the August 11, 1923, issue of the *Worker* proclaimed "Huiswoud Out to Organize Negro Labor." The ABB organizer was reported to be departing for Pittsburgh after spending three weeks organizing Negro workers of Chicago, where he urged African Americans "to join trade unions and resist the efforts of open-shop employers to make the Negro a weapon in breaking down standards of living." The ABB was described as having "branches in many states as well as in British Guiana and Trinidad . . . The brotherhood maintains the Crusader press service, sent to over 100 Negro papers twice weekly; sends organizers into the industrial centers, operates forums and classes, watches for open-shop abuse of the Negro and exposes the conditions in the south that force the Negro to flee to the north for safety and a livelihood."[56]

An essential part of the Harlem scene were the forums, book discussions, debates, and other types of programs at the YMCA, YWCA, public library, churches, and meeting halls. In typical Renaissance fashion Huiswoud and colleagues promoted and participated in community programs in addition to operating the People's Educational Forum and its successor, the Harlem Educational Forum. Debates were popular. At a program sponsored by the Harlem branch of the public library, Huiswoud debated George S. Schuyler, who had flirted with socialism but was becoming a conservative writer known for his sarcastic and satirical pen. According to Schuyler, "It was arranged in June, 1923 for me to debate Otto Huiswoud on the subject of the Negro and Communism. There was no other person around willing or able to debate him, all the others being intellectual Socialists. We had quite a turnout and the debate was stirring . . . I took the position that the Negro had difficulties enough being black without becoming Red; that an attempt was being made by communists to make a dupe out of the Negro which could only end in race war and his extermination."[57] Schuyler failed to mention Huiswoud's argument and the outcome of the debate. Huiswoud also debated Frank Crosswaith, a former political associate who had remained in the Socialist Party. According to Hermie, Huiswoud was judged the winner and awarded a framed copy of Rudyard Kipling's poem "If."[58] The poet's advice to a son on how to achieve manhood, such as keeping one's head when all about you are losing theirs and blaming you and not giving way to hate when hated, did not reveal Kipling's commitment to empire building. The irony of a prize by one of the British Empire's staunchest proponents of colonialism, however, was not lost on Huiswoud. Years later Hermie was to mark Kipling's death with her poem "Two Epitaphs in an English Graveyard" published in the *Negro Worker*. (See the epilogue to this book.)

While Huiswoud was wending his way from Moscow, Briggs was beginning negotiations with five African American leaders to sponsor a national race conference. After the defeat of an antilynching bill in Congress, William Monroe Trotter of the National Equal Rights League, in Boston, had recommended the formation of a council of Negro leaders. Dr. Matthew A. N. Shaw, president of the organization, issued an invitation to leaders of five other organizations, including the ABB, to devise ways to unify their forces.[59] Briggs responded with the suggestion for a United Front Negro Conference of Civil Rights Organizations, and on March 24, 1923, representatives of the following organizations signed a "Concordat" pledging their cooperation: Moore, Domingo, and Huiswoud of the ABB; George S. Schuyler of the Friends of Freedom; D. N. E. Campbell of the International Uplift League; James Weldon Johnson, Robert W. Bagnall, and Richetta G. Randolph of the NAACP; James L. Neill, Dr. Matthew A. N. Shaw, and William Monroe Trotter of the National Equal Rights League; and Dean Kelly Miller of Howard University, who signed on behalf of the "National Race Congress" because he was serving as chairman of the arrangements committee. Briggs served as secretary. An ambitious list of topics on which the conference was to focus was established. After a year of conferring, posturing, and organizing the "Sanhedrin," named by Miller from the ancient Hebrew name for a Supreme Council, was convened in Chicago on February 11–15, 1924.

Huiswoud and a second unidentified ABB representative were not alone in representing a radical perspective. The Workers Party sent five delegates. Announcement of the opening of the Sanhedrin was combined with news of a "supplementary" meeting the previous night at which Fort-Whiteman and Robert Minor spoke on Frederick Douglass as part of the "Negro Week" observance. The Sanhedrin, or All-Race Assembly, however, was not a gathering of radicals. Dean Kelly had secured the participation of a wide spectrum of eminent scholars, professionals, and businessmen and women—250 delegates from twenty states representing sixty-one national African American organizations. The session on labor in which the ABB and the Workers Party had the greatest interest did not meet their expectation, and they refused to be restricted by the chairman, Kelly Miller, in their attempt to bring the issue to the floor. Huiswoud "denounced the conspiracy to keep Labor from being heard and censured the leaders of the convention for providing no place for labor on the program."[60]

The Workers Party resolution in part called for the American Federation of Labor and other labor bodies to organize Negro workers on a basis of equality in the same unions with whites. The final wording of the resolution passed by the assembly stated that "the exploitation of Negro labor in the conflict between capital and organized labor is unfair and detrimental and that the principle of equal pay, recognition of Negro workers in fields where labor is organized, and community assistance to Negro workers in industrial centers and organized financial relief in farming centers are all highly desirable."[61] The ABB or Party resolutions on segregation, discrimination in schools, against the Ku Klux Klan, and encouraging friendship with Russia did not prevail. The two organizations did extend the nature of the debate, however, and contributed a perspective on issues that had to be faced ultimately by African Americans and the nation. Mark Solomon contends that despite such sectarian fervor, the Workers Party and ABB resolutions "were important contributions to the ongoing quest for equality . . . Unlike the other delegates, they represented a force that appeared to be external to the black community. But they were confident that their radicalism was true to the core of black needs and aspirations. And they were heard, as they took the floor repeatedly to press their program."[62] In fact they were heard so well that the Workers Party was barred from attending the subsequent and last meeting in Washington.

Huiswoud's trips to Chicago also involved attending meetings of the Farmer-Labor Party. The decision of the Comintern's American Commission regarding advocating for a labor party based on trade unions was pursued by the Workers Party, but it is questionable how serious they were about assuring the admittance of African Americans to unions. As early as March 1922 at the meeting of the Chicago Federation of Labor the communists began a series of alliances and were successful in gaining domination of the Farmer-Labor Federation. William Foster, who headed the Trade Union Education League and was elected chairman of the Workers Party in January 1924, played a key role in the negotiations, but as his tie to the communist movement became more evident, leaders in the Farmer-Labor Party distanced themselves. The conflict that ensued between the Workers Party and various players of the Farmer-Labor movement for leadership and control, particularly over the selection of a candidate for the office of president of the United States, was not simply a case of differences in ideology. A major factor was the old struggle between factions within the Communist Party. Foster, James Cannon, William Dunne, and Earl Browder were at loggerheads with Charles Ruthenberg, Jay Lovestone, and John Pepper regarding tactics, and the Comintern was called upon to settle the dispute. The CEC of the Party decided to send Foster, Cannon, Pepper, Ruthenberg, and a representative of the Anti-Third Party group to Moscow "to secure a decision and avoid a factional controversy."[63] In May the Comintern insisted upon the abandonment of the united front with the farmer-labor group. The failure of the Workers Party to retain positions of leadership and influence in the Farmer-Labor Party resulted in the Workers Party running its own candidates: Foster for president and Benjamin Gitlow for vice-president.

This internecine conflict had a detrimental effect not only on the relationship between the two political parties but on the development of work among African Americans. Much later a story circulated regarding repudiation of Huiswoud for his stand at the Farmer-Labor convention in St. Paul. One account drafted by Sen Katayama dated May 23, 1928, and presented by Otto Hall (a.k.a. Jones) to officials of the Comintern explained:

> At the Farmer-Labor Convention in St. Paul in 1924, which was under the control of our Party, a resolution on the Negro question which had been drawn up by the Negro Committee of our Party was presented by Comrade Huiswood [*sic*], a Negro delegate at the convention, calling for complete social equality, against lynching, etc. This was objected to by a Southern white farmer delegate who claimed to represent fifty thousand farmers, stating that they would not support a party which had in its platform social equality for the Negro. Upon this objection, the steering committee of our party agreed to take out of the resolution all of the "objectionable" points. This same farmer also made a speech before the convention, stating that the Negro did not want social equality but that all he wanted was an equal opportunity to earn a livelihood. Seeing that the resolution which he had presented had been changed by the Resolutions Committee, Comrade Huiswood took the floor to reply, in spite of the orders of the steering committee that he should not do so and strongly denounced the speaker from Texas. Both speeches were printed in the leading bourgeois newspapers of St. Paul and Minneapolis, commenting on the able speech of the Negro delegate in rebuking the farmer delegate from Texas.
>
> For this incident, Comrade Huiswood was censured and suspended from the Party for a period of one year. This suspension was not announced in any branch of the Party in which there were Negro members although it was announced in others.[64]

Mark Solomon has identified the resolution presented at the convention as a "Negro Equality" proposal prepared by the Negro Commission chaired by Robert Minor. The resolution "demanded the new party's support for full political and social equality through nondiscriminatory union membership, constitutional measures to assure equality at the ballot box and an end to segregation." Minor reported that a lone Communist defended the proposal.[65] Minor did not identify the lone defender but it can be assumed that it was Huiswoud. The only known statements by Huiswoud regarding the incident were oblique remarks made in 1928 and 1929. In response to challenges from comrades when he was making a report during a meeting of the American Commission in Moscow, he identified Arne Swaback as the person who pulled him down into his seat when he got up to speak at the convention. Swaback was a close ally of Foster, and it could have been assumed he was acting in support of Foster, who was chairman of the Party at the time. Earlier at a session of the Sixth Party Convention, Huiswoud indicated he had been denied work when the minority was in power.[66] He did not name Foster, but the implication was that his suspension occurred during the period when Foster was chairman of the Party.

The suspension of Huiswoud put the brakes on the organizational momentum developing in African American communities following the Fourth Congress and brought into question the commitment of the Party to implement the theses promulgated in Moscow. On October 13, 1924, the Negro Commission of the Party ("The Committee of Seven") addressed a document signed by Robert Minor and Gordon Owens to the CEC discussing the significance of the term "social equality." It pointed out that even "champions" of Negro rights in other organizations were aloof from the demand for "social equality" but that "the party of proletarian revolution, operating in a country where a racial caste-system is fundamentally rooted, cannot leave that caste system untouched." The Committee of Seven requested the CEC to rule that it was the duty of all Party members under all conditions to attack that caste system by demanding all forms of equality for Negroes, including open and emphatic declaration for "social equality." The committee then launched its criticism of the behavior of delegates at St. Paul by requesting an official ruling on whether Party representatives acted correctly:

> It will be remembered that this demand was not even brought on the floor of the convention, and this committee is uninformed as to whether the Communists on the resolutions committee at St. Paul presented the demand for "social equality" even in the committee-room, or whether it was eliminated by the C.E.C. in advance of the convention . . .
>
> As a second point, we should like to have an official ruling of the C.E.C. as to whether our Party representatives acted correctly in permitting the plank on Negroes' rights . . . to be taken back and reconsidered in the resolutions committee after it had been passed by the convention; and in permitting every mention of equality to be stricken out without our Party making protest on the floor . . . We point out that the Negro plank finally adopted is almost as evasive on this point as the platform of the Republican party, and does not even promise the Negro the political equality which Harding promised them in the southern city of Birmingham . . .

> We wish to emphasize . . . the need for the Communist Party to make a clear fight as the spokesman for such equality . . . so that we can go to the Negro working masses as their champion.[67]

This document and subsequent accounts of Huiswoud's suspension do not mention any appeal on behalf of Huiswoud. It is assumed that he accepted the discipline despite his anger.

Huiswoud maintained contact with his colleagues in Harlem and worked part-time jobs, mainly with Domingo, who had established a business importing tropical produce. Huiswoud was responsible for going to the docks to meet the incoming freighters from the Caribbean, unloading the produce, and supervising its distribution to stores in Brooklyn and Harlem. He also sold insurance. In 1925 the CEC apparently decided that his suspension was over, and Earl Browder, as acting secretary, wrote Huiswoud on April 25 that the CEC was placing him "in responsible charge of the activities in New York City and vicinity in the organization work preparatory to the American Negro Labor Congress" (ANLC) under the direction of the district executive committee.[68] Huiswoud's reply was reserved, indicating that he did not know whether he would be able to be responsible for the work but would do all in his power to further the work. He offered his criticism of the policy that was being pursued regarding the ANLC:

> It is my belief and that of the comrades here that a good deal of the publicity given may prove rather harmful and retard the success of this movement. It appears that the Party in its anxiety to promote this work has given publicity of such a nature that would easily tend to link up the Party with the American Negro Labor Congress; the result of which is necessarily detrimental to the success of the congress. I have also noticed that a meeting was held in Milwaukee under the auspices of the Trade Union Educational League. This to my mind is very ill-advised because of the fact that the Trade Union Educational League is known as a Communist organization and that to link up the two organizations at this stage of the game, will no doubt give the reactionaries an opportunity to try to stifle the growth of the American Negro Labor Congress.[69]

The Farmer-Labor experience provided Huiswoud with two lessons: the label "communist" created prejudgement of an organization, thereby diminishing opportunities to effectively reach potential participants; and second, Foster was not to be considered an ally. A second letter representing the New York and Philadelphia committees signed by Moore, Huiswoud, Aubrey Clifford Bailey (a.k.a. Harold Williams), and August Warreno was sent to the CEC on May 31 listing eleven points that should be considered for creating the proper image of the ANLC. The third point cited the Farmer-Labor debacle:

"We must always bear in mind that the reactionaries will undoubtedly employ the same tactics in connection with this congress as employed previously in connection with the St. Paul and similar conventions, namely, by 'exposing' its Communist character, thereby killing the movement at the very start."[70] On May 19 and June 13 Huiswoud was assured by Ruthenburg, the executive secretary, that the CEC had received and agreed with the criticism and had issued instructions to avoid establishing a close and formal connection between the Party and the ANLC.[71]

The leader selected as national organizer of the ANLC was not Huiswoud but Lovett Fort-Whiteman (a.k.a. James Jackson). During the same period that the Farmer-Labor meetings were in progress, Fort-Whiteman was in Moscow as a delegate to the Fifth Congress of the Comintern held from June 17 to July 8, 1924. During a discussion on the Negro question, his argument was similar to Huiswoud's at the Fourth Congress. He stated "that the Negro problem in the United States was psychological as well as economic, and covered all classes of Negroes." He reported on the Sanhedrin meetings held in Chicago earlier in the year and recommended that special literature directed to African Americans be prepared.[72] In a letter dated October 24 he reminded Grigori Zinoviev, president of the Comintern, of the resolution of the Fourth Congress to convene a World Negro Congress in Moscow and complained that the Workers Party had made "no serious or worthwhile efforts to carry Communist teaching to the great mass of American black workers." As an example of the Party's neglect he explained that the CEC had refused to pay his expenses to the Fifth Congress even though he was a full-fledged delegate. Financial support was provided "by individual Negro Communists, inspired by the belief that by sending one of their group to Moscow, he might be successful in getting the Comintern to take some practical steps helpful to our work among Negroes both in America and on a world scale." He revealed that he had recently submitted "suggestions to the Eastern Section of the Comintern in respect to . . . calling an American-Negro Labor Congress at Chicago, composed of delegates of the various Negro industrial and trade unions."[73]

The decision was made at the Fourth Enlarged Plenum of the ECCI that met July 12–13, 1924, to establish a standing Negro commission, including representatives of British, French, and Belgium parties, to organize propaganda among Negroes.[74] Fort-Whiteman, who was authorized by the CEC to remain in Moscow for an intensive course in organization, was evidently persuasive enough to gain support for launching the ANLC. In December the Comintern Secretariat wrote to the Workers Party Executive demanding action on the African American comrades' call for a Negro labor congress and requested an immediate reply regarding "the Party's attitude." The Comintern initiated action at the first joint meeting of the ECCI Secretariat and the Negro Commission on January 12, 1925. Fort-Whiteman was still in Moscow and attended that meeting. It was followed on January 16 by a memo to the Workers Party detailing the objectives, program, composition, and leadership. Fort-Whiteman was designated as the chief organizer.[75] The Party was informed on February 3 that the ECCI was sending $2,500 to support the organization work.[76] Later that year the Parity Commission of the Party unanimously adopted a resolution that incorporated a lengthy statement on "The American Negro and the Proletarian Revolution" for submission to the national convention to be held August 21, 1925. It included a description of the goals and composition of the ANLC that was scheduled to be organized on October 25.[77] A report at the convention on activities of the CEC clearly stated that their work carried on in connection with the ANLC was "in accord with the instructions of the Communist International."[78]

Pressure on the American Party to establish a front organization dedicated to winning African Americans' place in trade unions was consistent with the theses on tactics adopted by the Fifth Congress, known as the "Bolshevization of Communist Parties of the Communist International." The structure of the Russian Communist Party, organized with the industrial shop branch or party nucleus as the basic unit rather than the territorial or neighborhood unit prevalent in the United States, was promoted as a model for all national parties. The assumption was that the working class should be organized at the workplace where the conflict between the capitalist and the worker was sharpest and clearest. Party divisions along language and ethnic lines were to be eliminated. The American Party was still basically structured according to the territorial or neighborhood model inherited in 1919 from the Socialist Party, with many foreign-language federations that operated independent activities, newspapers, and social halls and clubs. The theses were a signal to the American Party to change its constitution and implement a complete restructuring along the lines of the Russian party despite the statement in the theses that "it would be the greatest mistake to transfer Russia's experience mechanically to other countries."[79] From the Comintern's perspective the absorption of an ethnic organization like the ABB would have been contrary to the proposed structural change. There was a major problem, however, with any plan based on organizing African Americans in American trade unions: racism in the United States posed a dilemma because most factory jobs and unions were closed to African Americans. The solution devised was to create a type of labor organization: to create the ANLC.

By 1925 Huiswoud, Briggs, and Moore had developed and solidified their political positions and moved beyond the precepts formulated when the ABB was originally established. Despite questions regarding the pace with which the Workers Party would implement the "Negro theses," the three committed themselves to the communist movement. During the first half of the decade they had presented their perspective not only to the Harlem community and members of the ABB but to other national and international bodies including the Workers Party, the UNIA, the Sanhedrin, the Farmer-Labor Party, and the Comintern. They perceived that the only organization ready to accept the challenge to combat racism and colonialism was the Comintern. Recognizing the influence that the Comintern exercised over the Workers Party, they mobilized their meager forces to exert pressure from within the Party and from outside through the Comintern. A pattern of appealing to the Comintern emerged similar to that resorted to by the major factions within the Party. According to Harry Haywood, when significant issues became mired in party pettiness Huiswoud would remind the comrades, "If you don't settle it here, we'll settle it in Moscow."[80] While many personal relationships were changed as political affiliations became more apparent, the friendship between Huiswoud, Briggs, Moore, and Domingo remained firm. Domingo's venture with a small business marketing tropical products and the identification of the three with the extreme radical Left did not cause conflict. It was Domingo who favorably described their collective contribution to the civil rights movement.

In the article "The Tropics in New York," which appeared in a special issue of *Survey Graphic* devoted to Harlem and was reprinted with a few minor changes as "Gift of the Black Tropics" in the *New Negro*, Domingo wrote of the current and historic presence of Caribbean peoples in New York and their contribution "to the wealth, power and prestige of the United States." The essay is most noted for its explanation of the difficulties endured following the arrival of Caribbean people "from countries in which they had experienced no legalized social or occupational disabilities" and its description of the gift they brought to America and to their African American kinsmen. He stated, "Despite his inconsiderable numbers, the black foreigner is a considerable factor and figure . . . Indeed, it is they who largely compose the few political and economic radicals in Harlem; without them the genuinely radical movement among New York Negroes would be unworthy of attention." He continued:

> They rebel against the "color line" as they find it in America. For while color and caste lines tend to converge in the islands, it is nevertheless true that because of the ratio of population, historical background and traditions of rebellions before and since their emancipation, West Indians of color do not have their activities, social, occupational and otherwise, determined by their race

... For this reason the West Indian has thrown himself whole-heartedly into the fight against lynching, discrimination and the other disabilities from which Negroes in America suffer ... Just as the West Indian has been a sort of leaven in the American loaf, so the American Negro is beginning to play a reciprocal role in the life of the foreign Negro communities ... This world-wide reaction of the darker races to their common as well as local grievances is one of the most significant facts of recent development ...

The outstanding contribution of West Indians to American Negro life is the insistent assertion of their manhood in an environment that demands too much servility and unprotesting acquiescence from men of African blood. This unwillingness to conform and be standardized, to accept tamely an inferior status and abdicate their humanity, finds an open expression in the activities of the foreign-born Negro in America.

Their dominant characteristic is that of blazing new paths, breaking the bonds that would fetter the feet of a virile people.[81]

While stressing the assertion of manhood Domingo was not unmindful of the contribution of Caribbean American women. He stated, "This freedom from spiritual inertia characterizes the women no less than the men, for it is largely through them that the occupational field has been broadened for colored women in New York."[82]

Domingo's essay was not unusual in its expression and content, but it was quite unique in its inclusion among poems, short stories, drama, and the focus on music and art intended to typify the creative expressions of the era. It brought some political leaven to the two collections that marked the Harlem Renaissance; it stands as a limited recognition of the "gift" that Caribbean people like Huiswoud, Briggs, Domingo, and Moore brought from four distant areas of the tropics to the political arena that was an integral part of the Harlem Renaissance. Domingo was not alone in his estimate of the contribution of Caribbean immigrants to Harlem. In January 1927 Hubert Harrison wrote in the *Pittsburgh Courier* that "almost every important development originating in Negro Harlem—from the Negro Manhood Movement to political representation in public office, from collecting Negro books to speaking on the streets, from demanding Federal control over lynching to agitation for Negroes on the police force—every one of these has either been fathered by West Indians or can count them among its originators." He singled out British West Indians, who "grow into spiritual participation with Negro-America and exchange cultural gifts with increasing facility. If the West Indian brings to the market a certain out-spoken and downright courage, he gains there a certain flexibility and tact which is necessary both for survival and success in the American atmosphere. And when the years bring their harvest it will be found that the mingling of West Indian with American

Negro has been highly beneficial to Harlem—and to America at large."[83] Essays focusing on the contributions of Caribbean Americans to Harlem and the United States would not have called attention to Huiswoud's and McKay's "gifts" to the Third International. Domingo and his colleagues recognized, however, the significance of the 1922 Moscow congress in placing the plight of all peoples of African descent on the international agenda. Wayne F. Cooper has noted that "the official stance of the Comintern regarding blacks in 1922 was influenced by West Indians, who were simultaneously much more nationalistic, class conscious, and international-minded than were American-born blacks."[84]

When the first version of Domingo's article was issued in March 1925, three of the four veteran radicals were positioned to wage their campaign against racism and colonialism on many fronts as functionaries of organizations allied with the Workers Party, such as the ANLC. Hermie was also now positioned to join the group. She had graduated from high school in 1924 and through Huiswoud had become friendly with his close comrades and exposed to radical politics along with the gifts of writers and artists in Harlem. When Huiswoud went to Chicago to help launch the ANLC he asked her to wait for him. And she did.

5. The Radicals and the Renaissance

As Hermie Dumont approached her twentieth birthday in 1925 she was beginning to appreciate that she was in the midst of a vibrant, eclectic, creative community. Bold print on the cover of the March 1925 *Survey Graphic* magazine declared "Harlem—Mecca of the New Negro" and included interesting short stories and other writings by people she had met or recognized from meetings, newspaper articles, or just walking down the street. A page of poems by Langston Hughes and the article by Otto's friend W. A. Domingo caught her attention. An avid reader, she spent much time in the 135th Street Public Library and had already read works by other writers who had made their way to Harlem and were represented in the magazine. Her favorite book, however, was not by an African American; it was special because it was her first gift from Otto. *The Gadfly* was by a British author, Ethel Lilian Boole Voynich, whose pen name was E. L. Voynich. Initially published in 1897, the story was set in Italy in the 1830s but was considered a reflection of revolutionary activity that might counter oppression in any nation. It was well received generally but grasped by Russians in both pre- and post-revolutionary periods as a classic. No doubt the self-sacrificing search for truth and justice as well as the anticlerical position of the protagonist also appealed to radicals in the United States.

Hermie's focus was on her future. The most critical moment arrived within a year, when Otto Huiswoud proposed marriage. His relationship with Anna Leve had ended in September 1924 and his affection for Hermie was deepening. He was keenly aware of the difference in their ages, thirty-two and twenty, as well as the fact that she had not considered their relationship a romantic one. When faced with having to go to Chicago in 1925 for several months he decided he must express his interest. He asked simply if she would wait for him. She accepted his question as the proposal it was meant to be, and plans were made for their marriage on his return. On September 30, 1926, they were married by the deputy city clerk in the Bronx, and a small wedding party gathered at her home. Richard B. Moore gave the toast, and the couple was off to a life unique in the annals of the Left. Her consent two years later to the invitation extended by Moore to join the Communist Party helped establish a union that could succeed only if there were mutual interest in communism in addition to affection for each other. Maturity had always been characteristic of Hermie, and she regarded marriage and joining the Party as appropriate and well-considered decisions. She was not concerned about the difference in the ages between herself and Otto, nor about his potential as a breadwinner. She has pointed out that even though Otto was twelve years older, she "had no idea of age. People were nice or not nice. They were old or not so old." Her explanation of her increase in affection for Otto was a typical Hermie response: "If you get exposed to the sun you get sunburned."[1] She had also become convinced that socialism was the answer to the social and economic problems facing the poor. Her exposure to political ideas began with her mother's interest in politics in Guyana, grew with her interest in social problems in high school, and was greatly expanded as Otto helped her understand political action. The true meaning of the life of a revolutionary was yet to dawn on her, but she felt ready to help Otto, the "kinsmen," and the Party to "meet the common foe."

Hermie was certainly not alone in her optimism and intent on looking forward. Despite the discriminatory barriers evident in New York there was no turning back for the thousands who had migrated to Harlem from tropical lands of the Caribbean or for the even greater mass of people who had thrown off the vestiges of slavery in the South to seek a new life in the North. She shared with the people of Harlem the sense of change that was occurring within them as well as in the few blocks gaining the approbation of "Mecca of the New Negro." The metamorphosis of Harlem from a few apartments on 134th Street to a mecca represented a keen transition for its inhabitants from southern sharecropping and small-town life to being part of an audacious, bustling, burgeoning community in the throes of building organizations, establishing businesses, erecting edifices of worship, writing poems and stories, creating paintings and sculptures, printing newspapers and journals, choreographing dances, staging theatrical productions, and sending forth a mighty sound of blues, jazz, and joy. Harlem became the venue for a remarkable confluence of diverse peoples from the English, French, Spanish, and Dutch cultures of the Caribbean as well as from the southern and northern

United States.² It was the crossroads where ideas were exchanged, experiences reevaluated, the status quo questioned, mores altered, identity strengthened, relationships adjusted, and creativity released. Unlike former New York City neighborhoods relegated to African American residents, Harlem emerged as a dynamic community of hope, inspiration, improvisation, and innovation. Rev. E. Ethelred Brown's humble church in the basement of a brownstone house was in keeping with the spirit of the times; it was no match, however, for the masterful architectural towers that housed large congregations. St. Mark's Methodist Episcopal Church (now St. Mark's Methodist Church), for example, which had worked its way uptown from a rented hall on Broadway and 37th Street in 1871 to 48th and then 53rd Street, constructed a prominent building on an entire block between 137th and 138th Streets on Edgecombe Avenue that provided a gymnasium and other facilities for community activities in addition to its large auditorium for worship. The building asserted Harlem's own lofty aspirations by using a neo-Gothic design in direct view of the Gothic-styled College of the City of New York prominently located on the hill overlooking Harlem.

Music played a significant role during the Renaissance. Harlem was most noted downtown for its contribution to the jazz scene, and acclaim was widespread for the great jazz musicians who played for white as well as African American audiences. But not as much was revealed about composers of classical works and arrangers of scores for dramatic works or the lyricists who provided Tin Pan Alley with words for popular songs. While Perry Bradford, James P. Johnson, Clarence Williams, and William Grant Still lived with their families in the new suburban community known as Merrick Park in Jamaica, Queens, they identified with Harlem and pursued their careers in both uptown and downtown Manhattan. Still, for example, worked with William Christopher Handy in Handy's publishing office, played jazz with Handy's and Deacon Johnson's orchestras, served as musical director at the African American–owned Black Swan Phonograph Company, and played the oboe in the orchestra of *Shuffle Along* in 1921.³ Later acclaimed by Leopold Stokowski as "one of our greatest American composers,"⁴ Still, who had been a student at Wilberforce University, incorporated African and African American themes in his symphonies, ballets, operas, choral works in much the same way as writers drew upon indigenous themes and experiences. He stated that he wanted "to employ an idiom that was unmistakenly Negroid because I wished to do my part in demonstrating to the world that the American Negro is capable of making a valuable contribution in the field of symphonic music, and I wanted to write a Negroid idiom, music that would help build more harmonious race relations."⁵ Lyricists like Andreamenentania Paul

Razafinkeriefo (a.k.a. Andy Razaf), a regular contributor to Briggs's *Crusader*, planted audacious ideas in songs such as "What Did I Do to Be So Black and Blue?"[6] Briggs devoted a regular column to performers of classical and religious music and carried advertisements of African American music companies. The musicians' works often employed themes they considered "African" that exemplified the innovative and race-oriented spirit of the Harlem Renaissance and inspired others engaged in creative pursuits. Thus community building in a new, attractive area added a fresh, pioneering, constructive cultural dimension that went beyond achieving satisfaction with improved housing for families and worship. The souls of Harlem folk were enriched by the outpouring of the arts and the expressions of protest that became an integral part of the territory.

New York was not the only northern city to receive a massive influx of African American residents. Why did it exert such a magnetic force? Why did the milieu in Harlem seem unique and become the focus of a special issue of *Survey Graphic*? The readership of the *Crisis*, the *Crusader*, the *Messenger*, the *Negro World*, and *Opportunity*, all published in New York but circulated across the country and some foreign nations, was a testament to the literacy the community commanded. Publications by African Americans in New York were directed toward a highly literate population. While the major motivation for mass migration to Harlem was economic, education, which had been systematically denied or limited in the South, was highly regarded and actively sought as an essential step to freedom from oppression. New York provided excellent schools. Children were required by law to attend elementary school and encouraged to complete high school, night schools were available for adults, and a free college education could be obtained in municipal colleges.

New York was not only a center of education; it was a center for publishing many types of books and newspapers in several languages, producing sheet music and piano player rolls, recording music, and broadcasting into homes via radio. It was a center for theatrical productions. Public libraries were open to everyone throughout the city. Bibliophiles like Arthur A. Schomburg, Hubert H. Harrison, and Richard B. Moore could dig through used bookstores and stalls downtown to expand their collections and thereby their knowledge of the history of Africans and peoples of African descent. Harlem also had its bookstore: George Young's Mecca of Literature Pertaining to Colored People. Harrison's constant admonition to "Read, Read, Read" could be fulfilled easily. Writing was also encouraged. Magazines and newspapers in Harlem, including the *Messenger* and the *Crusader*, sought poems and short stories and printed many of the first literary pieces submitted by young writers. Langston Hughes's first poems were published in the *Brownies' Book* and *Crisis* and his first short stories in the *Messenger*.⁷ Arna Bontemps has exclaimed, "When acceptances from Harpers; Harcourt, Brace; Viking; Boni & Liveright; Knopf; and other front line publishers began coming through in quick succession, the excitement among those of us who were writing was almost unbearable."⁸ As budding writers learned about Harlem they joined Harlem's growing literary vanguard and contributed to journals, magazines, newspapers, and books published in New York.

The New York literary scene presented an environment in which seedlings planted in the African American community during the second decade could blossom. In 1915 Du Bois had written in *The Negro* that "within their own souls they [African Americans] have arisen from apathy and timid complaint to open protest and more and more manly self-assertion. Where nine-tenths of them could not read or write in 1860, today over two-thirds can; they have 300 papers and periodicals, and their voice and expression are compelling attention." He went on to point out that "already in poetry, literature, music, and painting the work of Americans of Negro descent has gained notable recognition . . . They are today girding themselves to fight in the van of progress, not simply for their own right as men, but for . . . the emancipation of women, universal peace, democratic government, the socialization of wealth, and human brotherhood."⁹ Although Du Bois's observations were not centered on developments in New York, they do point to the growing literacy and interest in literary works that made the Harlem Renaissance possible. Most of the young African American writers and musicians came from small cities to the cosmopolitan city that represented the hub of the literary and music world. The significance of the era is not simply that African Americans demonstrated that they could master literary and musical forms but that they were able to pierce and open up the publishing curtain. It should be noted that a breakthrough occurred during this period because a few relatively new publishers like Alfred Knopf in New York and Charles Kellogg in Chicago were receptive to manuscripts by African Americans. The thoughts, feelings, attitudes, interests, and living conditions of African Americans would no longer be confined to their immediate communities as men and women were determined to overcome what Ralph Ellison's protagonist in *Invisible Man* referred to as the sense of "being outside of history."¹⁰ Publication downtown meant that the essential humanity of African Americans was now revealed, the sense of manhood asserted, and the cancer in the body of American civilization exposed to the world.

The careful nurturing of young writers on the part of leaders of the NAACP and the Urban League and the collaboration between uptown and downtown led to the collection of works by African Americans in the periodical *Survey*

Graphic and subsequently in the book *The New Negro.* In addition to ongoing encouragement and printing of young writers' works in the journals of those two organizations, influential individuals assisted writers in a variety of ways, including establishing contests and arranging contact with potential patrons or publishers. Charles S. Johnson, editor of *Opportunity,* and Jessie Fauset, literary editor of *Crisis,* were foremost in this role Langston Hughes labeled as "midwife."[11] In November 1924 Johnson organized a dinner intended to introduce uptown writers to downtown editors and publishers. Paul U. Kellogg, editor of *Survey Graphic,* was impressed by the young artists and writers as well as by the master of ceremonies, Alain Locke, an assistant professor of philosophy at Howard University in Washington, D.C. Kellogg was inspired to devote the 1925 special issue of the magazine to Harlem in a manner similar to special issues devoted to the "New Ireland" in 1921, "New Russia" in 1923, and "the newly awakened Mexico" in 1924. He invited Locke to be a collaborator in the selection and preparation of manuscripts.[12] Locke then edited a book-length expanded version, *The New Negro: An Interpretation,* which was published later that year by Albert and Charles Boni. The title "New Negro" was far from new; *The New Negro* by William Pickens, with the first chapter entitled "The Renaissance of the Negro Race," had appeared in 1916, and Hubert Harrison had edited a short-lived monthly magazine, the *New Negro,* in 1919. Even though Locke was not from New York, he caught the sense of rising assertiveness and expectations that had accompanied the New Negro movement in Harlem for ten years.

Both collections edited by Locke were acclaimed for documenting Harlem "as the sign and center of the renaissance of a people."[13] In order to accurately portray the New Negro free of the mask of the minstrel, Locke's selections needed to reveal assertiveness, self-respect, race consciousness, defiance, and expressions of protest. Locke recognized the race consciousness evident in "the present tone and temper of the Negro press, or by the shift in popular support from the officially recognized and orthodox spokesmen to those of the independent, popular, and often radical type who are unmistakable symptoms of a new order."[14] He was careful and cautious, however, to weigh the balance of his selections in favor of aesthetics over "revolutionary oratory" and "political flummery"; "self-direction" over "charity"; "buoyancy from within" over pressure of "conditions from without"; a "spiritual emancipation" over "the Negro problem." He warned that "this is indeed a critical stage of race relationships because of the likelihood, if the new temper is not understood, of engendering sharp group antagonism and a second crop of more calculated prejudice."[15] His attempt to retain a subtle touch was revealed when he altered the title and thereby the intent of Claude McKay's poem "The White

House" to "White Houses." Selections by McKay, W. A. Domingo, and J. A. Rogers were included in both the magazine and the book along with those by other outstanding writers of the period who revealed the conditions and thinking within African American life. But there was no place for the Harlem sage and early proponent of the New Negro, Hubert H. Harrison.

Locke's fear of contaminating art with propaganda fueled the debate on the relationship between the two and between beauty and truth. The fact that white American society set the standard and in Du Bois's view demanded "from its artists, literary and pictorial, racial prejudgment which deliberately distorts Truth and Justice as far as colored races are concerned" led him to the conclusion that all art was propaganda.[16] Du Bois's review of *The New Negro* presented his keen observations on the book and some of the history of the shift in the traditional attitude toward dealing with the "Negro Problem." It also served to restate his position that "with one point alone do I differ with the Editor. Mr. Locke has newly been seized with the idea that Beauty rather than Propaganda should be the object of Negro literature and art. His book proves the falseness of this thesis . . . yet, if Mr. Locke's thesis is insisted on too much it is going to turn the Negro renaissance into decadence. It is the fight for Life and Liberty that is giving birth to Negro literature and art today and when, turning from this fight or ignoring it, the young Negro tries to do pretty things or things that catch the passing fancy of the really unimportant critics and publishers about him, he will find that he has killed the soul of Beauty in his Art."[17]

Huiswoud, Briggs, and Moore welcomed the two collections with the focus on the New Negro, artistic and literary ties to Africa, contributions of Caribbean Americans, attention to the "Negro digging up his past," a bibliography by and about African Americans, and particularly the recognition of the African American's "new internationalism." The essay by W. E. B. Du Bois at the end of the book, "The Negro Mind Reaches Out," which had been substituted for his short story in the magazine, raised the question regarding his prophesy in 1899 that "the problem of the twentieth century was the problem of the color line." His review of the colonial hegemony by Portugal, Belgium, France, and England over Africa and the Caribbean, including their control over labor and certain African leaders who had been Europeanized, brought him to the same conclusion one-quarter of a century later. The three Caribbean crusaders could appreciate Du Bois's analysis of imperialism and especially his reference to the Caribbean: "Since the war not only has West Africa thus spoken but the colored West Indies have complained. They want Home Rule and they are demanding it. They asked after the war: Why was it that no black man sat in the Imperial conference? Why is it that one of the oldest parts of the empire lingers in political serfdom to England and industrial bondage to America? Why is there not a great British West Indian Federation, stretching from Bermuda to Honduras and Guiana, and ranking with the free dominions? The answer was clear and concise—Color."[18]

The trio of radicals had been intimately associated with the New Negro movement in Harlem for a decade and were keenly aware that it was motivated and driven by economic and social conditions. In 1918 Briggs had foreseen the economic and political tie to literary expressions when he dedicated his *Crusader* to the solution of the "Negro Problem" and a renaissance of Negro power and culture throughout the world. He and his colleagues did not expect to find in Locke, however, references to the economic underpinnings of the Harlem Renaissance or the polemical models that had promoted the transformation characterized by Locke as "from medieval America to modern."[19] They could be encouraged, however, by Du Bois's notion that "led by American Negroes, the Negroes of the world are reaching out hands toward each other to know, to sympathize, to inquire . . . We face, then, in the modern black American, the black West Indian, the black Frenchman, the black Spaniard and the black African a man gaining in knowledge and power and in the definite aim to end color slavery and give black folk a knowledge of modern culture."[20] They related to the aesthetic side of the movement but saw their role as internationalists who helped widen the debate to engage centers of action from Harlem to Africa, the Caribbean, and the USSR, and as realists who must confront the daily economic problems in the United States that poetry and art could not solve. They were convinced that the scales of justice would not respond quickly to acceptance of African peoples on the basis of demonstrated mastery of the arts. Their philosophy demanded agitation on all fronts.

While the extreme Left position represented by Huiswoud, Briggs, and Moore never gained a wide following, it broadened the spectrum of political activism among African Americans and influenced the direction of both the Harlem Renaissance and communism in the United States and abroad. Emanuel and Gross have maintained that "certain political spokesmen of the 1920s expressed the discontent and bitterness of the average Negro and proved to be still another contributing social force in the development of a new Negro literature." The confluence of forces "provided the proper social conditions for a literature of protest, of chauvinism, and of spontaneous expression."[21] Even Locke admitted that "the thinking Negro has shifted toward the Left with the world-trend, and there is an increasing group who affiliate with radical and liberal movements."[22] The New Negro movement in Harlem predated the 1917 Bolshevik Revolution and proceeded on a parallel course with the development of the Communist Party in the United States. While firm lines were drawn by 1925 between adherents of four political parties in Harlem, many new residents, particularly young writers (like their white counterparts), were open to examining and incorporating ideas of the Left and engaged in a mutual exchange with African American and white Marxists. Edmund Gaither and Arnold Rampersad have suggested, "Perhaps the most dramatic change wrought by the Harlem Renaissance was the sense that black artists gained by being part of a group linked by ethnic pride, political activism and a shared cultural lineage."[23] This appraisal not only acknowledges the influence of political activists but describes the forces that bonded African American radicals and linked them to the Harlem Renaissance.

In a rare study William Maxwell has called attention to the relationship between the New Negro and what he characterizes as the "Old Left." He commented on modern African American literature's debt to communism and communism's debt to modern African American literature: "The Old Left, normally sketched as a dire scene of white connivance and black self-cancellation, in truth promoted a spectrum of exchanges between black and white authors, genres, theories, and cultural institutions. Red interracialisms of word and deed . . . opened two-way channels between radical Harlem and Soviet Moscow, between the New Negro renaissance and proletarian literature." He proposed that communism's "rare sustenance for African-American initiative and cross-racial adventure was an urgent reason why scores of literary 'New Negroes' became 'Old Leftists.'" He cited "a gallery of black literary intellectuals" who were affiliated in some way with communism during the 1920s and 1930s and maintained talk in Harlem salons of "Communist drives against lynch law, 'white chauvinism,' and . . . imperial enemies of black freedom." He confirmed that the "New Negro's entrance onto the Old Left . . . was early, voluntary, and key to the formative modern instant in African American intellectual life" and that "Working-class Harlem internationalists impressed by both the Russian Revolution and a local pro-Soviet Left forged links between African-American writing and the Old Left while angling to jump-start Harlem's rebirth."[24] His last chapter referred to Winston James's statement crediting the actions of Briggs, Huiswoud, McKay, and Moore as evidence that "Caribbeans were among the most outspoken members of the Communist party, including on racism and on the 'Negro Question.'" Maxwell then concluded, "Let the record show that these vocal, adopted Harlemites, products of a special black diaspora linking the West Indies, uptown New York, and Soviet Moscow, also helped to initiate a practice of African-American literature as outspoken as any."[25]

Huiswoud, Moore, Domingo, and Briggs certainly qualified as "working-class Harlem internationalists." It is important to remember that when they arrived in New York between 1905 and 1912 there was no *Messenger, Crusader,* or *Negro World,* no Russian Revolution, no Black Mecca, no Harlem Renaissance. The publication of *The New Negro* helped establish a critical date associated with the Renaissance, but in 1925 participants were not concerned with defining or positioning the Renaissance in time. Almost a century later the debate continues as to whether the Renaissance should be confined to a period roughly between 1920 and 1935 or considered one of the peaks of florescence within a continuum of the African American experience. From the vantage point of the 1960s Moore judged that the "literary movement was no Minerva sprung full-fledged from the head of Jove, for while its immediate inspiration lay in the surrounding social conditions, its roots, too, went back through earlier Afro-American writers to the bards of ancient Africa."[26] Nevertheless, he recognized the historic impulse of the Renaissance and credited the radical publications and the activities associated with them as having given "rise to a cultural and social climate which caused Harlem to be known as 'The Mecca of the New Negro.'" He explained, "The movements which soon followed were nurtured in this cultural climate and militant temper which had been developed by the Harlem radicals and socialists."[27] The New Negro spirit and image Moore and his colleagues helped foster was in direct contrast to the nadir of the 1890s; Harlem's new-found voice and militancy of the teens, twenties, and thirties continued well beyond the decelerating force of the Great Depression. What mattered to the Harlem radicals at the time was the relief that could be found from racism that had existed from the founding of the country. Huiswoud, Briggs, and Moore focused on politics, and the mid-twenties marked a new phase in their commitment to Marxism. The American Negro Labor Congress promised to be a broader national organization than the African Blood Brotherhood: an opportunity to help organize a funded new radical organization committed to addressing the plight of African American workers. The circumscribed Brotherhood faded from the scene.

Huiswoud and Moore were sent to Chicago by the Workers Party to help prepare for the launching of the ANLC scheduled for October 25, 1925. The organization was characterized in promotional material as "not seeking to displace any other organization . . . is not a trade union, but seeks to strengthen all legitimate trade unions by bringing our working people into them and to win our equal rights within them."[28] Reports on attendance claimed an average attendance of six hundred per night but there were only thirty nine registered delegates. The largest number of delegates were from Chicago; others were from Alabama, California, Kansas, Louisiana, New York, Ohio,

Pennsylvania, and West Virginia. Aside from the ABB, the Negro Women's Household League, and a few other obscure organizations, the delegates represented labor organizations such as the Improved Janitors Union Local 66, Hod Carriers and Building Laborers Local 142, Freight and Express Handlers Local 1773, United Mine Workers Local 2012, and Amalgamated Clothing Workers Local 39.

Evidently Lovett Fort-Whiteman, national organizer of the congress, was either unaware of or disagreed with the strategy Huiswoud and Moore had insisted upon regarding the image of the organization. The program, publicity, and inclusion of white party members in the audience revealed ties to the communists and it was known that Fort-Whiteman had participated in the Sanhedrin conference as a delegate of the Workers Party. It is not that Fort-Whiteman was unaware of the concerns of the African American people. In an article, "The Negro in America," in the February 1925 issue of the *Communist International* he had complained that "the slow growth of Marxism among negroes had been wholly due to the inability both of the social democrats and the Communists to approach the negro on his own mental grounds, and to interpret his peculiar social situation in terms of the class struggle . . . The negro . . . wants to know how it [communism] can improve his social status, what bearing does it have on the common practice of lynching, political disfranchisement, segregation, industrial discrimination, etc." Yet he was so imbued with Russian culture that instead of arranging for entertainment by contributors to the Harlem Renaissance he included a one-act Pushkin play in Russian and a Russian ballet on the program. That too backfired; when the white dancers arrived and saw the audience they refused to dance.[29]

Fort-Whiteman continued as the national organizer, but John J. Ballam of the Central Executive Committee of the Workers Party was in charge of the organizational work for the ANLC. In his preliminary report on January 1, 1926, Ballam admitted that he was "not quite clear as to just what is expected nor exactly what my duties and relations to the ANLC are" and assumed that he was to assure a sound financial basis, establish the *Negro Champion*, utilize forces among the Negro comrades for propaganda and organization, and establish functioning local councils. Among his nine proposals were the "correction of attitude of indifference on part of Party rank and file and lower functionaries" through frequent articles on the Negro question by Fort-Whiteman, William Dunne, and Robert Minor, and continuation of the Party subsidy. His most revealing comments were regarding the contradiction in the ANLC constitution that claimed it was not a "rival organization" and pledged itself to create labor organizations, yet sought individual members and projected the formation of local councils. Ballam considered that the organization "was born with the disease of dual-union-itis" and would meet with the charge of "dual-unionism" if it attempted to organize the unorganized and unskilled Negro workers in the basic industries; it would also meet the hostility and opposition of all Negro petty-bourgeois and religious organizations if it attempted to organize Negro workers and farmers on a class basis. He favored "organizing the Negro workers and farmers for their protection as a Race" and making "a united front with all Negro organizations against Jim-Crowism; Segregation; peonage; black-beltism and all Racial discriminations at all times."[30] Evidently the concept of a united front organization dominated. Promotional material for Fort-Whiteman's tour to major northeast cities stressed that the ANLC aimed "to create a United Front of All existing Negro Organizations for the purpose of Uniting all forces for a common battle against Race Discrimination and for the right of Negroes to enter the Labor Unions and for the Unity of Negro and White workers in defense of their common interests."[31]

The ANLC limped along under a barrage of severe criticism from the African American press and organizations. Fort-Whiteman, remembered for his flamboyant appearance in a Russian *rebochka* [long belted tunic], high black boots, and fur hat, longed to be in the USSR. While he was still in Moscow for the Fifth Congress he appealed to the Secretariat to extend his time to permit research and writing a book on "Soviet Russia and the Darker Races." In July 1924, during his stay as a guest at the summer colony of the KUTV, he had also sought the assistance of W. E. B. Du Bois. His letter to Du Bois extolled the elimination of racial problems under the Soviet system and reported that he was conducting a study of social conditions in Russia.[32] On June 3, 1926, he proposed to the Party that he be sent back to Moscow and listed eleven objectives as the rationale. He included: "To make plans for extending the Congress work among the Negro agricultural workers and small farmers. To establish closer contact with the Krestintern. To make arrangements for negro students to be sent to the Agrarian Institute for short courses. To insist on the establishing of an African and Negro Bureau in the Comintern . . . To get further material . . . for my yet unfinished book, entitled 'Bolshevik Policy and Racial Problems.' To insist before the Comintern for the publication of a quarterly magazine for colonial peoples . . . To deal with the matter of a commercial treaty between the Soviet Union and the Negro Republic of Liberia." He was advised by Charles Ruthenberg, general secretary of the Party, that the Political Committee decided he was not to go to Moscow and recommended that he submit his proposal to the Eastern Department of the Comintern.[33] The party fraction in the ANLC began to question Fort-Whiteman's leadership, and many discussions on the weaknesses and improvement of the organization were held. On May 23, 1926, the ANLC was reorganized.

Lack of sufficient cadre to implement plans was a constant complaint. A request from William Weinstone to the Party for a Negro comrade to conduct work in a New York District was met with the response from CEC Negro Director Ballam: "You should find and develop a Negro comrade there to carry out this essential work . . . the solution is not for us to create a substitute for them in Chicago (it would take twenty years before one could be produced and he most likely would be mulatto). You should . . . force discipline thru your own agencies."[34] Weinstone persisted that an African American organizer was needed in New York because the Negro organizations were located in the city. He recommended on September 29, 1926, that Moore be assigned as a part-time organizer for the ANLC and that District 2 in New York would guarantee the balance of his wages in order to build up Negro work.[35] He mentioned Moore's role in the fight on behalf of Negro operators for the right to work in motion picture houses in Harlem but did not refer to the fact that Moore had lost his job due to absence during the time he devoted to the organization of the ANLC in Chicago. Moore assumed work as a functionary assigned to organize African Americans in New York City.

The ANLC, still based in Chicago, continued to experience problems. Roscoe Dungee, who was serving as acting secretary and editor of the *Negro Champion*, disappeared and James W. Ford, who had joined the Party in 1926, was brought in to cover the office. In preparation for a meeting of the national executive committee of the organization to be held on May 22, 1927, a year after the reorganization, a document on "Directions" was prepared for the Party fraction. Criticism stressed that the operation was on "too narrow a basis" with "Communist Party direction pressed too much to the forefront." Considerable blame was placed on Fort-Whiteman's "leftist sectarian policies and incompetent direction," which were considered largely responsible for the severe isolation from the wide non-Party masses. The Party fraction also expressed criticism of certain attitudes and actions of the Party Central Committee and considered that the CEC and its representative, Robert Minor, had failed to take note of and correct the policies and practice of Fort-Whiteman and his administration. Recommendations included accepting the resignation of Fort-Whiteman as general secretary, electing Moore as general secretary-organizer, increasing the staff, moving the headquarters to New York, and constituting a council of directors.[36] Considering that the major criticism was the failure to address burning issues such as lynchings, residential segregation and discriminations, the plight of southern Negro farmers, the recommendation to include special campaigns against the imperialist attack on China and the raid on the Soviet Trading Corporation in London seemed somewhat misguided. During a session of the general executive board of the ANLC, held from May 23 to May 26, Moore was elected to the head post. The office was moved to New York City when the Workers (Communist) Party headquarters were relocated there in 1927.

The ANLC was considered a national "auxiliary organization" of the Party. There were also local auxiliary organizations that attempted to address problems at a local level. In January 1928 Moore spearheaded the formation of the Harlem Tenants League. Hermie served as secretary and later described one of their street rallies held on May Day:

> Up till then, May 1st was tabu, but I went to the Police Precinct . . . with knocking knees to make the request of the Precinct head, who thought me a mere schoolgirl. We got the permit and when we gathered in front of our headquarters for the parade, I heard my name called. I was escorted to the Chief, who stepped out of his car, shook my hand and said he would lead off the parade!!! Which he did, turning us over to the Chief of the next Precinct waiting at Lenox & 135th . . . We had a big league and did a lot of good work.[37]

Subsequent activities of the League failed to elicit such cooperation by the police. They were more likely to be combatants when an eviction of a resident from an apartment took place and the League organized teams to carry the possessions that had been placed on the street back into the apartment. Members including Briggs, Domingo, Grace Campbell, A. Elizabeth Hendrickson, Cecil Hope, Otto Huiswoud, George Padmore, and Edward Welsh led rent strikes, protested against evictions and rent gouging, and lobbied for housing codes to improve conditions such as inadequate heat that were the responsibility of landlords.[38]

The Negro Workers Relief Committee, originally the Negro Committee for Miners Relief, was another auxiliary organization that was developed to solve a particular problem: to assist workers who lost their jobs during the miners' strike in Pennsylvania and workers who were victims of hurricanes in Florida and floods in Mississippi. The list of members of the executive committee was quite impressive, including William Pickens and W. E. B. Du Bois of the NAACP; prominent ministers of two large Harlem churches, Rev. William Lloyd Imes and Rev. J. W. Robinson; and communists Grace P. Campbell, chairman, Williana Burroughs, Briggs, Moore, Edward Doty, A. Elizabeth Hendrickson, Oliver J. Golden, and Henry Rosemond.

The portion of the population that the Party aimed to organize was "the masses"—a core concept in the communist lexicon. But was the ANLC, an organization committed to trade union activity, the most effective means to reach the African American masses? The civil rights battlefield was not exactly empty of battalions engaged in combating discrimination and colonialization. By 1920 the NAACP had already established its popular *Crisis* magazine, with a paid circulation of 94,000, a press service that released news to white and African American papers, 310 branches, 150 of which were in the South, and a membership that reached 88,000 by the end of the decade.[39] The UNIA, with its widely distributed *Negro World* and members in over one thousand branches in forty-two countries,[40] along with Randolph's efforts to organize the Pullman Porters were also ongoing mobilization efforts with which the Communists had to reckon. Efforts by the ANLC to coordinate and influence other organizations had only limited success. The congress did not have a clear strategy because the Party vacillated in its position toward noncommunist organizations, constantly shifting between building united fronts with other organizations and attacking them as enemies. African American communists had to cope with the dichotomy between the desire to influence liberal organizations from the inside and the assumed danger of association with "bourgeois" elements. It was not just capitalists the Party identified as its main target: they attacked socialists, social democrats, "petty-bourgeois intellectuals," nationalists, churchmen, and others, many of whom in the African American community shared some of the goals of the Party. African Americans were far more responsive to programs that attacked lynching and Jim Crow apartheid than tirades against the Fords and Rockefellers, and many resented attacks on Du Bois and Garvey.

Little ground could be gained by such a slim force attempting to develop a labor organization like the ANLC with branches throughout the nation while participating in Party activities that included recruitment of members for the Party. Despite the paucity of organizers, the Party considered attempts to influence noncommunist organizations an important part of Negro work. The UNIA, whose membership was considered to be "the masses," had local, national, and international units that could not be ignored. Early efforts to influence the UNIA by members of the ABB and the Party had not been successful, but the size of the UNIA and its misadventure with the Ku Klux Klan posed a challenge. A delegate of the Workers Party, Mrs. Olivia Whiteman, addressed the Fourth Annual International Convention of the UNIA, and National Chairman William Foster and Executive Secretary Charles Ruthenberg sent a long letter, dated August 14, 1924, urging the convention to reconsider a resolution that had been passed regarding the Ku Klux Klan.[41] Advice that the Klan was no friend of African Americans was not welcomed, and attacking Garvey seemed to be the only strategy available to the Party until factionalism within Garvey's movement presented an opportunity to gain allies. The competition for power in the UNIA became apparent when Garvey was taken into custody on February 5, 1925, following his conviction for mail fraud and sent to the Atlanta Federal Penitentiary. The Fifth Convention of the UNIA was scheduled to be held in Detroit in March 1926. ANLC representatives in Chicago made contact with UNIA leaders in Detroit, and Robert Minor and Fort-Whiteman spoke at one of the sessions. An article by Minor in the *Daily Worker* attacking the UNIA colonization scheme, however, created considerable tension and undercut the relationship they were trying to establish in what was considered a Garvey stronghold.[42] Subsequently, UNIA leadership in New York declared the Detroit meeting illegal and convened the convention in New York in August.

The August 12, 1926, report on Negro work submitted to the CEC indicated that Party leaders had discussed the split in UNIA leadership and decided to take an active role in the Fifth Annual Convention of the Negro Peoples of the World, held under the auspices of the UNIA in New York. One faction led by George O. Marke, supreme deputy next in command to Garvey, and George A. Weston, a leader of the New York division, was considered in a "sympathetic relationship" with ANLC delegates to the UNIA Convention (i.e., Fort-Whiteman, Moore, and Lionel Francis of Pittsburgh, a former member of the UNIA). The general policy of the Party was "to come to an understanding with the left wing of the UNIA for common work with the ultimate objective of forming one united front organization for the fight for the Negroes of this country." They set out "to clarify the Congress [convention] ideologically and get it into the orientation of the ANLC" and decided upon a series of resolutions to be introduced at the UNIA convention. The report indicated that "as a result of the discussion of the social and political status of the negro by Moore and Whiteman, they were elected on a convention committee of five to draw up a resolution."[43] The lengthy resolution that was adopted was entitled "The Social and Political Status of the Negro Peoples of the World; Means for its Improvement" and had sections describing conditions in Africa, the United States, Haiti, Caribbean islands, and colonies and Latin America and listed general remedial actions not likely to evoke contested debate. Clearly bearing the touch of Richard B. Moore, it included a resolution that "delegates be sent by all the Negro Peoples to the Conference called by the League against Colonial Suppression to be held next November in Brussels."[44]

Charles E. Ruthenberg, secretary-general of the Workers Party and member of the ECCI Presidium even entertained fantasies about collaborating with the UNIA on demands for the enforcement of the Thirteenth, Fourteenth, and Fifteenth Amendments to the U.S. Constitution, a campaign to organize a Tenant's League throughout the South, and a campaign to secure the freedom of Negro soldiers imprisoned in Texas as a result of race riots there.[45] The only known accomplishments were the passage of the resolution and a plan for Weston to attend the Brussels Congress. The Weston faction was embroiled in court cases involving UNIA property and lost their right to erect a new building on UNIA property. That battle probably diminished Weston's opportunity to go to Brussels.

Some of Garvey's adversaries thought they had heard the last of him after his deportation from the United States to Jamaica in 1927. While the UNIA continue to function in Harlem despite considerable factionalism that resulted in court cases, Garvey searched for another platform. In March 1929 he launched a new weekly newspaper, the *Blackman,* and in August formed another UNIA in Jamaica with a "mammoth parade" and a month-long convention. The Harlem radicals were still attentive to Garvey's popularity in the Caribbean as well as Harlem, and Huiswoud was sent to the UNIA convention as a representative of the ANLC. According to an interview conducted by the *Daily Worker* upon Huiswoud's return, he declared that practical problems confronting Negro workers had not been discussed. Instead, Garvey had expounded a new theory of African or "Race Imperialism" in which he said, "the UNIA is going through the course of establishing an empire—racial imperialism." Huiswoud reported, "As a delegate from the American Negro Labor Congress . . . I challenged his theme, his business schemes, and his sincerity. Exposing the fraud and pointing out the futility of his program, I outlined the program of the A.N.L.C. After my speech, he challenged me to a debate."[46] The debate, "The Negro Problem Can Only be Solved by International Labour Co-operation between White and Black Labour," with Huiswoud arguing the affirmative and Garvey the negative, was held on August 13 and was reportedly attended by about three thousand people. Robert Hill has indicated that "Garvey said he agreed to debate Huiswoud in order to 'destroy the effects' Huiswoud's remarks 'may have created in the minds of the other delegates.'"[47] Hermie recalled that "finding that Otto's arguments were beginning to convince his listeners, Garvey stopped the debate, demanded from the audience a standing vote in his favor which he received. When the meeting was dismissed, a few persons awaited Otto . . . declaring that they agreed with Otto 100% but dared not show it in Garvey's presence. They said they were trade unionists and needed guidance." They asked if Otto could help them form a strong trade union movement and he offered to return the next year if they would invite him officially. The next year he returned and held organizing meetings in Kingston and various parts of the country.[48]

Developing communist-supported organizations and affiliating with non-communist organizations were just two of the various strategies the Party used to extend the communist message. The African American cadre was tireless in disseminating its propaganda on street corners and halls, not just in Harlem but in as many large urban areas as they could command. Fort-Whiteman, Huiswoud, Moore, and Otto Hall went on speaking tours to cities primarily in the Northeast such as Boston, Rochester, Buffalo, Cleveland, Toledo, Youngstown, Detroit, Chicago, Chester, Pittsburgh, Philadelphia, Baltimore, Wilmington, Washington, D.C., and Wheeling. John Owens and his family were scheduled to cover western states in his "flivver" and trailer in 1926, speaking in Los Angeles, San Francisco, Seattle, Spokane, Butte, Denver, Pueblo, Kansas City, St. Louis, and Chicago.[49] As one of the main African American organizers for the Party, Huiswoud was frequently on the road thumbing a ride from city to city. Contrary to some reports, he only visited Buffalo. According to Hermie, he was never there on a regular basis. Attempts were made to arrange a two-week tour for Hubert Harrison to ten cities in Massachusetts, Rhode Island, Connecticut, New York, Pennsylvania, Maryland, and Virginia. The request from John Ballam on behalf of the Negro Committee of the CEC for $180 to cover expenses in April 1926 indicated, "Comrade Harrison would be invaluable in stimulating interest and increasing the organization for the American Negro Labor Congress. He is, however, not a trained or disciplined Communist and will require special consideration from us."[50] Any design to draw Harrison closer to the congress was dashed the following year when he died suddenly at the age of forty-four following an appendectomy. He had been scheduled to speak in Harlem the following week on "Soviet Russia and the Darker Races." Harlem mourned the loss of "one of its ablest, most brilliant and best-known figures,"[51] and African American socialists mourned the loss of their mentor.

Particularly during U.S. election campaigns they tried to raise speaking engagements to the level of Harrisonian persuasion. The Party ran candidates for political office in order to present the communist message even though they did not expect to win, and they included African American candidates on local, state, and national tickets. Nominations in the Harlem area, for example, included Grace Campbell for the U.S. Congress, Moore for the offices of congressman, New York State attorney general, state assemblyman and chief judge of the court of Appeals; Williana Burroughs for New York State lieutenant governor and New York City alderman and comptroller; Fort-Whiteman for state comptroller, Edward Welsh for state assemblyman, and Otto Hall for New York City comptroller. James Ford was nominated in 1932, 1936, and 1940 for the high office of vice-president of the United States. Huiswoud was not a citizen, yet he was nominated as a candidate for the state assembly at the Workers Party Convention in 1922 and shared with Grace Campbell the distinction of being the first African Americans to run for office on the Communist Party ticket.

Pamphlets, flyers, press releases, and articles in newspapers and journals were published and distributed extensively in all types of campaigns. The *Negro Champion* was created as the organ of the ANLC in 1925; ten thousand copies were printed, but the distribution and collection of payments was poor. Leaders of the ANLC had difficulty publishing the newspaper on a regular basis. According to Briggs, who served as editor, he took a leave of absence in 1927 to work for a "capitalist firm" in Trinidad.[52] In January 1929 Moore reported that because of lack of funds and time the *Champion* was not published from August 20, 1927 until May 1928, when George Padmore was secured to assist with the July and September issues and finally the return of Briggs was secured: "Since September 8th, the first issue brought out under his editorship, the Champion has been appearing with some degree of regularity." Moore stressed that "the carrying of historical articles which was begun must be continued again and measures must be taken at once to improve its distribution."[53] The *Negro Champion* was directed to an African American audience; articles in the *Daily Worker* and other communist publications increased the exposure of white comrades to problems and party activities in the African American community. Current news about African Americans was presented as an integral part of the Party policy and program. Huiswoud's cogent article, "The Negro and the Trade Unions," in the December 1928 issue of the *Communist,* for example, traced the historic involvement of African Americans in the labor movement, presented data on membership in various unions, reviewed the types of exclusion practiced against African American workers, and pressed for the organization of Negro workers in unions. He described the CEC's resolution in May 1928 on the role of the Party and the plan of the Red International of Labor Unions (RILU), or Profintern, for an International Negro Trade-Union Committee. He did not fail to mention, "The T.U.E.L. has too long neglected this important phase of its work."[54] In contrast to this article Huiswoud, Briggs, and others frequently did forgo the creative expression prevalent during the Renaissance and fell into the jargon so typical of Party journalism. Their writings were still strident and informative but no longer had the appeal of the *Crusader*.

Following the collapse of the *Crusader* in February 1922, Briggs had developed the Crusader News Service with the assistance of Domingo. The press service released news every week to about a hundred domestic and foreign newspapers with ties to the African Diaspora. It was an indirect but expanded and effective means of communicating with African American communities. Briggs considered "a powerful Negro Press as a first requisite of effective race defence" and had visions of his service conducting investigations and research, including translations of articles dealing with the Negro appearing in the European press and in foreign-language American newspapers and presenting firsthand reports on important events and legislation affecting the Negro. His appeal to the Party for a part-time stenographer in early 1923, at the time he was involved with preparation for the Sanhedrin, had been met with recommendations to secure voluntary assistance, and his request to The American Fund for Public Service in February 1924 for a grant was denied.[55] Robert Hill has indicated that the service lasted about two years.[56] Later in the decade, at the first meeting of the Party's Reorganized National Negro Committee on August 14, 1928, mention was made that the news service was to be revived under the title of the "Crusader."[57] Moore's motion at the August 17 meeting of the subcommittee on Negro work of the CEC clarified the way in which the service was reinstituted. He proposed "that a news service be started immediately and that we utilize the name Crusader News Service which has had a considerable prestige, which might be advantageous for us."[58] This time Briggs did get assistance; Hermie joined his staff. In fact, she became the staff for two years. He prepared the news stories, and she typed and mimeographed the news bulletin and took care of the mailing. She considered the service effective because it went to approximately two hundred African American editors who did not have resources: "The South lapped it up."[59]

There were few Huiswouds and Fort-Whitemans committed and prepared to operate as functionaries in the Party; both of them had been trained at the Rand School. Intense training to develop additional cadre was urgent. During the organizational period of the ANLC the number of active African American members in the Party increased, and Fort-Whiteman and others recruited African Americans for training in the USSR. The Comintern had responded to requests for training opportunities made by American representatives to the Fifth Congress, and as early as September 26, 1924, the Eastern Department notified the Party that $1,280 had been sent for the sole purpose of sending ten students to the Eastern University for two to three years. The guidelines included that the students should be in good health and free from infectious diseases, particularly venereal disease; should be "workers from the bench"; should be class conscious and actively participating in the revolutionary movement; and should be literate and expecting to conform to the strict discipline of the University. They were not required to be members of the Party but that was preferable.[60]

One of the first to register at the University of the Toilers of the East (KUTV) in November 1925 was Bankole Awoonor-Renner [a.k.a. Kweku Bankole], an Ashanti from the Gold Coast. He was in the United States as a student to attend Tuskegee Institute and Carnegie Institute of Technology and had become involved with the Youth Communist League (YCL) in Pittsburgh.[61] Other members of the group of students were Oliver John Golden [a.k.a. John Golden], Aubrey Bailey [a.k.a. Harold Williams and Dessalines], Roy Mahoney [a.k.a. Jim Farmer] and Otto Hall [a.k.a. Carl or John Jones]. Hall was endorsed to proceed to Russia by a joint meeting of the ANLC and the Polcom of the CEC on February 5, 1926,[62] and was joined by his younger brother, Haywood Hall [a.k.a. Harry Haywood] in the spring of 1926. The two places recommended for women were not filled at that time, so it does not appear that ten students were sent in the first group. It has been estimated that between sixty and ninety African Americans attended the KUTV and Lenin School from 1925 to 1938, including Howell V. Phillips, William Patterson [a.k.a. William Wilson], Marie Houston, Herbert Newton, and Maude White.[63] By the end of the decade Golden, Hall, Haywood, Patterson, White, and Williams had returned and were playing active leadership roles in the Party. Mark Solomon has pointed out that while the students experienced culture shock and studied under adverse physical conditions, "they were caught in a swirl of internationalism that . . . gave them a global frame of reference, built their self-confidence, and encouraged them to create and control their own agendas."[64]

Maude White is an example of a party member who gained self-confidence at the KUTV. According to Hermie she was not really ready for the rigors of the school: she was timid, fearful, and unsure of what to expect. In addition to the intense cold and the demanding program she was bullied by one of her American roommates. When she returned to New York three years later she was aggressive and fully prepared to organize in the trade union movement. Among her many assignments was her first, in 1930, as an organizer for the Needle Trades Workers' Industrial Union in New York. She was particularly effective in helping to improve conditions for women workers as well as waging a fight against racial discrimination within the union and the Party.[65]

Oliver John Golden, on the other hand, who was prepared to work on agrarian programs following his return from Moscow, was not afforded an opportunity to develop a program in the South. In the fall of 1927 Golden, who had studied at Tuskegee Institute in Alabama prior to attending the KUTV, presented a plan to the CEC of the Party. He reminded them that the ANLC program provided for organizational work among poor Negro farmers and agricultural workers who were historically the ally of the proletariat and that the leadership of the party recognized the importance of agrarian work but little was being done. He explained that "after Comrade Bandiere [of the Krestintern] was informed that I was a peasant and had studied scientific agriculture, he insisted that I work in the Krestintern in order to further my studies . . . Comrade Bandiere was very much disappointed when he was told that I had to return to America at once. He immediately undertook to give me a series of instructions on how to organize an agrarian movement." Golden proposed collecting data on the rural population—their demands, extent of organization, resources such as the NAACP, Tuskegee, Hampton, local organizations, and governmental agencies—and developing an agrarian movement as a phase of ANLC work in Oklahoma, Arkansas, Texas, Louisiana, Mississippi, Tennessee, and Kentucky. He proposed that he be placed in charge of the work.[66] Golden would have been aware that Negro land-grant agricultural and technical colleges supported by the federal government had spawned a network of African American agriculture specialists that might have been tapped. The Party rejected the plan and Golden continued to work with Moore, Huiswoud, Briggs, and others in New York. Moore lamented later that funds were not available and the proposal had been abandoned.[67] Huiswoud was more accusatory; he charged that despite Golden's training in Moscow the Party had assigned him to work in a Party cafeteria on Union Square.[68] Golden was to develop another plan, however, that benefited the USSR instead of African American farmers in the South.

William Patterson considered the education offered by the USSR to thousands of students from colonial countries "a priceless gift" and described contact with students who later became leaders in their homelands. In answer to the question why the Soviet Union would establish a school for foreign students when they could hardly provide for their own, he stated that the "imperialists had refined the techniques of miseducation to a fine art," and trained a limited number of their victims in simple clerical work. African American, African, Indian, and East Asian colonial youth had the slimmest chance of education beyond the earliest grades, and to the USSR educating these youth "represented the acceptance of responsibility to mankind, to international working-class solidarity—the essence of their philosophy."[69] While many observers would argue that the USSR's intent was indoctrination of the students, it should not be overlooked that the schools played a significant role in shaping resistance to colonialism. Woodford McClellan has concluded, "For all their own shortcomings, and despite the perverse agenda of the regime which controlled them, those schools played a generally positive role in the growing world wide assault on racism and colonialism."[70]

International exposure and informal education occurred at conferences, or congresses, as the Soviets preferred to call them, in addition to attending special schools in the USSR. Moore's opportunity to press forward the African American agenda came as a representative of the ANLC to the International Congress Against Colonial Oppression and Imperialism in Brussels, February 10–15, 1927. Willi (Wilhelm) Münzenberg of Germany has been credited with proposing a "colonial conference" in August 1926 in keeping with the view that it was in the interest of the proletarian revolution to assist oppressed nations in their fight for liberation. He borrowed the title "League for the Struggle Against Imperialism" from an organization that Chinese students in Moscow had founded in 1924 and announced in Germany the formation of a league against colonial terror and oppression. Invitations were not sent to the Comintern or communist parties, and communists representing other organizations were instructed to keep a low profile to encourage broad participation. Declarations of support were received from China, India, Egypt, the Sudan, South Africa, and other African countries, and the congress attracted 174 organizations from thirty-seven countries, as well as such well-known figures as Henri Barbusse of France, Albert Einstein of Germany, Jawaharlal Nehru of India, and Madame Sun Yat-sen of China. Huiswoud's mentors, Katayama and Rutgers, were also present.[71]

Manuel Gomez (Charles Phillips) was assigned to head the Anti-Imperialist Department of the U.S. Party, which reportedly had similar counterparts in all parties in major capitalist countries. He had operated under other names in the Mexican Communist Party for five years following his resistance to military draft into the American army during World War I and returned to the United States as Manuel Gomez in 1922. According to Gomez the Anti-Imperialist Department and subsequent International Congress and League sought to implement "the Leninist program of uniting all revolutionary working class movements in the home countries of imperialism with the National Liberation struggles in the oppressed colonial and semicolonial countries"[72] The theses formulated and introduced by Lenin at the Second Congress of the Comintern attended by Gomez had directed communist parties to aid revolutionary movements among the dependent, underprivileged nations and colonies and included reference to the "American Blacks." His claim is therefore not surprising that at one time it was expected the Anti-Imperialist Department would assume responsibility for the struggle against the oppression of Negroes. Eventually it was decided that the issue must be addressed by the entire Party organization. It was recommended that Moore should be a delegate to the congress "with a view to developing him as secretary of the ANLC, after his return."[73] In 1927 Moore and his colleagues were ecstatic to have another international platform to call attention to the plight of African Americans, African Caribbeans, and colonized peoples in Africa and to press for equality and freedom. Fort-Whiteman notified Ruthenberg that William Pickens, field-secretary of the NAACP, George Weston, president of the UNIA, and Hubert H. Harrison had agreed to attend the congress.[74]

Gomez has indicated that the delegation he headed included, in addition to Moore, Roger Baldwin, who represented the American Civil Liberties Union and the National Urban League, Chi Ch'ao-ting, a Chinese student, and Scott Nearing.[75] George Weston of the UNIA decided not to go, and even though Moore is listed only as a representative of the ANLC in the official list of delegates his name appeared in some records as representing both the ANLC and the UNIA. A disclaimer was issued in the *Negro World* that Moore had not been empowered to appear as a UNIA representative, but historic accounts have continued to link him to the UNIA because of the dual listing. William Pickens of the NAACP was listed as a delegate and a member of the executive committee of the congress but did not reach Brussels. On November 30, 1926, he wrote Fort-Whiteman from England, "Sorry you folks did not act promptly and unfailingly as I did—I did all I planned and more."[76] A second letter in December indicating that he still had not received instructions to proceed to Brussels helps explain why he missed the congress. Moore served as *rapporteur* of the committee on the Negro question, with Lamine Senghor of Senegal (representing the Comité de Défense de la Race Nègre) as chairman, Max Bloncourt of the French Antilles (Union Intercoloniale), Carlos Deambrosis Martins of Haiti (Unione Patriotica), Josiah Tshangana Gumede of South Africa (the African National Congress) and James La Guma (South African Non-European Trade Union Federation).

Like Huiswoud at the Fourth Congress of the Comintern in 1922, Moore was prepared to help structure a resolution. Senghor, Bloncourt, Martins, and Gumede made statements stressing the oppressive conditions in their areas, and Moore presented the introduction and "The Common Resolution on the Negro Question." It demanded complete political and economic independence for Haiti, Cuba, Santo Domingo, Puerto Rico, and the Virgin Islands and self-government for other Caribbean colonies, and also pressed for confederation of the British West Indies. The resolution set forth ten goals to achieve the emancipation of the Negro peoples of the world, including "complete freedom of the peoples of Africa and of African origin" and five measures to accomplish various freedoms and rights: the organization and coordination of Negro liberation movements; prosecution of the fight against imperialist ideologies of chauvinism, fascism, kukluxism, and race prejudice; admission of workers of all races into all unions; and unity with other suppressed peoples and classes for the fight against imperialism.⁷⁷ Several delegates, Gumede among them, went to Moscow from Brussels, but Moore visited his friend McKay in the south of France. McKay was experiencing financial problems, and Moore gave him what money he could spare. McKay gave Moore, however, a priceless gift, the poem "Pushkin," which he had written in Moscow (see poem placed at beginning of book).

When Moore returned to New York he engaged in an active campaign to promote the League against Imperialism and for National Independence (LAI) established by the congress. Not all observers of the League shared Moore's enthusiasm for the impact of the congress and organization that was formed. Gomez, who assumed the name Charles Shipman after leaving the Party, commented in his autobiography that he could not "say the congress accomplished anything."⁷⁸ Imanuel Geiss, however, in his study *The Pan-African Movement,* concluded that the congress and League "should neither be dismissed as a communist front organization nor inflated into part of a worldwide communist conspiracy." He recognized that "Münzenberg and the Comintern, with their keen sense of the forces of change at work in world history, had hit upon a theme pregnant with future possibilities at a time when European colonialism was still almost unchallenged . . . The Brussels congress served first and foremost to exchange information about conditions in various parts of the globe and to establish personal contacts."⁷⁹ Many diverse individuals and groups around the world could rally around the issue of imperialism. The 1927 congress—a peoples' league of nationalities—set the framework to counteract the League of Nation's acceptance of colonialism. Relationships and networks were initiated in Brussels that extended well beyond 1927 and helped challenge the power of imperialist nations.

Huiswoud and Moore were pleased when the Fourth Pan-African Congress was scheduled to be held in their own bailiwick in 1927, and they attended as delegates of the ANLC. Previous congresses had been held in Paris in 1919, London, Brussels and Paris in 1921, and in London and Lisbon in 1923. W. E. B. Du Bois had hoped to convene the fourth assembly in several Caribbean islands, but it was finally held from August 21 to 24 at Abyssinian Baptist Church in Harlem, with 208 delegates from eleven countries in attendance. Although William Pickens had not made it to Brussels, he gave a lengthy report on the International Congress Against Colonial Oppression and Imperialism. He tried to extend an opportunity for Moore to be included in the committee to give a special report on the Brussels Conference and for Huiswoud to be added to the resolution committee, but chairman Du Bois did not seem receptive to their inclusion and statements. Unionization of African American workers was a hotly debated issue, and Moore criticized the congress for not delving sufficiently into the African American workers' problems. The congress ended, however, with a statement urging "white workers of the world to realize that no program of labor uplift can be successfully carried through in Europe or America so long as colored labor is exploited and enslaved and deprived of all political power."[80]

There were also Party members who not only attended international conferences but contributed directly to the work of the Comintern or to the development of the USSR. The most notable in addition to Huiswoud and Fort-Whiteman were Williana Burroughs (a.k.a. Mary Adams), James W. Ford, Oliver John Golden, Malcolm Nurse (a.k.a. George Padmore), Robert Robinson, and Homer Smith (a.k.a. Chatwood Hall).[81] Probably the least known of these was Williana Jones Burroughs (1882–1945), who played a key role on Soviet radio during World War II. Burroughs lived most of her life in New York City, was a graduate of Hunter College, began teaching in 1902, and was employed as an elementary school teacher by the board of education from 1917 to 1933. She and a fellow union representative, Isadore Begun, attempted to defend another teacher named Blumberg at a meeting of the board. When Burroughs and Begun insisted on speaking without the board's acknowledgment of their presence, they were accused of creating disorder and dismissed for "conduct unbecoming a teacher." She and her husband, Charles Burroughs, a post office employee who had been a student of Du Bois when he taught at Wilberforce University, lived with their four children in Jamaica, New York. She taught at P. S. 48 in Queens and was active in the Merrick Park community as well as in Teachers' Union Local 555.[82] When she learned about the ANLC she became active in Harlem. She stated, "I wanted to get closer to the real struggle, closer to the basic organization of the working class in which I belong. I joined the Communist party."[83] From 1926 on she was involved with Huiswoud, Moore, and others in party meetings and campaigns, wrote for the *Daily Worker,* and was a contributing editor of the *Liberator* (Harlem) as Mary Adams. In the early thirties she served on the national council of the League of Struggle For Negro Rights as director of activities among women. She was also a party candidate as Williana Burroughs for the offices of alderman and comptroller of New York City and ran for the office of lieutenant governor on the New York State ticket the same year that Moore ran for chief judge of the court of appeals.[84] She always ran ahead of her ticket.

At the time Burroughs became active in the ANLC she was also involved as secretary of the Institute for Social Study, along with Moore as director. Among the council members were Hubert Harrison and Grace Campbell. The Institute did not seem to be affiliated with the Party even though some of the officers and council members were Party members. It was another avenue for educating the Harlem community on social problems—exploring the causes of oppression, world problems related to race, and "the means whereby complete social emancipation may be achieved."[85] Harrison was one of the featured lecturers. Along with his admonition to read he continually warned students that "before the Negroes of the western world can play any effective part they must first acquaint themselves with what is taking place in the larger world where millions are in motion."[86] This emphasis on international consciousness had been taken to heart by Burroughs as well as Moore and Huiswoud.

Burroughs attended the Sixth World Congress of the Comintern in the summer of 1928, and her two younger sons, nine-year-old Charles and six-year-old Neal, accompanied her.[87] The children attended a Pioneer camp during the summer. The Soviet commissar of education, Anatoli Lunacharsky, encouraged her to enroll the children in school in the USSR which she did. She returned home and visited them from time to time. She attended the congress of the League against Imperialism in Frankfurt, Germany, in July 1929 and worked for the English-language *Moscow News* in 1930. On September 8, 1930, she addressed the American Commission but did not mention Huiswoud as Browder and Haywood did. She stressed Party support for the social insurance bill in the U.S. Congress that would benefit workers who lost their jobs, the significance of women's work, training on the conduct of strikes, and mistakes the Party made in assignments. She sought a shift to a positive attitude in the choice and development of cadres and cautioned against assigning many jobs to one person, thereby making it impossible to conduct work satisfactorily.[88] In 1931 she returned to New York.

In 1937 Burroughs moved to Moscow, and in 1939 the Party representative to the ECCI sent a letter to the Cadre Department of the ECCI recommending Burroughs for the post as editor for the Soviet All-Union Radio Committee. In the spring of 1940 she requested permission to return to the United States with her sons but was asked not to leave because the number of American comrades in Moscow was so low. In September 1942 she requested an audience with Georgi Dimitrov, general secretary of the Comintern, to discuss questions connected with her work and personal concerns, stating that she had served in the VRK (the Soviet radio agency) as an announcer and editor for over five years. While her letter did not state health as a concern it was known that she "suffered from impaired health."[89] During World War II it was her voice that carried the English-language broadcasts on Soviet short wave radio. Because it was necessary for her to remain behind the front lines, she moved out of Moscow with the government when it retreated to Kuibyshev for safety. In 1945 she finally returned to New York in poor health with her son Neal. Since her husband had died in 1941 and their home in Jamaica, Queens, was sold, they lived with Hermie in Manhattan, where Burroughs died three months later, on Christmas Eve, 1945.[90] She was proud of the citation and thanks she received from the Committee on Radio and Radio Broadcasting Council of People's Commissars of the USSR for her "devoted work broadcasting on the Soviet radio, and in connection with the ninth year of her work in the All-Union Radio Committee."[91]

George Padmore (1902?–1959), whose birth name was Malcolm Ivan Meredith Nurse, also entered the international arena as a result of his association with the ANLC about a year later than Burroughs. A bright, handsome student at Howard University, he had arrived in New York on December 9, 1924, from Trinidad in order to study at Fisk University. In 1927 he enrolled at New York University, failed to attend classes, and then enrolled at the Law School of Howard University. He was well known and outspoken on the campus but did not confine his activities to Washington, D.C. One of his professors stated that he had "much more drive than most American Negroes" because he was a product of the "British system which did not completely silence their grievances at home."[92] He joined the Party in 1927[93] and traveled between Washington, D.C. and New York, where he assumed the pseudonym George Padmore. According to Hermie he was considered "an exciting addition" to their circle. He consulted her when he was trying to select a suitable pseudonym. She suggested "Padmore" after a Liberian minister and he responded, "By George, you've got it!"—at which point she added "George" to "Padmore." He liked the combination and it became his name for life.[94] He worked with Moore in the ANLC and Harlem Tenants League; edited and wrote articles, and edited the July and September 1928 issues of the *Negro Champion* while Briggs was away; participated in discussions of the Negro Commission as a visitor; served on national committees on Negro work during 1928 and 1929; campaigned on behalf of Party candidate William Z. Foster; and was sent to the Second Congress of the League against Imperialism in Frankfurt, Germany in July 1929. The record shows that he received $65 and Huiswoud $120 for wages for the period June 1 to June 25, 1928, from the national office of the Party, which means he was considered a functionary.[95] Interestingly, when James Ford wrote from Moscow regarding the establishment of the *Negro Worker* by the Profintern, Moore made a motion at a meeting of the National Sub-Committee on Negro Work of the CEC in August 1928 that Padmore be assigned to send news articles to the bulletin.[96] Later, Padmore was to have a career in Moscow as editor of the *Negro Worker*.

Despite the barrage of radical speeches and literature the communist message was not always well received in African American communities. Nonetheless, parts of the message found a sympathetic response among residents and fueled debates in the press and meeting places well beyond Party venues, especially among young writers and artists who were also searching for meaning in the American and African Diaspora experience. In explaining the African American's expanding interest in foreign affairs, Ira Reid credited, among other factors, "writers for the Socialist and Communist parties in various journals" with having "promoted interest in the problems of Negro peoples throughout the world."[97] The expressions of African American communists were part of life in Harlem during the Harlem Renaissance, and they were reflected in the art that began to reveal more clearly the lives of African Americans.

In his analysis of the failure of communists to gain and retain large numbers of members, Henry Lee Moon catalogued a series of inroads that they were successful in making. He described their untiring efforts: "Communists have devoted more attention and energy to work among colored citizens than any other non-Negro group seeking basic reform since the heyday of the Garrisonian Abolitionists. No other political party, no branch of the Christian church, no labor organization, no other reform or revolutionary movement has devoted as great a share of its resources to gaining adherents and spreading its influence among Negroes as has the Communist party." He went on to point out that their influence could not be measured in terms of membership, and that many Negro intellectuals and writers had been influenced by communist philosophy. "Communist activity has been an important factor in sharpening the Negro's fight for equal rights and in fostering his recognition in the labor movement, in the arts, and in the civic affairs of the community. Through their international connections the Communists have widely publicized the plight of the Negro in democratic America, to the painful embarrassment of American travelers in Europe, Asia, and Latin America." Moon's thesis was that African Americans did not consider communism the enemy; they knew "the *real* [his emphasis] enemy" as the "fiendish face of reaction. The face of death—death to the spirit as well as to the body . . . Offering no quarter, the Communists put the South on the defensive in the eyes of the whole civilized world. They stirred the imagination of Negroes and inspired the hope of ultimate justice. In churches, in conventions, in union halls, in street-corner meetings, Negroes were clamorous in expressing approval of this campaign." Moon also presented a strong case for the reasons communists encountered difficulties building membership among Negroes, including "the alien character of the movement, its domination from abroad by persons ignorant of the varied facets of race relations in this country, [and] the lack of understanding by its American agents of the true nature of the Negro problem in America," but he was willing to acknowledge that the communists had "performed a vital function as an irritant to the American conscience."[98]

Huiswoud knew Moon as one of the four disgruntled members of the twenty-two African Americans who went to the USSR in 1932 to appear in a movie. When the movie project was abandoned, the four had "accused the Soviet Union of betraying black people of the world" and returned home with negative press reports.[99] He could not have imagined that Moon, the head of public relations of the NAACP, would have presented a critique that credited the Party with an impact on the broader community. But, as Moon said in hindsight, "it is a matter of record that the Communists have generally fought for full recognition of Negro rights."[100] What is not usually acknowledged is the role of African American members in shaping and implementing Party campaigns and the connection between their activities and the Harlem Renaissance. In examining the communists' promotion of African American culture Mark Solomon has taken the position that "at times black culture was promoted by the left with a mechanical imposition of self-defined proletarian standards (thereby weakening the organic character of black art). But the Communists and their allies worked to advance African American culture shorn of the intrusive, racist influence of the dominant commercial cultural market . . . The convergence of the Marxist sensibility with black literature, painting, and drama opened the door to exploration of neglected and suppressed experiences of black militancy and resistance."[101] In the twenties it was difficult for Huiswoud and his colleagues to discern the significant role of radical politics in the Renaissance. In their efforts to engineer liberation from the vantage point of the socialist movement their focus was on adding their defiant voices to the many expressions emerging from Harlem at the time. While the communists abetted the shift toward militancy and an international perspective during the Harlem Renaissance, resistance to the status quo, whether in art or politics, emanated from within the African American community. That is what gave the period its force, passion, and authenticity.

As Huiswoud moved into the next decade he had one last tour to take as field organizer of the ANLC. The trade union leaders who had spoken to him in Jamaica followed through with a written invitation, and he was able to fulfill his promise to return early in 1930. Assistance in Jamaica was incorporated into a plan for Huiswoud to solicit participation of Caribbean workers in an international congress of Negro workers sponsored by the Profintern that was projected for July 1930 in Hamburg, Germany. He and Hermie embarked on an extensive tour of the Caribbean. In Jamaica Huiswoud reported success in holding mass meetings and organizing committees comprising thirteen occupations that were to be coordinated by the Jamaica Trades and Labor Union.[102] In addition to Jamaica they visited Haiti, Cuba, Columbia, Curaçao, Venezuela, Trinidad, British and Dutch Guiana, and Barbados.[103] The mass meeting at which Huiswoud was to have spoken in Trinidad was banned by the police, and he was ordered to leave the country. He was told by a police inspector, "We won't have any of you damn foreign agitators come in here to make trouble among our workers."[104] The trip was not a tourist's escape to sunny beaches; it was a small step toward a long-held vision of addressing the plight of the peoples of the Caribbean.

The tour was Hermie's first visit to the Caribbean since leaving British Guiana at the age of fourteen. The pleasant images of the tropics she considered home that she had carried with her for ten years were now tarnished by the stark poverty she noted in island after island and in the cities of northern South America. She expressed her dismay in articles she sent to Briggs as editor of the *Liberator,* which had replaced the *Negro Champion.* The article on Haiti was not designed to focus on women, yet her observations clearly indicated her interest in the role of women in protest movements. She described demonstrations in Port-au-Prince demanding the withdrawal of American troops when the Hoover Commission arrived: "Two demonstrations have been held here since the Commission arrived, and because of the vast numbers involved neither was broken up . . . A second demonstration was held on Sunday, March 2, in front of the hotel where the Commission is basking itself. This demonstration was composed wholly of Haitian women. Following the demonstration these women went to the chapel to pray for deliverance." Later in the article she described a mass protest meeting called by the Young Women Nationalist Organization that "brought out over 15,000 people, with house tops and trees crowded with spectators . . . Women were very numerous in the gathering."[105] Not only had Hermie joined the journalists of the Harlem Renaissance in painting a picture of the miserable conditions and protests by peoples of African descent, she had joined the protest movement. Unlike the wives of Briggs and Moore who were no longer with their husbands because they had not shared their spouse's passion for changing society, by 1930 Hermie had matured politically and was prepared to fully help Otto Huiswoud in his life's work.

6. The Struggle Within

Hermie became a member of the Workers (Communist) Party in September 1928, almost a decade after Huiswoud. She had joined the ANLC in 1925 and the Young Workers League in 1927. While her level of activity was completely different from Otto's, it was not long before she observed that the professed ideal of unity eluded Party deliberations. The atmosphere was often contentious. It is doubtful that she was aware, however, of the extent to which Huiswoud, Moore, and Briggs waged an internal battle to influence and implement Party and Comintern resolutions they perceived essential to the liberation of African American people. Nor was she privy to the pressure that was exerted against them to fall into line.

As the American Negro Labor Congress proceeded on its rocky course from 1925 to 1930, Huiswoud, Moore, Briggs, and other African American members achieved more influential leadership roles in the Party. Outside the inner circle the assumption was made that African Americans were gaining greater power with which to mobilize a strong fight for minority rights. The seemingly unified and consistent protests of the radicals broadcast primarily from street corners and organization halls were an integral part of the Harlem Renaissance scene. Their orations, however, were not recorded in the annals of the Party. Instead the records reveal that their rise to leadership and influence was frustrated and minimized by internal conflicts within the Party. Beneath the cloak of solidarity constant conflicts brewed, sapping their energy and complicating the work they hoped to accomplish. While the communist and Harlem Renaissance movements benefited from their voices, the Party did not fully accept or appreciate their perspective. An understanding of their commitment and contribution would be incomplete without understanding that they not only fought the police and opponents on the street but had to engage in bitter battles within the Party itself. The struggle within was unrelenting.

Life in the Communist Party never followed a predictable trajectory. Obviously the small African American cadre worked within the bureaucratic framework of the Party as members and paid functionaries, but their unique interests and agenda created a triangular relationship with the Party and the Comintern. The Party structure required African American work to be administered directly by the leadership of the Party, but the dynamics were complicated by the internal problems within each group and the pressures each tried to place on the other. The development of the ANLC as a national organization was not only hindered by its own internal problems but also affected by the factionalism that persisted in the American Party and the power plays and ideological shifts in the Russian Party and the Comintern. Between 1925 and 1929 three shifts or crises centered in Moscow affected the direction of the Workers Party and the work of Huiswoud, Briggs, and Moore.

The first shift in 1925, Bolshevization, created havoc within the Party because it destroyed the local power that the foreign federation fractions had enjoyed. In the broader area of Harlem alone there were branches as late as 1925 identified as English Harlem, Finnish Harlem, German West Harlem, Italian Harlem, Jewish Harlem, and Russian Harlem. The structural change to work-centered units drove many members away from the Party and in effect "Americanized" it. Party reorganization in Central Harlem was less disruptive than in foreign units. It resulted primarily in an adjustment of boundary lines and section leadership that created tension within the ranks. The segregated neighborhood was still the main staging area, and its residents were forced by society to see themselves as "Negroes" rather than "workers." Their identity as a racial or cultural group had been honed by history and re-enforced by the New Negro concept of the Harlem Renaissance. Bolshevization did not simply transfer organization agitation to the work place; it increased centralization and the power of the Comintern ECCI over national parties and the power of the central committees of the parties over the branches. In time it caused an unexpected shift in Negro work because it enabled the Comintern to impose implementation of the Resolution on the Negro Question of the Sixth Congress on the Party. Foreign members who manifested no interest or understanding of the condition of African American life in the United States and had adopted American patterns of discrimination could no longer ignore the issue of racism. Indirectly Bolshevization had a far-reaching effect on Party attitudes and programs directed against racism. It paved the way for the impact of the Resolution on the Negro Question of the Sixth Congress of the Comintern in 1928 and the Lovestone confrontation in 1929.

In preparation for the Sixth World Congress of the Comintern, scheduled to meet in Moscow between July 17 and September 1, 1928, the Anglo-American Secretariat headed by Petrovsky (Dr. Max Goldfarb, a.k.a. Bennett) appointed a subcommittee to draft a resolution on the Negro question for consideration by the Negro Commission of the congress that would in turn make recommendations to the entire congress. According to Harry Haywood, who was attending the Lenin School, the subcommittee included Nasanov, a young Siberian representative of the Young Communist International (YCI); Clarence Hathaway, an American Party member attending the Lenin School; and four African American students. Interestingly, Haywood identified only two of them—his brother, KUTV student Otto Hall (a.k.a. John Jones or Carl Jones) and himself. It is assumed that the other two students were Roy Mahoney (a.k.a. Jim Farmer) and Aubrey Bailey (a.k.a. Harold Williams). Robert Minor, U.S. representative to the Comintern, and William Dunne, U.S. representative to the Profintern, served exofficio, and James Ford, who was assigned to the Profintern, attended some sessions. Nikolai Nasanov had visited the United States previously and spoke English. He introduced Haywood to Soviet comrades in Moscow who shared an interest in the national question. Haywood explained, "they seemed to be pushing to have the matter reviewed at the forthcoming Sixth Congress of the Comintern And as it later became clear to me, they were anxious to recruit at least one Black to support their position." With Nasanov's "prodding," Haywood began to see merit in the argument that African Americans were an oppressed nation. He worked with Nasanov on a resolution incorporating the concept of nationalism as a "legitimate trend in the Black freedom movement" and supporting "the thesis that U.S. Blacks constituted an oppressed nation." Support for the concept was presented to the African American KUTV students by Sen Katayama, who informed them "Lenin had regarded U.S. Blacks as an oppressed nation." Haywood's brother, Otto Hall, also confirmed that the students had gotten "a similar impression from their meeting with Stalin at the Kremlin shortly after their arrival in the Soviet Union."[1]

Among the discussion papers prepared was a thirteen-page exposé, "The Party Attitude on Negro Work," dated May 23, 1928, by Otto Hall with a notation that it was drafted by Sen Katayama. It presented the attitude of the Party as one of complete confusion and misunderstanding of the importance of Negro work, then described several examples of mistakes, neglect, or missed opportunities by the Party, including Huiswoud's suspension following the

Farmer-Labor Party convention in 1924. Another example cited was an incident in Richmond, Virginia, the only place in the South where a Party branch had been established. At a mass meeting to raise money for a streetcar strike that involved both African American and white workers, the arrangements committee under the control of the Party attempted to segregate the audience by sending the African Americans to the gallery. When the African Americans protested and failed to gain their point, all of them left the meeting. Subsequently a letter was sent from the central committee expelling all the African Americans in the branch.

Of even greater interest in the Hall-Katayama article was the attention drawn to the policy of the Comintern drafted by Lenin and promulgated at the Second Congress that emphasized support for "the revolutionary movement among the subject nations (for example, Ireland, American Negroes, etc.) and in the colonies." The writers proposed that "the aim of the American Negro movement must ultimately be the establishment of the Soviet regime and the independent existence of the Negro people . . . The self-determination of the Negro race in America must be the ultimate aim and purpose of the task of the American Party."[2] Typical specific tasks related to social, economic, and political problems were enumerated, such as attacking "Jim Crow Law," lynching, barriers against African American workers by trade unions, and the unequal education in school systems, which spent $17.35 for each white pupil but only $0.90 for each African American pupil. The position paper was notable for its description of African Americans as a "national minority" and reference to the term "self-determination" that crept in as a goal of the Party.[3] Although it leaned toward Haywood's argument, Hall raised a strong voice opposing his brother's resolution during the sessions.

The contentious atmosphere, accusations, and differences of opinion on the Negro question were totally unlike the Fourth Congress attended by Huiswoud. Four discussion articles published in the *Communist International* revealed the diverse positions and the intensity of the debate. One article prepared by Andre Shiek,[4] an instructor who was a favorite among African American students, and a joint article by James Ford and William Patterson, who arrived to attend the KUTV just before the congress began, favored fighting for full equal political and social rights and argued against any program leading to separation. Haywood's discussion of the African American experience led to the conclusion that "while raising and fighting for full equal social and political rights . . . the party must support without reserve the right of national self-determination up to separation and the erection of an independent Negro state."[5] The fourth article was written by John Pepper (sometimes referred to as "John Swift"), who had been assigned in 1922–25 and 1928 to the American Party as the Comintern representative. Pepper, whose birth name was József Pogány, was a Hungarian who had become a pugnacious partisan of the Lovestone faction and also a proponent of the struggle for the right of national self-determination. During the Fifth Congress he had spoken against applying the principle of self-determination to the American Negro, but at the Sixth he described the Black Belt in the South as a colony of the United States. He stretched the argument to envision the establishment of a Soviet Negro Republic in the South.[6] It should be noted that only the articles by Shiek and Pepper were printed in the English version of the *Communist International*. The two articles by African Americans were not presented.

The Sixth Congress of the Comintern was attended by a twenty-member official delegation selected by the CEC of the American Party. Both factions vying for the favor of the Comintern were well represented: Foster with supporters Alexander Bittelman, James P. Cannon, William F. Dunne, Jack Johnstone, and Manuel Gomez; and Lovestone with supporters Pepper, William Weinstone, Bertram D. Wolfe, and two African Americans—Lovett Fort-Whiteman and Howell V. Phillips. The CEC also recommended that four Negro comrades who were in Moscow, Mahoney, Ford, Hall, and Haywood, be made fraternal delegates.[7] Haywood identified himself as the only Black member of the Foster group and Fort-Whiteman, Phillips, Hall, Mahoney, Williams, and Patterson as allied with the Lovestone group.[8] Joseph Z. Kornfeder (a.k.a. Joseph Zack and J. P. Collins), a member of the Anglo-American Secretariat and an ally of the Foster faction, alerted the Foster group to "Stalin's Self-determination Thesis" prior to their departure for the congress. The information, which he had learned from the secretary-general of the Profintern, was transmitted by code to Bittelman so they could "scoop the Lovestonites." Kornfeder later wrote that he was of the opinion that "neither faction at that time actually believed in the thing, but tossed it around as a factional football for Stalin's favor."[9]

Communications were also transmitted from New York to Moscow. Moore sent a cable to Ford seeking to appeal the Polcom's selection of Phillips and Whiteman as delegates, claiming the conference had recommended sending five African American delegates: Moore, Fulp, Doty, Ford, and Whiteman. He requested Ford to secure ECCI assistance requiring their selection.[10] Moore referred to resolutions passed at the meeting of the Party conference and National Fraction of Negro Work held May 28–31, 1928, which urged the central executive committee to send the five named delegates considered "the most capable and leading comrades who through active participation in this work and thorough bolshevist understanding will be able intelligently to take part in the deliberations of this important Congress." A second motion urged the CEC not to name students because they had been away from Party work but to invite them instead to participate in discussions.[11] Ford sent a communiqué to Petrovsky underscoring Moore's appeal in which he described the qualifications of the five candidates and proposed that they be brought to Moscow.[12] Even though the recommended five delegates had included Moore and the three alternates had included Huiswoud and Briggs,[13] the discussion articles and lengthy deliberations proceeded without input from either of those three African American veterans. Clearly their opinions were not wanted. Reactions by the two chosen delegates, Fort-Whiteman, who was eager to remain in the USSR, and Phillips, who was admitted to the Lenin School that year, were muted. Moore and Huiswoud, although left at home, were not forgotten. In one of Hall's speeches before the congress he referred to Moore as the "one who should have come over here with the delegation." He stated, "If it is true that this comrade has been guilty of any anti-Party activities he should be corrected. I say that we should bring this comrade here to Moscow because he is the official leader of the American Negro Labour Congress and I believe he can be saved for the Party."[14] Huiswoud's name was presented in a more favorable light. He was elected as a candidate member of the ECCI, the first African American to serve in that capacity.

The Negro Commission of the congress, chaired by Otto Kuusinen, had thirty-two delegates from eighteen countries. The American delegation included Ford and four African American students (Haywood, Hall, Mahoney, and Williams), along with Bittelman and Lovestone representing the opposing factions. It is odd that neither Fort-Whiteman nor Phillips were placed on the commission. The discussions during sessions of the Negro Commission and the congress were extensive and contributed modifications. Many American delegates spoke, as well as Katayama, who identified himself as having spent twenty-six years connected with the American movement and therefore had "a right to regard the American Party as mine." He stated, "We generally do not call the American Negroes a colonial people, but according to the II Congress decision the American Negroes are of the SUBJECT NATION and treated like that of Ireland . . . They are the best potential revolutionary factor in the American Communist movement . . . The CP of America should put up a propaganda slogan—the self-determination and complete independence of the American Negroes."[15] During the debate on whether to consider African Americans an oppressed nation or an oppressed racial minority, Haywood was the only African American to promote the national position.[16] Resolutions favoring that position were supported by Foster, Bittleman, Dunne, and Pepper. Ford and Hall led the opposition and were supported by Samuel Adams Darcy of the Young Communist League, who considered the resolution reactionary.¹⁷ Lovestone remained noncommittal. In the end the Nasanov-Haywood concept prevailed and was joined to the resolution on South Africa.

The lengthy twenty-six point resolution, among other things, defined the tasks of the Party, identified the Negro question as part of a world problem, proposed strengthening the ANLC, and called attention to women as a powerful force. Amid the strong criticisms of the Party, there was a positive citation of the Negro Miners Relief Committee and the Harlem Tenants League as "examples of joint organizations of action which may serve as a means of drawing the Negro masses into the struggle." The heart of the resolution can be found in part of the summary describing the important tasks to abolish "all kinds of social and political inequalities":

> It is the duty of the Communist Party to carry on the most energetic struggle against any exhibition of white chauvinism, to organize active resistance to lynching, to strengthen its work among Negro proletarians, to draw into its ranks the most conscious elements of the Negro workers, to fight for the acceptance of Negro workers in all organizations of white workers, and especially in the trade unions . . . to organize the masses of peasants and agricultural workers in the South in the South, to carry on work among the petty bourgeois Negro masses, to enlighten them regarding the utopian, reactionary character of petty bourgeois tendencies such as Garveyism and to carry on a struggle against the influence of such tendencies in the working class and peasantry.
>
> In those regions of the South in which compact Negro masses are living, it is essential to put forward the slogan of the Right of Self-determination for Negroes.¹⁸

Despite the many points listed, it was not a succinct, clear document on the new policy, and in 1930 the resolution was revisited and clarified by the Political Commission of the ECCI.

The discussions held by leaders in the Kremlin or by proponents and dissidents in the halls of the congress are not part of the record; many questions are left unanswered. Who was the theoretician who advanced the thesis? Did Joseph Z. Kornfeder's reminiscences correctly identify it as "Stalin's Thesis"? Was Nasanov, who later became head of the Negro Bureau, chosen for his skill at influencing the African American students who made up the majority of the subcommittee? Was Katayama attempting to manipulate Otto Hall's presentation to favor the theses despite Hall's opposition to the idea? The orchestration of the Resolution on the Negro Question occurred not solely during deliberations in Moscow but earlier with the selection of the African American delegates. The Party's central executive committee set the stage by deliberately ignoring recommendations for particular African Americans to be sent to Moscow as delegates. According to Ford they were not considered "because of their opposition to the present attitude of our Party to Negro work."[19] Even more puzzling is the fact that neither of the two official African American delegates was placed on the Negro Commission. It seems unusual, to say the least, that they were excluded from the process. It is not difficult to speculate why Pepper changed his argument drastically, but it is strange that all the other members of the delegation were so accepting and none was willing to defend the African American members who raised strong objections based on experiences in the United States. The overall conduct of the process makes it clear that the resolution was well engineered to satisfy a USSR official and that the responses of the American delegates were based on their need to curry favor with the leaders of the Comintern. The Comintern was prepared to entertain reports castigating the American Party for neglect, chauvinism, and factionalism, but it was not prepared to consider the logic of members of the group most affected by the policy. African American voices were heard and yet not heard.

The Comintern deliberations not only revised, expanded, and confused the Party's position on the Negro question, they revealed the difficulty, or perhaps recalcitrance, of the American Party to take on the centuries-old ingrained racism that permeated every aspect of American life. Philip S. Foner and James S. Allen have noted that the presentations made by Ford and Hall at the congress "present a devasting [sic] criticism of the American Party for its neglect of Negro work and for white chauvinism in its ranks. Ford held that more than in any other field Negro work was hampered by the factional struggle, by the racism of both factions." Ford also stated that his investigations of Comintern archives revealed that "during the last few years no less than 19 resolutions and documents upon the Negro Question have been sent by the Comintern to the American Party, and not a single one of them has been carried into effect or brought before the Party . . . The few Negro comrades we have in the Party have been making a fight for years to bring this question before our Party, and now we bring it before a Comintern Congress."[20] Hall charged that the Party had not "carried on a consistent and energetic fight against chauvinism in the past" and pointed to mistakes "due to the lack of close cooperation of the Party as a whole with the work of the Negro comrades."[21] The criticism was so pervasive throughout the speeches and position papers that Bukharin commented during his speech, "Almost all Negro comrades say in addition, that the survivals of race prejudice are still to be observed in some parties. I do not deny this fact . . . Even on the Commissions of the Comintern a wrong note is detected when questions concerning the Negro problem are discussed. I myself noticed this during a discussion on the South African question. We must put an end to this once and for all."²² Prejudice and inadequate attention to Negro work on the part of Party leaders was exposed without the presence of Huiswoud, Moore, or Briggs. The Comintern responded.

As news of the resolution reached the United States, African American Party members began to question whether the Comintern's action was a help or a hindrance to their work. At the meeting of the National Negro Committee on October 26, 1928, Huiswoud, who was the chairman, reported on decisions of the Polcom: he had been appointed head of the Negro Department and was to represent the Negro Committee on the Polcom, and a Commission of eleven had been named to study the Negro question and consider policies and personnel. Moore recommended the addition of Welsh and Golden to the commission; Briggs questioned why the editor of the *Champion* had been omitted, and it was recommended that the editor be included. Huiswoud also read a communication from the District Negro Committee requesting the National Committee to protest the publication of Pepper's article in the October issue of the *Communist*. The committee endorsed the sentiment expressed and reformulated the protest as a letter to be sent to the Polcom: "The committee feels that harm will result from the too close identification of the ANLC, Tenants League, Champion and Negro Workers Relief Committee being tied up too much with the Party in Swift's [Pepper's] pamphlet and the article in the Communist. We recommend that this pamphlet be withdrawn from circulation, in view of the fact that certain new theories have been advanced in this article." They also indicated that they wanted to know whether the policy formulated in the article had been accepted by the Party or was still in the stage of discussion.²³

Clearly the Party felt pressed to set changes in motion in the fall of 1928 even though the resolution was not published in the *Daily Worker* until February 12, 1929, or in the *Communist* until January 1930. It was also clear that the African American members had not accepted the entire position, were seeking to modify its interpretation, and were eager to distance the auxiliary organizations from the Pepper thesis. Over the years responsibility for Negro work had been assigned to a member of the CEC, such as Joseph Z. Kornfeder, Robert Minor, or John Ballam, but in 1928 one significant way the Party could demonstrate its response to the Comintern was to place an African American, Huiswoud, in charge of the Negro Department. According to Huiswoud, when he took charge "there was no functioning Negro Department though there was one comrade in charge. Very little connection had been established with the districts and no methods or plans devised to initiate activities throughout the Party to increase our Negro membership, and mobilize the entire Party behind the Negro work. Most of the districts paid very little attention to this important phase of Party activity and, since there was no coordination from the center and no specific instructions and advice to these various sections, no earnest attempt to work was made. Besides, most white comrades conceived of Negro work as the work of the Negro comrades."[24] Huiswoud set about the task of implementing a program on Negro work drawn up by the Party in April 1928 including the organization and coordination of district Negro Departments and supervision of various auxiliary organizations. In his report to the Sixth Party Convention held March 3–9, 1929, he continued to stress the weakness in trade union work and charged that the TUEL had "retreated before the anti-Negro policy of the labor aristocracy of the A.F. of L." He looked forward to change, however, with the recent formation of a Negro Department in the TUEL, directed by James W. Ford, who would work closely with the Negro Bureau of the Profintern.[25]

On November 15, 1928, the Party launched its Negro Commission to conduct a survey and prepare plans and proposals for Negro work, with the following members named by the Polcom: Mary Adams (Burroughs), John Ballam, William F. Dunne, John Golden, Otto Hall, Otto Huiswoud, Robert Minor, Richard B. Moore, Al Richman, John Swift (a.k.a. John Pepper) and Harold Williams. Grace Campbell was invited to remain in the meeting. Huiswoud was elected chairman. The Polcom's recommendation that Richman act as secretary was objected to by Moore, who stated that the "secretary should be a capable Negro comrade who has long experience in the work." Cyril Briggs was unanimously elected secretary but this was followed by a motion that "Richman serve as Technical Secretary to aid Comrade Briggs." Pepper then presented a lengthy description of the intentions of the Political Committee after his admission that the Party had not paid enough attention to Negro work because of the ignorance of most of the comrades, the few Negro comrades in the Party, the remnants of white chauvinism in the ranks, and the difficult and complicated nature of the work that was in need of much study. He called attention to the resolutions on the Negroes of South Africa and the United States at the Sixth Congress.

Pepper identified the basic shortcoming as the lack of trade union work: "Neither the Party nor the TUEL tackled that problem in a serious way." He referred to the ANLC as "a very sore spot in our work . . . it is unable to live and it is unable to die" and hoped the commission would offer concrete recommendations on its future. A second sore spot was that the Negro cadres, estimated to be only a few hundred, were "not on a very high level." He brought up the question of churches that "play a very big role in the life of the Negroes . . . In a certain respect they are social centers." After posing the two-fold problem on how to utilize those social centers and how to split the

Negro masses from the churches he pointedly stated, "We cannot tolerate, for example, that leading comrades should be members of churches." Various members added concerns that needed to be addressed, including suggestions related to the ongoing Harlem Renaissance. For example, Burroughs proposed studies on how Negroes in America make a living and their social and cultural traditions; Moore proposed an analysis of the imperialist structure and its ramifications on the Negro people, the ideology of race prejudice, race theories, white superiority, Negro history and culture, and African civilization; Richman suggested intensive study of national self-determination, Negro migration, the new Negro culture, and keeping in touch with the new Negro Bureau of the Profintern. Huiswoud stressed the significance of the decision on the ANLC. He stated that trade union work must be their first task and that the commission should make definite recommendations for the subcommittee on Negro work of the National Trade Union Committee. Briggs, Huiswoud, Pepper, Hall, and Moore were selected to bring in proposals on the Negro Department, ANLC, *Negro Champion,* instituting a news service, and trade union work.[26]

Moore's report on the ANLC at the meeting of the Negro Commission on January 3, 1929, indicated that the ANLC was still alive but not well. Local organizations had been maintained in Chicago, New York, Pittsburgh, and Philadelphia, and new locals initiated in Detroit, Kansas City, and Chester, Pennsylvania. Tours had been conducted to promote the anti-imperialist focus of the Brussels Conference and to agitate on issues such as the Mississippi flood disaster, the Gary, Indiana, school strike, the miners' strike, and the SS *Vestris* disaster.[27] The organization was not successful in issuing the *Negro Champion* regularly, following up on cooperative efforts with the UNIA, or assigning John Golden to begin work among farmers in the South primarily because of insufficient forces and funds and partly because some members, like Fort-Whiteman, had become pessimistic and initiated "liquidation activities." The contact that was supposed to penetrate the Pullman Porters had "turned out to be an agent of the Pullman porters working within" the ANLC. In his report, Moore considered the apparatus of the organization greatly improved within the last few months: "Instead of the one Negro Party functionary whose job it was to run the Congress, the Champion, Party work and all other activities, we now have a head of the Negro Department, a national organizer for the Congress, an editor of the Champion, two Party District organizers . . . a stenographer."[28]

The meeting was not without finger-pointing that revealed internal antagonisms. Moore alleged that he had found complete disorganization in the ANLC center and very few locals functioning. He added, however, that it was "not proper to blame the condition upon Comrade Whiteman alone, since he was not responsible for the direction of the work, but merely for certain tasks in execution. The direction . . . had been chiefly under the direction to Comrade Minor, who was the representative of the CEC in charge of Negro work." Moore also indicated that there was poor support by the Party and cited Chicago as an example where the Party had no committee on Negro work. George Padmore, a visitor at the meeting, called for a statement from Williams as to his attitude on liquidating the ANLC after the Comintern had decided that the ANLC was to be built. Pepper did not let Moore go unscathed. He called for a subcommittee to evaluate Moore's report. After a committee was established, Pepper reported, "Moore is instructed by the Secretariat to leave the church to which he belongs, but did not answer." Moore responded that he had made a statement previously and planned to notify the Political Committee the following day that he had decided to resign from the church in compliance with the decision of the Political Committee, not because he agreed with the perverted statements made about him but because his work was not yet fully understood even by communists.[29]

Moore had been a member of the Harlem Unitarian Church from the time it was organized by Rev. E. Ethelred Brown in 1920. The church frequently used a forum format that included lectures on atheism, agnosticism, "Jesus and Marx," and "The Church and the Negro Problem," instead of a traditional ecclesiastical service. Moore was a popular speaker and considered his social messages more political than religious. During the decade he had become a staunch atheist. To his way of thinking where better than the church to discuss the historic role the church had played in the oppression of the peoples of African descent? When a visiting minister expressed how he had found Jesus, for example, Moore countered with a lecture on how he had lost Jesus.[30] The Party failed to consider that historically the church in the African American community was a unique social as well as religious institution. The fact that the minister was a member of the Socialist party, stumped for Socialist candidates, and was employed by that party probably added to the objection raised to Moore's activities. There may have been unstated reasons for Pepper making an issue of Moore's church activities, but there was no question that Comintern policy was on Pepper's side. Not only was he the voice and ears of the Comintern in the United States, the Comintern had dealt with the question of religion in 1923. As a result of a controversy in Sweden a resolution had been passed at the Third Plenum of the Comintern that stated in part, "Communists demand that every citizen shall be free to acknowledge any religion he chooses or no religion, that is to be an atheist, which normally every conscious communist is." This freedom of religion assertion was followed, however, with the communist doctrine: "The communist party is obliged to train its members not only in the devoted pursuit of a particular political programme and economic demands and party statues; they must also have implanted in them the clear-cut and homogeneous world outlook of Marxism, of which atheism is an essential part . . . Active religious propaganda by leading comrades, especially intellectuals, is absolutely inadmissible, however up to date the form it takes."[31]

Moore's initial response to Pepper's charges had been submitted during the meeting of the Central Executive Committee Plenum on December 16, 1928. He stated for the record:

> I desire to protest against the misrepresentations of Comrade Pepper who misquoted me as saying that I am proud of my connection with the Church because it is a Liberal Left Church having 14 members. I stated that I was proud because of the Communist, atheist propaganda which I had conducted, pointing to debates in which I had taken the negative of such propositions as Resolved that Christianity Can Solve the Race Problem, holding Communism to be the solution, exposing the role of religion as "the opium of the people" and the Church as a force of capitalist-imperialist oppression, gaining the overwhelming vote of the 200 persons present, only 11 voting for the leader of the Church. The deliberate perversion of the attitude of the Negro comrades in relation to the church by Comrade Pepper to the Polcom was corrected by an overwhelming vote of the Negro Commission. This attitude was not as stated by Comrade Pepper that we should "concentrate our work around the church instead of in the factories, shops, etc." but actually was only how far the Party can utilize the church to reach the Negro masses there, especially in the South.
>
> I must protest also against Comrade Pepper's deliberate falsehood that I had resisted the decision of the Polcom to come out as a Communist until threatened with expulsion by the CEC. When the ANLC was reorganized in June 1927 the decision adopted by the Polcom was that I should not come out openly as a Communist and my Party card was changed by the DEC of the New York District accordingly. When the Party decided that I come out openly, I did so immediately, my speeches before and during the National Nominating Convention of the Party and my work in the election campaign is in proof . . .
>
> I demand finally that the campaign of misrepresentation calculated to remove me from responsible work and to drive me out of the party shall cease.[32]

At a meeting of the Political Committee on January 4 a motion by Robert Minor to orient work "predominantly toward the Negro working class masses and working class organizations and permit the approach to the church organizations to be only a very subordinate aspect of the work" passed but it was Pepper's motion that prevailed. Moore was instructed to carry out the

Polcom instructions to leave the church immediately, make a public statement giving the reasons for his break, attacking the church as one of the most dangerous instruments of capitalism and "religion in all its forms and of some religious ideology which masks itself with liberal or socialist phrases." Moore repeated his characterization of statements against him as misinterpretation and deliberate lies and that his connection was "simply to carry on the propaganda against religion at a point where it is most dangerous." He conceded: "Since my position, however, has been completely misinterpreted and as a result illusions may be fostered among the masses generally, and also among communists, I feel it necessary to withdraw from the church and have written a letter to the minister of the church to that effect."[33] Reverend Brown acknowledged Moore's withdrawal in his sermon, "Religious Liberalism in Harlem," on June 30, 1929: "Richard B. Moore who we all looked up to and whose stirring messages we all remember has recently withdrawn from us as he considers association with a religious movement inconsistent with his communist work." Interestingly, Brown also mentioned, "Grace Campbell is with us and yet not with us."[34]

The archival records of the church issue convey a simple Pepper-Moore controversy but it was the tip of an iceberg. Huiswoud and Hermie sometimes attended discussions at the church but he did not support Moore. He stated later in his report at the Party convention that some comrades had "a wrong policy toward the church. Their conception of the extent to which we could utilize the Negro church is based on an underestimation of the role of the church as an instrument of imperialism." He considered that trying to reach the masses from within the church detracted from the basic task of working in places of employment.[35] The true nature of the confrontation is somewhat revealed in deliberations that were running concurrently in the CEC Plenum sessions regarding the resolutions of the Sixth Congress. Moore's agitation on concerns beyond the church issue was displayed at the session of the Party on December 15, 1928. He commenced by referring to the danger of "pseudo-sophisticated dialectics" that begins with an analysis of objective conditions and "goes on to say my group has proven to be correct and always will be correct in the future." He asserted that such a species of dialectics "makes for the persistence of a factional atmosphere." Referring to the document dealing with Negro work prepared by the CEC majority he stated,

> Admission is made of the help of the Comintern in criticizing the weaknesses, the backwardness, the lack of proper estimation of Negro work in our Party, but it is to be pointed out that the CEC majority resisted the efforts of Negro comrades and other comrades in the Party to bring a correct orientation on

Negro work... All those comrades who were compelled by bitter necessity to make necessary criticism of the line of our party were labeled as anti-party and attacked in that connection. Now the program which was brought forward in the revision of the Party's line, you will find that the basic factors... were brought forward in my speech at the last convention where I pointed out the basic factors of the proletarianization of the Negro, the movement of the farmers to the cities, and the industrialization of the South... I pointed out that one of the serious shortcomings of our Party work was the failure to draw Negro comrades into leading positions for work; that Comrades Huiswood and Briggs and other comrades who had been allowed to practically drift out of the work of the Party completely, that they have to be drawn back. But the criticism was never accepted... Under pressure Comrades Huiswood and Briggs were drawn back into the work... Comrade Wolfe was against sending Negro students to Moscow. When I tried to get this cadre developed by proposing that Comrade Padmore be sent to school, Comrade Woolfe [sic] also objected that Comrade Padmore was a West Indian and would be likely to go back to West Indies.[36]

While incidents regarding Briggs were not cited by Moore, the climate in the Party was confirmed by a statement Briggs made in 1932 that he was "never out of Party, though inactive for a period of a year or so, as a direct result of open white chauvinism in the Party at that period, and resultant discouragement of all Negro members."[37] Moore criticized the choice of delegates that had been sent to the Sixth Congress: "We see that the recommendations made by the Negro comrades were ignored. Only two were sent and these are the weakest elements in the Party... When it was found out that Whitman [sic] could be expedient the Trotsky label was taken off him... Phillips who had broken discipline... was selected." Moore then complained that the *Daily Worker* failed to print news of a rent strike called by the Tenants League but the petty-bourgeois paper, the *Amsterdam News,* had run an article. Finally he got to the question of self-determination: "The whole Party has been confused by the erroneous and muddled formulation of the question. Comrade Pepper comes back here with a full-fledged black baby from Moscow... I say more Garveyism than Garvey himself... Here we have the central slogan of the Party: equal political and social rights completely ignored and self-determination put as the central slogan."[38]

Pepper's response was prompt: "Comrade Moore is accusing me of bringing a full fledged black baby with the slogan of self-determination and the Soviet Republic in the South... The mother of that baby is the Sixth Congress of the Comintern. The father of that baby... is the thesis of the Second Congress of the [Comintern] by Comrade Lenin... The role I played... was the role of the very modest midwife." He then mentioned that the Political Committee had forced Moore to come out openly as a communist and ridiculed Moore for his affiliation with the church. He concluded, "If Comrade Bittelman, Comrade Lovestone, Comrade Foster and myself, we all agree that Moore is a nationalist, not having the faintest idea about a Marxian conception of race and nationalist movements then certainly Comrade Moore something must be wrong with you . . . That finishes Comrade Moore."[39]

In a calmer and more focused manner Huiswoud complained about the generally negative view of the minority (Foster) group. He stated that the minority had discovered the Negro question at the Sixth Congress and suddenly developed out of a clear sky a platform on Negro work as laid down by the Comintern. He charged that "since the Minority's existence in the Party and during the period it was in power, it never had a policy on the Negro question . . . Negro comrades have been most critical of the CEC in so far as the shortcomings and underestimation of Negro work is concerned." He claimed the majority of the Party's central executive committee, however, always had a policy though at times not exactly correct and that "only people who try to do things make errors." He pointed to the misconception by the Party that Negro work is the work of Negro comrades and that Negroes are set aside to do only Negro work, while it is the duty of the Party as a whole to carry on Negro work. He criticized Moore for not assuming the leadership to call a meeting of the Tenants League fraction but joined him in the opinion that the policy on the Negro Workers Relief Committee was not carried out when the opportunities were ripe with the hurricane devastation in Florida.

Huiswoud approached the question of self-determination in a more analytical and accommodating manner than Moore, stating that everyone could express his own opinion within the higher bodies of the Party but should advocate the slogan of self-determination in other settings. He reviewed the basis for self-determination in the South and agreed completely with applying the slogan to a colonial situation like South Africa but obviously had reservations about applying it in the North. He described how the theses had struck as a

> thunderbolt when first broached in America because the Negro comrades never discussed it, because it was never presented to them. Naturally the first reaction to this slogan was one of opposition because of the very fact that when these conditions arise, the Negro comrades can register them first and foremost much better than any group in the Party because their ears are nearest to the ground and they have their fingers nearer to the pulse of the Negro masses . . . I say what

we must determine on the basis of the slogan is whether the Negro in America is a racial minority or national minority . . . In America, where the Negroes are a racial minority, where there is no thought, no expression whatever for the development of their own state or their own government, where on the contrary, the swing, the movement, the entire ideology of the Negro masses is for social, political and economic equality. That therefore our slogan in America must be based primarily on these questions. Social equality is the biggest thing so far as the Negro masses are concerned . . . The slogan today in America must be first and primarily that of social equality, that the question of self-determination . . . is a secondary slogan.[40]

He concluded by urging comrades to put into effect the demand of the Party and the Comintern on Negro work and not consider it something separate and apart from themselves, relegated only to Negro comrades.

The CEC agenda was geared primarily to the preparation of various theses for presentation at the forthcoming Party convention. The Party was expected not only to implement resolutions of the Sixth Congress but also to respond to the criticism of factionalism leveled by the Comintern. The Foster and Lovestone factions continued to jockey for the position of leadership and acceptance by the Comintern. Each faction offered resolutions but there was no compromising, no possible consensus; the votes were consistently along factional lines—except for Moore, who seems to have been the only African American entitled to vote. Moore voted several times with the Foster faction, but when they failed to vote on the motion by Benjamin Gitlow of the majority calling upon "the membership to accept all the decisions of the 6th World Congress of the CI without reservation" Moore changed his vote. He submitted a statement explaining his reasons:

> I realize that there is indeed a basic difference between the line of the minority and the line I could adopt . . . I, therefore, record my vote in favor of the motion to accept the decisions of the Sixth World congress without reservations. I record myself as abstaining from voting on either of the theses submitted, minority or majority, as both these contain propositions which I regard as unclear, confusing and not conducive to a correct and effective execution of the line of the CI or to the unification of our Party which is indispensable thereto . . . I am not what can be considered a good factionalist. I have tried and try still to be a good Bolshevik.[41]

Moore's position was odd, considering that he had clearly expressed his opposition to the Sixth Congress Theses on the Negro Question yet accepted the decisions of the congress without reservations. He attacked Lovestone and failed to support motions of the Lovestone group, which was probably contrary to Huiswoud's perspective as subsequent events would demonstrate.

At the Party convention in March, another step was taken to elevate the position of African American members. According to the *Negro Champion* of March 23, 1929, "Amidst scenes of the wildest enthusiasm on the part of its 104 delegates and thousands of visitors, the Sixth National Convention . . . placed the Communist Party in the vanguard of the Negro's struggle against white terrorism in this country." The article declared that unanimous support for a resolution denouncing lynching, Jim-Crowism, disfranchisement, and segregation, and also calling upon the workers of both races to unite in the struggle against the white oppressors of the Negro, was proof that the Party's "advocacy during the last election of full racial and political rights for the Negro was not a political maneuver but a studied and deliberate policy." Four African Americans were elected to the central executive committee, the highest body in the Party: Cyril Briggs, Otto Hall, John Henry, Otto Huiswoud. Edward Welsh was elected as "candidate" (alternate) to the CEC. "The convention also gave instructions to all party districts, sections and units to elect Negro members to leading positions as rapidly as possible."[42] It probably is not a coincidence that the election took place following the Sixth Congress deliberations on the Negro question and the receipt of the Comintern's open letter to the convention that mandated "drawing workers into the leadership."[43]

On the surface Huiswoud's second trip to Moscow was unrelated to his focus on securing rights for African peoples. As head of the Negro Department he was in the Party headquarters upper echelon but it is doubtful if he was aware of the campaign Stalin was waging to eliminate Bukharin as he had Trotsky or Stalin's growing animosity toward Jay Lovestone, who had assumed the position of secretary of the Party following the death of Charles Ruthenberg in 1927. For several years a philosophical conflict regarding the direction of the U.S. economy had been brewing among leaders of the Party and between the Comintern and the Party. One analysis argued that capitalism was well entrenched, and a second forecast a downturn of capitalism that would lead to inroads by communism. The debate reached a climax with the Comintern charging leaders of the American Party with promoting a doctrine of American "exceptionalism." This contentious climate helped set the tone when the struggle for leadership of the American Party and Stalin's struggle for leadership of the Russian Party were joined.

Of course, factionalism was not new nor was it a phenomena experienced solely by the American Party. As early as 1920 the ECCI had met in an enlarged meeting to review dissensions that had resulted in two American parties. The ECCI was convinced that there was no serious difference in principle between the two parties and that the "unity of the Communists is not only possible, but absolutely necessary." The letter to the American comrades stated, "The Executive Committee categorically insists on such unity."[44] Throughout the decade the Party was not able to overcome its dual conception, and leaders continually referred domestic disputes to the Comintern for adjudication, which rendered the Party ineffectual at home and subservient abroad. Instead of building strong, widely supported arguments tailored to the American reality, leaders of factions fed the fires of Soviet domination by seeking favor for their side. While there is no question regarding the Comintern's intent to dominate the national parties, the American Party established a submissive pattern early and revealed such weakness or confusion that the stage was set for the Comintern to take one final step to end factionalism.

The fierce dispute between the Foster and Lovestone forces was to develop into an entangled debacle loaded with undercover intrigue in New York and Moscow. Lovestone considered that he had triumphed over Foster when he succeeded in winning 95 out of 104 delegates to the Sixth Convention of the Party that took place in New York on March 1–9, 1929. Prior to the convention Philipp Dengel, a German communist, and Harry Pollitt, a British communist, were sent as representatives of the Comintern with an "Open Letter" that called for liquidating factionalism and drawing workers into the leadership along with confidential organizational proposals advising the convention to appoint Foster as new general secretary and requesting that the two chief factionalists, Lovestone and Bittleman, be assigned to the Comintern in Moscow.[45] The problem had begun two years earlier when Lovestone was in Moscow and had become friendly with Bukharin, whom Stalin was now determined to depose. It did not help that Stalin had interpreted Lovestone's statements and actions over the years as negative toward him. As the writing on the wall became clearer, Lovestone and his aides devised numerous strategies to win the favor of Stalin and the Comintern, including attacking Foster, arranging for a group of ten delegates to go to Moscow on March 23 to appeal the organizational proposals, and introducing a resolution denouncing Bukharin. A cable from the Party Secretariat to the ECCI on March 23 asserted lack of cooperation by members of the opposition and described the opposition's proposal for changes in leadership, including replacement of Stachel by Williamson, Huiswoud by Williams, Poyntz by Grecht, and Minor by Dunne.[46]

The African Americans chosen to accompany the delegation were Huiswoud and Edward Welsh, two of the five elected to the CEC just prior to the departure for Moscow. Welsh had been a Party candidate for the New York state legislature during the previous fall. Ella Reeve Bloor, William Miller, Tom Myerscough, Alex Noral, and William J. White also accompanied Party leaders

Lovestone, Benjamin Gitlow, and Max Bedacht. Gitlow has indicated that each delegate was supposed to be working in a factory but were "really chosen for their proletarian looks and political reliability." He pointed out that Huiswoud was the only one who was not born in the United States, but "being a Negro was considered a mark of distinction among us. We brought this delegation along, to prove to Moscow that the charges that we were a group of foreign-born Communists was false . . . We knew that the Comintern had repeatedly insisted that we must draw the native Americans into the Party if we really wanted to bring about its Americanization."[47] The proletarian dressing failed to impress the American Commission chaired by Kuusinen that convened in Moscow on April 12, 1929.

Stalin took a personal interest in the dispute and served as a member of the American Commission along with seven other Russians and four members of the Finnish, British, Hungarian, and German parties. Foster and William Weinstone had been called to Moscow to present the opposition's case. The sessions, which lasted until May 6, attracted over one hundred participants and spectators, including Bertram D. Wolfe and Harry M. Wicks, who were American representatives to the Comintern and Profintern respectively, as well as American students attending the Lenin School and leaders from other parties who were in Moscow. Following presentations by Gitlow and Foster the American delegates were cross-examined by members of the commission. Charges and countercharges peppered with nasty name-calling by both factions were exchanged, and eventually the attitude of comrades toward the "Negro Problem" was dragged into the debate. When Ed Welsh declared "Comrade Lovestone is our party, he has the respect of the membership," James Ford, a pro-Foster African American who was in Moscow at the time, injected that the Negro comrades had been poisoned by the Party leadership.[48] In fact the tie between the factional issue and the work among African Americans was placed before the American Commission prior to its deliberation. On March 22 Harold Williams, a former KUTV student, delegate to the national convention, and former supporter of the majority, sent a letter complaining that the Lovestone group had misrepresented the open letter. He charged that "the main consideration given to the leading Negro comrades is how best to employ them in the faction war. In this connection, comrades like Huiswoud and Hall were especially used for the factionalism of Lovestone and in mobilising Negro comrades for the faction." He concluded that "as long as the faction spirit and unprincipled groupings continue in the Party, Negro workers will be made a football and the real detailed tasks of realising a mass revolutionary Negro movement in the United States will not be achieved."[49]

At the April 12 meeting of the American Commission, Lozovsky asked whether it was not abnormal for there to be such a small number of Negro workers in the Party considering they were the most exploited. Huiswoud cited recent increased enrollments and responded, "It is abnormal; no one would claim otherwise. If anybody has been critical of the Party in its neglect of Negro work, certainly the Negro comrades have been in the forefront in this criticism . . . Particularly since the VIth Congress have we made this criticism and definite steps have been taken in getting Negro workers into the party." He went on to describe work in Alabama and Tennessee, where they had formed Party nuclei of white and Negro comrades who participated equally as functionaries of the units and met in the same hall, which was illegal in those states at that time. When asked by Harry Haywood about the implementation of the decisions on self-determination, Huiswoud replied that he had accepted the decision of the CI wholeheartedly. "I have made a statement in so far as my own opinion is concerned, just like all the other Negro comrades . . . the way in which the minority has issued the Slogan in America as the new line of the CI on the question—they would have us speak of self-determination in New York City, in Detroit, and so on. We pointed out that the main slogan must be racial equality, the question of self-determination is a Secondary Slogan to be applied in the South."[50]

On April 19 Huiswoud made a lengthy statement attacking the opposition for its lack of commitment and work benefiting African American workers. His attack revealed the intensity of the partisanship and some of the reasons animosity had been brewing for years. He criticized the manner in which Philipp Dengel, Comintern representative to the American Party, exhibited favoritism to the opposition before examining the true situation in the Party, the constant "hardened and crystallised" stands of the opposition in meetings of the Political Bureau regardless of the topic under consideration, the shift in the position of the Foster group on the open letter when they learned that Foster was being considered as leader for a revised administration, and the Foster group's failure to organize African Americans workers. He cited examples of white chauvinism in districts in which the opposition had a stronghold and also quoted an ally of Foster, William F. Dunne, who had "once said that he could understand Negroes being in the army as soldiers, but for a Negro to be an army officer is quite another story." He stated that since he "was in charge of the Negro work of the Party" he sought to answer the question of Negro work brought up by Foster:

> Comrades, it is true that our party as a whole has sadly neglected its Negro work . . . Did we make any criticism of the Party on that score? Plenty of it, it did not come from the Opposition however . . .

I pointed out the weaknesses in our Negro work and I also pointed out how since the VI World Congress, we have made a start in carrying out the line laid down by the VI World Congress . . . Now no one here, not even Foster, can deny that in the last six or seven months we have made certain definite gains. We have increased our Negro membership in the Party, we have started throughout the Party to build in every district, Negro departments, which take up the issues facing the Party in its Negro work . . .

This comrade wanted to know why I attacked the Opposition on their Negro work. Well I will tell you why. The comrades of the Opposition were in control of the trade union work of the Party. The T.U.E.L. published . . . a magazine called the "Labour Herald." Surely they had the opportunity to say at least a few lines about Negro work, about the organization of Negro workers in the trade union movement, I would like you to . . . show me one copy in which you treat the question of organization of Negro workers into the trade union movement . . . The opposition group rests upon the skilled workers, the building trades workers and they had the same ideas in the trade union movement that they brought into the Communist party . . . the same as that of the trade union bureaucracy who say organize the white workers first and the Negro workers will follow . . . Surely you cannot blame the Majority of not having done any work in the T.U.E.L. You had charge of the T.U.E.L. Why did you never wage a campaign against the bureaucrats of the A.F.L. who exclude Negroes because they are Negroes. This is one of the burning issues among the Negro workers, their exclusion from the trade unions because of color. This also serves as a powerful weapon in the hands of the Capitalists who use this fact to poison the minds of the Negro workers against the white workers . . .

Why is it that the comrades of the minority never take seriously the resolutions passed by the RILU regarding Negro work; nor the recommendations of the Negro Bureau of the RILU. This was left to the majority of the Polbureau. It was Comrade Gitlow who, in the Trade Union Committee, made a motion to have a Negro Department of the TUEL and Comrade Hall as director . . .

It was exactly at the period when Foster was in power that not a single stone was turned to do any Party work among the Negro masses . . . In so far as work among the Negro masses is concerned, if the minority is in power, if Comrade Foster is in power, we will have a repetition of what we had before. There will be no work done at all. There will be no work done because I know their attitude and I did not come into the Party yesterday. I came into the Party when the split took place from the Socialist Party. I helped to organise the Party; I am part of its flesh and blood, and I know what it means. I have seen the Party in action, I have gone deep into the work of the Party and I know what the action of the opposition will be when it comes into power. If the Commission recommends to the CI that a change in the leadership should be made, that Comrade Lovestone should be removed from the Party, this will be the most fatal blunder, so far as the life and activities [of] the Party are concerned; and the responsibility for this will rest upon the CI.[51]

Stalin's ire increased as the sessions proceeded, and on the last working day of the commission he strongly castigated both sides and ended by presenting a six-point solution that incorporated the original proposals of the Comintern except for handing control of the party to the Foster group. In New York, Minor, Stachel, Briggs, and others began notifying the delegation that the minority was spreading rumors of a Comintern position casting the majority as anticomintern. On May 3 the group sent a mixed signal giving assurances that they would stand by the Party convention actions and were willing to "carry out the forthcoming decision in letter and spirit" and "mobilize the entire membership in support of the CI decision."[52] The Lovestone faction decided not to wait for the subcommission report of Molotov, Kuusinen, and Gusev to be issued and presented a warning on May 9 that if the proposals of Stalin and Molotov were adopted the American Party membership would be forced to conclude that the ECCI desired to destroy the American central committee.[53] This move was viewed as a shift from a case of intraparty warfare to war against the Comintern, and the atmosphere became even more acrimonious.

On May 12 the "Address by the Executive Committee of the Communist International to All Members of the Communist Party of the United States," a message considered sharper than Stalin's speech, was adopted unanimously by the American Commission. It recommended immediate dissolution of all factions, removal of Lovestone and Bittelman from work in the American Party, reorganization and extension of the Secretariat, and commitment of Pepper's infractions to the International Control Commission. On May 14 the forty-member Presidium met for six hours. Kuusinen read the proposed Comintern Address, whereupon Gitlow introduced a letter signed by all members of the delegation stating that they could not vote for the Address because it would promote "demoralization, disintegration and chaos in the Party."[54]

Leading members of parties of various countries warned the delegates of the error of their thinking and implored them to reconsider. The words of Presidium member Katayama were particularly noted by Huiswoud. He cautioned the Americans: "Last Sunday you degraded yourselves . . . And today you bring a statement against the proposals . . . Comrades, you are breaking your necks . . . As a friend of the American party—I love the American party—do not fight this platform."[55] When the vote was taken there was only one vote cast against the Address—by the only American entitled to vote as a member of the Presidium—Gitlow. Each delegate was asked individually whether he or she accepted the decision of the Presidium. All maintained their position with the exception of Bedacht. But that was not the end. Katayama's words continued to ring in Huiswoud's ears; it was as if his friend was counseling him personally. On May 24 he joined Alex Noral and Mother Bloor in a statement retracting their position of May 14: "While still maintaining our disagreement with the Open Letter and its Organization instruction, and our conviction that they will not prove helpful to our Party, we, delegates to the C.I. elected by the Sixth National Convention of our Party, hereby categorically repudiate all charges of resistance to the Comintern decision, and call upon the Party membership to take no steps to resist or hinder the execution of the decisions of the ECCI. We pledge ourselves to this effect."[56]

Huiswoud had saved "breaking his neck" but would his role be maintained? The question was somewhat resolved when the central committee of the Party voted unanimously on May 18 to accept and endorse the Address and instructed the delegates in Moscow to withdraw opposition to it. Most party members accepted the Address and abandoned Lovestone. Lovestone, Gitlow, and Wolfe were removed from the positions they held in the Communist International and the Party by the ECCI and were later expelled by the Party. A new Secretariat was imposed with Bedacht as acting secretary and including Weinstone, Foster, and Minor. In September Foster became general secretary of the Trade Union Unity League (TUUL), successor to the TUEL. Pepper was recalled to Moscow and expelled for refusing to submit to instructions of the executive committee, deceiving the Party and the committee, and for instigating his followers to carry on factional work. His subsequent disappearance was attributed to execution by Stalin's forces.[57]

While the American Commission was in session the Enlarged International Trade Union Committee of Negro Workers (ITUC-NW) of the Profintern, chaired by Ford, was convened. The meeting on April 6, held prior to Huiswoud's statement in favor of the Lovestone leadership, was of particular interest because it brought Huiswoud and Foster together in another arena to discuss Negro work. Huiswoud's report on the status of Negro work pointed to the fact that only 150,000 Negro workers were organized out of 2 million concentrated in the large industrial cities of New York, Chicago, Pittsburg, Detroit, and Buffalo. He leveled his consistent allegation that the trade union department of the Party neglected this work and the Party had failed to fight against the discriminatory policies of the AFL. He identified the woman question as one of the biggest problems because a large proportion of trades, such as laundries, in which African American women predominated remained unorganized. On a more positive note he described the success of the Negro Miners Relief Committee, "the first time that such an appeal was made in the name of a definite Negro trade union group." Most of the work was being conducted on a territorial basis in neighborhoods and in churches. He admitted, "Even today after a long discussion on this question, there are some who think that the greatest attention must be paid to work in the churches. The reasons given by these comrades are that Negroes are spread over a number of enterprises . . . therefore we can reach the masses only in the churches where they assemble." He was optimistic that the Party had established a Negro Department and that TUEL was also organizing a department that could work closely with the Negro Committee of the Profintern to move from "theorising" to practical work.[58]

Foster countered with concessions and charges. He agreed that Negro work was in its initial stages and little had been done but attributed the poor performance to the fact that the Party and TUEL had just begun to understand the importance of the work. He argued that the political propaganda among Negroes was not connected with actual struggles and that the work was too local, limited mainly to New York. He complained, "There was a failure on the side of the Party to participate in the general work of the TUEL. Although there was a decision that the Negro Committee of the Party should participate in the work of the TUEL, this was never done. Comrade Huiswoud's statement that there was no program on Negro work is not true. After the Sixth Congress of the Comintern [1928] a program was worked out, presented to the CC of the Party, but was lost in committees. The reason for this is the underestimation of the Negro work." He stressed the significance of conducting work in the South despite the reign of terror there and conceded that "a difficult problem is white chauvinism."[59] The decision by the Comintern the following month on the leadership of the American Party altered the dynamics within the Party but not the relationship between Foster and Huiswoud.

At the conclusion of the sessions of the American Commission, Ed Welsh was assigned to return home from Moscow with Huiswoud. They traveled by train to Leningrad and by ship to Stettin, where they embarked for Holland to visit relatives of Huiswoud before returning to the United States.[60] They had left New York on the same side of the dispute but returned in disagreement. Theoretically factionalism was now dead but its vestiges continued to plague work in Harlem. Some African American comrades found it difficult to accept the shift in leadership. Divisiveness that had not previously existed developed in the Harlem Tenants League. Ed Welsh, Grace Campbell, and several other members who continued to support Lovestone attempted to take over the League but were not successful.[61] Later Campbell changed her position and continued her long alliance with Huiswoud, Moore, and Briggs.

While Huiswoud was out of the country Briggs served as acting head of the Negro Department, and in September 1929 he presented his analysis of Negro work during the previous ten years. He blamed the poor record on white chauvinism in both factions that had been unmasked at the Sixth Congress by Ford and "mercilessly condemned by that supreme revolutionary body":

> White chauvinism manifests itself in a general underestimation of the importance of the role of the Negro masses in the revolutionary struggles; in open or concealed opposition to doing work among the Negroes, in thinly veneered antagonism to Negro comrades and sympathizers; in failure to carry on anything but the most sporadic and feeble activities among these masses; in failure to come out openly and continually as the champion of the Negro masses in their racial and economic struggles; in failure to prosecute the fight in the reactionary trade unions for the removal of the color bar; in failure to mobilize and rally the broad masses of the white workers for active participation in the struggles of the Negro masses; in failure to draw capable Negro comrades into responsible and leading positions in the Party, in the left wing unions, in the Party auxiliaries, and in trying to excuse the failure to push the Negro comrades to the front with the rotten slander that existing Negro cadres are totally incapable and undeveloped.[62]

Briggs continued by pointing out the tendency to ignore leading Negro comrades when formulating policies on Negro work and cited a policy that had opposed the spontaneous mass migration from the South on the basis of the AFL argument that migration would hurt the economic position of northern white workers and result in the sharpening of racial antagonism with resultant race riots. He also decried the repudiation of social equality for the Negro that had taken place at a Party convention and the negative effect of the factional struggle on Negro work. Finally he applauded the Sixth Congress and the efforts that were being made to correct the shortcomings, including electing Negro comrades to the various Party bodies, exposure and expulsion of some comrades judged to be chauvinists, and the formation of a Negro Department in the TUEL with Otto Hall as head.[63]

Following his return from Moscow, Huiswoud continued as head of the Negro Department and served in other leadership roles. In mid-October at the first plenary session of the central committee of the Party, Huiswoud was elected to the Presidium of the Plenum along with Foster, Weinstone, Bedacht, and three others. He served as chairman of the Plenum the first day. The agenda consisted of four reports: on the Tenth Plenum of the ECCI in July by Robert Minor, on the general political and economic situation and tasks of the Party by Bedacht, on trade union work by Foster, and on Negro work by Huiswoud.[64] Minor had presented a report on the Party at the Tenth

Plenum on July 1. His review of Lovestone's opposition to the Comintern confirmed that the Negro question was neglected during factional rifts. He reported, "We find everywhere the tendency to look upon the Negro question as a sort of backward affair . . . Now the Negro comrades in the Party inevitably have a more acute ear for questions of this sort than any other comrades in the Party; and it is peculiarly interesting to note that the Negro comrades always tend to be against the C. C., no matter which C. C. is in power . . . The comrades instinctively feel the Party has not yet taken a proper revolutionary attitude towards the tremendous question of the Negroes, and the C. C., no matter which group may be in power, is always to blame for such condition."[65] The shifts in the opposition of African Americans to the group in power was no doubt a strategy to maintain pressure on leaders of the party. The statement reflects the general attitude of the Party toward Negro work as well as the independence that the African American cadre tried to exert.

Huiswoud's attempt to bury factionalism was expressed in his report at the plenary meeting of the CEC. In his introduction he described the paralyzing effect that the "vicious and unprincipled factional strife" had exerted on Negro work: "The Negro question was the 'political football' at Party Plenums and Conventions, each fraction charging the other with underestimation, neglect, incorrect political approach and willful sabotage . . . It was a deterrent to a careful analysis of the Negro question, the formulation of a correct program and the execution of decisions. Even decisions of the Comintern and the Red International of Labor Unions were sidetracked on one excuse or another." He then extolled the difference at the recent CEC Plenum where Negro work was an integral part of the discussions and reports: there had been the first careful examination of conditions facing Negroes in the South, attention to white chauvinism in the Party, and mobilization of the entire Party behind the program and consideration of a new field of activity—the West Indies. Huiswoud had finally realized one of his lifelong goals—"Practical steps taken toward organizing these low-paid and terribly exploited workers . . . It is the duty of our Party to take the initiative in organizing these workers and leading them in the struggle against world imperialism."[66] In fact, Huiswoud had already made a trip to Jamaica to attend the UNIA convention and assess the revolutionary climate. Agitation on behalf of the peoples of the Caribbean had been joined with the Party's pursuit of freedom for African Americans.

African American Party leaders must have experienced considerable stress at times. Despite the intention to have minutes of meetings reflect only the action taken during business sessions, the minutes reveal evidence of irritability and antagonisms within the group. The strange minutes of the August 14, 1928, meeting of the National Negro Committee, for example, reported "personal antagonisms which are quite marked between: Moore and Padmore; Moore and Rosemond; Moore and Williams . . . Huiswood plays a cuatious [sic] game between the two groups."⁶⁷ Even Huiswud could lose his cool demeanor. When Henry Rosemond was needling him at the Sixth Party Convention in 1929 to tell why he had left and returned to the Party, he called Rosemond "a baby in more than one sense of the word." As the confrontation proceeded Huiswoud insisted he had never left the Party and said that there was a period when the minority was in power that he was inactive and asked, "What the hell else could you do, Rosemond, when you had to buck up against a stone wall, when there was deliberate sabotage and no opportunity given for work?"⁶⁸ In response to Haywood's interruption when he was speaking at the meeting of the American Commission during the Lovestone problem, Huiswoud exclaimed, "Listen Hayward [sic] you had better keep quiet, you don't know a damned thing about the American Party."⁶⁹ Huiswoud, Moore, and Briggs, however, were able to retain their friendship throughout the decade despite their differences.

Reports and articles by Huiswoud and Briggs following the establishment of the Negro Department applauded the Sixth Congress and the Comintern for pressuring the American Party to correct its program to reach the Negro masses but avoided references to self-determination for the "Negro Nation." It was not the term that was the problem. They had discussed self-determination a decade earlier, but the designation of a "Black Belt" in the South that conferred characteristics of nationhood on African Americans in the country seemed outlandish. Moore had already blurted out his initial reaction, but Huiswoud was more restrained and formulated a rational, documented article, "World Aspects of the Negro Question," that appeared in the *Communist* in February 1930. He proposed, "We must take into consideration the National-colonial character of the Negro question in Africa and the West Indies and the racial character of this question in the United States." First he dealt with the distinction between the social democrat and communist views of the Negro question and reasserted that the Negro question was not only a class question but a race question. The Negro masses were not only subjected to the ordinary forms of exploitation as other workers, but were also "the victims of a brutal caste system which holds them as an inferior servile class . . . social outcasts. In order to maintain its policy of repression, violence and exploitation of the Negro the bourgeoisie creates a false racial ideology among the whites and fosters contempt and hatred for the Negro. The idea of 'superior' and 'inferior' races is the theoretical justification for their policy of super-exploitation of the Negro race."⁷⁰

Throughout the article Huiswoud attempted to clarify the difference between groups in the African Diaspora according to certain common features, including majority of population and a common language and culture. He divided the regions into: "(A) The United States and some Latin American countries, in which the Negro population is a minority. (B) Africa and the West Indies, where the Negro population is the majority... (C) The independent Negro nations (Haiti and Liberia), which are in reality semi-colonies of American imperialism." He found that countries in Africa and the Caribbean had all the characteristic features of the national-colonial question but that the Negro in America was a racial minority, had no language and culture distinct from the dominant racial group, and had as its only distinguishing feature its racial origin. He described the size of the population and the territory, major industries, working conditions in the three areas, the potential for radical activities, and stressed that the "peculiar forms of racial exploitation of the Negro masses provide the basis for a race liberation movement which must be actively supported by the Communist Party."

In Huiswoud's discussion of the Caribbean, class rather than race was identified as an issue. He referred to the numerous spontaneous strikes as indicators of the mood of the masses and predicted that "under such circumstances the Communist Parties can build a broad movement for the fight for the right of self-determination, giving proletarian leadership to the struggle for a 'Federated West Indies.'" He noted the migratory movement of Negroes in the South from rural areas to both southern and northern industrial cities and the failure of white workers blinded by race hatred to see the common interest between them and the Negro workers. This was a basis for organizing Negro workers in the "new revolutionary trade unions under the leadership of the Trade Union Unity League." He commented upon racial separation, through segregation, as an effective means of reducing the Negro to a social outcast and warned that segregation also created the basis for the development of a group of real estate brokers, merchants, and bankers that enabled the Negro bourgeoisie under the deceptive slogan of "race loyalty" to establish an ideological influence over the Negro masses and divert their militancy into reformist channels.[71]

Huiswoud's approach was to present some facts of the life experienced by Africans, Caribbean peoples, and African Americans that he believed were crucial in determining attitudes and policies of the Communist Party. He never attacked the Sixth Congress theses or used key terms such as "Black Belt" or "nation within a nation." The term "self-determination" was used only in the context of his description of the Caribbean. Nonetheless, his definition of the Negro in the United States as an oppressed racial minority was interpreted as a renunciation of the theses.[72] The article was honest in presenting the position Huiswoud, Moore, or Briggs might have taken had they been afforded an opportunity during the deliberations in Moscow, but in 1930 it was considered not only untimely but heresy. The Party was now faced with the dilemma of having the head of the Negro Department publicly take exception to the policy on the Negro question pronounced by the Comintern and adopted by the Party.

One response was a counterarticle by Haywood in the August issue of the *Communist.* Haywood described how Nasanov and he searched through the Party press and documents for some discussion on the Negro question following the congress but there had been none until Huiswoud's article. He stated, "It was the first article in a year to broach the theoretical aspects of the question," and they decided that a reply afforded an excellent opportunity to clarify the theses and settle accounts with Sik [Shiek].[73] His long article, "Against Bourgeois-Liberal Distortions of Leninism on the Negro Question in the United States," asserted that Huiswoud "not only revives the opportunist formula 'race' question, but attempts to give it a theoretical basis. In this manner he places himself in direct opposition to the CI line, giving objective support to the rankest chauvinism. Attempting to prove that the Negro question in the United States is a race question as opposed to a national question, Comrade Huiswoud, together with his co-'thinkers' prove instead their absolute desertion of the Marxian-Leninist position on this question and inevitably slide down into the swamp of the most sterile bourgeois liberalism."[74] Of course this condemnation did not replace the discipline that such defiance demanded.

Haywood not only acted as a student advocate, he assumed a position of greater influence. While still a student at the Lenin School following the Sixth Congress he was a paid "practicant" in the Negro Bureau of the ECCI. He informed the U.S. Party in September 1929 that the bureau had been reorganized as the Negro Section of the Eastern Secretariat of the ECCI and complained about a lack of communication between the Negro Bureau and the Negro Department of the Party. He demanded that the Party forward information on its Negro work, its fight against white chauvinism, and an assessment of "moods among the Negro comrades." He took an active role in formulating the revision of the Negro question in 1930 and pressing for implementation.[75]

On September 6, 1930, Earl Browder reported to William Weinstone, the American representative to the Comintern, that Huiswoud, who had been the leader of Negro work in the party for ten years, was one of the foremost to reject the slogan of self-determination. Browder commented that he had witnessed some merit derived from the slogan already: "This goes to the very roots of the Garvey movement and rapidly brings the best elements from it into the party." The critical issue was the future of the ANLC. Some party members favored liquidating the organization, but Party leaders considered such an approach wrong. Browder stressed the need for a mass organization dealing specifically with the Negro question.[76] In his reply of September 8, Weinstone agreed with Browder on the need for an organization such as a "League to Fight for Rights for Negroes." He thought the major problem was that they had not sufficiently taken up the grievances and abuses of Negroes.[77] At the September 9 session of the American Commission of the ECCI, Haywood took exception to the Party's interpretation of the self-determination slogan and its plan to continue a separate organization committed to Negro rights. His argument was based upon the danger of "a mixed class" organization that would foster petty-bourgeois narrowness and isolationist tendencies. He charged that the unhealthy division of so-called party and Negro work was largely responsible for the petty-bourgeois orientation of some of the leading Negro comrades in the ANLC and cited Huiswoud's position calling for an organizational divorce between the party and the ANLC as an example of petty-bourgeois moods.[78] The Party proceeded to transform the ANLC into the League of Struggle for Negro Rights in November 1930, with Langston Hughes as president and Richard B. Moore as general secretary. Despite the shift to a definition casting the Negro people as a "nation," Negro work was no longer to be centered in a Negro congress or organization. Instead, white members were to join the African American's struggle for equality in an interracial League. Haywood was to find himself at the helm of the organization two years later, when Moore resigned to work for the International Labor Defense.

On October 1, 1930, Max Bedacht complained to Weinstone that the struggle over the Negro question had not ended with the convention action but was a continuous one. He described the resistance of leading comrades in the Negro Section who were "against the policy of the C.I., especially in regard to self determination. Where it was impossible to convince the comrades and where the comrades persisted in continuing their propaganda against the policy of the Central Committee we had to shift these comrades from supremely responsible positions in the Negro Department to other sections of Party work . . . In their private letters to the District they attempt to undermine the confidence of the comrades in the policy of the Central Committee and of the C.I." He then presented the current problem: "Now, we are confronted with a rumor that the E.C.C.I. has taken up this question, has condemned the Central Committee and has promoted some comrades involved to 'high positions'. Especially mentioned are: Huiswood and Williams. I take it for granted that the basis for this rumor is that these comrades are to be called to Moscow to be made functionaries in the apparatus there. But I certainly also take it for granted that this was not meant as promotion, but partly as an attempt to strengthen the Negro Department in Moscow and partly as an attempt to help us against these comrades." Even though Bedacht did not think Padmore's letter on which the rumors were based "contained the political interpretation of the ECCI's call for Houiswood [sic] and Williams" he sought clarification in order to contend with the rumors.[79]

A follow-up letter of October 30 from Earl Browder to Weinstone indicated that some satisfactory understanding had been reached on the Resolution on the Negro Question at a special meeting of the Pol Bureau with five or six leading comrades. They had studied the resolution and expressed their complete agreement, but two Negro comrades thought the introduction was too complimentary to the past history of the Party on Negro work. Browder stated:

> We were all especially pleased with Comrade Huiswood's attitude. He made a speech which was a very open and honest examination of his own deviations on the Negro question and a concrete analysis of the reasons for his previous wrong views, and a very convincing statement that he agrees with the line of the Party. He had already clarified his position very much before the arrival of this Resolution and the new Resolution completed the job. He himself says that he is still not thoroughly grounded in many of the basic problems involved, such as the agrarian question and the whole national question, which he had only in the past months begun seriously to study. He, however, already sees the complete erroneousness of his past position, and is rapidly consolidating himself on the Party line.[80]

Browder also noted that work among the Negro masses was still inadequate and unsatisfactory but was optimistic that "with the liquidation of the differences among the Negro elements, and between some of them and the Party, we will be able rapidly to overcome the worst of these weaknesses."

Hermie was aware of Otto's article, but not the entire controversy, and she was proud that he had carefully expressed opinions that were important not just to him personally but that needed to be considered for the progress of the movement. Not only had he argued on behalf of Lovestone and against the Black Belt thesis, which turned out to be incorrect positions as far as the Comintern was concerned, it seemed he and his close colleagues were moving out of favor in the Party just as they had been finally placed in significant roles of leadership. She worried what the price of expressing one's principles would be.

7. Harlem Goes to Moscow and Paris

Punishment? Removal? Reward? Reeducation? Reassignment based on credentials to fill a significant post? Hermie did not know what precipitated their long journey to the east or who had made the decision for Otto and her to go to Moscow, but she was delighted and content to be embarking on the novel odyssey. It was exhilarating to be transported suddenly from the "Black Mecca" to the "Red Mecca," to view with one's own eyes the vast Kremlin and Red Square, to witness the bold socialist experiment, to experience life among the stalwart Russian people, and most importantly, to share with Otto the place and progress of *the* Revolution. Despite her conviction that James Ford had helped instigate the removal of Otto from his leadership role in the American Party, she viewed their work in Moscow as a logical next step in the efforts to emancipate people of color around the world.

On November 19, 1930, Randolph (William W. Weinstone), the American representative to the ECCI, notified the Secretariat of the Party that the Political Committee had decided Huiswoud should come to Moscow but the Eastern Department had opposed his working in the Negro Bureau. An agreement on where he would work would have to be reached.[1] Correspondence dated December 6, 1930, to the CEC from the ECCI signed by Z. (Zigmas Aleksa) Angaretis of the International Control Commission and countersigned by Weinstone referred again to the objection by the Eastern Secretariat to Huiswoud's possible assignment in the Negro Bureau. That secretariat was the unit responsible for the Negro Subcommittee, of which Nikolai Nasanov served as chairman and Harry Haywood as vice-chairman prior to Haywood's departure for the United States in early November. The letter did not refer to the relationship between the Negro Bureau and the Party's Negro Department;

it expressed the Secretariat's fear that since Huiswoud "would be the only Negro comrade in the Bureau he would be the practical head and they did not think it advisable for one with his deviation to head the bureau as it might be misinterpreted by the party as condoning the opposition to self determination." The writer commented that he was glad to learn of Huiswoud's change of attitude on the question of self-determination. It was also stated that Huiswoud's wife should not accompany him because it was impossible to obtain living accommodations: "I am looking around for a job for her and if successful . . . I shall wire for her to come . . . The room question demands that no one be sent here upon the responsibility of the party without the approval of the Comintern."[2] The arrival of both Huiswouds five days later suggests they were already en route when Otto's assignment became an issue. A room was found for them in a Russian Trade Union hotel for foreign trade unionists.

Moscow on December 11, 1930, might have given the illusion of a beautiful winter wonderland but it was not long before both of them were afflicted with influenza. They received good medical care but had a problem obtaining meals provided at the Hotel Lux restaurant. Fortunately Juliette Stuart Poyntz, one of Hermie's former teachers at the Workers School in New York, and Shura, the maid of Ethel and Fred Ellis, helped care for them. Polyntz was working in the Woman's Commission in the Comintern, and Fred Ellis was working as a cartoonist for the Russian Trade Union organ *Trud* ("Labor"). Life in Moscow was organized in relation to the workplace. Housing, meals, and political and social contacts were determined by one's job assignment. The Huiswouds were later moved to the apartment of a trade union functionary who was away for a half year and then to a large one-room apartment with the use of communal kitchen and bath. The building was occupied by foreign trade unionists and their families. Hermie was assigned a dormitory room when she entered the Lenin School as a full-time student; Otto continued to live at the apartment when he was in Moscow.[3] Contrary to concerns about available housing expressed in communications from the ECCI, housing accommodations were satisfactory for their entire stay in Moscow.

A job was found for Hermie. She was assigned to work with translators in the International Lenin School, using her clerical skills and proficiency in English. For a few months in 1930 she had worked as a stenographer for the Central Control Commission of the Party and considered her new assignment in Moscow a "transfer."[4] Otto was assigned to work in the Anglo-American Section of the Red International of Labor Unions (RILU, or Profintern), not the Negro Bureau of the Comintern established in December 1928. The concern expressed by leaders of the American Party regarding rumors circulating based on a personal letter from George Padmore in Moscow that the Party was being condemned by the ECCI, Harry Haywood's criticism of Huiswoud at a meeting of the American Commission, and the subsequent objections to Huiswoud's assignment by the Eastern Secretariat evidently forced a change in the original plans for him to work in the Comintern. It would have been logical to have an African American in the Negro Bureau of the Comintern and Padmore in the International Trade Union Committee of Negro Workers (ITUC-NW) of the Profintern. Apparently Haywood, a student at the Lenin School, played a key role in raising sufficient doubt regarding the Comintern's consideration of Huiswoud's placement in the Negro Bureau.

The Fourth Congress of the Profintern held in March–April 1928 had recommended the establishment of a Profintern International Bureau of Negro Workers charged with "the work of drawing Negro workers into the trade unions, the creation of new independent Negro unions, the setting up of connection with Negro workers of the whole world and the unification of the wide masses of Negro Workers on the basis of class struggle." Also included was a charge to publish a special bulletin and convene an international conference of Negro workers at the end of 1929.[5] When the British government refused to allow the conference to meet in London the venue was changed to Hamburg. The vision of an international conference promulgated in the Resolution on the Negro Question that Huiswoud had helped draft in 1922 finally materialized in 1930, but Huiswoud was not there. He had traveled to the Caribbean to help recruit delegates for the conference and had hoped to be present but his assignment to the European scene did not occur until after the conference.

Despite Huiswoud's placement in the Anglo-American Section of the Profintern his reception by the Eastern Secretariat of the Comintern was still a problem. Toward the end of December he made a report to the Secretariat on the American Negro Labor Congress Convention that had been held in St. Louis on November 15–16, 1930, to launch the League of Struggle for Negro Rights (LSNR). Huiswoud prefaced his report with a statement on his own position regarding the question of self-determination and the Comintern Resolution on the Negro Question:

> In February 1930, I wrote an article in the "Communist" in which I developed a line in direct opposition to that of the C.I. as contained in the October (1928) Resolution on the Negro question. My statement was to the effect that, unlike in Africa and the West Indies, the Negro question in America was a race question and not a national question; that the oppression of the Negro in America was of a racial rather than a national colonial character, and that therefore, there was no basis for the slogan of Self-determination in the USA. My error in this respect was of a two-fold character. First, because of the prominence of the racial

distinctions and social antagonisms in the Negro question in America, I over emphasised this peculiarity of the Negro question in the USA, and secondly, my complete failure to take into consideration the difference in the position of the Negro peasantry in the south from that of the Negro industrial worker of the north. Thus I failed to understand that the agrarian problem is the very basis of the Negro national movement; that the Negro question in the United States is the question of an oppressed nation and that only through the achievement of the right of self-determination in the "Black Belt," can the oppressed Negro peasantry attain their equal rights. My opposition to the slogan of Self-determination therefore, was based on my lack of understanding of the character of the oppression of the Negro masses in the south. Here, I must say that this question was never clarified before the Party, but there was never any discussion of this important question, and that my article was allowed to appear without even being criticised. The October resolution was simply formally accepted by the Party.

Huiswoud went on to say that the recent resolution of the CI had clarified the whole question and that the three basic demands set forth in the resolution, "1. Confiscation of land by Negro farmers. 2. Establishment of the state unity of the 'Black Belt', and 3. The right of self-determination" had given concrete expression to the meaning of the slogan on self-determination. He stated, "In a recent meeting of the Political committee of the CP, USA, I have accepted fully the CI Resolution on this question, recognising my past error. I wish to restate here my full acceptance of the decisions of the CI on the Negro question."[6]

Huiswoud's brief report on the ANLC attributed the lack of success in obtaining a wide response to the fact that it did not participate in the everyday struggles of the workers, was a "highly centralized disciplinary" organization trying to combine programs of a liberation movement with trade union and defense organizations, and was oriented to the North. He reiterated that it had not received full support from the Party and that the Party membership had not yet learned that "work in non-Party mass organisations is also Communist work and that a movement based on the struggle for Negro rights must be a joint movement of Negro and white workers." The League of Struggle for Negro Rights was intended to be a joint organization of Negro and white workers and farmers who subscribed to its program of the struggle for equal rights and the right of self-determination. In the South its tasks were to include "aid in the formation of tenant-farmer, sharecropper and agricultural labourer organisations."[7] The Negro Bureau's response to Huiswoud's report did not comment on his revised attitude but expressed dissatisfaction with the Party's "old line of relegating Negro work to a special organization, instead of mobilising the Party, revolutionary unions and

United Farmers League, to organise and lead the struggles of the Negro workers and farmers." The Bureau listed eight recommendations to "make the line of the Comintern on the Negro question clear to the Party membership."[8]

Huiswoud also reported on the state of the Party and the unions to the Anglo-American Secretariat on January 11, 1931. He stated that the Party had made certain gains but that a report of the last Plenum had estimated a loss of twenty to fifty percent of the members in their unions. He viewed their shortcomings as a lack of focus, inadequate utilization of their forces, and the method by which union leaders were continually shifted and changed without the workers in the union having any say: "It is all imposed from the top down by our party fractions in the unions." He also criticized the manner in which comrades were selected for work with the unemployed: "Instead of giving political direction to this work, we pick out comrades whom we cannot put anywhere else and put them into this important work." He touched again upon the perspective held by Party members that working in different non-Party organizations was not perceived as working among the masses and that when they did engage in that work, "they go into these organizations like Brahmins—they are the superior beings and the other workers simply happen to be there." In discussing problems in the needle trade unions he cited an example of a leading comrade who insisted, "There is no discrimination in the shops against the Negroes but the only thing is that they are paid lower wages. That is all."[9]

Other hurdles that Huiswoud might have faced are unknown, for he and Hermie were welcomed warmly and seemed to adapt to the Soviet scene quite smoothly. They were aware that the Russian people were experiencing many hardships, and they expected to live in makeshift quarters, eat cafeteria-type meals, and limit their personal belongings. At first Hermie had difficulty with the idea of having a maid in the egalitarian USSR. Ethel Ellis urged that she employ their maid, Shura, when they moved, and Hermie found she gained a wonderful Russian mother substitute. "Soon, as my mother did in New York, Shura was running our home and, surreptitiously, our lives . . . When we returned home, Shura had washed and ironed whatever soiled laundry there was, she had cleaned house, marketed and there was a hot meal ready." The hot meal was actually for Otto because meals were not provided for workers in the Profintern, whereas Hermie's meals were provided in the dining room at her workplace. Shura's services were most valuable for shopping because there was no refrigeration and it was necessary to shop daily. She was quite adept at maneuvering the complex shopping at stores for rationed foods, closed groceries established solely for foreign workers, and the Arbat farmers' market offering surplus fresh produce.¹⁰ Among those welcoming the Huiswouds on their arrival was Williana Burroughs, who had worked closely with them in the U.S. Party and was employed by the *Moscow News.* Hermie has stated that Burroughs sought to have two of her younger children, Charles and Neal, educated in a society free of the racism prevailing in the United States, and "in 1931 she returned home leaving me 'in charge' of her two sons. We saw Charles almost weekly as he was at a boarding school in Moscow but Neal attended school near Leningrad."¹¹ Thus within a short time the Huiswouds were settled in Moscow with work assignments, a comfortable apartment, a maid, two "sons," and for Hermie, a new name—Helen Davis.

Hermie worked for two years with translators at the Lenin School. The typical week was one day off following five days of work. In 1931 she also worked on her free days with Ivy Low Litvinov, the English wife of Maxim Litvinov, the minister of foreign affairs. Ivy Litvinov worked at home, translating writings of Marx and Lenin into English from German and Russian texts. Hermie discontinued working on the project when she sensed an English rather than a Russian attitude toward fellow workers of color. Frequently Hermie devoted her free day to a voluntary project, or *subbotnik,* such as carting stones and dirt in a wheelbarrow for the bed of a new railway line, cleaning the Park of Culture and Rest in preparation for May Day 1931, helping on the construction of Moscow University, carting away dirt excavated for construction of the Moscow subway, weeding vegetable patches, threshing wheat, picking tobacco, or unloading a train load of potatoes. She has stated that she appreciated all the work she did because it made her conscious of the tremendous tasks entailed in production.¹²

Hermie attended classes at the Lenin School at night while she was working there. The classes, taught by Soviet professors, were provided for comrades from foreign countries who worked for the Comintern, Profintern, or foreign language units. Otto Huiswoud never attended the Lenin School or the KUTV; it was Hermie who was a student at the Lenin School. She and Peggy Dennis, wife of Eugene Dennis (Frank Waldron), were the two Americans selected by a Comintern commission to attend the regular day program in the fall of 1932. According to Peggy Dennis they studied the writings of Marx, Engels, Lenin, and Stalin, as well as the history of the Russian Revolution and the Russian Party, and also visited factories and villages to glimpse Soviet life; but they never had "direct contact and conversation with ordinary Soviet citizens."¹³ Other sources list the fourteen-month curriculum as including political economy, history of the Comintern, Leninism, historical materialism, party-building, military science, current politics, the English language, and "practical work."¹⁴

Huiswoud's assignment was far more complex, significant, and difficult to trace. Evidence of his work may be inferred from Peggy Dennis's account of her work as a "referent" for the Anglo-American Section of the Profintern. In her autobiography she described the workplace and responsibilities: "In a sprawling, colonnaded white building on the banks of the Moscow river, the Profintern was to its affiliated, independent Left federations in sixty-one countries very much what the Comintern was to the Communist Parties abroad . . . As the Section's research worker I followed the American and British newspapers and magazines, I built up an extensive clipping file and prepared data . . . gave reports to our weekly Sections meetings . . . wrote articles for the Profintern's news bulletin and for Soviet newspapers and radio."[15] This description and that of George Padmore provide clues to Huiswoud's responsibilities. It would appear that in the beginning his major responsibility was to collect data, prepare reports, and coordinate activities related to the work of the Profintern concerned with organization of workers in the African Diaspora.

In *The Life and Struggles of Negro Toilers* Padmore described the Profintern as the only international organization that conducted "a consistent and permanent struggle against white chauvinism, for equal rights for the labour movement in the colonial and semi-colonial countries, for the correct solution of the national-race problem." It is interesting that he placed so much emphasis on white chauvinism and was quite blunt in claiming the Profintern had "to some extent succeeded in overcoming white chauvinism in its ranks," and "corrected the mistakes of its American section which formerly ignored work among the Negroes."[16] His statements assigning special responsibility to "revolutionary unions to bring the white workers into the struggle on behalf of the Negro demands" echoed the position that had been expressed frequently by African American comrades. Huiswoud must have been disappointed and annoyed by the conflict over his assignment, but he could only have viewed the role granted him by the Profintern to implement such a mission on the international level as a reward. It was an appropriate sequel to his leadership at the national level and completely consistent with the struggle he had mounted for years within the movement.

Throughout the twenties African Americans had been involved with the Comintern primarily as delegates to conferences or students at the University of the Toilers of the East (KUTV), founded in 1921, or the International Lenin School (ILS), founded in 1926, but the next decade witnessed the assignment of African Americans to posts in the Profintern. Two years after James W. Ford joined the party in Chicago he was launched on a meteoric rise in Moscow as a delegate to the Fourth Profintern Congress in March–

April 1928, where he was elected to its executive committee. While serving on the committee he attended the Sixth Congress of the Comintern, held from July to September 1928; the Tenth Enlarged Plenum of the executive committee in July 1929; and in the same month, the Second Congress of the League against Imperialism in Frankfurt where he was elected to the general council and its executive committee.[17] The Profintern assigned Ford to establish an office for the International Trade Union Committee of Negro Workers (ITUC-NW) and make arrangements for the Hamburg conference advanced at the Fourth Congress of the Profintern. Later George Padmore was added to the team. Padmore had attended the League against Imperialism and for National Independence congress with Ford and returned home. On a second trip with William Z. Foster in December 1929 to report to the Profintern on the establishment of the Trade Union Unity League (TUUL) in August and its Cleveland convention, the United States refused to grant Padmore a reentry permit.[18] By that turn of events Padmore was employed by the Profintern. As of January 1, 1930, he was certified as "a manager of Negro Workers' Committee."[19] With the transfer of Huiswoud to Moscow in December 1930 African American comrades could claim not just one man on the international front but three: Ford, Padmore, and Huiswoud.

Ford arrived in Hamburg on November 16, 1929, to establish an office for the ITUC-NW and develop relationships with various cooperating units such as the International of Seamen and Harbour Workers (ISH), the bureau of the Revolutionary Trade Union Opposition, the Hamburg Party, the League against Imperialism, and the printer used by the German party. The conference, held July 7–8, 1930, was attended by seventeen delegates representing South Africa, Nigeria, Gambia, Sierra Leone, the Gold Coast, the Cameroons, Jamaica, Trinidad, and the United States. It not only served as a networking meeting to establish the committee but generated contacts beyond the participants, published propaganda bulletins, letters, and journals to expose the oppressive living conditions of workers in various colonies, and inspired the creation of communist or sympathetic cadres throughout Africa, the Caribbean, and the United States. At the conference the provisional committee became the nine-member executive committee with Ford as general secretary.

In a letter dated February 13, 1931, from Padmore to Ford, Padmore delineated the central and most important function in Hamburg: "a) to work among the Negro seamen who arrived in Hamburg trying to build up cadres among them so that they can be used by us in establishing direct contacts with the colonies and b) making indirect connections with all working class organizations as well as individuals in those parts of Africa and the West Indies where we have no sections or adherents of the RILU at the present time." He went on to indicate that his office would take care of the United States, "where conditions are very bad in the movement," and advised that the name *Negro Worker* would be assigned to the committee's publication, the *International Negro Workers' Review,* begun in January.[20] In November 1928 J. A. Rogers announced in the *Pittsburgh Courier* the appearance in France of a new publication, *L'Ouvrier Nègre* ("The Negro Worker"),[21] but that publication issued by Red Aid International (MOPR) ceased after the establishment of the ITUC-NW. Thus, issue number 3 of the ITUC-NW's publication carried a new title, the *Negro Worker.*

The mode of operation of the ITUC-NW was similar to David Walker's reliance on African American seamen to distribute protest literature in the South one hundred years earlier. Seamen in major ports of Europe, such as Hamburg, Antwerp, Rotterdam, London, Liverpool, and Marseille, were to be the contact to distribute literature, develop potential converts, and establish links to local subcommittees in Africa and the Caribbean. The pattern of relying on seamen to reach the far corners of the globe was widely used by the colonial section of the International of Seamen and Harbour Workers (ISH). The ITUC-NW office was established in a building at 8 Rothesoodstrasse that served as one of the most active headquarters of the Communist Party in Germany and a center for Comintern activities. It was strategically located just a few streets from the harbor, and the front part of the building housed the International Seamen's Club, unofficially referred to as the "Red Marine." It was the model for clubs established for seamen in port cities on the continent.[22]

Correspondence and reports throughout the year from Ford in Hamburg to Padmore at the Negro Bureau of the Profintern revealed tremendous activity and distribution of hundreds of materials but also problems such as shortage of personnel, lack of cooperation by communist units or individuals, failure of writers to supply regular articles for the journal, difficulty in sending and receiving mail, the lack of key local contacts in certain countries, complications due to a spy, and the difficulty seamen had going ashore in some African ports where the ships had to anchor offshore, not to mention surveillance and investigation by the police. In April, Ford informed Padmore that his work "consisted of organizing the colonial section with sub-groups, Chinese, Indian and Negro. Each sub section has charge of carrying out the tasks with regards to organization and agitation among the seamen of its group," including arranging excursions to visit Soviet ships, taking up grievances of the seamen and placing them before the International of Seamen and Harbour Workers Secretariat, discussing with the seamen the general situation in their respective countries, and briefing European comrades directly connected with colonial work. As a concrete example of an object lesson on ship organization he described a meeting with a group of seamen on board their ship where they discussed the Scottsboro case. He had a resolution drawn up that they enthusiastically endorsed.[23] In August, Padmore reminded Ford of the focus of his work, informed him of the appointment of an editorial board to be "politically responsible for the line" of the *Negro Worker,* and requested that he send a report of the committee's work and a plan for the next six months. In September 1931, Ford was assigned back to the United States, and Padmore arrived in Hamburg around December 1 to assume direct responsibility for the work of the ITUC-NW and editorship of the *Negro Worker.*

Meanwhile, among the materials Huiswoud prepared were two articles on British Guiana and one on the Congo for the *Negro Worker,* and one on "The Effects of Unemployment on the Negro Masses in the U.S.A." for *International Press Correspondence (Inprecorr).* He chaired meetings of the Negro Committee of the Profintern to help the International Red Aid develop an international program for the defense of the Scottsboro case. He also participated in meetings of the Negro Bureau on the situation in the South African Federation of Trade Unions (AFTU).[24] It is not clear what his title was during 1931. In 1932 he was listed as chairman of the Trade Union Committee of Negro Workers with a salary of 275 rubles, raised to 300 rubles in September.[25] When Padmore shifted to Hamburg reports were submitted to Huiswoud.

Padmore's first report on November 16, 1931, reveals a continuation of problems: the office was "in a perfect mess"; he could not find Ford's files; a key comrade in Berlin had a "bureaucrate [sic] attitude" and "behaved like a real chauvinist;" he could not work in the seamen's club because it was being raided daily; articles for the *Negro Worker* were desperately needed; and there was concern that "K's [Kouyaté's] method of struggling against the opportunists, Faure and others, took on too much of a black versus mulatto affair and lacked real political contents."[26] Huiswoud's lengthy report during sessions of the Eighth Central Soviet of the Profintern in December reflected tremendous frustration: "The national sections of the RILU in spite of the adoption of the resolutions at the 5th Congress on the work among the Negro workers have not translated this resolution into action. . . . With the result that we find that in these colonies, practically no work on the part of the sections of the RILU, not even in the metropolitan countries. We must ask our French comrades, since the 5th Congress of the RILU, to give us an idea of what work was done among the French colonists, what work has been done by the French section of the RILU among the 50,000 Negro workers in France." He continued by castigating the British: "our British comrades have not up to date taken the first steps in beginning some actual work amongst the colonies."[27] This problem had been noted seven years earlier by Ho Chi Minh at the Fifth Congress of the Comintern: "As for our Communist Parties in Great Britain, Holland, Belgium, and other countries—what have they done to cope with the colonial invasions . . . from the day they accepted Lenin's political program to educate the working class of their countries in the spirit of just internationalism, and that of close contact with the working masses in the colonies? What our Parties have done in this domain is almost worthless."[28]

In his report Huiswoud granted that there was the beginning of some work in the United States and cited how six thousand African American miners, nearly one-fifth of the total strikers, participated in the miners' strike in Pennsylvania. He considered the work of the TUUL among African Americans, however, "too abstract, too general" and not attempting to draw workers in basic industries into the TUUL and the communist movement. He also reported on the implications of unemployment among workers in the United States, South Africa, Rhodesia, Sierra Leone, and Cuba where workers from Jamaica and Haiti were being returned home; taxation in South Africa, West Africa, and the Belgian Congo; strikes in South Africa and Haiti; and enrollment in the West African Army. He asserted that while the Negro Committee of the Profintern could register progress particularly in widening its contacts and rendering political and organizational aid to workers in the colonies, its work had been "largely of a propagandist character" and "not able to make even at the present time, Africa the centre of gravity of its work and to begin actually the organizational work on this Continent."[29] To Huiswoud it was necessary to carry the struggle into the heart of Africa and for national sections of the Profintern to become involved in drawing together workers of both races in the battle against colonialism and imperialism.

Some of the discontent Huiswoud expressed in the Profintern session was reiterated months later in the report on the United States presented at the Twelfth Plenary Session of the Executive Committee of the Comintern on September 9, 1932. He described graphically the economic plight of African American workers who had been hit the hardest by unemployment in both the North and South. He used the workers' activities at Camp Hill in Alabama, the Scottsboro case, and the miners' strike to illustrate the readiness of African Americans to fight for their rights and the good opportunities for revolutionary labor unions to organize those workers despite bourgeois anticommunist organizations such as The National Negro Organization for Struggle against Communists and Atheists and the Association for Struggle against Radicalism and Communism among Negroes. He asked, "Since the time of the eleventh plenary session, are we entitled to say that the Party has actually improved upon its work among Negroes?" His response was negative: "Our red labor unions which, according to the task assigned to them by the fourteenth plenary session of our Party, should have become a genuine arena for our work among the Negroes, have done practically nothing up to the present moment in the matter organizing the Negro workers . . . We have not yet learned how to fight the battles of the Negro masses on the ground of their everyday demands and needs." He stressed the laxity of the Party regarding work in the South and the lack of attention given to training new staff drawn from the rank and file. He pressed for an energetic campaign against lynching and Negro disfranchisement.[30]

Throughout 1932 the activities and publications of the ITUC-NW proceeded with some accomplishments along with many frustrations. Success depended not only upon the publication and widespread distribution of literature exposing atrocities perpetrated throughout Africa, the colonies, and the United States but also on the cooperation of other organizations both in and outside the Profintern. Their ambitious plan assigned to one functionary establishment of ITUC-NW subcommittees in the ports and colonies, the organization of Negro workers' trade unions, and the training of cadres with the assistance of Profintern sections and national parties. It was also expected that a relationship would be established with a host of related communist organizations such as the AFTU, CGTU, ILD, ILU, ISH, KUTV, LAI, MOPR, and TUUL. It is not surprising that there were constant complaints of lack of cooperation. One example noted "the RILU Sections despite all the appeals of the RILU have not rendered any real assistance to the HC [Hamburg Committee, or ITUC-NW] during 1932. In the case of the French and USA sections instead of helping they have just sabotaged and hindered us as has been indicated in the case of the sub-committee."[31] Padmore had confided in Huiswoud almost one year earlier how difficult it was to find indigenous revolutionary recruits: "But when we ask them to begin the work, they say for their justification: We have no one, who can begin the work . . . The Communists do not appear from nowhere, or from African woods . . . You must not be excited by paper achievements. We must say frankly we do have nothing in Africa. We do not gather prepared bolsheviks on the banks of Congo or Nile."[32]

The year had begun with an account in the January–February 1932 issue of the *Negro Worker* of raids on the committee office and confiscation of publications by the Hamburg police during December.[33] The year ended with a similar raid and with Padmore's arrest, two-week detention, and deportation. Padmore's letter in March to Moscow from Paris indicated that following his release from prison in Hamburg he was placed on a British ship with a British Criminal Investigation Division (CID) agent and landed in Britain without funds. He was followed by CID officers the entire time. He found some humor in his predicament: "Our propaganda in Africa has certain [*sic*] been successful. The C. I. D. officers had a list of all our stuff to be confiscated wherever found. They made inquiries about 'the famous' Mr. G. P., whom I professed not to know, only having read about (laughter). They were very bitter in their denunciation of this 'bastard.'" As soon as Arnold Ward of the Negro Welfare Association (NWA) of London arranged a loan he left England for France. He was staying with an Indo-Chinese comrade introduced by Garan Kouyaté and after long discussions with some comrades decided to continue the work from Paris using space provided by the French Negro Sub-Committee. He explained, "There is no difficulty in printing the 'N.W.' here as the French know that 'their' blacks don't read English & they have no particular love for the England [*sic*]." There were suggestions for security and a plea for immediate money to be able to continue the work: "My position here is one like a rat just rescued from drowning awaiting the sun."[34] Hence the operation was established in Paris with the *Negro Worker* printed there and distributed to various ports.

The Profintern Secretariat reviewed Padmore's report covering November 1931 to December 1932 and found achievements such as establishing contacts and forming groups of seamen in Great Britain and France as well as numerous shortcomings. They were particularly concerned about "insufficient consolidation of the connections established and feeble leadership in the organisation of sub-committees," etc. They reminded him of the measures listed in the 1931 resolution establishing the committee and emphasized that "the inactivity of the TUUL has considerably hindered the development of work in the West Indies." The usual types of recommendations were made, such as building "trade union groups appropriate to the enterprises, plantations and nature of employment"; building "agitation and propaganda activity around the concrete questions that arise in each colony"; strengthening the subcommittees in France and Britain to involve Negro workers in a united front with white and colored workers; organizing subcommittees in Trinidad and South Africa and laying stress upon the organization of the unemployed." The International of Seamen and Harbour Workers was reminded again of its responsibility to carry on the whole work "connected with the organisation of Negro seamen in the motherlands and colonies . . . It is the task of the Hamburg Committee to render systematic aid and collaboration to the ISH in the mobilisation of the masses of Negro seamen."[35]

The "Resolution on the Report on the Work of the Hamburg Committee" by the Profintern Secretariat was followed by a letter to Padmore in March 1933 from "J" indicating that "as a result of the last events" the committee would be working under a new name in its new sphere, International Committee for Mutual Aid to Negro Workers, and offered "comradely criticism:"

> In connection with the change we must stress the importance of our connection with you. We cannot allow such a situation as existed before to continue, namely, your activities must be based on a skillful combination of legal, semi-legal and illegal methods of work as the occasion arises. We want to call your attention in a comradely manner to the fact that you must radically change your method of work. Concretely and firstly not to leave so many traces of yourself not in your mass work but on a quite personal basis. Not only should not you speak in open meetings but create an *"active"* around you through which you must work in your present place and in the other place.
>
> It is important to stress here the absolute necessity for collective work and not individualist business relationships. In this respect there is much to be required of you in the way of quitting some of your inclinations in this direction. You have a good opportunity for collective work now . . .
>
> On the same basis of comradely criticism we must draw your attention to the fact that it is the general opinion that you are not entirely blameless in regard to the incidents in the other place. We advise you comradely to treat our proposals in this letter seriously and avoid further complication on this head in your future work . . .
>
> We want to draw your attention to the question of selection of students. It is intolerable for you to send people that you don't know. And we find ourselves in a difficult position in regard to your last choice . . . As a rule you have no right to send people whom you have not thoroughly investigated from every aspect.
>
> We are rather astonished at your information that you have sent somebody to the WI [West Indies], on your own account. We would like to know what reason you had to send this person on your own initiative. Whose advice did you act on? It is true the American comrades have been passive in this respect but it is wrong to send somebody whom we don't know and whom you also probably don't know well, on such responsible work . . .
>
> The WI affair and the student affair show that you have not orientated yourself correctly in accordance with our requirements and our special situation.[36]

The Profintern's letter went on to recommend using the French comrades and "our" organizations, stressing caution in sending mail and warning against mentioning work in private letters. A subsequent letter dated June 5 from "Jack" in a friendly tone requested information on Padmore's relationship with the French comrades in the Confederation General du Travail Unitaire (CGTU) and on Kouyaté and the publication of *Le Cri des Nègres*. A second letter the same date from "Zus. [Alexander Zusmanovich] & M." commented on the scarcity of Padmore's letters for the last months and also inquired about the French publication *Cri,* his present connections with the Negro Welfare Association in London, and the Liberian question.[37] Huiswoud was not mentioned in the correspondence probably because at the time he was out of Moscow on a special mission. His involvement was yet to come.

Life in the Party was always serious but there were occasional lighter moments. For the Huiswouds work in the USSR was interspersed with cultural events. Huiswoud was able to obtain plush first-tier center box seats reserved for Soviet government officials and special guests at the Bolshoi Theater that had been reserved for the tsar. They visited Leningrad as tourists. In February 1932 Hermie traveled to Germany to renew her passport. While they were in Europe Huiswoud traveled with a Dutch passport but Hermie used her U.S. passport, which required renewal periodically at an embassy of the United States. That summer they rented a room in a dacha available to employees of the Profintern in the Silver Forest above the banks of the Moscow River, where they went on free days. Many friends visited them to enjoy the beach and picnics in the meadow. It was there that they met Maria Ulianova, the surviving sister of Lenin, who gave them "special attention when she learned that Otto had spoken to her brother, Lenin, on his sickbed shortly before his death." Hermie described her as "a charming, soft-spoken, tiny elderly lady who lived in a little cottage. The wooden building was decorated with fretwork in typical Russian design. There was a little garden in front paled off with white pickets . . . To complete the Russian picture, there was a cherry tree and two birch trees like sentinels overlooking the pallisades [*sic*] that dropped down to the river. Our hostess offered us cake made from the cherries . . . I felt as if we were in a scene of one of Checkov's plays."[38] In October of that year Hermie spent her annual one-month vacation in the republic of Georgia to undergo a "mineral water and mountain air cure." The trip entailed four days of train travel "across the Trans-Caucasus to the Caspian Sea, through the desert with camel caravans, oases and cliff dwellers, down to Baku and the oil fields then across Georgia to Tiflis and then once more westward across the Caucasus to Borzhom on the Turkish border."[39]

In the summer of 1932 the scene was enlivened by the arrival of twenty-two African Americans who had been recruited to act in a movie, *Black and White,* to be produced by the Meschrabpom Film Corporation in Moscow. The group had been recruited by the Co-operating Committee for Production of a Soviet Film on Negro Life, an interracial and international committee chaired by W. A. Domingo.[40] Langston Hughes, invited to join the group as a scriptwriter, and two recruits with stage experience were the only professionals prepared to work on such a project. The others who had enlisted were not established actors. They were volunteers eager to spend a free summer in the USSR and willing to pay their own advance $90 fare to Leningrad. They set sail on the large steamship *Europa* from New York on June 14 for Bremerhaven, Germany, where they proceeded to Berlin, Stettin, Helsinki, Leningrad, and Moscow. Louise Thompson Patterson, who assisted in recruitment and arrangements, described them as a "gay group of young adventurers."[41] They partied all the way and were thrilled by the terrific reception they received, the accommodations in the prime Grand Hotel located one block from Red Square, the fine food despite famine in parts of the land, and the payment of four hundred rubles per month. Hughes singled out the one missing homelike provision—"And no Jim-Crow."[42]

Keen disappointment was soon to follow for the Soviets as well as for the budding actors. Patterson noted that "it was hard for the Russians to believe they were facing twenty-two Negroes—for we were of all color shades from mulatto to black. Then we didn't square with their concept of working class folk, for we were students, writers, professionals and white collar workers who first saw the inside of a steel mill or any factory in the USSR . . . and they were to find out quickly that most of the group knew no Negro folk songs, some could not carry a tune nor dance a step."[43] More important was the bitter reality that the script was ill-conceived because the scenarist had no personal experience with the United States and relied on literature like *Uncle Tom's Cabin*. In Hughes's judgment the script was "a pathetic hodgepodge of good intentions and faulty facts . . . improbable to the point of ludicrousness"[44] and did not lend itself to a rewrite.

Some accounts of the film debacle attributed the cancellation of the film to the Soviets' foreign policy at the time, but Hughes, who knew the serious deficits of the script, stated, "So when the best minds of the Soviet film industry declared the scenario of *Black and White* artistically weak and unsound; and when they said that they felt it could not do justice to the oppressed and segregated Negroes of the world, or serve to further enlighten Soviet movie audiences, there could hardly have been a better reason for the postponement of the film."[45] Hermie also recognized that the deficiency was not due solely to lack of knowledge about African American life: "My experience at the time was that Russians interpreting such matters artistically, held a stereotyped view of what workers and bosses behaved and looked like, as well as black people."[46] African Americans were passionate about overcoming stereotyped images, and the group could not have been associated with such a portrayal in discrimination-free Russia, where the group had found, as Patterson put it, "our color a badge of honor."[47] While attempts were being made to remedy the script the group was sent on an excursion to Odessa to cruise the Black Sea. When the final decision was made to abandon the project the group was offered several options: a ten-day tour of Central Asia, passage home via Paris, or remaining in the USSR. Most of the group selected the tour, conducted by Huiswoud; Hughes and six others extended their stay in Moscow. The longest stays were by Homer Smith, who remained for fourteen years during which time he served as a consultant to the postal system and journalist for American newspapers, and Wyland Rudd, who worked in the theater, became a Soviet citizen, and died there in 1952.

While on tour to Central Asia the group visited African American agronomists working on two-year contracts in the Tashkent area. After Oliver John Golden's scheme to develop a program in the South was not accepted by the Party he conceived of recruiting African American agriculture specialists to assist the USSR. He sought the assistance of George Washington Carver, head of the agriculture department of Tuskegee Normal and Industrial Institute, to recruit specialists in all branches of agriculture. The contracts signed with the USSR Ministry of Agriculture stipulated a salary of one hundred fifty to two hundred dollars per month, sick benefit insurance, free medical and hospital service, and a month's vacation with full pay and free transportation to summer resorts.[48] The terms were well beyond those available to African Americans in the United States. Golden returned to the USSR in 1931 with a group that included Welton Curry, Frank Faison, C. T. Hopkins, A. M. Overton, Bernard Powers, John Sutton, George Tynes, Joseph J. Roane, and Charles N. Young, some of whom were graduates of Hampton Institute, Tuskegee Institute, Howard University, and Wilberforce University. Many were assigned with Golden to an experimental station in Yangi-Yul, a small village in Uzbekistan about forty arduous miles from the capital, Tashkent, and almost four thousand miles from Moscow. They grew cotton, sugar beets, peanuts, and other crops and were credited with introducing an important new strain of cotton. A few experts extended their contracts; some married Russian women. Tynes, who bred poultry on various farms, chose to remain and became a Soviet citizen. Sutton worked on an improved strain of rice at the Rice Institute and remained there until 1938.[49] Later he explained to Elton Fax that the family of the Russian woman he married had no objection to him, a Black man. "After all, the Russians worship the memory of Pushkin, who . . . went out of his way to extoll the virtues of his African ancestry. My being an *American,* however, did raise a few doubts with them."[50] Golden's first wife, Bessie (known as Jane), who had accompanied him to Moscow when he attended the KUTV, had died there in 1925. On the second trip he was accompanied by Bertha Bialek, who was active in the Party in New York. In 1934 they were moved from Yangi-Yul to Tashkent, where he taught at the Tashkent Institute of Irrigation and Mechanization of Agriculture and she taught English at the Institute of Foreign Languages and the Central Asia State University.[51] Golden had worked with Huiswoud, Moore, Briggs, and Burroughs in the Party in New York, and Huiswoud was delighted to visit the project in 1932 with the theater group.

Langston Hughes left the group in Ashkhabad to explore Central Asia on his own for five months. He returned to Tashkent and spent a bitter cold Christmas 1932 with the Goldens in Yangi-Yul. Then he returned to Moscow to work as a member of the International Union of Revolutionary Writers. During this period he produced some of his most controversial works. Like McKay, who had been invited to be an author in residence ten years earlier, Hughes found the USSR to be the first place he could make a living as a writer and feel free of the burden of race. He remarked that he found himself forgetting that the Russians were white folks.[52] Contrary to McKay, however, his relationship with the Huiswouds evolved in a positive manner, and during his sojourn in Moscow a lifetime friendship was established. Hermie recalled his arrival after several years without contact:

> As the key was turning in the door, I heard a gusty boyish laughter which proved to have come from Langston. He was still chuckling gleefully as they entered—my husband, he and Loren Miller. He flung himself full length on his back on the divan after greetings were exchanged, with a contented sigh . . . They had just come from the Kremlin where the group had been received by Stalin . . .
>
> We had taken a summer place in the Silver Forest . . . Many a day, during the month of July, some of the group would come out to visit, swim and later romp in the forest. Almost on every occasion Langston would be among them. I remember one day, while sitting on the beach, a group of children surrounded us and posed the usual children's questions . . . Langston was amazed to learn that that little boy, that distance away knew all about the Scottsboro Boys . . . Other children joined in the conversation and they told us they had sent a petition from their school pleading for the Scottsboro Boys' release . . .
>
> During those months of his stay in Moscow, he kept busy writing. Now and again, he would show me a short story manuscript which resulted in "The Ways of White folks."[53]

While Hughes was in the USSR he wrote the poem "Goodbye, Christ," which would haunt him in later years. It is not surprising that five poems and an essay found their way, undoubtedly through the Huiswouds, to the *Negro Worker*. The poem might not have been noticed if it had not been reprinted in *Negro* by Nancy Cunard in 1934. In 1933 he wrote to Carl Van Vechten that he liked some of the poems written then "as well as anything I ever did."[54] But in the McCarthy era his responses were disclaimers regarding publication. When the attack on Hughes arose he did not identify who might have been responsible for including the poem in the November–December 1932 issue of the *Negro Worker;* he insisted that it appeared without his knowledge or permission.[55] Clearly his aim was to maintain his integrity, his voice as a writer, and the close friendship established with the Huiswouds. Huiswoud was in South Africa part of the time Hughes was in Moscow, and Hermie and "Lang," as she called him, continued to attend any theatrical production that could fit into their schedules—Shakespeare, the Jewish and Gypsy repertory theaters, opera, ballet, symphony concerts. They were pals who thoroughly enjoyed the Russian cultural scene. They often visited friends, and the night before Hughes departed for home there was a lively farewell party at the Ellises. On June 7 friends gathered for a grand send-off at the Moscow railway station.[56] Had Hughes been able to see the report by the police of the International Settlement on "Movements of James Langston Hughes, American Nigger Writer, in Japan" filed by the American consulate general in Shanghai on August 28, 1933, he would have been reminded that he was not far from home in the United States.[57]

The Russian children's reference to the Scottsboro Boys that had impressed Hughes was an indication of the extensive publicity about the trial of nine young African American men accused of raping two white women on a train in Alabama on March 25, 1931. The International Labor Defense (ILD) had not only taken charge of the legal defense but had mounted national and international campaigns to pressure the United States to adhere to justice instead of southern mores. As Henry Lee Moon has pointed out, Scottsboro represented to the communists "much more than a defense of nine unfortunate lads. It was an attack on the system which had exploited them, fostered the poverty and ignorance in which they were reared and finally victimized them by legal proceedings which were a mockery of justice."[58] In the United States there were mass rallies all over the country. Huiswoud, Moore, and Briggs contributed wholeheartedly to the campaigns even though they were operating miles apart. Moore made four cross-country tours to raise money and sympathy for the defense, some with relatives of the boys and one of the accusers, Ruby Bates, who had recanted and admitted that rape had never taken place. He accompanied four of the mothers of the accused to the White House in May 1934 to seek the intervention of President Franklin Roosevelt but the president refused to see them. J. Louis Engdahl toured sixteen countries in Europe for six months with one of the mothers, Mrs. Ada Wright, and died of exhaustion and pneumonia on November 21, 1933, after they arrived in Moscow. Despite the reversal of the testimony of one of the women who accused the young men, the case dragged on for over nineteen years, with appeals to the Supreme Court before the last of the young men,

Andrew Wright, who was nineteen years old when arrested, was released. Hughes, like many other writers, added to the protests with poems, essays, and a play that became part of the legacy of the Harlem Renaissance.

At the end of 1932 Huiswoud was to revisit problems associated with the Resolution on the Negro Question promulgated in 1928. This time it was in connection with South Africa. In his article "World Aspects of the Negro Question," which had been so roundly attacked, he had noted that the Negro question in Africa had all the characteristic features of the national-colonial question. At the outset he had accepted that the resolution applied to South Africa, but white communists who had been in leadership there for years resisted the proposed change in policy on the basis that it substituted a form of nationalism for the struggle of both races against class differences.

Josiah Gumede, a founding father and leader of the African National Congress (ANC), and James La Guma, a representative of the Communist Party of South Africa, had both attended the 1927 League against Imperialism congress in Brussels and served with Moore on the Committee on the Negro Question. They visited the USSR following the congress and were also invited to return to Moscow for the tenth anniversary of the Bolshevik revolution. On both occasions discussions on the severe situation in South Africa were held with various Comintern officials. A draft "Resolution on the South African Question" drawn up by the ECCI was circulated for consideration in South Africa prior to the Comintern's Sixth Congress to be held in Moscow. Strong opposing arguments were put forth prior and during the congress. Stephen Ellis and Tsepo Sechaba have described the dismay of many South African communists because "they were being instructed to forego work with the group still seen as the vanguard, white workers, in favour of working with blacks—not for an immediate socialist transition, their objective, but for a black-governed republic. In the context of South Africa in 1928 it appeared an almost preposterous aim."[59] On the other hand, La Guma recognized the potential of the growing militancy and strike action on the part of Africans to fight for their own liberation: "The argument that the movement depends to a large extent if not solely upon the European workers does not carry much weight if we bear in mind the opposition of the part of the rank and file European labour to co-operation with Blacks, and their further realisation that their privileges and concessions are obtained at the expense of the Black workers."[60] The resolution called for South Africa to "combine the fight against all anti-native laws with the general political slogan in the fight against British domination, the slogan of *an independent native South African republic as a stage towards a workers' and peasants' republic, with full, equal rights for all races, black, coloured and white.*"[61]

Once the resolution was passed, Sidney P. Bunting, chairman of the party executive committee along with other white leaders in opposition, resolved to try to implement it but the result was continued dissension in the Party, expulsions, and a loss in membership. The difference in opinion on the new direction was not the only complication. Demands for Bolshevization and the campaign against an alleged "right danger" were judged by some party members as Comintern policies that added to the Party's internal strife.[62] Surely the harassment of communists by the South African government was a factor that affected Party growth and stabilization, along with the complexities of the brutal, segregated life of the African workers, whose lives were constantly in jeopardy. To be a Black Communist in South Africa was to court deportation, detention, or death. When large numbers did join the party around an issue during mass rallies or demonstrations, the Party did not have the ability to sustain work or to train cadres. It was not long before the South African Party was in disarray, along with various related organizations.

An American, Eugene Dennis, was designated by the Comintern to evaluate the situation in South Africa and try to reverse the damage. He went there in the spring of 1932 after a similar assignment for a year in the Philippines. His ambitious mission included organizing the work of the central committee, guiding the Politburo, establishing functioning organizations, preparing a national recruiting program, establishing an illegal Party apparatus, and arranging for selecting and sending students to Moscow schools.[63] His reports from South Africa dealt with problems in the unions as well as in the Party and occasionally referred to the "International Trade Union Committee of Negro Workers" or the "Hamburg Committee"(ITUC-NW). For example, he clarified in one report on September 13, 1932, that the Profintern had issued instructions from the Profintern to have the Seamen and Harbour Workers Union (S&HWU) in Cape Town, a section of the African Federation of Trade Unions, apply for affiliation to the ITUC-NW. When he learned that they had applied for affiliation, he instructed comrades "to apply for affiliation to the International Seamen and Harbour Workers Union and for the union to maintain *fraternal* relations with the Hamburg Committee in accordance with the line laid down by the Polit Commission in January . . . Namely, that in those countries where sections of the RILU are already in existence, i.e. TUUL in the USA, AFTU in South Africa—all trade union groups, unions, etc. organized shall *not* affiliate to the Hamburg Committee." He declared that the policy was "fundamentally correct and until instructed by the CI, the directives of Profintern which if universally applied will lay the basis for building a Black International Trade Union Centre—will not be acted upon." He went on to state that the organizational activities in South West Africa, Tanganyika, Nyasaland, and Portuguese East Africa carried on through the Seamen and Harbour Workers Union were being directed from the center in South Africa.⁶⁴ Obviously the policy of the Comintern as interpreted by Dennis was intended to limit the power of the ITUC-NW.

Huiswoud and the Hamburg Committee of the Profintern had been monitoring the situation in the African Federation of Trade Unions. Among their sources of information was T. Jackson (Albert Nzula), a member of the committee who had been secretary of the federation in 1929. Just a month before Dennis's report, Huiswoud reported at the August 9 meeting of the Negro Committee that the AFTU had diminished to a skeleton organization and measures had to be taken to overcome its imminent collapse. Committee members considered that the AFTU was underestimating the work of "reformist" groups and questioned the tactics the union might use for a proposed United Front Conference.⁶⁵ Jackson's report to the Negro Bureau of the Profintern on August 26 implied that prejudice might be one reason the federation had very few white members. He mentioned that the majority of the dock workers' unions and most of the railway workers were white and both groups were chauvinistic. On the other hand, he found that the mainly Dutch Unemployed Workers' Union (UWU) committee encouraged the native workers to participate in the movement.⁶⁶ Evidently race relations in South Africa was not the only problem. The seeming divergence of interpretations on turf and responsibilities reflected the confusion and conflict that could exist within the multilayered central bureaucracy as well as in hinterland operations. By the end of the year Huiswoud was dispatched to South Africa by the Profintern to assess and assist the AFTU.

Huiswoud was a good candidate for such a mission. He spoke English and Dutch and his appearance allowed him to move about in various groups without being too noticeable. His report, dated July 2, 1933, confirmed that the AFTU as a national organization was "practically non-existant," its situation "catastrophic." Organizational weaknesses in Cape Town, Durban, and Johannesburg among the miners, agriculture workers, laundry workers, and the unemployed were identified. The working conditions that were mentioned, such as the miners' workday that ran from 3 A.M. to 4 P.M. and the restriction permitting the unemployed only seven days to find work in an area, suggested that there were many factors beyond the control of the AFTU that inhibited party activity. A major problem was that party work depended entirely upon local forces, "most of whom have received no training whatever and are carrying on activities without any real conception of the proper methods of work and the tasks to be carried out." The growing unemployment was perceived as a potential for the rapid development of a strong unemployment movement, but it required a persistent struggle in the ranks "against the attitude that it is of no use organizing the white unemployed because they are white chauvinists and it is impossible to draw them in for a real joint struggle with the native workers."

Within the few months that Huiswoud was in South Africa, structures, elections, programs of work, and activities such as go-slow strikes and hunger marches were organized, organizers were appointed, and preparation made for conferences for marine, mine, agricultural, and railroad transport workers. United front unemployment conferences were held in Johannesburg, Cape Town, and Durban. An underlying problem was revealed in the statement that putting the first steps into effect required "a relentless struggle against the traditional resistance toward mass trade union work . . . against the underestimation of and the wrong policies pursued in the united front struggles and the left sectarian attitude towards work in the reformist and national reformist unions and organizations."[67] While Huiswoud's report did not cite the portion of the 1928 Comintern resolution that urged the Party to pay particular attention to national organizations such as the African National Congress, it was clear that many South African comrades did not appreciate either the growing strength of the ANC nor an infiltration strategy. The resolution was quite specific: "The Party while retaining its full independence, should participate in these organisations, should seek to broaden and extend their activity. Our aim should be to transform the African National Congress into a fighting nationalist revolutionary organisation."[68] How long could the shot in the arm administered by Dennis and Huiswoud last? The major task of developing "a real revolutionary Trade Union Center in South Africa" required training of cadres.

Recruitment of students for various levels of education within the communist system was always mentioned as an essential part of the operation, and the ITUC-NW constantly strove to identify potential candidates who might be recommended for either school in Moscow. A confidential letter from a South African student, J. Warren (Moses Kotane), on November 30, 1932, revealed that even at the highest level students' experiences were not free of racial problems. He complained that "a nasty opinion prevails in the American section . . . the AUTHORITIVE body of all the English speaking sections in the Communist International." He stated, "The opinion PREVALENT in the American section of the Communist International about the Negroes does not differ very much to that of Bunting, that is, the Negroes are merely opportunists and place-seekers in the Communist movement." After pointing out that the African American students were mostly still young boys who had joined the movement only three to six months previously and were not representatives of American Negro workers, he addressed the main thrust of his letter, which was to convey how ill-prepared he felt to assume leadership in South Africa:

> The Comintern speaks about the Negroes taking the leadership of the Communist movement in South Africa. Why? Because they are the majority . . . 6 to 1. But so far as Communism and Communist theory is concerned the whites are the ideological leaders. First because most of them are all European products brought up under different circumstances and inherit a historical tradition peculiar to European capitalism and European working class struggles as such. Joanes has had a chance of almost 3 years training in the ILS and sent to S. Africa well equipped theoretically. I being a Negro who the CI proposes to take the leadership, and despite the fact that I have had no training and education prior to joining the revolutionary movement, I am only given 1 year's training in the ILS and shipped back to South Africa, with heavy responsibility [sic] on my shoulders. The absurdity of this responsibility lies in the fact that I who have had no sufficient training (theoretically and politically) I am supposed to supervise the Communist movement in South Africa. How can I? . . .
>
> For we cannot hold the movement back until such time when the Negroes will have advanced to be the ideological leaders of it.
>
> So my work in the AFTU can be nothing but subordinate to those above me. NOT because I am a Negro but because theoretically they are super to me, of course due to historical reasons, for instance experience, education and environment. Let us not simply say that the Negroes must take the leadership irrespective of the situation . . . The ideological expressions have been and will be that of the whites, though they are the minority in leadership.
>
> I will take a stand in any question insofar as I can reason my point out, BEYOND THAT I CANNOT BE HELD RESPONSIBLE.
>
> So in your letter to South Africa, you have to recommend me to a subordinate position in the AFTU as well as in the Party.
>
> To consider me as a leader would be a MOCKERY to Negro people and the Communist movement in South Africa in particular.[69]

He concluded by requesting that the letter be shared with the Comintern's Eastern Secretariat and the Profintern's Negro Bureau for discussion. Dennis's report of January 17, 1933, had only one cryptic reference to Warren: "You will be interested to know that Warren is now safe with his family."[70]

On Huiswoud's return from South Africa he was met with a serious personnel problem in the ITUC-NW. In August 1933 he was dispatched to Paris to inquire into the activities of Padmore and Tiemoko Garan Kouyaté.[71] The Comintern had received reports that Kouyaté was consorting with agents of the French police, and the operation under Padmore's direction was feared to be subject to exposure. Padmore met Kouyaté initially in 1929 at the Second Congress of the League against Imperialism in Frankfurt and again at the conference sponsored by the ITUC-NW in Hamburg in 1930. Kouyaté had worked with Ford, was on the executive committee of the ITUC-NW, and was a contributing editor of the *Negro Worker*. Padmore and Kouyaté became close coworkers and friends after Padmore assumed leadership following Ford's departure.

Kouyaté entered the international scene as an associate of Lamine Senghor, a leader of the Comité de Défense de la Race Nègre (CDRN) who had served with Moore on the Committee on the Negro Question at the 1927 League against Imperialism congress. Since 1921 a series of organizations had evolved from the Union Intercoloniale, considered the first association to unite intellectuals from the French colonies residing in Paris. The Manifesto of the Union stated that "with the assistance of French comrades who sympathize with our cause, it seeks to rally all the native people of the colonies now living in France."[72] Imanuel Geiss has listed as active members the Vietnamese Nguyen Ai Quoc [a.k.a. Ho Chi Minh], who occupied a key position, the Algerians Hadjali Abdelkader and Messali Hadu, and the West Africans Lamine Senghor, Émile Faure, and Timeko Garan Kouyaté.[73] It was Ho Chi Minh who had pressed the Comintern on the colonial question at the Fifth Congress in 1924, declaring, "It is not enough, as has been done so far, to work out long theses and pass high-sounding resolutions which are, after the congress, sent to the museums." He went on to propose concrete measures including regular articles on colonial questions in *l'Humanité,* increased propaganda and recruitment in colonial countries, sending comrades from colonial countries to study at the KUTV, negotiating with the United General Confederation of Labour on organizing workers in France from colonial countries, and making it a duty for Party members to pay greater attention to colonial questions. After presenting facts on the horrible economic and social conditions in Indochina and many areas in Africa he concluded by quoting René Maran on the negative changes that had resulted from colonial destruction in Equatorial Africa. He urged the Comintern to help the people in colonies to organize and supply them with leading cadres.[74]

By 1927 the Comité de Défense de la Race Nègre had been formed in Paris along lines similar to the Committee for the Defense of the Vietnamese Workers, in Marseilles. Leadership of the Comité was shared by Senghor, Kouyaté, a student from the Sudan, another African, and three émigrés from the French Caribbean. One of Senghor's activities was to organize African dock workers and seamen in French ports. He was involved in establishing a communist-operated international building for seamen to which he took Claude McKay when it was opened in Marseilles.[75] In May 1927 he founded the Ligue de

Défense de la Race Nègre (LDRN), which began publication of its journal, *La Race Nègre,* in June. This publication and similar ones were distributed to émigrés residing in France and in ports, especially Marseille, as mentioned in McKay's novel of the period, *Banjo.*[76] Both Senghor and Kouyaté were members of the French Communist Party (PCF), and when Senghor died in November of that year his mantle was assumed by Kouyaté. Kouyaté served as secretary general of the LDRN from 1927 to 1931.[77] Imanuel Geiss has stated that Kouyaté submitted a draft programme for the LDRN emulating the example of the Indo-Chinese revolutionaries, with their demand for national independence. He voiced the demand for independence for Africa and proposed that the LDRN seek "to set up a unitary negro state embracing the entire continent of Black Africa and the West Indies."[78]

In 1931 an arrangement was made by the International of Seamen and Harbour Workers for Kouyaté to undertake special work in Marseille.[79] The decision was made to create another organization, Union des Travailleurs Nègres, with a new journal, *Le Cri des Nègres.* It appears that while the split was intended to disassociate the organization and its journal from the Comité de Défense de la Race Nègre, the debt of the previous journal continued as a responsibility of the new organization. The first issue of *Cri* appeared in August 1931, and in June 1933 Kouyaté was still trying to account for the previous debt, the current commingling of funds of the organization with expenses associated with the publication of *Cri,* and the problem created by "the one in charge [who] had been excluded as a policeman."[80] From the beginning of 1932 to the fall of 1933 serious questions regarding Kouyaté's administration of the work among French colonials were being asked by Huiswoud, members of the Central Colonial Section, the Union and the communist fraction of the Union, and Julien Racamond, who was a national secretary of the Confederation General du Travail Unitaire and a member of the French Party's central committee. As part of his responsibilities Padmore had delegated certain activities to Kouyaté for work among the French. In May 1932 he advised Kouyaté not to wait until the Confederation acted but to proceed to organize a committee called the Séction Française du Comité International Syndical des Nègres, and to develop and submit a plan of work and a budget. "You must be the secretary and responsible organizer . . . I have already expressed *my* opinion: it is you who must be responsible for this work." Padmore explained that up until that time the orientation of the Confederation had been toward North Africa and Arab Africa, and that when F. [presumably James Ford] was there he interested himself only in America; henceforward the *Negro Worker* would be directed to "the English Negroes, just as the 'Cri des Nègres' must be for the French Negroes."[81]

Padmore's letter to Kouyaté did not carry the same tone and criticism regarding the content of *Cri* that Huiswoud had written to the colonial commission of the Confederation the previous February 16. Huiswoud outlined eleven severe deficiencies, in particular the absence of articles treating trade union problems and organization. He stressed the need to include and defend the specific claims of Negro workers on board ships and on plantations; reserve more space for the fight against the colonial politics of the imperialist powers; familiarize workers with the life of the working class in the Soviet Union and the way in which the USSR resolved the national question; encourage correspondence with readers; and develop a column on international news that would tie the fight of the workers of capitalist countries with those of the colonial workers. His evaluation also commented on style: the articles were too long, too general, and should be written in a simple manner. He closed by requesting a report on the circulation, subscribers, penetration, and agents in the colonies and the influence and circulation in France.[82]

Almost a year later, eleven members of the Central Colonial Section reviewed *Cri*, queried Kouyaté, and commented in a similar vein. The previous issue was criticized as too theoretical and not sufficiently simple but the major problem was the financial control and the fact that the editorial board was composed of the same twelve comrades who headed the Union. Kouyaté's lack of numbers on journals sold, the financial deficit, his responses regarding lack of control over a comrade, Danaé Narcisse, and his resistance to suggestions to improve the operation brought the meeting to a close with the comment that "a communist cannot say that he will disengage from his responsibilities."[83] Comrades attempting to verify Kouyaté's accounts of activities in Marseille learned that the owner of the café where he met with sailors was close to the police; comrades in Marseille whose addresses Kouyaté had given them could not be located; there were reports that Danaé was observed walking with "policemen who had arrested the Chinese who were to be expelled."[84]

By September members of the communist faction were discussing "l'Affaire Kouyaté" and planning that the general secretary would announce Kouyaté's sabotage and present his letter of resignation at the next meeting, and that *Cri* would publish an article on Kouyaté's attitude within the Union.[85] Kouyaté's fiery response, dated November 24, 1933, stated in part: "I am warning you that in case of defamation I will sue you before the bourgeois correctional tribunal where the culpability of your paper will be exposed, all your credentials shown and the author of the article might also be incriminated by the more conscious Negroes. My patience is reaching its limits with your provocations and continual threat . . . We will see if I am 'the agent of the bourgeoisie' as Radi says or better, if the Negro mass follows me." He added a postscript: "The

Colonial Section would do much better to pay me my 2650 francs instead of trying to rush toward action which the political consequences are beyond your understanding because Kouyaté is the name of a well-known family which is able to defend itself by all means."[86]

Had Padmore been implicated in the charges brought against Kouyaté it is not likely that the Profintern would have sent Huiswoud to Paris to warn Padmore of the danger presented by Kouyaté's associations. Padmore did not receive the warning kindly. No doubt he was already annoyed with the criticism of his work by the Profintern Secretariat. To Huiswoud's surprise and dismay Padmore resented being told with whom he should associate and refused to go to Moscow to discuss the problem. The die was cast for the Comintern to expel Padmore as well as Kouyaté. In the August/September 1933 issue of the *Negro Worker,* Padmore announced his "Au Revoir." He urged the "Black toilers of the world" to support the journal that he characterized as facing bankruptcy: "It is high time for the Negroes to stop depending on other people to fight their battles . . . Help the new editor to overcome the present financial difficulties and to carry on the militant traditions of the *Negro Worker*—the only international voice of the Negro Peoples."[87] The Executive Control Commission of the Comintern took action on February 23, 1934, including among the charges that "despite repeated warnings, Padmore did not break connections with already exposed provocateur Kouyaté and lived in the flat of provocateur Jacques." It "decided to exclude Padmore from the Communist Party for his connections with provocateurs, ties with bourgeois organizations on the question of Liberia, for false attitudes towards the national question (instead of class unity he aimed for race unity) and for not handing over of Committee files, where he worked."[88] Months later Padmore released his version of his "resignation" and recriminations were hurled back and forth in the media.[89] Subsequently he conducted his agitation against colonialism in London; the Profintern's loss was the Pan-African Movement's gain. Now there was only one African American left to carry the torch—it was Huiswoud's turn to edit the *Negro Worker.*

The task of investigating the possibility of carrying on the work of the Committee and publication of the *Negro Worker* fell to Huiswoud. In September Huiswoud submitted a report based on discussions with leading comrades and a meeting with the Colonial Commission. The conclusion was that it would be impossible to continue the work of the committee unless a special functionary were assigned, but the comrades agreed that there was not a single individual available who was qualified either politically or technically due to the lack of forces and the language difficulty. If the work was to be continued, the RILU had to provide someone. Huiswoud presented a budget and raised the question regarding a suitable location. He favored a European port with traffic to African ports where close contact could be maintained with maritime workers in a seamen's interclub organization, to help facilitate work among the colonial workers. Bordeaux, Antwerp, Amsterdam, and Rotterdam were considered.[90] Evidently the best person the Profintern could find to continue the work of the ITUC-NW was Huiswoud, and Antwerp was chosen as the city in which to resume the cat and mouse game with the Belgium, Dutch, English, and French authorities.

This decision marked the end of the Moscow era for the Huiswouds. Otto bade a final farewell to his mentor and friend, Sen Katayama, who died on November 5, 1933. It was a sad moment but Huiswoud was glad that he was in Moscow to join the solemn tribute to the "devoted fighter for the cause of the world revolution."[91] The Huiswouds left Moscow in February 1934. Hermie returned to New York to visit her mother for a few months while Otto went to Paris to reorganize the affairs of the organization. He set up an office as the Crusader News Agency at Marche St. Jacques 9 in Antwerp. When Hermie rejoined him they rented rooms at Rue Osy 6 and resumed issuing the *Negro Worker* in May 1934. He had used the name Edward Mason for Comintern missions but assumed the name Charles Woodson as secretary of the ITUC-NW and editor of the *Negro Worker;* Hermie continued as Helen Davis. No mention was made of Hermie except for articles signed "Helen Davis," but she was the sole staff member who typed the copy and assisted with the layout for the next three years.

The abrupt shift in leadership and editorship did not result in a fresh approach. On the contrary, the organization struggled with more acute versions of the same problems Ford and Padmore had experienced, and the journal continued with the same format and hackneyed expressions. Huiswoud's reports all stressed the difficulty of starting "from the ground up," the lack of technical help, the paucity of contacts in Africa and the Caribbean, poor communications from contacts in the field and in Moscow, and the lack of articles. In May 1934 he mentioned that discussions with Belgian friends regarding the Congo revealed that they had only two or three contacts there. "Even here in the country itself they have no contacts with those who live here and the seamen . . . The main trouble is that the responsible people do not pay the slightest attention to this question and have to date not been able to form a functioning colonial commission." Similar discussions with Dutch friends regarding the Dutch West Indies and marine workers disclosed a lack of concrete action. Huiswoud submitted plans that could be employed to institute activities to Belgium, Dutch, and French colleagues. He stressed the absolute necessity for continuing the publication of *Cri des Nègres.*[92]

Subsequent reports on July 26 and August 23 indicated improved contacts with Africa and the Caribbean, particularly Gold Coast and Trinidad. On a trip to England he discovered that the Negro Welfare Association was "not what has been reported . . . It has only about 30 members in London and the activities carried on are very sporadic and ineffective." He worked out a program that would strengthen the Association and use seamen to establish connections with the colonies. In an attempt to move the British "away from abstract agitation to concrete, practical organizational work" he centered the work among colonial seamen in Cardiff, where there were about two hundred colonial seamen in the unemployed movement, and in London. He held a number of interviews with workers from the Congo on ships in Antwerp and expected to have regular meetings and give them some form of training. He also secured two salesmen from West Africa who were to arrive in October to take over their posts. Little had been heard from South Africa or France. He warned that friends coming through Antwerp should make contact with him only through the responsible person in charge of the seamen's Interclub.[93]

Several months after settling in Antwerp, both Huiswouds were arrested and instructed to pack their belongings. According to Hermie she had completed the copy for the September issue of the *Negro Worker* and was able to slip it undetected under garments in one valise. They were taken for interrogation, but the man in charge asked very few questions and apologized for the investigation saying, "We had nothing to do with this. It is the British who pressed us." They were imprisoned for eight days and taken every afternoon to an office building for further interrogation. On September 11 they were transferred to Brussels, and the following day put on a train to a "sort of no-mans-land on the border between Belgium and Holland." Hermie described the last steps of the deportation:

> The numerous suitcases [6] of ours would have been a problem but the guards solved it. There were 6 whites, I believe all Dutch, who were being deported as well. Just young men without baggage and they were each ordered to take one piece of our luggage to the Dutch Customs House a few yards away. It was a comical sight to see these 6 whites trudging along with the baggage and OEH and I walking leisurely behind. At the Customs, after a few formalities, including the lifting of some Paul Robeson and Marian Anderson gramophone records, we were free to enter Holland . . . From Maastricht . . . we entrained for Amsterdam . . . We rented two rooms—one used as dwelling and the other as office space. By October first, the September 1934 issue of The Negro Worker was rolling off the press. There was, actually, no break in publication. Contacts, held earlier, continued the distribution of the journal without a hitch.[94]

Having to reestablish the operation in Amsterdam was another setback. Evidently during this period Huiswoud was ill. Reference was made to his health in an unsigned letter from Moscow dated December 4. That letter and a second one in February urged Huiswoud to press contacts in Nigeria, Gold Coast [Ghana], South Africa, Liberia, Paris, and London to send students to Moscow.[95] Evidently this "honorable task" could not be fulfilled; subsequent reports from Huiswoud detailed how recruitment plans were not progressing. Finally, he wrote on June 24, 1935, "It is one thing for you at that distance to accuse us of exchanging 'polite phrases . . . but not doing a thing in this matter' and another to be on the spot and actually know the situation. We might be clear on one point right now. We are not ready to pick up people from the streets and send. The tragic results of this method is still fresh in our memory." He concluded by assuring that "we, as well as you, are fully aware of the crying need of reinforcements."[96] His reports on April 11 and June 24 reiterated that situations in South Africa, France, and England were not healthy. He judged that despite offers of concrete directives to leaders in Great Britain, "the NWA merely flounders around. The main reasons for this, is the almost complete lack of attention paid to colonial work (particularly Africa) on the part of the highest circles. Thus the leadership is devolved on the shoulders of a few good and willing N. comrades, but who are untrained." His one bit of good news was from British Guiana. He urgently requested that arrangements be made for him to go to Moscow for discussions of present and future activities.[97]

Frustration had mounted regarding the journal as well as the failure to produce students for training in Moscow. Despite bans that were imposed by several countries on the *Negro Worker,* Huiswoud was able to devise indirect methods of distribution, and he seemed satisfied that two thousand copies were reaching intended areas. His letter of June 24 showed his disgust, however, with the lack of cooperation particularly by comrades in the United States. While he did not use his earlier strong characterization of "sabotage," he phrased it as "not merely neglect." He charged, "But our friends there are too 'Busy' to answer our numerous letters . . . In the last *10 months,* we have written several letters to J. F.; E. B.; H. H.; Ben D; [presumably James Ford, Earl Browder, Harry Haywood, and Benjamin Davis] besides several others. We wrote them concretely requesting cooperation in the form of articles and material; we made proposals to them regarding the work in the W.I. and the aid they could give us in this; we asked them to send us their publications. To all this NOT A SINGLE ANSWER! That they have received the letters we know. THE ONLY THING WE GOT IN REPLY FROM ALL OUR EFFORTS WAS FORD'S SPEECH WHICH WAS published in the NW."⁹⁸ Huiswoud was finally authorized to go to Moscow in November.

Discussions in Moscow must have concluded with the decision to move the center back to Paris. Huiswoud had pointed out the inherent weakness in not having an official address to which readers could write or submit articles. From the time the journal was moved from Hamburg no address had been listed except for a few issues that carried an address in Copenhagen and later New York because conditions in Belgium and the Netherlands necessitated a clandestine operation. The operation was never located in Copenhagen or New York, and using addresses there would have been impractical. In December the Huiswouds moved to Paris and began the process of reestablishing headquarters and contacts for the third time at Office 316, 40 rue de Colisee.⁹⁹ In his first report from Paris Huiswoud raised the question as to whether it had been possible to secure a person from the United States to take charge of the activities in Moscow as proposed and agreed upon. He also recommended that the date for a proposed conference be postponed to the first week in July to mark the sixth anniversary of the conference at which the ITUC-NW was created.¹⁰⁰

Huiswoud's report for the year of 1936, issued January 1937, indicated success in widening the committee's connections and functioning in a more normal manner with an open, legal address that enabled shifting "its basis of operation from merely individual contacts to one of close connection, relationship and active cooperation with Negro unions, cultural and national liberation organizations in the colonies, the United States and in some European countries." Initiative had been taken to render advice on concrete problems facing a wide range of specified organizations in South Africa, West Africa, Trinidad, British Guiana, London, Holland, and France. Examples cited included the initiation and support of the Hands Off Abyssinia committees; the Scottsboro campaign; and trade union activity in the colonies that incorporated demands, slogans, and methods of work suggested by the committee. A special appeal had been made for organizations to affiliate with the committee, but that had not produced the expected results. He lamented that the projected conference had been called off "though the delegates had already been selected and preparations made to participate. This . . . did not serve to enhance the prestige of the Committee."¹⁰¹

The report warrants study not just for the accomplishments listed for the year but the honest evaluation and projection Huiswoud presented after working with the committee for six years of its existence:

> At the outset, it must be stated that the Committee has up to now functioned merely as a paper organization, in the sense that all its work which is supposed

to cover so many countries, wide apart, and the work of the NEGRO WORKER is done by the Secretary and his technical help, and that it had no connecting local committees in the countries of operation. It must be recalled here that by decision and the circumstances under which its work was carried on, the Committee was restricted to general propaganda activities and mainly through the medium of THE NEGRO WORKER. Under these circumstances it could never have functioned as a living, bona fide organization . . .

From the experiences of the past activities of the Committee and its failure to attract wide support from the Negro masses our conclusions can be no other than that the Committee is much too narrow in aim, purpose and scope, to serve the needs of the Negro people. They did not see in it the instrument that would effectively aid them in their struggles to improve their living conditions and to secure their rights. Besides, the specific features and character of the developing Liberation movements in the colonies precludes a trade union committee from functioning as a co-ordinating force, giving assistance, advice and leadership to the growing anti-imperialist movements.

While we must recognize the fact that in most of the colonies strike struggles are fast increasing and steady progress is being made in trade union organization, especially in South Africa and the West Indies, nevertheless the major development in organization among the Native people today is on a much wider basis—the struggle for elementary democratic rights—political rights, the right of free press, speech and organization, against specific colonial slave laws and economic exploitation. The demand for and the activities to gain self-government is gaining ground especially among the natives of the larger and most important West Indian colonies.

The indignation of the colonial toilers against the increasing political and social discriminatory laws . . . find their expression in the developing and growing National Liberation organizations. To this must be added that the Italian fascists war on Abyssinia, has profoundly affected large strata of the Negro people everywhere imbuing them with a certain political consciousness as to the necessity of struggle for liberation from imperialist domination . . . This increasing political consciousness and mood for struggle can be properly guided and directed provided the suitable organizational medium which corresponds to, reflects and serves the needs and demands of the masses is employed.

Huiswoud identified the most important and active movements of the national liberation struggles in the colonies. Interestingly he included the presence in the United States of "numerous organizations of West Indians, working for and supporting the natives in the Islands in their struggle for democratic rights and self-government." Then he proposed a ten-point program of demands and described a new international coordinating committee of Negro liberation movements and a transformed *Negro Worker* that would carry out the task.[102] Unfortunately his revisions were pronounced too late. The last issue of the *Negro Worker* was volume 7, number 7, September/October 1937. On March 23, 1937, a visa was requested by the Comintern Secretariat for Huiswoud to travel to Moscow to report on the International Negro Committee.[103] It was to be his last trip to Moscow. War clouds were gathering and the demise of the Profintern in December 1937 meant that the ITUC-NW, having no other bases of support, would be phased out in 1938.

How is a periodical edited by a "New Negro" who entered the political arena as an associate of the *Messenger* and *Crusader* groups in Harlem to be judged? What was the effect of an international journal that aimed to "discuss the day to day problems of the Negro toilers and connect these up with the international struggles and problems of the workers"? To what extent did the hackneyed style of leftist "agitprop" journalism constrain the language and format? Du Bois had argued that art was propaganda, but there was no proponent who insisted that propaganda should be art. Even the secretary general of the Communist Party of Great Britain, Harry Pollitt, noted in 1933 that party members had developed a psychology that they were not carrying out the Party line unless certain words occurred every other minute. He noticed that comrades who in England could talk to workers simply and clearly returned from the Lenin School speaking a foreign language.[104] Despite its style the *Negro Worker* conveyed a deep concern for millions of poor, oppressed peoples of African heritage throughout the world. It can be viewed as a historic collection of the atrocities wrought by colonialism and a call to redress the cruelty and callousness imposed by European and American corporations and governments. But to whom did it speak? Did it incorporate a humanistic expression? Did it have a touch of soul?

Huiswoud strove to put a face on the victims and to include more personal, individual accounts but recognized that "the journal did not sufficiently reflect the burning, vital issues of today in the colonies." He attributed that shortcoming to the fact that the editors did not "receive sufficient live material direct from the colonies written in the midst of activities and struggles taking place." He judged from letters, requests, and reprints of the journal's articles in the Negro press that the *Negro Worker* was gaining influence but admitted that the journal had not yet succeeded in deeply penetrating the Negro world. He went further: "One of the basic shortcomings of the journal was the lengthy and dry theoretical articles it contained. This could only interest a few revolutionaries and intellectuals, but not the average Negro toiler . . . The lack of light and popular articles and material dealing with certain social phases of Negro life is quite apparent. We have set ourselves the task of bridging this gap as quickly as possible."[105] It is not clear why Huiswoud did not alter the style of the *Negro Worker* when he assumed editorship. His criticism of earlier editions of *Cri* and the *Negro Worker* reveals his conviction that those periodicals should have been more appealing and appropriate for workers of diverse languages and backgrounds. With such a clandestine, impromptu method of distribution and little mention of the journal in contemporary literature it is difficult, if not impossible, to evaluate its impact. His brief assessment is the best available. Clearly the *Negro Worker* should not be dismissed. It was a significant effort on an international scale to provide information, bolster courage, encourage organization, and evoke a vision of self-determination and self-government for thousands of people living under colonialism.

The Huiswouds' sojourn in Paris from 1936 to 1938 was not without intangible compensation. Otto and Hermie were again face to face with the Harlem Renaissance. The experiences of the African Diaspora that kindled the Renaissance had contributed to its spread. Many African Americans who were part of the Harlem scene and were intrigued by the promise of socialism and the experiment in the USSR found their way, however, not to the land of Pushkin but to the "City of Light" that had proclaimed, "Liberté! Égalité! Fraternité!" American soldiers helped spread the word that the French treated them with respect, and jazz musicians found their music to be in great demand. Paris became the European venue to inspire, cultivate, and expand the Harlem Renaissance. Not only did Paris attract African American tourists, artists and writers settled there because they could study and work better where they had a sense of freedom and were appreciated. McKay preferred what he called "sinister Marseille," but Paris lured untold hundreds from Harlem to study, work, and play.

It was understandable yet ironic that France had such a favorable reputation among "New Negroes" who were seeking to adjust their self-image, identify with the glorious past of Africa, and correct the ignominious record that had been perpetuated by Western historians. Paris was represented as the pinnacle of culture, and it had become a crossroads of creative expression drawing artists and writers from all over the world. Nonetheless, it was also the seat of a colonial power that extracted wealth from nations in Asia, Africa, and the Caribbean. As Brent Hayes Edwards put it, "In part, black and brown encounters on the Seine were uneasy because of the African-American habit of thinking about Paris as a liberating cosmopolis, as free of racism, at precisely the height of French colonial exploitation."[106] René Maran wrote an open letter attacking Alain Locke's article in *Opportunity* for his uncritical admiration of France.[107] Michel Fabre has singled out two African American writers who acknowledged the hypocrisy of imperialist France: Du Bois's study of the racial situation of African American troops on the European front during World War I "correctly identified the harmful effects of French colonization"; and McKay's *Banjo* brought out the "different forms of colonialization, of which cultural assimilation is perhaps the most harmful."[108] Interestingly, McKay had renounced the duplicity of the French prior to his sojourn in France. While in the USSR in 1923 he described the naive response of African American tourists:

> At present a Negro who travels round Europe notes that France and Italy treat him much more hospitably than England . . . American Negroes are beginning to believe that one imperialist exploiter can be better than another. The black intelligentsia of America looks upon France as the foremost cultured nation of the world; the single great country where all citizens enjoy equal rights before the law, without respect to race or color or skin color . . .
>
> Thus, the sympathy of the Negro intelligentsia is completely on the side of France. It is well informed about the barbarous acts of the Belgians in the Congo, but it knows nothing at all about the barbarous acts of the French in Senegal, about the organized robbery of native workers, about the forced enlistment of recruits, or about the fact that the population is reduced to extreme poverty and hunger, or about the total annihilation of whole tribes. It is possible that the Negro intelligentsia does not want to know about all this.[109]

Documents circulated during the nineteenth and early twentieth century by the people of Indochina were vivid in testifying to the brutalization of the people and the eradication of their culture by the French. One "Proclamation to the People" in 1926 detailed the effects of colonization and stated, "Oh! Our freedom is lost. We expect nothing from the concept of equality. The more we speak up, the more we suffer. And yet the twenty-five million of Hong Lac's children [Vietnamese people] are as intelligent as anyone else. What a shame that they have accepted for more than seventy years the role of beast of burden. To live in these conditions is a shame. It is better to die rather than to lead such a life."[110] Similar ideas were expressed in a long poem, "An Appeal to the Soul of the Nation," by a fifteen-year-old high-school student: "In such quandaries, what is left of human dignity / In such state, what remains of the land? / The present predicament makes my heart wither / Our mountains and rivers prompt my tears to roll down . . . I summon the old soul to come home to our mountains and rivers."[111] Truong Buu Lam has documented that jail and death were the fate of many who dared oppose French rule. Those who were able to organize and protest in the metropolitan center of the French empire found they had common cause with the peoples from Africa and the Caribbean.

Students in Paris from French colonies in the Caribbean and Africa had their own tales of colonialism to tell and were more sensitive than African

Americans to the negative attitudes toward people of color held by the French. They saw liberating ideas, however, in the literature of the Harlem Renaissance in the same way that writers in Harlem had been stimulated by René Maran's novel *Batouala* in 1922. Lilyan Kesteloot's *Black Writers in French* has presented an excellent study of the influence of the Harlem Renaissance on French black writers of the period. "American jazz, the blues, and Negro dancing, reaching Paris via recordings and the cinema as well as in the nightclubs where expatriate American black performed, were testimony to the cultural vitality of black America . . . Black American writers visited Paris, and some met the black students there . . . The realism and unashamed self-acceptance of 'The New Negro,' typified in the poetry and novels of Langston Hughes and Claude McKay, provided a background for what later crystallized as 'negritude,' the French version of black self-awareness."[112] In tracing the evolution of Negritude, Kesteloot described how the French Caribbean students in Paris created their Renaissance by revolting against the earlier West Indian literature that mimicked French literature. Instead they began to "express themselves not in relation to the literature or the society of France, but in relation to colonized Negro societies. She noted that "particularly between 1918 and 1940, West Indian and African students who came to Paris found themselves in extraordinary intellectual and political ferment." Examination of the role of communism and the "prestige of the Third International" led her to the observation: "To intellectuals in Paris, communists seemed to be the only people publicly to protest the lynchings and other crimes committed against the blacks in America."[113] To a greater degree than Harlem, Paris became the center of exchange of militant ideas among peoples of the African Diaspora not solely through the literature that was generated but in personal contacts and the multitude of journals published in French and English. Paris was a cosmopolitan world that offered surrealism, Marxism, communism, the appreciation of African art, fresh studies in anthropology and ethnology, the defense of the Scottsboro Boys, and attacks on colonialism and imperialism. It harbored René Maran and Aimé Césaire from Martinique, Leon Damas from French Guiana, Dr. Jean Price-Mars and Jacques Roumain from Haiti, Leopold Senghor from Senegal, and Nicolas Guillén from Cuba; it was the world to which Hermie and Otto Huiswoud could enthusiastically relate.

In Paris the Huiswouds, Jacques Roumain and Thyra Edwards attended the opening of the Spanish Pavillion of the 1937 World's Fair, where Picasso's painting *Guernica* was unveiled. In July Langston Hughes showed up at the Second International Writers' Congress and was to be associated with some of the Huiswouds' fondest memories of Paris. Hughes had left California, where he was working with William Grant Still on the opera *Trou-*

bled Island, to participate in the congress and cover the Americans in the International Brigade on the front lines of the Spanish Civil War as a correspondent for the *Baltimore Afro-American* newspaper. His speech at the congress, entitled "Too Much of Race," appeared under a different title in the September/October issue of the *Negro Worker*.[114] His two weeks in Paris were a feast of renewing old acquaintances and making new ones. He visited the Huiswouds almost daily. Jacques and Nicolle Roumain, Nicolas Guillén, René Maran, or Henri and Retna Cartier-Bresson were the companions they were most likely to meet in restaurants for dinner. When Hughes and Guillén, who was covering the Spanish Civil War for a Cuban journal, left for Madrid they were accompanied to the railroad station by Roumain, Nancy Cunard, the Huiswouds, and several others for a warm farewell. In November Hughes made his way back to Paris, and they all had fun together again even though they were saddened by the discouraging news from the Spanish front.

On Christmas Eve 1937 Hughes and the Huiswouds attended the midnight supper given by Felix Merlin, a metal worker from Martinique who was the mayor of a Paris suburb. In 1935 he had been elected to the municipal council of Epinay-sur-Seine and served as second assistant to the mayor; in 1936 he was elected mayor on the Communist Party ticket in the Popular Front Elections.[115] Hughes spent Christmas Day with the Huiswouds, enjoying the dinner Hermie cooked, and the following day he was back with a Dutch wooden shoe filled with blooming miniature red tulips and two tickets for *Manon.* He and Hermie attended the opera at the Opera Comique before joining Otto to devour leftovers from the Christmas dinner. He commented in his autobiography, *I Wonder as I Wander,* that "it was a wonderful home-cooked dinner" but failed to mention the names of his hosts.[116] In mid-January he returned to New York but was back in Paris the following July for a peace conference sponsored by the International Association of Writers for the Defense of Culture. This time Hughes spent two months in Paris writing and visiting friends, including the Huiswouds. In September his poem "Madrid—1937," which he had written while at the front, was recorded in Paris for broadcast to the troops in Spain. Hermie read the "News Item" that prefaced the poem and Hughes read the poem. They never knew whether it was broadcast. Arnold Rampersad has considered that Hughes "responded to the deadly drama of Madrid" with "renewed brilliance. His most passionate sense of the violence and the heroism of Spain inspired three strong poems."[117] One was "Madrid—1937," yet the poem remained unpublished until 1973.

As World War II thundered closer there were signals that the time had come to leave the City of Light. Hermie applied for her passport on April 29, 1938, and was ready to leave for New York in September on the French liner *De Grasse*.[118] Hughes left Le Havre ahead of Hermie on September 10 to take advantage of engagements in London and caught the *De Grasse* in Liverpool. Huiswoud wound up the ITUC-NW business and left by undisclosed transport for Mexico, where he waited for an opportune moment to enter the United States. While biding his time, he pursued a long-standing interest he had in examining the difference between the life of people of African heritage in Mexico and the United States. He conducted original research and wrote an essay, "Negro Slave Revolts in Mexico." It was an amazing historical account free of communist jargon and written before recent histories on the subject. He planned to show it to Hughes and hoped to publish it but never did.

The Huiswouds were friends with Hughes for the rest of their lives. He sent them copies of his books, clippings, and programs. They maintained contact mostly through letters and cards that included reports about their mutual friends Guillén, the Roumains, Thyra Edwards, Louise Patterson, and the Cartier-Bressons. In September 1938 Hughes wrote, "Hermie, I wish I was in Montmartre!" In December 1965 he inquired, "Remember our Christmas in Paris?"[119] In one letter following Hermie's mother's death Hermie referred to Jacques Roumain and Langston as her mother's "sons" and wrote, "It might interest you to know that it was in our kitchen (!) that Jacques wrote the first chapter and I recall very vividly how he stood in the doorway reading it to me."[120] In December 1954 she commented, "I keep track of you through one or another source and sometimes look back on the carefree days when Jacques and Henri and Nicolas and the many others were still young and full of hope for a bright future. Hope is still with those left but future is now past and present is tryingly somber and the world is not quite so brave anymore."[121] Even more poignant was her letter following Otto's death in December 1961 when she wrote, "Funny I got to thinking yesterday about myself—an African poem I once read long ago runs something like this: Mother, who will weep when you are dead since you have no children? Well yesterday I was thinking of poems and of René Maran whom I'd met in Rome in 1959 and last year when in Paris I learned of his death and from him to the African poem and then suddenly it struck me—yes who will weep for *me*? I thought of O's death and the several hundreds who came to his funeral and the grown people who wept."[122] Otto and Hermie Huiswoud had spent eight years working for the Comintern. Who there would weep for them?

Rand School Class of 1918–19. Otto Huiswoud is in the last row, third from right. Instructors, *left to right, second row:* Ella Wolfe, David P. Berenberg, Alexander Trachtenberg, Dr. Scott Nearing, Bertha Howell Mailly, Eugene Wood, Louis P. Lochner. (Courtesy of Tamiment Library/Robert F. Wagner Labor Archives, New York University.)

Otto Huiswoud and Claude McKay at the Fourth Congress of the Communist International (Comintern), Moscow, 1922. (Courtesy of the Yale Collection of American Literature, Beinecke Rare Book and Manuscript Library, Yale University.)

American Negro Labor Congress organizing meeting in Chicago, 1925. *Left to right, seated:* Otto Huiswoud and Richard B. Moore. (H. Huiswoud Papers.)

Class on "World Problems of Race" organized by Richard B. Moore (*extreme left*) with lecture by Hubert H. Harrison (*seated in front*). W. A. Domingo (*front row center*) is ready to present gifts to Harrison. Otto Huiswoud and Williana Burroughs were also in the audience. September 9, 1926. (Courtesy of Jeffrey B. Perry, Wesleyan University Press, and Charles Richardson.)

Langston Hughes (*standing*) and Otto Huiswoud (*seated center*) with unidentified companions in the Tashkent area, Uzbekestan, USSR, October 1932. (Courtesy of the Yale Collection of American Literature, Beinecke Rare Book and Manuscript Library, Yale University, and the Harold Ober Associates.)

The African American Film Group's visit to agricultural projects conducted by African American agronomists, Tashkent, USSR, 1932. Langston Hughes (*standing second from left*); Otto Huiswoud (*standing second from right*). (H. Huiswoud Papers.)

Oliver John Golden, circa 1926, organizer of a team of fifteen African American agriculture specialists in 1931 under contract with the USSR for development of products in Uzbekistan. He and his family remained in the USSR. (Courtesy of Lily Golden.)

Langston Hughes. (H. Huiswoud Papers.)

Otto Huiswoud, Paris, 1936.
(H. Huiswoud Papers.)

Hermina Huiswoud, Paris,
1936. (H. Huiswoud Papers.)

Anti-Imperialist International Congress, Paris, 1937. *Left to right, seated:* Louise Thompson Patterson, *fourth; second row,* William L. Patterson, *fifth;* Felix Merlin, mayor of Epinay-sur-Seine, a suburb of Paris, *sixth;* and Otto Huiswoud, *seventh.* (H. Huiswoud Papers.)

Otto Huiswoud (*center*) speaking at El Gran Maceo society in Santa Clara, Las Villas, Cuba, October 18, 1946. Hermina Huiswood on right. (H. Huiswoud Papers.)

Otto and Hermina Huiswoud in Havana, Cuba, 1946. (H. Huiswoud Papers.)

Richard B. Moore in front of his Frederick Douglass Book Center on 125th Street, Harlem, 1955. Photo taken by Langston Hughes. (Author's possession.)

Otto Huiswoud, Amsterdam, the Netherlands, circa 1955. (H. Huiswoud Papers.)

Hermina Huiswoud, Amsterdam, the Netherlands. (H. Huiswoud Papers.)

Elementary school in Paramaribo, Suriname, named for Otto Huiswoud. (H. Huiswoud Papers.)

Joyce Moore Turner (author) and Hermina Huiswoud, Amsterdam, the Netherlands, 1987. (Author's possession.)

8. Home to Amsterdam

As Hermie sat among the stoic, silent Dutch residents of the Wittenberg nursing home musing on their past, resigned to their future, hoping for an occasional visitor, waiting for the next meal and death, she thought about her thirty-four years traveling the globe with Otto and her thirty-six years in Holland since his death in 1961. For years she had claimed she was alone but not lonely; in 1997, however, she had to admit she was not alone but lonely. What a difference a fall had made! Slipping in the hallway outside her apartment had transformed her life from one of independence to one of dependency. She had traveled a long way from New Amsterdam in British Guiana to Amsterdam in the Netherlands. Her husband's journey had been even longer: starting in 1910 from Dutch Guiana in South America, he headed for Amsterdam but detoured to the cosmopolitan North American city formerly known as New Amsterdam and its northern section, which still bore the Dutch name Harlem. Ultimately his road led to old Amsterdam, his original destination.

Although they had escaped World War II in Europe the years between Moscow and Amsterdam turned into painful days of separation, illness, and internment. When Huiswoud returned to New York in 1938 from Moscow after a half-year detour in Mexico, he was diagnosed as suffering from tuberculosis of the kidney and underwent surgery to remove one kidney. Following a prolonged illness with pneumonia the doctor recommended convalescing in a warm climate, and he left New York in January 1941 for "home" in Dutch Guiana with his family. On arrival he was met by the port police, who promptly interned him in spite of his illness. The Netherlands was already involved in World War II, and Huiswoud was to experience it in the Dutch colony he had hoped to liberate. He was detained at the convent at Copieweg and then sent to an internment camp constructed for prisoners of war, where he was imprisoned under wartime security restrictions for almost two years without explanation, charges, trial, or representation. German internees and German-Jewish refugees were also sent to the camp, and Huiswoud set up a protest that led to the fascists being separated from the antifascists.[1] Hermie could not visit him and her mail to him was intercepted.

On September 27, 1942, Otto wrote Hermie about his release:

My dearest Honi,

   This is a special letter. It's written in a happy frame of mind. It's to announce to you that I've returned home. It occurred Friday evening. It happened suddenly. On Friday afternoon I was told that it was all over and that I could go home immediately.

   You can imagine what such a happy tiding meant to me and what an effect it had. You can also imagine how pleased and happy the family and friends were when I returned to the City.

   I know that you too will be overjoyed when you read this and that you will share my happiness.

   A number of relatives and friends have called to express their best wishes. I never knew that so many people knew me. Of course a number of people here have contributed greatly to attain the desired end . . .

   Please inform Atty. Stevens that I received his letter concerning the visa. I was indeed very pleased to get that news, which came on the 23rd, thus two days before the other great news . . .

   My birthday greeting to Mater [Hermie's mother] . . . Best wishes darling. Our reunion is getting closer and closer.

   With best wishes for your good health. Regards to friends.

   With love and many kisses.
   Otto[2]

The New York lawyer and friend, Hope Stevens, whom Hermie had retained to assist in Huiswoud's case, discouraged immediate travel because of difficulties with transportation. For the duration of the war Huiswoud remained in Dutch Guiana, where he worked for M. R. Kent and Company as manager of the shipchandlers department from May 1943 to July 1945. It was not until September 1946 that he and Hermie managed to meet in Cuba, where they decided that he would not return to New York. Instead she would join him in the Netherlands, where he had the right of citizenship. Huiswoud left Paramaribo in October 1947 for Amsterdam, and Hermie moved there in 1949. They had endured eight long years of separation before they could settle down to a more "normal" life as Dutch citizens. In 1952 Huiswoud was ill for months, yet during that year he contemplated starting a bookselling business. He wrote his old friend Richard B. Moore for advice, but the venture did not develop. Instead he obtained a civil service position as a clerk for the national Post, Telephone and Telegraph Service. While Hermie was alone in New York she had worked several jobs, including assistant to Moore, who was editing the Pathway Press edition of *Life and Times of Frederick Douglass;* secretary for the Negro Labor Victory Committee; and assistant to Gwendolyn Bennett, director of the George Washington Carver School for adult education. Mayme Brown and Elizabeth Catlett were also associated with the school, and both became lifelong friends of Hermie's. After she moved to Amsterdam she taught English on a private basis and worked as a secretary for the K.L.M. International Pilots Association. She and Otto confined their political activity to working in the organization Ons Suriname. As president, Huiswoud helped transform the social organization to one with activities on behalf of independence for Dutch Guiana. He founded and edited *De Koerier,* the organization's publication.

Although W. A. Domingo had not taken the communist path as Huiswoud had, he shared a similar fate when he traveled to his birthplace, Jamaica, in 1941. The governor of Jamaica cited letters Domingo had sent to Jamaica as evidence of his intent to "impede the policy of the imperial and local governments in relation to the war effort," "excite opposition to the policy of the Imperial Government of allowing the United States to establish defense bases in Jamaica," and "foster among the Colonial population of Jamaica feelings of . . . racial animosity." He was detained by the British in the Up-Park Internment Camp for twenty months.[3] Huiswoud and Domingo, having retained their Dutch and English citizenships, had evoked the wrath of colonial governments, but Lovett Fort-Whiteman, who had been one of the first African Americans to join the Communist Party, had the most tragic fate of all: he evoked the wrath of Stalin's henchmen. Not much was reported or known about him after the Sixth Congress in 1928. He remained in the USSR and appeared in a photograph in the *Negro Worker* in 1933 as a teacher in a Moscow public school.[4] Brief mention was made of him in minutes of a subcommittee of Party leaders in Moscow on August 25, 1935 recommending that Patterson and Ford hold a meeting to discuss reported efforts of Lovett Fort-Whiteman "to mislead some of the Negro comrades."[5] Perhaps allegations of "left sectarianism" and Trotskyism stuck. Years later Homer Smith and Robert Robinson mentioned Fort-Whiteman's disappearance in their autobiographies, but it was not until recent publication of Russian documents in *The Soviet World of American Communism* that his fate was revealed. Evidence now exists that he was sentenced to five years in internal exile for "anti-Soviet agitation" by the People's Commissariat of Internal Affairs (NKVD) on July 1, 1937, and sent to the city of Semipalatinsk in Kazakhstan, where he worked as a teacher in local schools. On May 8, 1938, his punishment was changed to five years hard labor and he was sent to a prison labor camp in northeastern Siberia. He died there on January 13, 1939.[6]

Cyril Briggs and Moore stayed home during the war and experienced a different type of separation. Both were expelled from the Communist Party in 1942, allegedly for their "nationalist tendencies." Briggs moved to Los Angeles in 1944 and was later readmitted to the Party. Moore never sought to be readmitted. He opened the small Frederick Douglass Book Center in 1942 on 125th Street in the heart of Harlem and devoted his energy to programs on African and African American history and developing organizations dedicated to the independence of Caribbean nations. He was joined in some of these organizational efforts by others of Caribbean background, including W. A. Domingo, Rev. E. Ethelred Brown, J. A. Rogers, and George A. Weston, who had not been attracted to the Communist Party but were passionate about destroying colonialism.

African Americans who elected to cast their lot with the communists had to ask themselves repeatedly whether they were accomplishing their mission to change the world. There was no question regarding their motivation, for they were convinced that the disappointment they experienced after coming to New York was due to prejudice against all people of color that developed as part of the European justification for the enslavement of Africans and the conquest of Africa and the Americas. They were also convinced that the concept of race was invented by conquerors who sought to exploit human as well as natural resources of various lands. Studies on race by anthropologists such as Franz Boas reinforced their conviction that the "problem" did not lie in the color of the African skin but in the European mind. Even though the Caribbean immigrants had not had the benefit of higher education, their intense study of history revealed that the United States, founded on the economic base of chattel slavery, not only compromised the Declaration of Independence by counting each African American as three fifths of a person in the Constitution but failed to "correct" its view of African Americans as human beings with unalienable rights after emancipation. Protests by African Americans against the treatment of citizens of African heritage had prevailed throughout the history of the country, but the situation remained a blight on the total society that required reeducation and change on the part of the white population. When the immigrants from the Caribbean arrived in New York, the city was undergoing what has been described as assembling "the first global nation."⁷ Throngs of immigrants pressed by poverty, persecution, and political unrest who managed to escape from pogroms and oppression in Eastern Europe were also arriving at the city's gateway. The evils and dislocations of the industrial revolution were being challenged, and many immigrants as well as native-born Americans put their hopes in the promise of socialism. The Caribbean émigrés also dared to envision a society built on a truer base of equality.

Huiswoud, Domingo, and Moore embraced socialism in their quest for a "New Emancipation."⁸ They recognized that racism had to be attacked by white as well as African American radicals. The editors of the *Messenger* described the doubly difficult task Negro radicals encountered: "They must educate the radicals to the realization of the fact that capital is ever weaving a net work of lies around Negroes, and, to educate Negroes so that they may understand their class interests. Negroes must learn to differentiate between white capitalists and white workers, as yet they only see white men against black men . . . Organized labor must harness the discontent of Negroes and direct it into working-class channels for working-class emancipation."⁹ In an article that McKay quoted in *The Negroes in America* Domingo pronounced the litmus test: "One can boldly say that in America the Negro question is the touchstone, the measure by which the sincerity of American radicalism can be measured."¹⁰ When the self-educated Harlem soapboxers experienced difficulty combining their view of the flaws in American democracy with certain positions the socialists expounded they struggled to integrate issues related to class, caste, and race with the interpretations presented by the Socialist Party. They also recognized that their mission was not only to castigate well-identified perpetrators of discrimination and subjugation but also to help build a self-image that would counteract the disfiguring badge of inferiority.

It was pure coincidence that their search coincided with the birth of the USSR and the American Communist Party. It was a propitious time in their lives. As they learned about Marxism and Lenin's concept of imperialism they felt that their response to racism and imperialism was justified and that intransigent and unyielding institutional discrimination required a radical remedy. They perceived that the radical Left of communism widened the spectrum of organizations engaged in fighting for equality for Africans, African Americans, and African Caribbeans, and they believed that an alliance with the Comintern would provide a broader international platform for their cause. Often overlooked was the fact that their radicalization occurred in the United States, unlike many European immigrants who arrived with socialist concepts and a core of experienced writers, editors, and printers. In addition to their youth and tenacity, the immigrants from the Caribbean brought to the socialist movement an international outlook of the Diaspora. Their tiny, powerless nations had provided them with an orientation to the sea, an understanding of global relationships, an openness to unlimited possibilities.

Having accepted Marxism as their weapon Huiswoud and his comrades threw themselves wholeheartedly into the political fray. They found that not only were they attempting to interpret communist positions to African Americans but they were also constantly having to interpret the African American experience to their white comrades. Gradually it became clear that the Comintern was more responsive to pressure on issues related to African American life than was the American Party. During the early twenties it was leaders of the Comintern who questioned a party whose membership did not adequately reflect the American masses, especially African Americans, whom they considered to be the most oppressed of the proletariat. They questioned a party in which the majority of the members did not speak English and that lacked a strong English press. It was the voice of Moscow that helped force the American Party into restructuring and reordering its priorities to include the Negro question. The plight of African Americans and peoples under colonial domination was subsumed under the Comintern's broad agenda oriented to the preservation of the USSR and world revolution, but the influence the USSR hoped to create required covering a multitude of bases on a global scale. It was the old case of the squeaky wheel getting the grease: small as the African American cadre was, their constant pressure gave priority and perspective to the Negro question. Had the focus of the Comintern been purely theoretical the Negro question would have been part of a minority question in the United States and incorporated the oppression of Native Americans and Hispanic Americans. Instead the Comintern focus was limited to the adverse conditions of African Americans, largely because they were both advocates and victims staking a claim in their own liberation on the international stage. In evaluating the impact of "Moscow gold" on USSR-USA relations there should be recognition of the contribution it made to opportunities the Comintern provided for low-income African Americans to enter the international arena—to travel to foreign countries, to meet and exchange ideas with people from different lands and cultures, to work with emerging African leaders, to experience treatment based on equality, to be exposed to philosophical and theoretical ideas, and last but not least to express the plight and vision of the African American people. Huiswoud and McKay were the first African Americans to present the case for peoples of the African Diaspora to the Third International. Their presence at the Fourth Congress of the Comintern was significant in establishing the direction of Negro work both in and outside the United States for two decades. Huiswoud's participation in the congress convinced him that he had chosen the correct path to emancipation.

The same year that Huiswoud and McKay laid the groundwork for Negro work at the Fourth Congress, the Comintern urged all parties to establish women's departments. According to Kate Weigand, the American Party established a Woman's Bureau but failed to give it power to create or implement a program for women's liberation, and it was not until the mid-1930s that the communists began to consider the woman question in earnest. Despite male domination of Party leadership and the African American cadre, traces of sensitivity can be observed among African American leaders. Immigrants from the Caribbean like Briggs, Domingo, Moore, Harrison, and Hermie Dumont never forgot the role their mothers or step-mother, sisters or aunts had played in providing for their development and migration to the United States. They shared concerns regarding the sacrifices African American women made for their families and the extremely harsh conditions under which they worked in domestic service, farms, and laundries. These concerns were expressed by McKay, Huiswoud, and Williana Burroughs, who directed women's activities for the League of Struggle for Negro Rights. As early as 1920 the *Emancipator* reported that one of the demands of Panama workers on strike was that "female employees shall receive the same rate of pay as male employees for the performance of a similar class of work."[11] In 1923 McKay wrote in *The Negroes in America*, "The Negro question is inseparably connected with the question of woman's liberation," and Huiswoud identified the woman question as "one of the biggest problems" at the April 6, 1929, meeting of the International Trade Union Committee of Negro Workers in Moscow. The effect of racism on African American women, however, had yet to be seriously addressed.

Weigand claimed that years later, women used the Party's approach to African Americans and racism as a model to strengthen and refine their earlier liberation efforts: "Progressive women forced the Communist Party to rethink its narrowly economic understanding of women's oppression, to clarify the relationship of gender oppression to race and class oppression, and to acknowledge that women's so-called personal problems had political solutions."[12] In 1949 Claudia Jones was still calling for "An End to the Neglect of the Problems of the Negro Woman!" In that essay she sought to clarify the relationship between issues of gender and race and articulated the perspective of African American women: "A developing consciousness of the woman question today . . . must not fail to recognize that the Negro question in the United States is *prior* to, and not equal to, the woman question; that only to the extent that we fight all chauvinist expressions and actions as regards the Negro people and fight for the full equality of the Negro people, can women as a whole advance their struggle for equal rights."[13] It can be claimed that the women's movement benefited from the work of the early African American leaders, but it cannot be said that the plight of African American women was addressed by the Party during the early years.

Life in a communist party was extremely demanding. To be a communist was to be a target in a hostile environment, subject to harassment by government officials and rejection by most of the public. To be a functionary was to accept a life of frugality; wages were meager and irregular. The lifestyle often led to physical exhaustion and ill health, as Huiswoud, Moore, and Burroughs were to experience. Despite the implications of comradeship there was little comfort being a member of the Party. In addition to work in the local unit, there were committees on section, district, state, and national levels; committees, subcommittees, and commissions for special issues and cases such as the Tom Mooney, Angelo Herndon, and Scottsboro Boys campaigns; and front organizations and their fractions. The pace was frenzied, the pitch feverish, the mood cantankerous. Meetings went on for hours, with long speeches, heated exchanges, and much wrangling. The commitment demanded of members was often beyond the capacity of workers engaged in hard manual labor and domestic service for long hours. Not only were working hours long, African American workers were in a precarious position, always at risk of losing their jobs. Joining the Communist Party was not like joining the Democratic or Republican Parties. In addition to the exposure to European Marxism and Leninism, a cultural chasm had to be crossed. The New York scene incorporated many cultural elements of Eastern Europe, and the milieu was compounded by slogans and signs in strange Hebrew characters, sounds of Yiddish conversations and songs, and unfamiliar dishes such as kasha, borscht, blintzes, and potato latkes. Camps like Nitgedaiget, Unity, and Kinderland were foreign islands of respite during the summer. Evidently their Caribbean experience had not only prepared Huiswoud, Moore, and Briggs to participate in debate and deliberations, it had prepared them to enter the intellectual, social, and cultural world of cosmopolitan New York and beyond.

Party committees, conventions, and international congresses provided a sense of involvement and participation in decision making. International congresses in particular gave legitimacy to resolutions promulgated by the Comintern and created the illusion of a democratic process—theoretically from the bottom up. The Party operated in a culture that thrived on intellectual exchange, yet it was permeated with traditional Russian autocracy and the acceptance of suffering. The Russian Revolution was successful in removing the ruling monarch and reducing the influence of the Russian Orthodox

Church but not in eradicating authoritarian, autocratic modes of operation. Opportunities were provided for airing opinions, but loyalty, trust, and discipline were demanded once final decisions had been reached. The overall tenor was not truly democratic and concealed a sense of being constantly under siege from within as well as from outside. The trust that was expected of members was rarely practiced by leaders. It was very easy to be considered too Right or too Left, a reformist or nationalist, an opportunist or deviationist, a proponent of Trotskyism, Bukharinism, Lovestoneism, or Buntingism. At the Sixth Congress in 1928 Bukharin warned that leadership in the parties was overcentralized, that it was difficult to promote the selection of cadres without more local initiative, and that the tendency to dictate rather than persuade was not in a communist spirit. He stated, "We have learnt well how to conduct operations against every kind of deviation; we do it brilliantly. But as for a real study of the problems, genuine argumentation and not a mechanical fight against opponents—that we have still to learn."[14] His words fell on deaf ears, and his voice was soon silenced.

The labeling and demonizing of outcasts was only one technique for containing dissent, assuring conformity, and keeping the revolutionary train on track. Resolutions at congresses were manipulated at various stages of development. Representatives of the Comintern, such as József Pogány (a.k.a. John Pepper), were assigned to the national parties to act as an integral part of the leadership. They did not simply advise; they spoke, wrote, and voted as authorities on the local scene, represented the Party at Comintern congresses, and in Pepper's case helped to foster factionalism by advocating on behalf of issues and individuals. Representatives from the parties were also assigned to the Comintern as a means of indoctrination and communication between the parties and the Comintern.

The fierce factionalism of the American Party added another problematic dimension. Negotiating one's way through the maze of internal party politics was hazardous, especially for African Americans with an agenda of their own. The road was rocky as well as slippery; there was no map. There were times they had to compromise, but defiance was a trait they maintained inside as well as outside the Party. Contrary to assessments like that of Roger Kanet, who credited the communists with infiltrating the African Blood Brotherhood,[15] or others who considered African Americans to be dupes of the communists, Mark Naison found that "their actions confound the image of the black Communist as puppet or automaton, unwilling to take initiatives without direct orders from the top."[16] He credited the initial African American members of the Party, who joined largely because of the Communist International's commitment to support "racial and national movements against imperialism," with transforming the American Party: "By the end of the decade, this inner party struggle had, with Soviet help, elevated the organization of blacks into a matter of top political priority and transformed a previously apathetic white membership into a force willing to bring the Party's message to black communities."[17] Party records and published accounts confirm that despite many obstacles, African Americans maneuvered and fought constantly to establish and implement programs that would benefit the African American community and African and Caribbean colonies. They were actually thorns in the side of the American Party.

Charges and admissions of white chauvinism appear repeatedly throughout the record of the two decades. Given the harsh organizational environment and abundant evidence of racial prejudice in the Party it is curious that Huiswoud and his colleagues elected to stay the course. They perceived a radical difference between battling for the cause of justice and equality in the American and Soviet arenas. Prejudice and its oppressive consequences were a condition of life for people of color in America, and complaints of white chauvinism would have fallen on deaf or uncomprehending ears in the typical daily setting. Communists, however, extended the hand of comradeship to African Americans. The family of Oliver Golden has passed down his story that "the first white American to take his hand and shake it as an equal was a Communist."[18] Some white members of the Party such as Robert Minor understood the dehumanizing effect of racial barriers. In describing the plight of African American workers reduced to working as scabs for less pay than a white worker, he wrote of his own experiences growing up in the South. He recalled that the daily press assumed as fact that the entire Negro race was a lower order of beings than white people, and in his first twenty-one years he had never known a white person who did not believe this to be true. "I had never known a white worker who would be willing to work side-by-side with a Negro doing the same kind of work. As a member of a trade union, in which there were several 'socialists,' I had never known a trade unionist who would not have felt himself mortally insulted with a proposal to admit a Negro to membership."[19]

Claude McKay had foreseen how the hostility of white workers would deter the recruitment of African Americans by the Party. In 1922 he explained, "The blacks are hostile to Communism because they regard it as a 'white' working-class movement and they consider the white workers their greatest enemy, who draw the color line against them in factory and office and lynch and burn them at the stake for being colored. Only the best and broadest minded Negro leaders who can combine Communist ideas with a deep sympathy for and understanding of the black man's grievances will reach the masses with revolutionary propaganda. There are few such leaders today."[20]

The cry for unity and the vision of "Black and White Together" were convincing enough to some African Americans to raise the possibility of a "new day." The attack on white chauvinism is testament to the expectation communists set that theirs was a world in which racial barriers did not or should not exist. African American communists were convinced they could hold their white comrades to the high expectation set by the Party, albeit with the help of a powerful foreign nation that condemned exploitation based on race. Their impression proved to be correct to some extent, for as Robert Hill has assessed, "Comintern prodding did move the American leadership toward a forthright espousal of full civil rights for blacks. The Communist party helped popularize the cause of black rights among liberal and radical whites in the labor movement and elsewhere, an infusion of considerable significance in the later development of the civil rights coalition in the United States."[21] In communism African Americans found a commitment to help solve problems facing peoples of African heritage that was at least amenable to their criticism. They were protagonists who continued to fight on this battlefield strewn with land mines because they were convinced the Party was the best vehicle to accomplish the liberation of African peoples around the world. The relationship was symbiotic—they needed the movement, and the movement needed them.

Otto Huiswoud was a charter member of the Party who had been trained as an organizer at the Rand School and influenced by Hubert H. Harrison, Sen Katayama, and Sebald Justinus Rutgers. He was hardly a raw recruit fresh off the streets of Harlem. Cyril Briggs was an experienced journalist with an extensive record of radical newspaper and magazine publications. Richard Moore's experience was limited to stumping as a socialist but his skill as a speaker was to gain him the reputation as one the best orators in the Party. The "gifts" that W. A. Domingo claimed they brought from the tropics were augmented by skills that were useful to the Party as well as for their own purposes. They studied and argued their way into positions of leadership but seldom experienced a sense of success. Reports are replete enumerating scarce resources, limited achievements, lack of cooperation, and utter frustration.

In view of the Party's practice of negative self-criticism it is difficult to evaluate the extent to which goals were realistic and projects proceeded according to plan. It is also impossible to judge the extent to which factionalism played a role in Negro work. Not only had Huiswoud entered the Party on the side of the Ruthenberg forces, his early experience in the Farmer-Labor Party reinforced his antipathy to the Foster camp. Throughout his involvement with the Party he consistently condemned the Foster forces for inadequate pressure on unions to accept African American workers and insisted that Negro work was not the sole responsibility of African American members of the Party. As early as 1920 his mentor, Harrison, had countered Foster's advice that "the best Negro leaders must join heartily in destroying the pernicious anti-union attitude so deeply rooted among their people." Harrison responded, "It is up to the white unions of the American Federation of Labor and the great railroad brotherhoods themselves and not up to the Negro leaders to change this deep seated aversion which American Negroes have for white American labor."[22] Huiswoud's insistence that Foster's deeds should conform to Party policies and pronouncements regarding African American workers ultimately led to his involvement in the Lovestone debacle. Some members tried to distance themselves from the factional fight. Moore claimed he "was not a good factionalist;" Otto Hall pointed to his record of criticizing both the minority and the majority; Minor described how some African American members frequently shifted their support for the two factions. But was it possible to be beyond factionalism and have allies? How important was Negro work?

The fact that Huiswoud, Moore, and Briggs have received so little mention in memoirs and histories of the Party may be an indication of how the Party viewed them and the program for which they labored. Huiswoud was practically invisible. There was no reference to him in Foster's *History of the Communist Party of the United States* or in Ella Reeve Bloor's autobiography, *We Are Many.* James P. Cannon reminisced that "American communists in the early Twenties . . . had nothing to start with on the Negro Question but an inadequate *theory,* a false or indifferent *attitude* and the adherence of a few individual Negroes of radical or revolutionary bent." He failed, however, to remember who those few African Americans were. In describing the delegates to the Fourth Congress he mentioned "a Negro delegate whose name has escaped me, who seemed to support the leftist faction."[23] When he described the 1929 Lovestone delegation "chosen for their proletarian looks and political reliability," Benjamin Gitlow had slightly more to offer: "Otto Huiswoud, a Negro Communist who had been a paid Party official almost from the organization of the Party in 1919 . . . Each one of them was a native-born American with the exception of Huiswoud, who was a West Indian."[24] Unstated was the fact that it would have been unwise to send a delegation to Moscow without an African American on the heels of the Sixth Congress Resolution on the Negro Question. Hermie, who attended the Lenin School with Peggy Dennis, was named in Peggy's autobiography but no mention was made of Otto even though he worked in the Anglo-American Section of the

Profintern as she did and he was sent to South Africa when her husband, Eugene, was stationed there by the Comintern.[25]

It is conceivable that Huiswoud was not remembered as having participated in founding meetings because he was a reticent novice, spoke with a heavy Dutch accent, had a light complexion, and was accompanied by Anna Leve. His involvement as a functionary, however, began very early. Leve, who became a charter member with Huiswoud in 1919 and lived with him until 1924, indicated that he worked most of the time as a full-time party functionary. Surely his subsequent roles merited recognition. It would be a mistake to assume that Huiswoud was mute because he was modest, had a quiet manner, and chose his modus operandi carefully. He shared the social consciousness that drove militants to join the Socialist and Communist Parties as well as the passion that fired their meetings. While dedicated to the cause of liberation within the African Diaspora, his voice was not confined to matters related to Negro work. At the Sixth National Convention of the Workers (Communist) Party in March 1929 he was elected, for example, chairman of a committee on Trotskyism.[26] Along with other African American comrades, he actively raised questions, presented ideas, debated issues, and offered suggestions and criticisms on matters discussed in party committees, meetings, conferences, and plenums as he moved to various positions within the U.S. Communist Party, the Comintern, and the Profintern. It is ironic that an organization so involved in cleansing itself of chauvinism should provide so little notice of his presence. Modest as he was, he reminded members of the American Commission of the Comintern in 1929 that he entered the Party at its inception: "I helped organize the Party; I am part of its flesh and blood."[27] Ignored in the annals of the American Left, Otto Huiswoud stands nevertheless as a pioneer in the American communist movement. The question remains whether he was relegated to a nonperson status because his positions were not in complete agreement with some of the leaders, or because his reports to the Party, the Comintern, and Profintern did not paint the rosy picture that the leaders might have preferred, or because the leaders of the Party were not truly serious about the significance of Negro work.

During the twenty years Huiswoud was in the vanguard of the communist front he faced serious condemnation on at least three occasions. He was considered out of step for his insistence on social equality at the Farmer-Labor Party convention in 1924; for distinguishing between applying the colonial question (self-determination) to the United States and South Africa in 1928; and for his advocacy of Lovestone as a leader of the American Party in 1929. Moore and Briggs also faced condemnation and ultimately expulsion for their perspectives on Negro work. Clearly the Party did not appreciate the positions of Huiswoud, Briggs, and Moore on various issues and continuously sought ways to control their activities. While Huiswoud's assignment to Moscow during the thirties expanded his responsibilities and contribution, it also removed him from Harlem. The impact of the Caribbean veterans in Harlem was further eroded by Moore's assignment to the International Labor Defense. He was constantly on the road from coast to coast on behalf of the Scottsboro and Tom Mooney cases and was assigned to Boston reportedly to reduce his influence in Harlem. When he returned to Harlem he was again in conflict with the Party. His position favoring demands for jobs for African Americans in 125th Street stores, for example, was in direct opposition to the Party's insistence that such demands would result in the loss of jobs for white workers. Briggs, who had remained in Harlem, was removed as Editor of the *Liberator* allegedly because of statements in the paper regarding Party-Garvey conflicts at meetings, "exposure of a white chauvinistic incident at the Coney Island Workers Club," and exposure of "reformist slogans of Negro Business." Briggs admitted that he deserved criticism but noted that the process of his isolation began with the assignment of Ford to the section and that such severe changes had not been made by the Party in the case of the *Freiheit* or other publications that had made serious mistakes.[28] While each of the trio continued to work toward their goal of liberation for the peoples of African heritage, their collaborative efforts were substantially reduced and their impact in Harlem minimized.

Undoubtedly the shift in the interpretation of the Negro question in 1928 was the most threatening and puzzling. Events surrounding the development of the Resolution on the Negro Question at the Sixth Congress of the Comintern open a window on the complexity surrounding the establishment of policies that were to guide the program in the African American community. It seemed to the African American members that the solution to the American Party's neglect and misunderstanding of the commitment required for the emancipation of African Americans was simply greater pressure by the Comintern. Yet the scramble for power in both the Russian and American Parties became the significant factors in determining the direction the correction would take and drowned out the voice of African American members. Huiswoud survived each crisis but the role he might have played in the Negro Bureau of the Comintern was denied him by proponents of the 1928 Resolution on the Negro Question.

Slowly Huiswoud, Briggs, and Moore were able to find some merit in applying the self-determination argument to African Americans in the United States, especially when Comintern action accomplished significant movement on the part of the American Party. The Comintern had heeded the insistence of the African American cadre that the Negro question was not solely the work of African American members. The Comintern could command that white American communists become involved in the struggle for African American liberation. But it could not dictate an understanding of the African American community—the role and significance of various institutions, the psyche developed by decades of brutal terrorism, or the perspective of most African Americans that true liberation should mean social and economic equality *within* American society. Confusion prevailed regarding the new road map to socialism. In a philosophy that posited the concept of a nation within a nation, how was a nationalist to be defined? Thirty-four years later Briggs and Harry Haywood, who were still advocates of self-determination, continued to mull over the issue. Briggs raised the questions, "Why did our Negro nation analysis have so little appeal to the Negro people? . . . And aside from the factors of white chauvinism, why was there such a big turn-over in our Negro membership, larger even than that of others? . . . Was it correct to wholly differentiate between Negroes in the Black Belt and Negroes in the North, to say that the first were a nation and the second a national minority? . . . Did we go about it the right way?"[29] Experiences like Huiswoud's were always a test of balancing one's own convictions against the accommodations that had to be made to continue to use the Party and Comintern as allies in the fight for freedom.

The African American cadre's frustration and their demeaning by some Party leaders was somewhat neutralized by the Scottsboro case. The search for a meaningful connection with the African American community during the twenties was finally realized in the thirties. Success was due more to the Party's focus on the tragedy and trauma of Scottsboro than on promulgating the Soviet philosophy of a nation in the "Black Belt." The case became the symbol of the oppression of African Americans and provided the impetus the Party needed to convert Negro work conducted by a small African American cadre to a national cause célèbre engaged in by the entire Party. The three crusaders' voices were sounded on all fronts: Briggs's in the New York press, Moore's on nationwide tours covering hundreds of cities, and Huiswoud's on the international scene wherever he and the *Negro Worker* reached a wide audience. The case dramatically transformed work in minuscule local tenant organizations into hundreds of mass demonstrations on a variety of issues important to African American communities. Most importantly, the campaign expanded opportunities to organize in the South. It provided a breakthrough and resulted in the most successful period of acceptance of the Party and recruitment among African Americans. It has been widely recognized, as claimed by Michael Dawson, that "Scottsboro was instrumental in helping to build the reputation of the Communist Party among grassroots African Americans . . . The party's membership in New York grew slowly, while its influence (as it did around the country) grew rapidly during the early 1930s. By mid-1930 in New York and elsewhere in urban black America, communists were major players. Their ideological influence far exceeded their numbers, as their work especially influenced intellectual and cultural elites."[30] Scottsboro made its mark on the Harlem Renaissance and gave the Caribbean crusaders some sense of accomplishment.

Communist Party comrades who worked with Huiswoud, Moore, and Briggs might have had short memories when they wrote their memoirs, but the three veterans were never forgotten by the Federal Bureau of Investigation. Records of their activities occur far more frequently in government archives than in biographies and histories. Beginning in 1920 surveillance was part of their lives. For decades agents followed them, conducted inquiries and investigations, tapped their telephones, and opened their mail. As the years went by, increasing numbers of disillusioned ex-members were willing to testify against them, and anticommunist organizations conducted their own investigations and exposures. The Department of Justice and the Department of State were provided information by American embassies and agencies from other nations along with unsolicited communications from dissidents. State Department records reveal, for example, a June 28, 1938, memorandum from the American embassy in London reporting that a French communist had informed a friend of his in Trinidad that there was a movement in New York in support of strikers in Trinidad. It was suggested that labor disturbances in the West Indies might have been organized by Huiswoud. The July 8 reply from Washington indicated that information on Huiswoud was confirmed by Hermine [sic] Huiswoud's application for a passport in Paris stating she resided with her husband. It went on to say that Huiswoud's presence was not necessary in the United States because Ford, Patterson, Haywood, Ben D. Amis, Manning Johnson, Moore, and Briggs were there:

> Some of these persons came from the West Indies originally and any one of them is quite capable of directing a supporting movement in this country . . . The open supporting movement in the United States for elements in the West Indies would probably be found in the National Negro Congress . . . active last December in organizing mass support in this country in protest against the massacre of Haitian laborers in the Dominican Republic. Currently it is active in arranging lectures for W. Algernon Crawford, editor of the *Barbados Observer,* who is now in New York regarding conditions in the West Indies.[31]

The amazing part of the State Department response was the admission that African American communists were considered effective: "The amazing part of this set-up . . . is the wide-spread approval of Negroes for its objectives . . . Most of the non-communist Negro newspapers in the United States while cognizant of the Communist influence in this organization frequently praise its program as one to which any Negro could subscribe."

The records are replete with such examples, which suggests large expenditures over decades by the federal government. They never reveal, however, the impact of the surveillance on the individuals long after their communist activities had ceased or the nation had begun to come to terms with some of its racist practices. Hermie always felt that she was being watched, and even at the age of ninety-two she insisted on conducting conversations in the park. A lifetime of paranoia was the price many paid for affiliation with the Communist Party.

After many years studying the surveillance of African Americans conducted during the teens, Theodore Kornweibel Jr. observed that the "New Crowd Negro" faced a formidable force and that "the guardians of politics and the capitalist way of life saw nothing positive to be gained from racial change or reform." He stated, "The post war months were the most militant era of African-American history until the modern civil rights period but the political intelligence establishment born in World War I was able to block that militancy by making the maintenance of white supremacy part of the nation's security agenda, thus legitimizing the suppression of racial activism."[32] He reached the conclusion:

> Given the intensity of investigation, surveillance, and infiltration, if prosecutable offenses had been committed by Randolph, Briggs, or other black radicals, the Justice Department would have acted with vigor and dispatch. The conclusion is inescapable: The federal intelligence partners, led by the Justice Department's Bureau of Investigation, knew that even strident racial advocacy and self-defense were lawful. But their distaste for black militancy was so profound that they persisted in harassing individuals engaged in legal, if unpopular, activities. The even handed administration of justice was sacrificed. Federal injustice prevailed. And it established a pattern of hostility to racial and civil rights progress that persisted for the next fifty years.[33]

The programs, protests, and propaganda in which Huiswoud, Briggs, and Moore engaged stressed the political rather than the aesthetic and were radical for the times but hardly revolutionary. In hindsight the objectives of such organizations as the African Blood Brotherhood, American Negro Labor Congress, Harlem Tenants League, and the Scottsboro Campaign were achievable within the legal framework of the U.S. Constitution, but it was the position and passion of the militants of the twenties and thirties that helped push an acceptance of civil rights into the body politic of the sixties and seventies. As they reviewed the statistics of lynchings in 1920 the militants could hardly foresee the changes that would occur within forty years, nor were they inclined to wait half a century. John Ballam described Moore as "a valuable and energetic comrade but . . . impatient."[34] The Caribbean contingent serves as an example of a broader group of impatient African Americans. The records of the Communist Party contain many names of African American members, both men and women, who worked with Huiswoud, Moore, and Briggs and remain unknown, not to mention thousands who cast their lot with the NAACP, UNIA, other militant organizations, and the Pan-African movement. The human rights movement required thousands of partisans and a variety of approaches.

Otto and Hermie Huiswoud, Domingo, Moore, and Briggs gained the respect of many people in Harlem, the Caribbean, and Africa. Friends and acquaintances not only referred to their steadfast commitment, consistency, persuasiveness, and remarkable knowledge of history but also described a side not apparent in archival records. All of them were known for their wit, keen sense of humor, integrity, and concern for others. Serious as they were, they had the ability to kid each other and laugh at themselves. There were marked differences noted as well: Huiswoud the quiet thinker who shunned the limelight, Hermie the efficient collaborator and facilitator who got things done, Moore the bibliophile and extemporaneous "orator of electrifying passion and clarity,"[35] Domingo the astute businessman and caustic and effective writer and speaker, Briggs the clever writer who used the absurd to shock and call attention to the ridiculous position of the opponent. Their names were frequently linked—a testament to the fact that they could work together and maintain their comradeship despite the contentious atmosphere within many organizations.

How did the Huiswouds, Briggs, and Moore view their two decades devoted to communist organizations? Otto Huiswoud left no papers and none of them wrote an autobiography. Obviously there were keen disappointments that Negro work was not more extensive and effective. The conversations, interviews, and writings of Hermie, Moore, and Briggs clearly reveal, however, that they never regretted taking the communist road. They all remained steadfast in their conviction that socialism was a preferred solution to racism and colonial oppression. They thought of themselves as New Negroes, internationalists, proponents of trade unionism, co-operatives and collectivism, advocates of self-determination for peoples whose rights to nationhood had been thwarted by colonialism—as Marxists. Neither Huiswoud, Briggs, nor Moore ever used names other than their own in their work in Harlem; they presented themselves as proponents of socialism and communism. During his years in Harlem Huiswoud's name was pronounced "Huiswood" instead of the Dutch pronunciation (to rhyme with "loud") and was often spelled that way—a case of mispronunciation and misspelling rather than hidden identity. He used other names, such as J. Billings, Otto Woods, Edward Lee Mason, or Charles Woodson, only when he was associated with the Comintern.

The trio felt that they had worked hard to promote socialism and had helped to change some of the horrible conditions they encountered in the United States. Hermie always downplayed the significance of her "background" office management role and expressed pride in Otto's contribution. For Otto, highlights were his meeting with Lenin, his friendship with Katayama, participation at the Fourth Congress, and his working in Moscow; for Hermie, it was life with Otto, editing and writing for the *Negro Worker,* and their involvement with Ons Suriname; for Moore, it was attendance at the First Congress of the League against Imperialism, his work on behalf of the Scottsboro Boys, the pressure he exerted to advance the knowledge of African American history, and ultimately, the independence of Barbados and other Caribbean nations. They felt that they had contributed to a significant world movement despite the enmity they aroused; and also despite the failure of many comrades to grasp an understanding of racism; the lack of clarity on whether front organizations were to be simply African American units of the Party, coordinating bodies involving noncommunist labor organizations, or community organizations; the internecine battles that sapped the vitality of the movement; the vacillations in policy; and Stalin's betrayal and reign of terror. It should be noted that they shared a deep disdain for those they considered "turncoats" and purposely kept their criticisms of the Party and the Comintern to themselves. Occasionally they would make comments on particular individuals, but they were not willing to attack the Party, the Comintern, or the USSR.

The Comintern and its trade union arm, the Profintern, have been considered by some proponents to be the center of inspiration and the driving force behind the revolutionary attack on colonialism. Surely Huiswoud and his fellow comrades counted on the significant role both organizations played in exposing and attempting to dismantle the power that European nations exerted over Asia, Africa, the Caribbean, and parts of the Americas. A close examination of the genesis of anticolonialism in Harlem reveals, however, that the political and cultural upheaval during the Harlem Renaissance originated within the experience of the triangular African-Caribbean-American Diaspora, not within European socialism. The politically oriented Caribbean settlers in Harlem who were radicalized during the early 1900s attempted to graft the "Negro Problem" onto the socialist platform because they envisioned a socialism that was inclusive of all peoples in its outlook and actions.

The defiance and concerns of the Harlem Renaissance catapulted a host of individuals into the Soviet orbit.

It was not only in Harlem and other metropolitan areas in the United States where radical reactions developed in response to oppression based on race. A core of rebellious African and Caribbean writers and activists from French colonies who asserted their African heritage as well as their civil rights assembled in France. Many of them were in communication with Harlem writers, and an exchange of ideas and literature took place between France and Harlem. A similar shift from European models to an appreciation and celebration of indigenous subjects was in progress in Mexico. Diego Rivera proudly claimed that his mother passed on to him the "traits of three races: white, red and black" and asserted that the heritage of Mexico derived from those three well-springs and incorporated images drawn from them in his art. According to Rivera the shift in orientation that he and his colleagues and disciples effected were dubbed by European and American art critics the "Mexican Renaissance."[36] These radical changes in literature and art were not inspired by Soviet models, even though many of the writers and artists in Harlem, France, and Mexico were associated with the radical international political movement. Their concern about social problems and their heritage was derived from their personal experiences and informed their art; it also developed the recognition that change in society required a political component.

Although the contribution of African American communists in the Harlem Renaissance cannot be quantified, they can be given credit for helping to advance the social, economic, and political rights of African Americans. They were models of radical thought and activity and inspired others, especially writers, to think and act in a militant manner. They stimulated community political action by running as candidates and supporting campaigns of African American candidates on local, state, and national tickets on a scale that had not been conducted previously. Their activities helped set a pattern of involvement and voting that ultimately resulted in the election of candidates who were responsive to the needs of Harlem such as Benjamin Davis Jr., Adam Clayton Powell Jr., and Vito Marcantonio. They raised issues such as housing and employment to which noncommunist politicians, landlords, store and movie house owners had to respond, and they fought against lynching and campaigned in national and international arenas on behalf of Angelo Herndon and the Scottsboro Boys. Their voices were heard not only on the corners of Harlem but in national and international forums. They brought the plight of the people of the African Diaspora to international tribunals, including subsequent appeals during the launching of the United Nations in San Francisco. Last but not least they were at the forefront of demanding workers' rights at a critical time of industrialization and unionization. The slogan "Black and White Together" was not proclaimed at the workplace by any group other than the communists; the constant complaint registered by Huiswoud and others contributed to a multitude of voices that helped break down barriers in the unions and at the workplace. This agitation was generated within the spirit of the Harlem Renaissance; it also contributed to the success of the Harlem Renaissance.

Perhaps history will find a way to evaluate the role of the Caribbean crusaders during the Harlem Renaissance. A clear picture cannot depend solely upon the number of African Americans who joined and maintained membership in the Communist Party or the number and distribution of the *Crusader,* the Crusader News Service bulletins, the *Emancipator, Negro Champion, Liberator,* or *Negro Worker.* As participants in the Harlem Renaissance Huiswoud, Briggs, and Moore should be viewed as radical polemicists who helped advance arguments for equal rights and justice not only in publications directed toward African Americans but also in publications read by a much wider audience. In addition to unrecorded orations on corner soapboxes and meeting halls, their voice was present in the *Daily Worker, Communist, International Press Correspondence,* and other organs. They raised the level of militancy by adding a radical component to the protests mounted by the NAACP, UNIA, Socialist, Pan-African, and other movements dedicated to moving the civil rights and anticolonial movements forward in the United States and abroad. They were a vanguard for civil and worker's rights when they could not even become a member of most unions, eat in Child's Restaurant in Harlem, or ride in the front of a bus in the South. They may not have converted many recruits to their political party, but their influence was out of proportion to their number. Their effectiveness may be discovered in the strength of their protests during a critical period of transforming the battle for civil rights in the United States.

Many forces were at work during this critical period and subsequent developments should not be attributed to any one group. It is not too much of a leap, however, to tie the Caribbean crusaders to the works of other writers. Margaret Walker has reminded students of the Harlem Renaissance that the thirties, the decade of the socially conscious writer, was the era when the New Negro came of age and "grew away from the status of the exotic, the accidentally unusual Negro . . . They were the poets of social protest who began to catch a glimmer of a global perspective, who as spokesmen for their race did not beg the question of their humanity, and who cried out to other peoples over the earth to recognize race prejudice as a weapon that is as dangerous as the atomic bomb in the threat to annihilation of culture and peace in the western world."³⁷ The poets of the thirties could not have "come of age" as she claimed had there not been the political agitation of the previous two decades.

The Harlem Renaissance was a period of psychological repositioning in the Diaspora. Its deep roots were in the experience of forced removal, dispersal, and enslavement of African peoples; its expression ranged in degrees of protest and the diversity of assertions of the group's humanity; its timing was attuned to a blossoming and flowering that had occurred before and would occur again. The acceleration of literary and artistic creativity was stimulated by the same forces that propelled the rise of the militant New Negro. Race, the problem of the twentieth century, was the theme at the core of artistic as well as political outpourings; literary and political expressions were not isolated but an integral part of the culture. There was a constant interaction, a dynamic energy, a rejuvenated race consciousness and pride that wove an intricate tapestry combining threads of art, architecture, music, dance, theater, literature, and history with journalism and oratory. The Caribbean militants represented a vociferous arm of protest of the Harlem Renaissance—assuming a fearless stance if they must die while asserting the political aspect of a broad movement. They strove for a system that would assure equality and justice in the United States and independence of African and Caribbean nations.

Moore returned to Barbados as an honored guest of the government after an absence of almost sixty years to witness the lowering of the British flag and the raising of the new Barbados flag at midnight on November 29, 1966. Huiswoud did not live to see full independence for Suriname in 1975, but an elementary school in Suriname was named for him in recognition of his contribution to independence. Hermie wished that Otto could have witnessed the passage of the series of civil rights acts in the United States and the independence observances across the Caribbean and on the continent of Africa. Then he too would have known that the sacrifice was not in vain.

After Otto's death on February 20, 1961, Hermie had a difficult decision to make. Should she return to the United States or remain in Holland? Her mother had died and she had no close relatives. Her first impulse was to return, but she carefully considered that the Netherlands had made the change from a colonial power to an open, democratic society. It had instituted many social benefits for its citizens and could tolerate a variety of political opinions, including Communist Party representatives in the legislature. She decided to remain in Holland. Not only had her childhood years prepared her to be independent, curious, and flexible, life with Otto had demanded a high degree of courage, commitment, and change. When asked how she felt about the many times they had been separated and the mystery surrounding some of his activities, she responded, "That was the life of the wife of a revolutionary." It was a life she could gladly accept because she shared his vision. Otto's long voyage to Amsterdam had determined that his destination would become ultimately Hermie's home. She was eternally grateful that he had jumped ship along the way and she could share his dedication to the liberation of people of the African Diaspora.

Epilogue

On October 8, 1995, Hermie Huiswoud celebrated her ninetieth birthday. A large, jolly group gathered—all age groups, different nationalities, friends from different periods of her life—to pay tribute to a feisty, jovial woman who had shown deep interest in their lives and had shared the life of one they also honored. Despite the absence of Otto for thirty-four years, he was still in their minds and hearts; not as a communist, for he had not been associated with the Dutch Communist Party and most of them were unaware of his political affiliations during the twenties and thirties in the United States and the Soviet Union. They were mindful of Otto's as well as Hermie's devotion to the independence movement of the former colonies of the Dutch and other European nations and particularly to the Huiswouds' leadership in the organization Ons Suriname. Each celebrant had brought one flower in accordance with Hermie's instructions to avoid gifts or multiple bouquets so typical of Dutch hospitality. The result was an enormous beautiful bouquet of diverse shapes and colors, symbolic of the circle of friends and the life that Hermie had lived.

Hermie was a wonderful raconteur, spinning long tales with many related tangents. She always denied there was a story to tell about her life. She felt strongly that it was Otto whose story had been omitted or misrepresented in historical accounts. She was proud of Otto's contribution and thought his story and that of Harrison, Domingo, Briggs, and Moore had been grossly neglected. Her attempts to write a biography had failed because she did not have sufficient documents to construct an accurate account. The second disappointment was even more bitter; she had lived long enough to witness the fall of the Soviet Union. The vision of a more equitable society had been grossly miscarried by Stalin, and the Cold War had created more instruments of war than a satisfying life of peace. She summed up her despair in a few words: "After seventy years the people of Russia are still suffering. This is not how we thought it would turn out."

Hermie's goal had been to live to the year 2000. She said she had been born shortly after the beginning of the twentieth century and was curious to see how it ended. Otto's and her life had traversed the African Diaspora from the so-called New World to the Old and had been dedicated to changing the relationship between those worlds. While she had not been attentive to the 1917 Russian Revolution, it had made an impact on society in general and her life in particular. Unlike Otto she had the satisfaction of witnessing changes in patterns of systemic discrimination in the United States and colonialization in the Caribbean and Africa. As an activist turned observer she continued to follow world events assiduously every day in newspapers, magazines, and Dutch and British newscasts on radio and television. By 1990 it was clear to Hermie that the gains in equality and justice were threatened. During her last year spent in the Wittenburg nursing facility she resented the dependence that had been forced upon her and decried the fate of the world. She lost the desire as well as physical endurance to face the millennium.

On April 21, 1998, Hermie died at the age of ninety-two. Her dear friend Magda Bon Bruno wrote, "We cannot forget her fight against injustice and racism all over the world, as well as her interest in literature and politics." Indeed she did have a story to tell.

Two Epitaphs in an English Graveyard
HELEN DAVIS [HERMINA HUISWOUD]

Here lies the remains of a man called Great
By those who wish to perpetuate
The state of profits vast, and booty yields
From stolen mines and forests and golden fields—

KIPLING
The imperialist who vowed that East
The West could never meet.
For him the East must ever bear a bondage yoke
Obscured by the western "civilizing" cloak.

The coloured race shall ever be
A burden to the whites, said he
He left unsaid—the true:
That Negroes, Indians and others too,
Sustain the white imperialist crew.

SLEEP KIPLING
To your class you have been a glory—
Those who oppress with rule so gory.
Your talented mind
Helped serve your kind

To build that which is falsely called by Tory
"A Commonwealth of British Nations."

* * *

And here lies another, a true, a noble hero.
One from the East who came West
Defending those in bondage leashed,
Fighting to the end and giving his best—

SAKLATVALA
This Indian fraternized with those oppressed
Tho' he with worldly goods was born possessed,
For the freedom of his people he placed on high,
A loyalty no imperialist gold could buy.

He earned the rulers' hate untold
For advocating fearlessly and bold
The freedom of the labouring man,
The unity of coloured man with white man.

SLEEP ON SAK.
Your labours have not been in vain.
Though you cannot view the gain,
The time will come when life's at best
When East shall meet and join with West.

The Negro Worker, March 1936

[This poem was written on the deaths of Rudyard Kipling and Shapurji Saklatvala, who died within two days of each other in January 1936. Hermina (Hermie) Huiswoud explained that both men were born in Bombay but Kipling became one of the most outstanding exponents of British imperialism, whereas Saklatvala became a staunch opponent. Saklatvala joined the Socialist Party in 1910 and the Communist Party in 1920. He served in the British House of Commons from 1922 to 1929 but was denied the opportunity to return to the land of his birth.]

Notes

Introduction

1. For a bibliography on Caribbean migration, see Brana-Shute, *Bibliography of Caribbean Migration*. An excellent overview may be gleaned from W. James, *Holding Aloft the Banner*, 9–49.
2. Knight, *Caribbean,* 27–65. See also Crosby, *Columbian Exchange.*
3. Richardson, *Caribbean.*
4. See Curtin, *Atlantic Slave Trade* and *Rise and Fall.*
5. Look Lai, *Indentured Labor, Caribbean Sugar;* Laurence, *Question of Labour.*
6. Lumsden, *Barbados American Connection.*
7. W. James, *Holding Aloft the Banner,* 40–49.
8. Ibid., 12.
9. Lewis, *Labour in the West Indies.*
10. See Albert and Graves, *Crisis and Change* and *World Sugar Economy.*
11. Knight, *Caribbean,* 275–306.
12. W. James, *Holding Aloft the Banner,* 76.
13. Anderson, *This Was Harlem.*
14. See Huggins, *Harlem Renaissance;* Anderson, *This Was Harlem;* W. James, *Holding Aloft the Banner.*

Prologue

1. Hermina Dumont Huiswoud preferred the name "Hermie" and used her given name only on legal documents. According to baptism record number 694, page 118, 1905, of the Mission Chapel, New Amsterdam, British Guiana, Hermina Alicia was born to Hermann R. C. V. Dumont and Alice Janet Dumont on October 8, 1905, and baptized on November 19, 1905.

Chapter 1: The Caribbean Comes to Harlem

1. W. James, *Holding Aloft the Banner,* 43.
2. C. Johnson, "Black Workers," 641.
3. W. James, *Holding Aloft the Banner,* 356; Knight and Palmer, *Modern Caribbean,* 212.
4. C. Johnson, "Black Workers," 641.
5. Huiswoud Papers, "Women," (McCoy and Moore).
6. Thurman, *Negro Life in New York's Harlem,* 7.
7. J. Johnson, *Black Manhattan,* 48; Watkins-Owens, *Blood Relations,* 40.
8. Huiswoud Papers, "Women" (Little White Girl).
9. Huiswoud Papers, "Re: Otto Eduard Huiswoud."
10. Gruening, "New York," 263.
11. Ibid., 259.
12. Rogers, *World's Great Men of Color,* 2:617.
13. Moore, "Hubert Henry Harrison," 292–340; Samuels, *Five Afro-Caribbean Voices,* 27–39.
14. P. James, "Hubert H. Harrison," 83.
15. Foner, *American Socialism and Black Americans,* 206–11.
16. Harrison, "Socialism and the Negro," 65.
17. Ibid., 66–68.
18. Du Bois, "Socialism and the Negro Problem," 338.
19. Ibid., 337–40.
20. Perry, *Harrison Reader,* 10.
21. W. James, *Holding Aloft the Banner,* 126.
22. Moore, "Hubert Henry Harrison," 293.
23. Ibid.
24. Rand School of Social Science Records.
25. Kublin, *Asian Revolutionary,* 7, 13, 18, 24.
26. Ibid., 176.
27. Ibid., 85.
28. Ibid., 232, 239.
29. Yamanouchi, *S. J. Rutgers and a Case Study,* 362.
30. Rutgers, "The Left Wing," 97.
31. Yamanouchi, *S. J. Rutgers and a Case Study,* 351–52.
32. Ibid., 361–63; Riddell, *Founding the Communist International,* 14; Klehr, "James W. Ford," 351.
33. Shipman, *It Had to Be Revolution,* 128.
34. Ibid., 123–24. Gomez was born Charles Phillips. He assumed the name Manuel Gomez during his communist activities in Mexico and the name Charles Shipman after he left the Communist Party.
35. *Rand School News,* April 1919 and June 1919 (Rand School of Social Science Records).
36. Ibid., Sept. 1919. Huiswoud's membership in the Socialist Party was also confirmed in a letter from Anna Leve to Hermie Huiswoud dated June 7, 1973, in which she wrote, "When I came to New York in 1918 he was a member."
37. *Trow's General Directory,* 1916.

38. Huiswoud Papers, "Women" (Grace Campbell). McKay would have left New York by the time Hermie visited Campbell's home, and W. A. Domingo would have been present.

Chapter 2: Uptown and Downtown

1. Thurman, *Infants of the Spring,* 222.
2. Clark, *Dark Ghetto,* 141.
3. Davis, "Growing Up in the New Negro Renaissance," 429.
4. J. Johnson, *Black Manhattan,* 146.
5. Du Bois, *Souls of Black Folk,* 204–5.
6. Ibid., 13.
7. Hill, "Introduction," *Crusader,* 1:vi.
8. See Turner and Turner, *Richard B. Moore.*
9. Hill, *Garvey Papers,* 1:527–28.
10. RA, 495/261/2133/7–9 (outline prepared by Briggs for the CPUSA and the Comintern); Briggs, "Autobiography" (an unpublished brief outline of the autobiography Briggs never wrote; courtesy of Mark Solomon); Hill, "Introduction," *Crusader,* 1:vii–viii.
11. Draper Papers, Cyril Briggs to Theodore Draper, June 4, 1958.
12. Ibid., March 17, 1958.
13. Hill, "Introduction," *Crusader,* 1:x, xxii, xiii.
14. Foner, "Cyril V. Briggs," 2. Courtesy of Philip Foner.
15. FBI File, 100-375204-19.
16. Hill, "Aims of the Crusader," *Crusader,* 1:75 (Nov. 1918). Citations to unsigned articles in the *Crusader* are to the three-volume facsimile reprint edited by Robert A. Hill.
17. RA, 495/261/2133/10.
18. Reid, *Negro Immigrant,* 84, 163.
19. Ibid., 84. Reid noted that the test for literacy established by the 1927 Immigration Act was a Biblical passage: "He hath also prepared for him the instruments of death; he ordaineth his arrows against the persecutors. Behold, he travaileth with iniquity and hath conceived mischief, and brought forth falsehood. He made a pit, and digged it, and is fallen into the ditch which he made."
20. W. James, *Holding Aloft the Banner,* 76.
21. Thorne, "Negro and His Descendants," 308–12.
22. W. James, *Holding Aloft the Banner,* 50.
23. Kublin, *Asian Revolutionary,* 235.
24. Burns and Sanders, *New York,* 243.
25. Draper, *Roots of American Communism,* 13.
26. Debouzy, *In the Shadow of the Statue of Liberty,* 3.
27. Draper, *Roots of American Communism,* 31. It is assumed that the representatives of the seven English-speaking sections included Americans who joined with foreign language members to establish the Party.
28. Ibid., 34–35.
29. *Emancipator* 1 (March 20, 1920): 4.
30. Morais and Cahn, *Gene Debs,* 63.
31. Ibid., 86.

32. Teitelbaum, *Schooling for "Good Rebels,"* 14.
33. Silver, "Public Speaking," 737–39.
34. Teitelbaum, *Schooling for "Good Rebels,"* 20. The Rand School was owned and controlled by the American Socialist Society, not the Socialist Party.
35. Ibid., 18, 35, 37, 40–41, 177.
36. Morais and Cahn, *Gene Debs,* 89.
37. Leinenweber, "Socialists in the Streets," 152–57, 166. The population of Harlem was still predominately white at that time.
38. Shannon, *Socialist Party of America,* 47.
39. Ibid., 49–50.
40. Morais and Cahn, *Gene Debs,* 77.
41. Gitlow, *I Confess,* 14–15.
42. Shannon, *Socialist Party of America,* 52.
43. Saltmarsh, *Scott Nearing,* 138.
44. Trachtenberg, *American Labor Year Book 1919–1920,* 109, 302.
45. Perry, "Hubert Henry Harrison," 421–23.
46. Harrison, *When Africa Awakes,* 43.
47. Perry, "Hubert Henry Harrison," 520–22; Harrison, *When Africa Awakes,* 43.
48. Foner, *American Socialism and Black Americans,* 267.
49. Appiah and Gates, "Chandler Owen," 1472.
50. Franklin and Meier, *Black Leaders,* 140–43.
51. Foner, *American Socialism and Black Americans,* 277.
52. Miller, "Socialist Party and the Negro," 227.
53. Franklin and Meier, *Black Leaders,* 143.
54. "Negroes Organizing in Socialist Party," *Messenger* 2 (July 1918): 8.
55. *New International* 1 (Feb. 1918): 7. Courtesy of Akito Yamanouchi.
56. Socialist Party Records, "Minutes" for Oct. 10, 1917; Feb. 27, 1918; March 27, 1918; May 1, 1918; Sept. 4, 1918. Chandler Owen was drafted by the army and Thomas Potter was appointed as district organizer on March 3, 1919. The Independent Political League was short-lived.
57. Blossom, "Rand School," 22.
58. *Rand School News,* Nov. 1918; Feb. 1919; Sept. 1919; Sept. 1920 (Rand School of Social Science Records).
59. Huiswoud Papers, "Benefit for a Sick Comrade" (ticket).
60. Foner, "Cyril V. Briggs," 8.
61. Moore, "Afro-Americans and Radical Politics," 217.
62. J. Johnson, *Black Manhattan,* 246.
63. Waskow, *From Race Riot to Sit-In,* 12, 177.
64. Hill, "The Negro Candidates," *Crusader,* 1:10 (Sept. 1918).
65. Hill, "Africa for the Africans," "Aims of the Crusader," "Race Catechism," *Crusader,* 1:3, 6, 13 (Sept. 1918).
66. Hill, "Sowing Dissension," *Crusader,* 1:32.
67. Hill, "Make Their Cause Your Own," *Crusader,* 1:368 (July 1919).
68. Cyril Briggs to American Fund for Public Service, New York, Feb. 26, 1924. Courtesy of Jeffrey Perry.

69. J. Turner, "Richard B. Moore," 34.
70. Draper Papers, Cyril Briggs to Theodore Draper, Los Angeles, June 4, 1958.
71. Hill, "The African Blood Brotherhood," *Crusader*, 2:731, 746 (June 1920).
72. Huiswoud Papers, "Otto Eduard Huiswoud," 13–15.

Chapter 3: "If We Must Die"

1. Huiswoud Papers, "Otto Eduard Huiswoud," 13.
2. Hill, "General Introduction," *Garvey Papers*, 1:xxxviii.
3. Ibid.
4. Anderson, *This Was Harlem*, 122.
5. J. Turner, "Richard B. Moore," 25, 38; Moore, "Critics and Opponents of Marcus Garvey," 217.
6. Harrison, *When Africa Awakes*, 10.
7. J. Johnson, *Black Manhattan*, 253.
8. Hill, *Garvey Papers*, 1:528–29.
9. Moore, "Africa Conscious Harlem," 167.
10. W. James, *Holding Aloft the Banner*, 365–66.
11. W. James, *Fierce Hatred of Injustice*, 152–61. McKay's date and place of birth have been established as September 15, 1889, in the village of Nairne Castle in the James Hill district of Clarendon by Winston James, who located his birth certificate.
12. Cooper, *Passion of Claude McKay*, 48.
13. McKay, *Long Way from Home*, 95.
14. Ibid.
15. Ibid., 31.
16. Domingo, "If We Must Die."
17. Work, *Negro Year Book*, 101.
18. Du Bois, "Triumph," 308.
19. Emanuel and Gross, *Dark Symphony*, 65.
20. Davis and Redding, *Cavalcade*, 233.
21. W. Turner, "Joel Augustus Rogers," 34.
22. Harrison, *When Africa Awakes*, 135–36.
23. Rogers, *From "Superman" to Man*, 3rd ed., 116.
24. Ibid., 5th ed., 117–18.
25. Rogers, *World's Great Men of Color*, 1:ix–xi.
26. W. Turner, "Joel Augustus Rogers," 36.
27. Brown Papers (UUA), "Harlem Unitarian Church," 5.
28. Brown Papers (Schomburg), "Religious Liberalism in Harlem," 46.
29. Brown Papers (UUA), "Harlem Unitarian Church," 4–5.
30. Morrison-Reed, *Black Pioneers*, 71.
31. Brown Papers (UUA), "Harlem Unitarian Church," 4.
32. Holmes, *Revolutionary Function*, 217, 221.
33. Brown Papers (Schomburg), "Fifteen Years in the Unitarian Ministry," 69–70.
34. Brown, "Labor Conditions in Jamaica," 349–60.
35. Draper Papers, "Meetings with Lenin," by S. J. Rutgers. This handwritten document

seems to be a translation of an article in Dutch by Rutgers, "Een ontmoeting met Lenin," *Communisme* 4 (Juni 1936), 390–97.

36. Katayama, "Morris Hillquit," 6.

37. Buhle and Georgakas, "Communist Party, USA," 147; Draper, *Roots of American Communism*, 144–45; Draper, *American Communism and Soviet Russia*, 18; "National Left Wing Conference," *Revolutionary Age* 1–2 (July 5, 1919) 4–5.

38. Buhle and Georgakas, "Communist Party, USA," 148; Weinstone, "Formative Period of CPUSA," 16–17.

39. Huiswoud Papers, Anna Leve to Hermie Huiswoud, New York, April 4, 1971, and June 7, 1973.

40. Johnpoll, *Documentary History*, 238.

41. Gitlow, *I Confess*, 522.

42. Brown Papers (UUA), "Harlem Community Church Membership Roll," 1; Brown Papers (Schomburg), "Religious Liberalism in Harlem," 48.

43. Kornweibel, "Seeing Red," 168–71.

44. Domingo, "Did Bolshevism Stop," 27.

45. Domingo, "Will Bolshevism Free America?" 86.

46. Domingo, "Socialism," 22.

47. J. Turner, "Richard B. Moore," 33–34.

48. Senate of the State of New York, *Revolutionary Radicalism*, 1489–1510.

49. "Grace Campbell," *Messenger* 2 (Nov. 1920): 138–39.

50. W. James, *Holding Aloft the Banner*, 174.

51. Huiswoud Papers, "Otto Eduard Huiswoud," 21.

52. "Our Reason for Being," *Emancipator* 1 (Mar. 13, 1920): 4.

53. NA, File 672, OG 258421, March 11, 1920.

54. NA, Group 65, 329359, Sept. 7, 1920; 329357, Sept. 4, 1920.

55. Draper Papers, Interview of W. A. Domingo, Jan 18, 1958; Moore, "Critics and Opponents," 230.

56. Ibid.

57. Hill, "Cyril Briggs," 45–46.

58. J. Turner, "Richard B. Moore," 31.

59. Senate of the State of New York, *Revolutionary Radicalism*, 2004.

60. Kornweibel, "Seeing Red," 12.

61. NA, OG208369, Jan. 31, 1920. Courtesy of Kornweibel.

62. Kornweibel, "Seeing Red," 133.

63. Ibid., 136.

64. NA, RG 65, 198940-145, May 31, 1921.

65. Kornweibel, "Seeing Red," 146, 145.

66. Ibid., 31.

67. Ibid., 77, 91.

68. Ibid., 86–87.

69. Kerlin, *Voice of the Negro*, 151.

70. Kornweibel, "Seeing Red," xiv, 23, 37.

71. "Negro—A Menace to Radicalism," *Messenger* 2 (May–June 1919): 20.

72. J. Turner, "Richard B. Moore," 33–34.

73. Kornweibel, "Seeing Red," 92.
74. Hill, "Congress, the Lusk Committee," *Crusader* 2:506–7 (Nov. 1919).
75. Senate of the State of New York, *Revolutionary Radicalism*, 1476.
76. NA, Dept. of State, (unidentified), Courtesy of Robert A. Hill; "Scotland Yard Detectives Grill Rogers," *Amsterdam News* (Aug. 19, 1925): 3.
77. Moore, "Afro-Americans," 217–18. The date of the meeting was determined from an announcement in the *New York Call* that Algernon Lee was the speaker for May 15, 1921.
78. "W.S. Harlem Br. Workers Party Meets," *Worker,* July 15, 1922, 2; "Harlem West Side Branch," *Worker,* Aug. 5, 1922, 5.
79. RA, 515/1/1600/32.
80. RA, 515/1/1598/9; 495/261/2133/9; Draper Papers, Briggs to Theodore Draper, March 17, 1958, 4.
81. Cooper, *Claude McKay,* 402n17.
82. McKay, *Long Way from Home,* 109; Cooper, *Claude McKay,* 402 n17; RA, 515/1/93/89.
83. RA, 495/261/2133/10.
84. J. Turner, "Richard B. Moore," 46. See W. James, *Holding Aloft the Banner,* 161–62.
85. Naison, *Communists in Harlem,* 5.
86. Cooper, *Claude McKay,* 115.
87. NA, 202600-2265, Sept. 15, 1921.
88. RA, 515/1/93/77.
89. McKay, *Negroes in America,* 89.
90. McKay, *Long Way from Home,* 109. Joseph P. Fanning was a socialist cigar store owner at 122 West 135th Street.
91. Cooper, *Passion of Claude McKay,* 54.
92. Kornweibel, "Seeing Red," 141–42.
93. FBI File, 61-50-493, Nov. 27, 1923.
94. McKay, *Long Way from Home,* 150.
95. J. Turner, "Richard B. Moore," 47.
96. Kornweibel, "Seeing Red," 125–26.
97. C. Johnson, "The Negro Renaissance," 227–28.
98. Hughes Papers, Hermie Huiswoud to Langston Hughes, Amsterdam, Sept. 18, 1961.

Chapter 4: Gift of the Tropics

1. McKay, *Harlem Shadows,* 50.
2. Hill, "Tulsa Riot," *Crusader* 4 (July 1921).
3. *New York Call,* June 2, 1921, 5.
4. Oklahoma [State] Commission, "Tulsa Race Riot," 12. Courtesy of Vivian Clark.
5. J. Johnson, "Exploited Negro," 108.
6. Hill, "A.B.B. Activities" and "Tulsa Riot," *Crusader,* 4:1176–77, 1173–74 (July 1921).
7. Kornweibel, *Federal Surveillance,* Reel 17, Survey 179.
8. Ibid., Survey 183.
9. Ibid., Survey 178.
10. NA, OG202600-2031-9, Aug. 26, 1921.
11. Kornweibel, *Federal Surveillance,* Reel 18, 861.00.

12. Hill, "Aims of the Crusader," *Crusader,* 1:75 (Nov. 1918).
13. Ellsworth, *Death in a Promised Land,* 89, 90, 94, xvi–xvii.
14. Brophy, *Reconstructing the Dreamland,* xvii, 8, 7.
15. "Panel Calls for Reparations in Tulsa Race Riot," *Arizona Daily Star,* Feb. 5, 2000, 1, 12.
16. Oklahoma Commission, *Tulsa Race Riot,* 19.
17. Riddell, *Founding the Communist International,* 8.
18. Ibid., 91.
19. Adler, *Theses, Resolutions and Manifestos,* 79.
20. Foner and Allen, *American Communism and Black Americans,* 8.
21. d'Encausse, *Great Challenge,* 12, 47, 62, 73.
22. Degras, *Communist International,* 1:398–99.
23. Kornweibel, *Federal Surveillance,* Reel 17, Survey 184.
24. Foner and Allen, *American Communism and Black Americans,* 9.
25. McKay, "Soviet Russia and the Negro," 63 64.
26. McKay, *Long Way from Home,* 156–57.
27. van het Reve, *Mijn rode jaren,* 164–67. Courtesy of and translation from Dutch by Magda Bon Bruno.
28. NA, RG65, BS202600-2265, Sept. 15, 1921.
29. McKay, *Long Way from Home,* 160–61.
30. RA, 515/1/93/77–78. "Wallunyus" was probably Alan Wallenius, a member of the ECCI.
31. Cannon, *First Ten Years,* 68.
32. Kornweibel, *Federal Surveillance,* Reel 18, Case File 861.00, Nov., 28, 1922.
33. Degras, *Communist International,* 1:265.
34. Stokes, "Communist International and the Negro," 1. Stokes did not identify the source of the "comprehensive report."
35. "Report on the Negro Question," *Inprecorr* (Jan. 5, 1923): 14–17.
36. Ibid., 21, 22.
37. RA, 515/1/93/84–85.
38. RA, 515/1/93/84A.
39. RA. 515/1/93/88. McKay's letter was addressed to "Kolaroff" but "Kolorov" is the spelling found in other references.
40. Cannon, *First Ten Years,* 64–71; Eastman, *Love and Revolution,* 333.
41. Johnpoll, *Documentary History,* 382–92.
42. Degras, *Communist International,* 1:375.
43. van het Reve, *Mijn rode jaren,* 172–74. Courtesy of and translation from Dutch by Magda Bon Bruno.
44. McKay, *Long Way from Home,* 206.
45. Draper, *Roots of American Communism,* 386.
46. McKay, *Negroes in America,* 4.
47. McKay, *Long Way from Home,* 177.
48. Cooper, *Passion of Claude McKay,* 126.
49. Foner, *American Socialism and Black Americans,* 205.
50. RA, 515/1/164/7.

51. NA, Dept. of State, 861.00/9909. Courtesy of Robert A. Hill.
52. RA, 515/1/174.
53. RA, 495/155/17/10.
54. "Negroes' Wrongs Aired at Moscow," *New York Amsterdam News,* Dec. 6, 1922, 1.
55. NA, Dept. of State, 61-40-401, July 2, 1923.
56. "Huiswoud Out to Organize Negro Labor," *Daily Worker,* Aug. 11, 1923.
57. Schuyler, *Black and Conservative,* 145–46.
58. Huiswoud Papers, "Otto Eduard Huiswoud," 12.
59. Solomon, *Cry Was Unity,* 29–30.
60. "Great All-Race Negro Congress Opening," *Daily Worker,* Feb. 11, 1924, 1; "Labor Fights Machine Rule," *Daily Worker,* Feb. 15, 1924, 3.
61. "What Finally Got Thru," *Daily Worker,* Feb. 18, 1924, 3.
62. Solomon, *Cry Was Unity,* 32–33.
63. Klehr, Haynes, and Anderson, *Soviet World of American Communism,* 26. Only Foster, Pepper, and Moissaye Olgin went to Moscow to present the three opinions within the CEC.
64. RA, 515/1/1233/99. The Huiswoud incident was cited along with other examples of negative attitudes and behavior by members of the Communist Party in the United States. A similar account was included in document RA, 495/155/59/88–89. Briggs also referred to this incident in his article in *Communist* 8 (Sept. 1929): 496.
65. Solomon, *Cry Was Unity,* 36–37.
66. RA, 495/37/26/143; 515/1/1580/173.
67. RA, 515/1/359/9–16.
68. RA, 515/1/474. The individuals responsible for the decision on Huiswoud's suspension, the meetings held, and the exact dates of the suspension are unknown. At the time William Z. Foster was chairman and Charles E. Ruthenburg was executive secretary of the Party.
69. RA, 515/1/513/111–13.
70. RA, 515/1/504/1–3.
71. RA, 515/1/474/145, 146.
72. Degras, *Communist International,* 2:97.
73. Solomon, *Cry Was Unity,* 46–47. There is evidence that Fort-Whiteman attended and spoke at the Fifth Congress, but his name does not appear on a list of delegates attending the congress.
74. Degras, *Communist International,* 2:164.
75. Solomon, *Cry Was Unity,* 49.
76. Klehr, Haynes, and Anderson, *Soviet World of American Communism,* 125–27. Document 25 indicates sums allocated for a pamphlet, ads, traveling expenses, salary for two organizers, and office expenses for three months. It is possible that the two organizers were Fort-Whiteman and Huiswoud.
77. RA, 515/1/450/49.
78. RA, 515/1/449/79.
79. McDermott and Agnew, *Comintern,* 133.
80. J. Turner, "Richard B. Moore," 56.
81. Domingo, "Gift of the Black Tropics," 341, 344–49.

82. Ibid., 345.
83. Perry, *Harrison Reader,* 252–53.
84. Cooper, *Claude McKay,* 180–91.

Chapter 5: The Radicals and the Renaissance

1. Interview of Hermina Huiswoud by Joyce Turner, Audiotape, Amsterdam, October 12, 1995.
2. Most of the Spanish-speaking residents congregated in East Harlem, and the area under consideration was referred to as Central Harlem.
3. Southern, *Music of Black Americans,* 455.
4. Ibid., 462.
5. Murchison, "Dean of Afro-American Composers," 49.
6. Vincent, *Keep Cool,* 17.
7. Hughes, *Big Sea,* 72, 234.
8. Emanuel and Gross, *Dark Symphony,* 64.
9. Du Bois, *Negro,* 231.
10. Ellison, *Invisible Man,* 439.
11. Hughes, *Big Sea,* 218.
12. "The Gist of It," *Survey Graphic* 6 (Mar. 1925): 627.
13. Locke, "Harlem," 629.
14. Ibid., 630.
15. Locke, "Enter the New Negro," 632.
16. Moon, *Emerging Thought,* 367.
17. Du Bois, "Locke, Alain," 79.
18. Du Bois, "Negro Mind Reaches Out," 401.
19. Locke, "Harlem," 630.
20. Du Bois, "Negro Mind Reaches Out," 412–13.
21. Emanuel and Gross, *Dark Symphony,* 64–65.
22. Locke, "Enter the New Negro," 633.
23. Gaither and Rampersad, "Harlem Renaissance," 527.
24. Maxwell, *New Negro, Old Left,* 1, 2, 6, 9.
25. Ibid., 202.
26. Moore, "Africa Conscious Harlem," 169.
27. Moore, "Afro-Americans and Radical Politics," 218.
28. RA, 515/1/575
29. Jackson, "Negro in America," 51; Haywood, *Black Bolshevik,* 144.
30. RA, 515/1/819/1–2.
31. RA, 515/1/819/15.
32. RA, 515/1/273/167. Aptheker, *Correspondence,* 289–90.
33. RA, 515/1/720/3–4.
34. RA, 515/1/819/11.
35. RA, 515/1/819/53.
36. RA, 515/1/819/4.
37. Huiswoud Papers, "Letter to the Editor."

38. J. Turner, "Richard B. Moore," 55–56.
39. Hughes, *Fight for Freedom*, 49–50, 197.
40. W. James, *Holding Aloft the Banner*, 365–66.
41. Foner and Allen, *American Communism and Black Americans*, 83–86; RA, 515/1/359/2.
42. RA, 515/1/819/30.
43. RA, 515/1/819/55; 515/1/819/43
44. RA, 515/1/819/56–59.
45. RA, 515/1/819/48–49.
46. "Huiswoud Shows Garvey's Latest Political Tricks," *Daily Worker,* Sept. 27, 1929, 3; Hill, *Garvey Papers,* 7:341–43.
47. Hill, *Garvey Papers,* 7:344n1.
48. Huiswoud Papers, "Re: Otto Eduard Huiswoud," 5–6.
49. RA, 515/1/819/32.
50. RA, 515/1/819/2.
51. *Amsterdam News,* Dec. 21, 1927.
52. RA, 495/261/2133/11.
53. RA, 515/1/1685/2–3.
54. Huiswoud, "The Negro and the Trade Unions," 770–75.
55. RA, 515/1/204/12.
56. Hill, "Cyril Briggs," 46.
57. RA, 515/1/1366/5.
58. RA, 515/1/1366/10.
59. Interview of Hermina Huiswoud by Joyce Turner, Audiotape, Amsterdam, Oct. 12, 1995.
60. RA, 515/1/255/26.
61. McClellan, "Africans and Black Americans," 373. Courtesy of Robert A. Hill.
62. RA, 515/1/819/8.
63. McClellan, "African and Black Americans," 375; Haywood, *Black Bolshevik,* 153–54.
64. Solomon, *Cry Was Unity,* 91.
65. See Solomon, "Rediscovering a Lost Legacy," 6–9. The NTWIU was the communist counter organization to the ILGWU of the AFL.
66. RA, 515/1/1267/20–21.
67. RA, 515/1/1685/2.
68. RA, 495/37/26/136.
69. Patterson, *Man Who Cried Genocide,* 101, 103.
70. McClellan, "Africans and Black Americans," 388.
71. Gross, *Willi Münzenberg,* 184–85, 189.
72. Shipman, *It Had to Be Revolution,* 153–54.
73. RA, 515/1/207/64.
74. RA, 515/1/720/11–12.
75. Shipman, *It Had to Be Revolution,* 162. Scott Nearing was not listed in the official proceedings of the congress.
76. RA, 515/1/720/22.
77. Moore, "Statement," 146. See 143–46 for the complete statement by Moore. In some

of his writings Moore listed Timeko Garan Kouyaté as a delegate, but his name does not appear in the official list of delegates. He was a delegate to the subsequent congress in 1929.

78. Shipman, *It Had to Be Revolution,* 162.

79. Geiss, *Pan-Africanist Movement,* 324–26.

80. "Pickens Addresses Pan-African Congress, *Daily Worker,* Aug. 23, 1927, 6; "Negro Congress Wants U.S. Navy to Leave Haiti," *Daily Worker,* Aug. 25, 1927, 2; "Pan-African Congress favors Unionization," *Daily Worker,* Aug. 30, 1927, 2. The resolution also appears in Aptheker, *Documentary History,* 3:548–49.

81. Robert Robinson wrote an autobiography, *Black on Red,* that described his unhappy years in the Soviet Union; Homer Smith described his experiences in *Black Man in Red Russia.* Evidently Smith decided to distance himself from the group that traveled to the USSR to make the movie *Black and White,* because his version regarding his arrival is quite different. According to Langston Hughes and Hermie Huiswoud, Smith was a member of the group.

82. Huiswoud Papers, Burroughs obituaries: *New York Herald Tribune,* Dec. 29, 1945; *Daily Worker,* Dec. 31, 1945; *New York Amsterdam News,* Jan. 5, 1946.

83. CPUSA election campaign biographical notes. Courtesy of John Earl Haynes.

84. CPUSA election campaign flyer. Courtesy of John Earl Haynes.

85. Perry, "Hubert Henry Harrison," 120.

86. Harrison, *When Africa Awakes,* 103.

87. *Daily Worker,* Oct. 1, 1928, 1. The caption under a picture of Williana Burroughs and her two sons on the front page identified her as a delegate to the Sixth Congress but her name was not included in a CP document listing delegates, nor was she mentioned by Harry Haywood in his autobiography. Her obituary identified the congress she attended as the seventh but the sixth was held in 1928 and the seventh not until 1935. There is no doubt, however, that she and her sons went to Moscow in 1928.

88. RA, 495/37/68/45–46. Courtesy of John Earl Haynes.

89. Klehr, Haynes, and Firsov, *Secret World of American Communism,* 200–202.

90. Huiswoud Papers, "Women" (Burroughs).

91. Huiswoud Papers, Burroughs Obituary, *New York Amsterdam News,* Jan. 5, 1946.

92. Hooker, *Black Revolutionary,* 7.

93. RA, 515/1/1600/33; On the Party's Sixth National Convention delegate registration form in 1929, Padmore indicated that he was twenty-four years old and had joined the Party in 1927. His biographer, James R. Hooker, thought he was probably born in 1902 in Arouca District, Tacarigua, Trinidad, which would have made him closer to age twenty-seven.

94. J. Turner, "Richard B. Moore," 104n43.

95. RA, 515/1/1231/30.

96. RA, 515/1/1366/10.

97. Reid, *Negro Immigrant,* 141.

98. Moon, *Balance of Power,* 120, 124–27.

99. Patterson, "With Langston Hughes," 156.

100. Moon, *Balance of Power,* 127.

101. Solomon, *Cry Was Unity,* 306.

102. Huiswood [sic], "A.N.L.C. Organizes Labor Unions in West Indies," *Liberator* (Harlem), Dec. 7, 1929, 3.
103. Huiswoud Papers, "Re: Otto Eduard Huiswoud," 6.
104. "Trinidad Orders Huiswood Out," *Liberator* (Harlem), May 10, 1930, 1.
105. Dumont, "Notes on the West Indies," *Liberator* (Harlem), March 15, 1930, 3.

Chapter 6: The Struggle Within

1. Haywood, *Black Bolshevik*, 218–19, 228–30.
2. RA, 515/1/1283/96, 103–4, 106.
3. RA, 515/1/1283/96.
4. Shiek was also referred to as Endre Sik by Harry Haywood and William Patterson.
5. Foner and Allen, *American Communism and Black Americans*, 177.
6. Draper, *American Communism and Soviet Russia*, 347; Foner and Allen, *American Communism and Black Americans*. 179.
7. RA, 515/1/1248/12.
8. Haywood, *Black Bolshevik*, 253.
9. Draper Papers, Joseph Z. Kornfeder to Theodore Draper, April 18, 1958.
10. RA, 495/155/66/5.
11. RA, 515/1/1291/14.
12. RA, 495/155/66/6.
13. RA, 495/155/59/12.
14. Foner and Allen, *American Communism and Black Americans*, 183.
15. RA, 493/1/285/4.
16. Haywood, *Black Bolshevik*, 253.
17. Solomon Papers, Samuel A. Darcy to Mark Solomon, Harvey Cedars, N.J., June, 2, 1974.
18. Foner and Allen, *American Communism and Black Americans*, 197; see Solomon, *Cry Was Unity*, chapter 5, and Foner and Allen, *American Communism and Black Americans*, chapter 6, for a detailed discussion and related documents on the Sixth Congress.
19. RA, 495/155/59/12.
20. Foner and Allen, *American Communism and Black Americans*, 180–82.
21. Ibid., 183.
22. "Bukharin's Speech," *Daily Worker*, Sept. 5, 1928, 3.
23. RA, 515/1/1366/17–19.
24. Foner and Allen, *American Communist and Black Americans*, 203.
25. Ibid., 205.
26. RA, 515/1/1271/22–29.
27. Following the sinking of the *Vestris* during an Atlantic storm in November 1928, the ANLC rallied to the defense of African American seamen who were charged with cowardice by authorities. Evidence pointed to heroic behavior as well as the terrible conditions under which they worked, and Huiswoud, Moore, and others organized a mass protest meeting in Harlem attended by twelve hundred people. See Solomon, *Cry Was Unity* and *Inprecor* (Jan. 18, 1929): 63.
28. RA, 515/1/1685/1–3. The meeting of the Negro Commission was attended by Moore,

Pepper, Burroughs, King, Lamb, Williams, Huiswoud, Golden, and Padmore—visitor. The minutes were signed by Cyril Briggs, secretary.

29. RA, 515/1/1685/1, 5, 6.

30. Brown Papers (UUA), "Hubert Harrison Memorial Church" (brochure), Sept. 1929, 10–11. The name of the church was changed on May 6, 1928, from Harlem Community Church to the Hubert Harrison Memorial Church in honor of Harrison, who died in 1927. In 1937 it was renamed the Harlem Unitarian Church.

31. Degras, *Communist International,* 2:38.

32. RA, 515/1/1272/12–13, 46–47.

33. RA, 515/1/1628/8.

34. Brown Papers (Schomburg), "Religious Liberalism in Harlem," 48.

35. Foner and Allen, *American Communism and Black Americans,* 205.

36. RA, 515/1/1274/154–55

37. RA, 495/261/2133/12.

38. RA, 515/1/1274/156–57, 159.

39. Ibid., 160–62.

40. Ibid., 171–76.

41. RA, 515/1/1272/22–23.

42. "5 Negro Workers on Communist Executive," *Negro Champion,* March 23, 1929, 1–2.

43. Draper, *American Communism and Soviet Russia,* 398.

44. "The Communist International to the American Comrades," *Communist International,* 1920, 2495–96.

45. Draper, *American Communism and Soviet Russia,* 398–99.

46. RA, 495/37/51/63.

47. Gitlow, *I Confess,* 522–23.

48. Morgan, *Covert Life,* 87.

49. RA, 495/37/53/79.

50. RA, 495/37/23/116–18.

51. RA, 495/37/26/131–44.

52. RA, 495/3/140. Courtesy of John Earl Haynes.

53. Draper, *American Communism and Soviet Russia,* 413.

54. Ibid., 414–15, 418.

55. Morgan, *Covert Life,* 95.

56. RA, 515/1/1818/68.

57. Klehr, Haynes, and Firsov, *Secret World of American Communism,* 174–75.

58. RA, 534/3/450/1–2.

59. Ibid., 2.

60. Draper Papers, "Interview with Edward Welsh," New York, May 20, 1958.

61. Briggs, "Lovestoneites."

62. Foner and Allen, *American Communism and Black Americans,* 216.

63. Ibid., 216–17. Both James Ford and Otto Hall were referred to in documents as director of the TUEL Negro Department but it seems Hall functioned in the role most of the time. Ford was in Moscow and Hamburg much of the time.

64. "Communist Party Plenum Upholds Comintern Line," *Daily Worker,* Oct. 15, 1929, 1.

65. *Inprecorr* 9 (Sept. 19, 1929): 51, 1112.
66. Foner and Allen, *American Communism and Black Americans,* 219–20.
67. RA, 515/1/1266/5. The minutes appear to have been recorded by a woman identified as M. King.
68. RA, 515/1/1580/173.
69. RA, 495/37/26/136.
70. Huiswoud, "World Aspects," 132–33.
71. Ibid., 133, 140–46.
72. Ibid., 141.
73. Haywood, *Black Bolshevik,* 321–22.
74. Foner and Shapiro, *American Communism and Black Americans,* 18.
75. Solomon, *Cry Was Unity,* 83–84.
76. RA, 495/37/65/69–70. Courtesy of John Earl Haynes.
77. RA, 495/37/68/43.
78. RA, 495/37/65/147–48. Courtesy of John Earl Haynes. It is not known whether the American Commission made any recommendations regarding Huiswoud's assignment or the fate of the ANLC.
79. RA, 515/1/1872/48.
80. RA, 515/1/1872/51.

Chapter 7: Harlem Goes to Moscow and Paris

1. RA, 515/1/1870/137.
2. RA, 515/1/1870/169. Courtesy of John Earl Haynes. The letter was probably written by William Weinstone, who had worked with Huiswoud in the CPUSA.
3. Huiswoud Papers, "Women" (Shura).
4. RA, 495/261/1408/10, 18.
5. RA, 495/155/53/1.
6. RA, 495/155/87/441–2.
7. RA, 495/155/87/443–44.
8. RA, 495/155/87/463–64.
9. RA, 495/72/94/140–45. Courtesy of John Earl Haynes.
10. Huiswoud Papers, "Women" (Shura).
11. Ibid. (Burroughs).
12. Ibid. (Mme. Litvinov). Hermie used the pronoun "I," so it is not presumed that Otto was involved with these cited *subbotniks*.
13. Dennis, *Autobiography,* 69–70.
14. McClellan, "Africans and Black Americans," 375.
15. Dennis, *Autobiography,* 68–69.
16. Padmore, *Life and Struggles,* 122–23.
17. Lazitch, "James W. Ford," 103.
18. Hooker, *Black Revolutionary,* 14.
19. RA, 495/261/1380/5. Translation from Russian by Sergey Listikov.
20. RA, 534/3/668/57.
21. Foner and Allen, *American Communism and Black Americans,* 151.

22. Italiaander, *Schwarze Haut*, 56–57. Courtesy of and translation from German by Ingeborg Bauer Knight.
23. RA, 534/3/669/145.
24. RA, 534/3/668/8–11, 13–15.
25. RA, 534/8/227/5, 119.
26. RA, 534/3/668/120.
27. RA, 534/2/65/208–10.
28. Ho Chi Minh, *Selected Writings*, 26.
29. RA, 534/2/65/212.
30. NA, Dept. of State, 800.00B-Communist International/140.
31. RA, 534/3/753/141.
32. RA, 534/3/754/9, 15.
33. "Our First Anniversary," *Negro Worker* 2 (Jan.–Feb. 1932): 2.
34. RA, 534/3/895/126–29.
35. RA, 534/3/753/20 23.
36. RA, 534/3/895/7.
37. RA, 534/3/895/1–2.
38. Huiswoud Papers, "Women" (Maria Ulianova).
39. Ibid. (Shura).
40. Berry, *Langston Hughes*, 155.
41. Patterson, "With Langston Hughes," 152. Louise Thompson Patterson had not married William Patterson when she took the trip.
42. Berry, *Good Morning Revolution*, 73.
43. Patterson, "With Langston Hughes," 155.
44. Hughes, *I Wonder as I Wander*, 76.
45. Berry, *Good Morning Revolution*, 74.
46. Huiswoud Papers, "Women" (Louise Thompson Patterson).
47. Patterson, "With Langston Hughes," 156.
48. Golden, *My Long Journey Home*, 202.
49. Huiswoud Papers, "Women" (Louise Thompson Patterson); Khanga, *Soul to Soul*, 67–68, 73–75, 85–86; Blakely, *Russia and the Negro*, 96–97.
50. Fax, *Through Black Eyes*, 133.
51. Golden, *My Long Journey Home*, 15, 17. Oliver John Golden was referred to as John Golden in Party records. Following his death in 1940 from a kidney disease, Bertha and their daughter, Lily, continued to live in Tashkent. Lily studied history at Moscow University, completed her PhD with a specialty in African music, and became the first researcher at the Institute of African Studies when it was opened by the Academy of Sciences in 1959. She continues to write and lecture on an international circuit. Her daughter, Yelena Khanga, is a noted journalist who hosts her own TV program in Moscow. Both Lily and Yelena have written autobiographies of interest.
52. Berry, *Good Morning Revolution*, 75.
53. Huiswoud Papers, Hermie Huiswoud to Milton Meltzer, Amsterdam, Nov. 20, 1967.
54. Bernard, *Remember Me to Harlem*, 104.
55. Berry, *Good Morning Revolution*, 159.
56. Huiswoud Papers, Hermie Huiswoud to Milton Meltzer, Amsterdam, Nov. 20, 1967.

57. NA, Dept. of State, 800.00B-Hughes, Langston/7.
58. Moon, *Balance of Power,* 124.
59. Ellis and Sechaba, *Comrades against Apartheid,* 19.
60. Bunting, *Moses Kotane,* 39.
61. "The South African Question," *Communist International* 6 (Dec. 15, 1928): 55.
62. Roux, *Time Longer Than Rope,* 256.
63. Davidson et al., *South Africa,* 2:21.
64. RA, 495/64/119/21.
65. RA, 534/3/753/1.
66. RA, 534/3/668/13.
67. RA, 534/3/895/49–66.
68. "The South African Question," *Communist International* 6 (Dec. 15, 1928): 55.
69. RA, 495/64/119/34–36. Also, Davidson et al., *South Africa,* 2:66–68.
70. RA, 495/64/126/60.
71. Kouyaté's first name is sometimes spelled Timeko.
72. Ho Chi Minh, *Selected Writings,* 21.
73. Geiss, *Pan-Africanist Movement,* 307.
74. Ho Chi Minh *Selected Writings,* 29, 36. Ho Chi Minh identified René Maran as an African, but he was from Martinique.
75. McKay, *Long Way from Home,* 278–79.
76. McKay, *Banjo,* 74–76.
77. Langley, "Pan-Africanism in Paris, 1924–36, 84–85, 87.
78. Geiss, *Pan-African Movement,* 310–11.
79. RA, 534/3/669/187.
80. RA, 517/1/1515/3–5.
81. RA, 534/3/755/61–63.
82. RA, 534/3/754/115–17.
83. RA, 517/1/1504/23. Danaé Narcisse was evidently not a new recruit. He had attended the 1927 anti-imperialism congress in Brussels representing the Inter-koloniale Vereinigung, Sektion der alten Kolonien und schwarzen Volker, two years before Kouyaté attended the 1929 congress.
84. RA, 517/1/1515/1–2.
85. RA, 517/1/1515/27, 28.
86. RA, 517/1/1515/32–33. Translation from French by Daphne Volle.
87. "Au Revoir," *Negro Worker* 4 (Aug.–Sept. 1933): 18.
88. RA, 495/64/132/13. Translation from Russian by Sergey Listikov.
89. See *Crisis,* October 1935.
90. RA, 534/3/895/120–21.
91. "Obituary," (Sen Katayama) *Inprecorr* (Nov. 10, 1933): 1108.
92. RA, 534/3/986/1.
93. RA, 534/3/986/8, 3.
94. Huiswoud Papers, "Otto Eduard Huiswoud." See also NA, Dept. of State, 800.00B-Huiswoud, Otto E./1, 2.
95. RA, 495/64/138/89; 495/155/102/2.
96. RA, 495/155/102/9. The particular incident referred to by Otto Huiswoud is not

mentioned in the available records, but it is assumed that there is some connection with events resulting from recruitment by George Padmore for which he was chastised by "J" in March 1933.

97. RA, 495/155/102/9, 5.
98. RA, 495/155/102/8, 9.
99. NA, Dept. of State, 844G.00.27 GDG.
100. RA, 534/3/1103/11.
101. RA, 534/3/1103/59, 60, 63.
102. RA, 534/3/1103/60–66.
103. RA, 495/261/6668.
104. McDermott, *Comintern*, 106.
105. RA, 543/3/1103/65–66.
106. Edwards, "Three Ways to Translate," 291.
107. Langley, "Pan-Africanism in Paris," 75.
108. Fabre, *From Harlem to Paris*, 2–3.
109. McKay, *Negroes in America*, 50, 52.
110. Lam, *Colonialism Experienced*, 249.
111. Ibid., 230. These few lines are from a poem by Chieu Hon Nuoc in 1926.
112. Kesteloot, *Black Writers in French*, xvi–xvii, translator's introduction.
113. Ibid., 7, 9, 48–49.
114. See Berry, *Good Morning Revolution*, 101–4.
115. "Negro Worker Elected in Paris," *Negro Worker* 5 (July–Aug. 1935): 29.
116. Hughes, *I Wonder as I Wander*, 400.
117. Rampersad, *Life of Langston Hughes*, 1:350; see Berry, *Good Morning Revolution*, 111–12.
118. NA, Dept. of State, 844G.00/27.GDG.
119. Huiswoud Papers, Langston Hughes to Hermie Huiswoud, New York, Sept. 27, 1938, and Dec. 6, 1965.
120. Hughes Papers, Hermie Huiswoud to Langston Hughes, New York, July 29, 1947.
121. Ibid., Amsterdam, Dec. 11, 1954.
122. Ibid., Dec. 4, 1961.

Chapter 8: Home to Amsterdam

1. Huiswoud Papers, "Re: Otto Eduard Huiswoud," 6.
2. Huiswoud Papers, Otto Huiswoud to Hermie Huiswoud, Paramaribo, Dutch Guiana, September 27, 1942.
3. J. Turner, "Richard Moore," 77.
4. *Negro Worker*, 3 (Apr.–May 1933): 23.
5. Klehr, Haynes, and Firsov, *Soviet World of American Communism*, 223.
6. Ibid., 222.
7. Burns, *New York*, 220.
8. "Our Reason For Being," *Emancipator* 1 (Mar. 13, 1920): 4.
9. "Negro—A Menace to Radicalism," *Messenger* 2 (May–June 1919): 20.
10. McKay, *Negroes in America*, 40.

11. *Emancipator* 1 (Mar. 20, 1920): 2.
12. Weigand, *Red Feminism,* 27.
13. Jones, "End to Neglect," 15.
14. Degras, *Communist International,* 2:447.
15. Kanet, "Comintern," 94.
16. Naison, *Communists in Harlem,* 72.
17. Ibid., 3–4.
18. Khanga, *Soul to Soul,* 49.
19. Minor Papers, "Negro 1924–1925" (notes by Robert Minor).
20. Cooper, *Passion of Claude McKay,* 91.
21. Hill, *Garvey Papers,* 5:854.
22. Harrison, "Negro in Industry," 83.
23. Cannon, *First Ten Years,* 230, 67.
24. Gitlow, *I Confess,* 522–23.
25. Dennis, *Autobiography,* 70.
26. "Lovestone Makes Report," *Daily Worker,* March 8, 1929, 1.
27. RA, 494/37/26/131–44.
28. RA, 515/1/3/60/24, 28.
29. Haywood Papers, Briggs to Harry Haywood, [Los Angeles, California] June 10, 1962, 1.
30. Dawson, *Black Visions,* 187, 191.
31. NA, Dept. of State, 844G.00/27 GDG.
32. Kornweibel, *"Investigate Everything,"* 276.
33. Kornweibel, *"Seeing Red,"* 182.
34. RA, 515/1/819/3.
35. Cooper, *Claude McKay,* 106–7.
36. Rivera, *My Art, My Life,* 1, 78.
37. Walker, "New Poets," 181–82.

Selected Bibliography

Manuscript Collections

Egbert Ethelred Brown Papers. Schomburg Center for Research in Black Culture, New York Public Library.
Egbert Ethelred Brown Papers. Unitarian Universalist Association Archives, Boston.
Theodore Draper Papers. Robert W. Woodruff Library, Emory University.
Harry Haywood Papers. Schomburg Center for Research in Black Culture, New York Public Library.
Langston Hughes Papers. James Weldon Johnson Collection, Beinecke Rare Book and Manuscript Library, Yale University.
Hermina Dumont Huiswoud Papers. In the possession of the author. To be placed at Tamiment Institute Library at New York University.
Robert Minor Papers. Rare Book and Manuscript Library, Columbia University.
Rand School of Social Science Records, 1901–56. Collection 13. Tamiment Institute Library and Robert F. Wagner Labor Archives, New York University.
Socialist Party Records. Tamiment Institute Library and Robert F. Wagner Labor Archives, New York University.

Government Archival Documents

UNITED STATES

Federal Bureau of Investigation. Records on Hermina and Otto Huiswoud, Cyril Briggs, W. A. Domingo, and Richard B. Moore obtained through the Freedom of Information Act were of limited use due to extensive deletions and incorrect accounts.
Library of Congress Manuscript Division. Communist Party USA—Records of the CPUSA (microfilm copies of Russian State Archive of Social and Political History Fond 515, Opis 1).
National Archives. Records of the State Department.

RUSSIA

The Russian State Archive of Social and Political History (RGASPI), formerly the Russian Center for the Preservation and Study of Documents of Recent History (RtsKhID-NI), designates documents according to Fond, the number of the collection; Opis, the subseries of the collection; Delo, the file; and List, the page. The archive uses the four terms in sequence to identify documents. All documents from the archive referred to in this account follow the sequence Fond/Opis/Delo/List after the letters RA, for Russian State Archive. For example, "RA, 495/261/2133/7–9" refers to Russian State Archive, Fond 495, Opis 261, Delo 2133, List (pages) 7–9. In some cases the page number was not available. The collections used in this study are as follows:

Fond 493	Opis 1	Sixth Congress of the Comintern
Fond 495	Opis 3	Political Secretariat, ECCI
	Opis 4	Political Commission of the Political Secretariat, ECCI
	Opis 7	Permanent Commission, ECCI
	Opis 17	Secretariat of the ECCI
	Opis 37	American Commission, ECCI
	Opis 64	Communist Party, South Africa
	Opis 72	Anglo-American Secretariat
	Opis 155	Eastern Secretariat Negro Department
	Opis 261	Personal files
Fond 515	Opis 1	Communist Party USA
Fond 517	Opis 1	Communist Party France
Fond 521		Sen Katayama personal papers
Fond 531		Lenin School
Fond 534	Opis 1	Profintern Congresses
	Opis 2	Session of Central Soviet, RILU International conferences organized by RILU
	Opis 3	Executive Bureau, RILU
	Opis 5	RILU International Propaganda Committee
	Opis 6	RILU
	Opis 8	RILU

Articles and Essays

Appiah, Kwame Anthony, and Henry Louis Gates Jr., eds. "Chandler Owen." In *Africana: The Encyclopedia of African and African American Experience.* New York: Basic Civitas Books, 1999.

Blossom, F. A. "Rand School." *Messenger* 2 (Jan. 1918): 22.

Briggs, Cyril. "Lovestoneites in Action" *Daily Worker,* Oct. 30, 1929, 4.

———. "Tulsa Riot and the African Blood Brotherhood." *Crusader* 4 (July 1921): 10. (For Briggs's unsigned articles in the *Crusader,* see Hill, *The Crusader,* in the book section of the bibliography.)

Brown, E. Ethelred. "Labor Conditions in Jamaica Prior to 1917." *Journal of Negro History* 4 (Oct. 1919): 349–60.
Buhle, Paul, and Dan Georgakas. "Communist Party, USA." In *Encyclopedia of the American Left,* ed. Mari Jo Buhle, Paul Buhle, and Dan Georgakas. Urbana: University of Illinois Press, 1992.
Davis, Arthur P. "Growing Up in the New Negro Renaissance." In *Cavalcade: Negro American Writing from 1760 to the Present,* ed. Arthur P. Davis and Saunders Redding. Boston: Houghton Mifflin, 1971.
Domingo, W. A. "Did Bolshevism Stop Race Riots in Russia?" *Messenger* 2 (Sept. 1919), 26–27.
———. "Gift of the Black Tropics." In *The New Negro: An Interpretation,* ed. Alain Locke. New York: Albert and Charles Boni, 1925.
———. "If We Must Die." *Messenger* 2 (Sept. 1919), 4.
———. "Socialism: The Negroes' Hope." *Messenger* 2 (July 1919), 22.S
———. "Will Bolshevism Free America?" *Messenger* 3 (Sept. 1920), 85.
Du Bois, W. E. Burghardt. "Locke, Alain, ed. *The New Negro.*" In *Book Reviews by W. E. B. Du Bois,* ed. Herbert Aptheker. Millwood, N.Y.: KTO Press, 1977.
———. "The Negro Mind Reaches Out." In *The New Negro,* ed. Alain Locke. New York: Albert and Charles Boni, 1925.
———. "Socialism and the Negro Problem." In *W. E. B. Du Bois: A Reader,* ed. Meyer Weinberg. New York: Harper and Row, 1970.
———. "Triumph." In *W. E. B. Du Bois: A Reader,* ed. Meyer Weinberg. New York: Harper and Row, 1970.
Edwards, Brent Hayes. "Three Ways to Translate the Harlem Renaissance." In *Temples for Tomorrow: Looking Back at the Harlem Renaissance,* ed. Geneviève Fabre and Michel Feith. Bloomington: Indiana University Press, 2001.
Foner, Philip S. "Cyril V. Briggs: From the African Blood Brotherhood to the Communist Party." Paper presented at the annual meeting of the Association for the Study of Afro-American Life and History, Los Angeles, Oct. 14, 1978.
Gaither, Edmund, and Arnold Rampersad. "Harlem Renaissance." In *The Encyclopedia of New York City,* ed. Kenneth T. Jackson. New Haven: Yale University Press, 1995.
Gruening, Ernest H. "New York: I. The City—Work of Man." In *These United States: Portraits of America from the 1920s,* ed. Daniel H. Borus. Ithaca: Cornell University Press, 1992.
Harrison, Hubert H. "The Negro in Industry," review of *The Great Strike and Its Lessons* by William Z. Foster, *Negro World* 9 (Aug. 21, 1920). In *A Hubert Harrison Reader,* ed. Jeffrey B. Perry. Middletown, Conn.: Wesleyan University Press, 2001.
———. "Socialism and the Negro." *International Socialist Review* 13 (July 1912): 65–68.
Hill, Robert A. "Cyril Briggs." In *Biographical Dictionary of the American Left,* ed. Bernard K. Johnpoll and Harvey Klehr. Westport, Conn.: Greenwood Press, 1986.
Huiswoud, Otto. "The Negro and the Trade Unions." *Communist* 7 (Dec. 1928): 770–75.
———. "World Aspects of the Negro Question." *Communist* 9 (Feb. 1920): 132–47.
Jackson, James. "The Negro in America." The Communist International 8 (Feb. 1925): 50–51.
James, Portia. "Hubert H. Harrison and the New Negro Movement." *Western Journal of Black Studies* 13 (1989): 82–90.

Johnson, Charles S. "Black Workers and the City." *Survey Graphic* 6 (Mar. 1925): 641–43, 718–21.

———. "The Negro Renaissance and Its Significance." In *Remembering the Harlem Renaissance,* ed. Cary D. Wintz. New York: Garland Publishing, 1996.

Johnson, James Weldon. "Exploited Negro." In *American Labor Year Book, 1921–1922.* New York: Rand School of Social Science, 1922.

Jones, Claudia. "An End to the Neglect of the Problems of the Negro Woman!" *Political Affairs* (June 1949); reprinted by the National Women's Commission, C.P.U.S.A. (n.d.).

Kanet, Roger E. "The Comintern and the 'Negro Question': Communist Policy in the United States and Africa, 1921–1941." *Survey* 19 (autumn 1973): 86–122.

Katayama, Sen. "Morris Hillquit and the Left Wing." *Revolutionary Age* (July 26, 1919): 6.

Langley, J. Ayo. "Pan-Africanism in Paris, 1924–36." *Journal of Modern African Studies* 7 (1969): 69–94.

Lazitch, Branco, with Milorad M. Drachkovitch, eds. "James W. Ford." In *Biographical Dictionary of the Comintern,* ed. Branko Lazitch. Stanford: Hoover Institution Press, 1973.

Leinenweber, Charles. "Socialists in the Streets: The New York City Socialist Party in Working Class Neighborhoods, 1908–1918." *Science and Society* 41 (summer 1977): 152–71.

Locke, Alain. "Enter the New Negro." *Survey Graphic* 6 (Mar. 1925): 631–34.

———. "Harlem." *Survey Graphic* 7 (Mar. 1925): 629–30.

McClellan, Woodford. "Africans and Black Americans in Comintern Schools, 1925–1934." *International Journal of African Historical Studies* 26 (spring 1993): 371–90.

McKay, Claude. "Soviet Russia and the Negro." *Crisis* 27 (Dec. 1923–Jan. 1924): 61–65.

Miller, Sally M. "The Socialist Party and the Negro, 1901–1920." *Journal of Negro History* 56 (July 1971): 220–39.

Moore, Richard B. "Africa Conscious Harlem." In *Richard B. Moore, Caribbean Militant in Harlem: Collected Writings 1920–1972,* ed. W. Burghardt Turner and Joyce Moore Turner. Bloomington: Indiana University Press, 1988.

———. "Afro-Americans and Radical Politics." In *Richard B. Moore, Caribbean Militant in Harlem: Collected Writings 1920–1972,* ed. W. Burghardt Turner and Joyce Moore Turner. Bloomington: Indiana University Press, 1988.

———. "The Critics and Opponents of Marcus Garvey." In *Marcus Garvey and the Vision of Africa,* ed. John Henrik Clarke. New York: Random House, 1974.

———. "Hubert Henry Harrison." In *Dictionary of American Negro Biography,* ed. Rayford W. Logan and Michael R. Winston. New York: W. W. Norton, 1982.

———. "Statement and Resolution at Congress of the League Against Imperialism and For National Independence, Brussels, February 1927." In *Richard B. Moore, Caribbean Militant in Harlem: Collected Writings 1920–1972,* ed. W. Burghardt Turner and Joyce Moore Turner. Bloomington: Indiana University Press, 1988.

Murchison, Gayle. "'Dean of Afro-American Composers' or 'Harlem Renaissance Man': The New Negro and the Musical Poetics of William Grant Still." In *William Grant Still: A Study in Contradictions,* ed. Catherine Parsons Smith. Berkeley: University of California Press, 2000.

Patterson, Louise Thompson. "With Langston Hughes in the USSR." *Freedomways* 8 (spring 1968): 152–58.

Rutgers, S. J. "The Left Wing." *International Socialist Review* 17 (Aug. 1916): 96–98.
Silver, Grace. "Public Speaking." *International Socialist Review* 13 (Apr. 1913): 737–39.
Solomon, Mark. "Rediscovering a Lost Legacy: Black Women Radicals Maude White and Louise Thompson Patterson." *Abafazi* 6 (fall/winter 1995): 6–13.
Thorne, A. A. "The Negro and His Descendants in British Guiana." In *Negro: An Anthology,* ed. Nancy Cunard. New York: Frederick Ungar Publishing, 1970.
Turner, Joyce Moore. "Richard B. Moore and His Works." In *Richard B. Moore, Caribbean Militant in Harlem: Collected Writings 1920–1972,* ed. W. Burghardt Turner and Joyce Moore Turner. Bloomington: Indiana University Press, 1988.
Turner, W. Burghardt. "Joel Augustus Rogers: An Afro-American Historian." *Negro History Bulletin* 35 (Feb. 1972): 34–38; reprinted in *Black Scholar* 6 (Jan.–Feb. 1975): 32–38.
Walker, Margaret. "New Poets." In *Remembering the Harlem Renaissance,* ed. Carl D. Wintz. New York: Garland Publishing, 1996.
Weinstone, William. "Formative Period of CPUSA." In *Highlights of a Fighting History: 60 Years of the Communist Party USA,* ed. Philip Bart. New York: International Publishers, 1979.

Books

Adler, Alan, ed. *Theses, Resolutions and Manifestos of the First Four Congresses of the Third International.* Atlantic Highlands: Humanities Press, 1969.
Albert, Bill, and Adrian Graves, eds. *Crisis and Change in the International Sugar Economy, 1860–1914.* Edinburgh: ISC Press, 1984.
———. *The World Sugar Economy in War and Depression, 1914–40.* London: Routledge, 1988.
Anderson, Jervis A. *This Was Harlem: A Cultural Portrait, 1900–1950.* New York: Farrar Straus Giroux, 1991.
Aptheker, Herbert, ed. *The Correspondence of W. E. B. Du Bois. Vol. 1, Selections.* Amherst: University of Massachusetts Press, 1973.
———. *A Documentary History of the Negro People in the United States.* Vol. 3, 1910–1932. Secaucus, N.J.: Citadel Press, 1977.
Bernard, Emily, ed. *Remember Me to Harlem: The Letters of Langston Hughes and Carl Van Vechten.* New York: Vantage Books, 2002.
Berry, Faith, ed. *Good Morning Revolution: Uncollected Writings of Social Protest by Langston Hughes.* New York: Citadel Press, 1992.
———. *Langston Hughes: Before and Beyond Harlem.* Westport, Conn.: Lawrence Hill, 1983.
Blakely, Allison. *Russia and the Negro.* Washington, D.C.: Howard University Press, 1986.
Brana-Shute, Rosemary, comp. and ed. *A Bibliography of Caribbean Migration and Caribbean Immigrant Communities.* Gainesville: The Center for Latin American Studies, University of Florida, 1983.
Brophy, Alfred L. *Reconstructing the Dreamland: The Tulsa Riot of 1921.* New York: Oxford University Press, 2002.
Bunting, Brian. *Moses Kotane: South African Revolutionary.* London: Inkululeko Publications, 1975.

Burns, Ric, and James Sanders. *New York: An Illustrated History.* New York: Alfred A. Knopf, 1999.
Cannon, James P. *The First Ten Years of American Communism.* New York: Pathfinder Press, 1962.
Clark, Kenneth B. *Dark Ghetto: Dilemmas of Social Power.* New York: Harper and Row, 1965.
Cooper, Wayne F. *Claude McKay: Rebel Sojourner in the Harlem Renaissance.* Baton Rouge: Louisiana State University Press, 1987.
———, ed. *The Passion of Claude McKay: Selected Poetry and Prose, 1912–1948.* New York: Schoeken Books, 1973.
Crosby, Alfred W., Jr. *The Columbian Exchange: Biological and Cultural Consequences of 1492.* Westport: Greenwood Publishing, 1972.
Curtin, Philip D. *The Atlantic Slave Trade: A Census.* Madison: University of Wisconsin Press, 1969.
———. *The Rise and Fall of the Plantation Complex. Essays in Atlantic History.* New York: Cambridge University Press, 1990.
Davidson, Apollon, Irina Filatova, Valentin Gorodnov, and Sheridan Johns, eds. *South Africa and the Communist International: A Documentary History.* Vol. 2. Portland, Ore.: Frank Cass, 2003.
Davis, Arthur P., and Saunders Redding, eds. *Cavalcade: Negro American Writing from 1760 to the Present.* Boston: Houghton Mifflin, 1971.
Dawson, Michael C. *Black Visions: The Roots of Contemporary African-American Political Ideologies.* Chicago: University of Chicago Press, 2001.
Debouzy, Marianne, ed. *In the Shadow of the Statue of Liberty.* Urbana: University of Illinois Press, 1992.
Degras, Jane, ed. *The Communist International 1919–1943 Documents.* Vol. 1, 1919–1922. London: Oxford University Press, 1956.
———. *The Communist International 1919–1943 Documents.* Vol. 2, 1923–1928. London: Oxford University Press, 1960.
d'Encausse, Hélène Carrère. *The Great Challenge: Nationalities and the Bolshevik State 1917–1930.* New York: Holmes and Meier, 1992.
Dennis, Peggy. *The Autobiography of an American Communist: A Personal View of a Political Life 1925–1975.* Westport: Lawrence Hill, 1977.
Draper, Theodore. *American Communism and Soviet Russia.* New York: Viking Press, 1960.
———. *The Roots of American Communism.* New York: Viking Press, 1957.
Du Bois, W. E. Burghardt. *The Negro.* New York: Henry Holt, 1915.
———. *The Souls of Black Folk: Essays and Sketches.* Chicago: A.C. McClurg, 1909.
Eastman, Max. *Love and Revolution: My Journey through an Epoch.* New York: Random House, 1964.
Ellis, Stephen, and Tsepo Sechaba. *Comrades against Apartheid: The ANC and the South African Communist Party in Exile.* Bloomington: Indiana University Press, 1992.
Ellison, Ralph. *The Invisible Man.* New York: Random House, 1952.
Ellsworth, Scott. *Death in a Promised Land: The Tulsa Race Riot of 1921.* Baton Rouge: Louisiana State University Press, 1982.

Emanuel, James A., and Theodore L. Gross, eds. *Dark Symphony: Negro Literature in America.* New York: Free Press, 1968.

Fabre, Michel. *From Harlem to Paris: Black American Writers in France, 1840–1980.* Urbana: University of Illinois Press, 1991.

Fax, Elton C. *Through Black Eyes: Journeys of a Black Artist to East Africa and Russia.* New York: Dodd, Mead, 1974.

Foner, Philip S. *American Socialism and Black Americans: From the Age of Jackson to World War II.* Westport: Greenwood Press, 1977.

Foner, Philip S., and James S. Allen, eds. *American Communism and Black Americans: A Documentary History, 1919–1929.* Philadelphia: Temple University Press, 1987.

Foner, Philip S., and Herbert Shapiro, eds. *American Communism and Black Americans: A Documentary History, 1930–1934.* Philadelphia: Temple University Press, 1991.

Franklin, John Hope, and August Meier, eds. *Black Leaders of the Twentieth Century.* Urbana: University of Illinois Press, 1982.

Geiss, Imanuel. *The Pan-African Movement.* London: Methuen, 1968.

Gitlow, Benjamin. *I Confess: The Truth About American Communism.* New York: E. P. Dutton, 1940.

Golden, Lily. *My Long Journey Home.* Chicago: Third World Press, 2002.

Gross, Babette. *Willi Münzenberg: A Political Biography.* East Lansing: Michigan State University Press, 1974.

Harrison, Hubert H. *When Africa Awakes: The "Inside Story" of the Stirring and Strivings of the New Negro in the Western World.* New York: Porro Press, 1920.

Haywood, Harry. *Black Bolshevik: Autobiography of an Afro-American Communist.* Chicago: Liberator Press, 1978.

Hill, Robert A., ed. *The Crusader, Cyril V. Briggs, editor. A Facsimile of the Periodical Edited with a New Introduction and Index by Robert A. Hill.* 3 vols. New York and London: Garland, 1987.

———. *The Marcus Garvey and Universal Negro Improvement Association Papers.* Vol. 1, 1826–August 1919. Berkeley: University of California Press, 1983.

———. *The Marcus Garvey and Universal Negro Improvement Association Papers.* Vol. 5, September 1922–August 1924. Berkeley: University of California Press, 1986.

———. *The Marcus Garvey and Universal Negro Improvement Association Papers.* Vol. 7, November 1927–August 1940. Berkeley: University of California Press, 1990.

Ho Chi Minh. *Selected Writings 1920–1969.* Hanoi: Foreign Languages Publishing House, 1973.

Holmes, Rev. John Haynes. *The Revolutionary Function of the Modern Church.* New York: G.P. Putnam's Sons, 1912.

Hooker, James R. *Black Revolutionary: George Padmore's Path from Communism to Pan-Africanism.* New York: Praeger, 1970.

Huggins, Nathan I. *Harlem Renaissance.* New York: Oxford University Press, 1971.

Hughes, Langston. *The Big Sea.* New York: Hill and Wang, 1940.

———. *Fight for Freedom: The Story of the NAACP.* New York: W. W. Norton, 1962.

———. *I Wonder as I Wander: An Autobiographical Journey.* New York: Hill and Wang, 1956.

Italiaander, Rolf. *Schwarze Haut im roten Griff.* Düsseldorf: Econ-Verlag, 1962.
James, Winston. *A Fierce Hatred of Injustice: Claude McKay's Jamaica and His Poetry of Rebellion.* London: Verso, 2000.
———. *Holding Aloft the Banner of Ethiopia: Caribbean Radicalism in Early Twentieth-Century America.* London: Verso, 1998.
Johnpoll, Bernard K. *Documentary History of the Communist Party of the United States.* Westport, Conn.: Greenwood Press, 1994.
Johnson, James Weldon. *Black Manhattan.* New York: Atheneum, 1968.
Kerlin, Robert. *The Voice of the Negro, October 25, 1919.* New York: Arno Press, 1968.
Kesteloot, Lilyan. *Black Writers in French: A Literary History of Negritude.* Philadelphia: Temple University Press, 1974.
Khanga, Yelena, with Susan Jacoby. *Soul to Soul: A Black Russian American Family 1865–1992.* New York: W. W. Norton, 1992.
Klehr, Harvey, John Earl Haynes, and Kyrill M. Anderson. *The Soviet World of American Communism.* New Haven: Yale University Press, 1998.
Klehr, Harvey, John Earl Haynes, and Fridrikh Igorevich Firsov. *The Secret World of American Communism.* New Haven: Yale University Press, 1995.
Knight, Franklin W. *The Caribbean: The Genesis of a Fragmented Nationalism.* 2nd ed. New York: Oxford University Press, 1990.
Knight, Franklin W., and Colin A. Palmer, eds. *The Modern Caribbean.* Chapel Hill: University of North Carolina Press, 1989.
Kornweibel, Theodore, Jr., ed. *Federal Surveillance of Afro-Americans 1917–1925.* Microfilm Reels 17, 18. Frederick, Md.: University Publications of America, 1986.
———. *"Investigate Everything": Federal Efforts to Compel Black Loyalty during World War I.* Bloomington: Indiana University Press, 2002.
———. *"Seeing Red": Federal Campaigns against Black Militancy, 1919–1925.* Bloomington: Indiana University Press, 1998.
Kublin, Hyman. *Asian Revolutionary: The Life of Sen Katayama.* Princeton: Princeton University Press, 1964.
Lam, Truong Buu. *Colonialism Experienced: Vietnamese Writings on Colonialism, 1900–1931.* Ann Arbor: University of Michigan Press, 2000.
Laurence, K. O. *A Question of Labour. Indentured Immigration into Trinidad and British Guiana, 1875–1917.* Kingston, Jamaica: Ian Randle Publishers, 1994.
Lewis, Arthur. *Labour in the West Indies.* London: Fabian Society, 1937.
Locke, Alain, ed. *The New Negro.* New York: Albert and Charles Boni, 1925.
Look Lai, Walton. *Indentured Labor, Caribbean Sugar. Chinese and Indian Migrants to the British West Indies, 1838–1918.* Baltimore: Johns Hopkins University Press, 1993.
Lumsden, May. *The Barbados American Connection.* London: Macmillan Publishers, 1983.
Maxwell, William J. *New Negro, Old Left: African American Writing and Communism between the Wars.* New York: Columbia University Press, 1999.
McDermott, Kevin, and Jeremy Agnew. *The Comintern: A History of International Communism from Lenin to Stalin.* London: Macmillan, 1996.
McKay, Claude. *Banjo: A Story without a Plot.* New York: Harper and Brothers, 1929.
———. *Harlem Shadows: The Poems of Claude McKay.* New York: Harcourt, Brace, 1922.
———. *A Long Way from Home.* New York: Harcourt Brace and World, 1970.

———. *The Negroes in America*. Part Washington, N.Y.: Kennikat Press, 1979.
Moon, Henry Lee. *Balance of Power: The Negro Vote*. Garden City, N.Y.: Doubleday, 1949.
———, ed. *The Emerging Thought of W. E. B. Du Bois*. New York: Simon and Schuster, 1972.
Morais, Herbert M., and William Cahn. *Gene Debs: The Story of a Fighting American*. New York: International Publishers, 1948.
Morgan, Ted. *A Covert Life: Jay Lovestone, Communist, Anti-Communist and Spymaster*. New York: Random House, 1999.
Morrison-Reed, Mark D. *Black Pioneers in a White Denomination*. Boston: Beacon Press, 1984.
Naison, Mark. *Communists in Harlem during the Depression*. Urbana: University of Illinois Press, 1983.
Oklahoma Commission to Study the Tulsa Riot of 1921. *Tulsa Race Riot*. Oklahoma City: Oklahoma Historical Society, 2000.
Padmore, George. *The Life and Struggles of Negro Toilers*. London: R.I.L.U. Magazine for the International Trade Union Committee of Negro Workers, 1931.
Patterson, William L. *The Man Who Cried Genocide: An Autobiography*. New York: International Publishers, 1971.
Perry, Jeffrey B., ed. *A Hubert Henry Harrison Reader*. Middletown, Conn.: Wesleyan University Press, 2001.
Rampersad, Arnold. *The Life of Langston Hughes: I, Too, Sing America*. Vol. 1: 1902–1941. New York: Oxford University Press, 1986.
Reid, Ira De A. *The Negro Immigrant: His Background, Characteristics and Social Adjustment, 1899–1937*. New York: AMS Press, 1968.
Richardson, Bonham C. *The Caribbean in the Wider World, 1492–1992. A Regional Geography*. New York: Cambridge University Press, 1992.
Ridell, John. Ed. *Founding the Communist International: Proceedings and Documents of the First Congress, March 1919*. New York: Anchor Foundation, 1987.
Rivera, Diego, with Gladys March. *My Art, My Life: An Autobiography*. New York: Dover Publications, 1991.
Rogers, J. A. *From "Superman" to Man*. 3rd ed. Chicago: J. A. Rogers, 1917.
———. *From "Superman" to Man*. 5th ed. New York: Joel A. Rogers, 1965.
———. *World's Great Men of Color*. Vols. 1 and 2. New York: J. A. Rogers, 1947.
Roux, Edward. *Time Longer Than Rope: A History of the Black Man's Struggle for Freedom in South Africa*. Madison: The University of Wisconsin Press, 1964.
Saltmarsh, John A. *Scott Nearing: An Intellectual Biography*. Philadelphia: Temple University Press, 1991.
Samuels, Wilfred D. *Five Afro-Caribbean Voices in American Culture 1917–1929*. Boulder: Belmont Books, 1977.
Schuyler, George S. *Black and Conservative: The Autobiography of George S. Schuyler*. New Rochelle, N.Y.: Arlington House, 1966.
Senate of the State of New York. [Lusk Committee.] *Revolutionary Radicalism: Its History, Purpose and Tactics with an Exposition and Discussion of the Steps Being Taken and Required to Curb It*. Report of the Joint Legislative Committee Investigating Seditious Activities. Part 1, vol. 2. Albany: J. B. Lyon, 1920.

Shannon, David A. *The Socialist Party of America: A History.* New York: Macmillan, 1955.

Shipman, Charles. *It Had to Be Revolution: Memoirs of an American Radical.* Ithaca: Cornell University Press, 1993.

Solomon, Mark. *The Cry Was Unity: Communists and African Americans, 1917–1936.* Jackson: University Press of Mississippi, 1998.

Southern, Eileen. *The Music of Black Americans: A History.* New York: W. W. Norton, 1971.

Teitelbaum, Kenneth. *Schooling for "Good Rebels": Socialist Education for Children in the United States, 1900–1920.* Philadelphia: Temple University Press, 1993.

Thurman, Wallace. *Infants of the Spring.* New York: Macaulay, 1932; reprint, New York: AMS Press, 1975.

———. *Negro Life in New York's Harlem: A Lively Picture of a Popular and Interesting Section.* Little Blue Book No. 494. Girard, Kans.: Haldeman-Julius Publications, n.d.

Trachtenberg, Alexander, ed. *The American Labor Year Book 1919–1920.* New York: Rand School of Social Science, n.d.

Trow's General Directory of the Boroughs of Manhattan, Bronx, City of New York. New York: R. L. Polk, 1916 and 1917.

Turner, W. Burghardt, and Joyce Moore Turner, eds. *Richard B. Moore, Caribbean Militant in Harlem: Collected Writings, 1920–1972.* Bloomington: Indiana University Press, 1988.

van het Reve, Gerard J. M. *Mijn rode jaren. Herinneringer van een ex-Bolsjewiek.* Utrecht, The Netherlands: Ambo, 1967.

Vincent, Ted. *Keep Cool: The Black Activists Who Built the Jazz Age.* London, Pluto Press, 1995.

Waskow, Arthur I. *From Race Riot to Sit-In, 1919 and the 1960s: A Study in the Connections between Conflict and Violence.* Garden City, N.Y.: Doubleday Anchor, 1967.

Watkins-Owens, Irma. *Blood Relations: Caribbean Immigrants and the Harlem Community, 1900–1930.* Bloomington: Indiana University Press, 1996.

Weigand, Kate. *Red Feminism.* Baltimore: Johns Hopkins University Press, 2001.

Work, Monroe N. The Negro Year Book 1918–1919. Tuskegee Institute, Ala.: Negro Year Book Publishing, 1919.

Yamanouchi, Akito. *S. J. Rutgers and a Case Study of the International History of Socialism: Association with Sen Katayama, the Bolsheviks and the American Left Wing.* Kyoto: Minerva Shobo, 1996.

Dissertation

Perry, Jeffrey Babcock. "Hubert Henry Harrison, 'The Father of Harlem Radicalism': The Early Years—1883 through the Founding of the Liberty League and *The Voice* in 1917." PhD diss., Columbia University, 1986. Facsimile. Ann Arbor: University Microfilms International, 1999.

Index

Adams, Mary. *See* Burroughs, Williana
African American agronomists in USSR, 202–3
African Blood Brotherhood (ABB): aims of, 56–57; and Communist Party, 89; *Crusader,* organ of, 57; founding of, 55; officers of, 57; and Sanhedrin, 113; and Tulsa riot, 93–94
African Federation of Trade Unions (AFTU), 207–8
African National Congress, 208
Allen, James S., 161
American Negro Labor Congress (ANLC): evaluation of, 135, 163–65, 189; founding of, 132; and KUTV students, 142; leaders of, 118–19, 133–36; *Negro Champion,* organ of, 133, 141, 162, 164; reorganization of, 135; termination of, 184; and UNIA, 137
Anderson, Jervis, xviii
Awoonor-Renner, Bankole, 143

Bagnall, Robert W., 8, 113
Bailey, Aubrey. *See* Williams, Harold
Baldwin, Roger, 146
Ballam, John, 133–35, 140, 162, 163–65, 242
Bates, Ruby, 204
Bedacht, Max, 105, 173 177, 179, 184–85
Bennett, Gwendolyn, 227
Berenberg, David P., 53
Berger, Victor, 43
Bialek, Bertha, 202–3
Billings, J. *See* Huiswoud, Otto

Bittelman, Alexander, 158–59, 169, 172, 176
Black and White (film), 200–201
Bloncourt, Max, 146
Bloor, Ella Reeve, 172, 177, 236
Boas, Franz, 53, 228
bolshevization, 119, 155–56
Bontemps, Arna, 127
Boudin, L. B., 73
Bradford, Perry, 125
Braithwaite, Isaac Newton, 61
Briggs, Cyril: and ABB, 57, 94, 95, 99; and *Amsterdam News,* 36–37; background, 35–36; on bolshevism, 76; *Colored American Review,* editor of, 36; and Communist Party, 86–87, 141, 154–55, 162–65, 171, 179, 228, 235, 237–38; *Crusader,* editor of, xix, 37, 55–56, 59; and Crusader News Service, 59, 111, 141–42; description of, 57, 242; and *Emancipator,* 78, 79; and FBI, 82, 84, 240–41; on Fourth Comintern Congress, 111; and Garvey, Marcus, 80, 89; and Harlem Renaissance, 121–22, 130; and Harlem Tenants League, 136; *Liberator,* editor of, 59, 153, 238; McKay, Claude, on, 105; migration to United States, 35, 71; *Negro Champion,* editor of, 59, 141, 162; Negro work (1929), report on, 179; radicalization, xvii; and Sixth Comintern Congress, 159; and Stokes, Rose Pastor, 95; on TUEL, 179
Brophy, Alfred L., 95–96
Browder, Earl, 114, 117–18, 183–85
Brown, Rev. E. Ethelred: and African Blood

Brotherhood, 57; background, 68–70; and Domingo, W. A., 69; and Garvey, Marcus, 80; Harlem Community Church founded by, 68–70, 79; and Harlem Renaissance, 70–71; on Harrison, Hubert, 68; and Holmes, John Haynes, 69–70; "Labor Conditions in Jamaica Prior to 1917," 70; migration to U.S., 68–69, 71; on Moore, Richard B., 167; and People's Educational Forum, 79; and Socialist Party, 53, 69–70
Brown, Mayme, 227
Bruce, John E., 63
Bruno, Magda Bon, 250
Bukharin, Nikolai I., 73, 102, 106, 171–72, 233
Bunting, Sidney P., 102, 205–6
Burrell, Benjamin E., 57
Burrell, Theophilus, 56–57
Burroughs, Williana, 203; and ANLC, 148, 163–64; as candidate for public office, 140, 148; and Communist Party, 163–65, 148; on Communist Party, 149; death, 150; employment, 148; and Huiswoud, Hermina, 150, 191; and League against Imperialism Congress (1929), 149; LSNR director for women activities, 148; as *Moscow News* writer, 149; and New York City Board of Education conflict, 148; and Sixth Comintern Congress, 149; and sons Charles and Neal, 149–50, 191; as Soviet Radio (VRK) announcer and editor, 49–150, 191; and women's issues, 149
Byrnes, James F., 82

Caffey, Francis G., 82
Campbell, Grace P.: and ABB, 57, 77, 89, 94; background, 77–78; Brown, Ethelred, on, 77; as candidate for public office, 53, 77, 86, 140; and Communist Party, 86, 163; Empire Friendly Shelter operated by, 77; employment, 77; and Harlem Community Church, 69, 167; and Harlem Tenants League, 136, 178; and Institute for Social Study, 148; and McKay, Claude, 66, 88, 90; Negro Workers Relief Committee chairman, 136; and People's Educational Forum, 53; social gatherings of, 25; and Socialist Party, 53, 77–78
Campbell, Martin Luther, 53, 69
Cannon, James P., 102, 105, 106, 114, 158
Carpenter, Clarence, 53
Carr, John. *See* Katterfeld, Ludwig E.
Cartier-Bresson, Henri, 223–24
Cartier-Bresson, Retna, 223–24

Carver, George Washington, 202
Catlett, Elizabeth, 227
Césaire, Aimé, 222
Challenge, 80–81
Chaplin, Charlie, 7
chauvinism. *See* Communist Party USA
Clark, Kenneth B., 28
Colored Socialist Club, 16–18, 42
Comintern: American Commission, deliberations of (1929), 172–77; policy on religion, 165–66
Comintern Congresses: First (1919), 96–97; Second (1920), 98; Third (1921), 98–99; Fourth (1922), 96, 100–108; Fifth (1924), 118; Sixth, (1928) 156–62
Comité de Défense de la Race Nègre, 210
Committee for the Defense of the Vietnamese Workers, 210
Communist International. *See* Comintern
Communist Party USA: African American candidates for public office, 140–41; CEC, African Americans elected to, 171; chauvinism in, 103–4, 161–62, 174, 178, 179, 180, 234–35; and Comintern, 97, 106; factionalism within, 72–74, 106, 114, 158–59, 170, 171–77, 180; and Farmer-Labor Party, 114–16; founding of, 71, 73; Harlem Branch of, 86; life within, 140–41, 180–81, 232–33; Negro Commission (1924), 116–17, (1928), 163–65; restructuring of, 107–8, 119, 155; and women's issues, 149, 153, 160, 177, 231–32
Confederation General du Travail Unitaire, 199
Cooper, Wayne F., 87, 122
Corey, Lewis. *See* Fraina, Louis C.
Crawford, W. Algernon, 240
Cri des Nègres, 199–200, 211–12, 214
Crisis, 31–32, 81
Crosswaith, Frank, 52, 69, 78, 96, 112
Crusader, 32, 55, 57, 80–81
Crusader News Agency, 214
Crusader News Service, 111, 112
Cunard, Nancy, 201, 223

Damas, Leon, 222
Darcy, Samuel Adams, 159–60
Davis, Arthur P., 29
Davis, Benjamin, Jr., 244
Davis, Helen. *See* Huiswoud, Hermina
Dawson, Michael, 239–40
Debs, Eugene V., 43, 44, 45, 47, 50
d'Encausse, Hélène Carrère, 98

Dengel, Philipp, 172, 174
Dennis, Eugene, 191, 206, 208, 209, 237
Dennis, Peggy, 191, 236
Dimitrov, Georgi, 149
Domingo, Eulalie, 70
Domingo, Wilfred A.: and ABB, 57, 94; arrest in Jamaica, 227; background, 34–35, 39; on bolshevism, 74–77; and British Jamaican Benevolent Society, 35; and Brown, Ethelred, 69; business of, 13, 86, 117, 120; on Caribbean American contributions, 120–21, 235; Cooperative Committee for Production of a Soviet Film on Negro Life chairman, 200; and Crusader News Service, 141; description of, 242; and *Emancipator,* 59, 78; and FBI, 82, 83, 84; "Gift of the Black Tropics," 120; and Harlem Community Church, 69–70; Harlem Renaissance contributor, 121–22, 131–32, 245; and Harrison, Hubert, 35, 49; internment in Jamaica, 227; Liberty League assistant secretary, 49; marriage, 35; and McKay, Claude, 66, 88, 108; and *Messenger,* 59, 79; migration to United States, 34, 71; and *Negro World,* 59, 63, 79; as orator, 44; and People's Educational Forum, 53; on racism in unions, 42; radicalization of, xvii–xviii, 32–33; and Randolph, A. Philip, 35; and Rand School, 52, 76; and Sanhedrin, 113; "Socialism Imperiled or the Negro—A Potential Menace to American Radicalism," 76–77; and Socialist Party, 46, 47, 96, 97, 110, 229; on women's issues, 231
Doty, Edward, 158
Draper, Theodore, 41–42, 86
Du Bois, W. E. B.: on African American literacy, 127; and *Crisis,* 31; and Fourth Pan-American Congress, 147; on French imperialism, 220–21; "The Negro Mind Reaches Out," 129–30; *The New Negro,* review of, 129; and People's Educational Forum, 53; on propaganda, 52; on racism, 30–32, 54, 65; on Socialist Party, 17–18, 110; *The Souls of Black Folk,* 31
Dungee, Roscoe, 135
Dunne, William, 114, 133, 156, 158–59, 163–65, 172, 174

Eastman, Max, 90, 106
Edwards, Brent Hayes, 220
Edwards, Thyra, 222, 224
Einstein, Albert, 145

Ellis, Ethel, 187, 190
Ellis, Fred, 187
Ellison, Ralph, 127
Emancipator, 78–79, 80–81, 105, 231
Emanuel, James A., 130
Engdahl, J. Louis, 204

Fabre, Michel, 220–21
Fanning, Joseph P., 88, 94
Farmer-Labor Party, 114–16
Faure, Émile, 210
Fauset, Jessie, 128
Fax, Elton, 202
Federal Bureau of Investigation (FBI), 81–84, 240–41
Ferris, William H., 53, 63
Flynn, Elizabeth Gurley, 18, 53
Foner, Philip S., 16, 50, 161
Ford, James: ANLC, 135; as candidate for public office, 140; and Comintern, 148; and Communist Party, 192–93; and Fort-Whiteman, Lovett, 227; and ITUC-NW, 177, 193–95, 210, 211; and Lovestone crisis, 173; and Negro question, 156–59, 161; and *Negro Worker,* 150; and TUEL, 163
Fortune, T. Thomas, 63
Fort-Whiteman, Lovett: and ANLC, 119, 132–34, 135, 140; arrest in St. Louis, 79; as candidate for public office, 140; and Comintern, 118, 134; and Communist Party, 87; death, 227–28; Du Bois, W. E. B., correspondence with, 134; as Fifth Comintern Congress delegate, 118, 134; and *Messenger,* 52; "The Negro in America," 133; and Negro question, 158–59; Rand School, 75, 142; and Sanhedrin, 113; and Socialist Party, 52; and UNIA, 138
Foster, William: as candidate for public office, 114; and Huiswoud, Otto, 116, 178; and Lovestone crisis, 170–79; on Moore, Richard B., 169; on Negro question, 158–59; and Padmore, George, 150; and UNIA, 137; as Workers Party chairman, 114
Fraina, Louis C., 22, 73
Francis, Lionel, 138
Franke, Genosse, 100
Franklin, John Hope, 95

Gaither, Edmund, 131
Garvey, Marcus, xvii–xviii; and Briggs, Cyril, 89; and Brown, Ethelred, 80; and Communist Party, 137–38; and Domingo, W. A., 61, 79–80; and Huiswoud, Otto,

139; indictment of, 96; migration to United States, 60, 71; *Negro World,* founder of, 62–63; Universal Negro Improvement Association (UNIA), founder of, 60–62
Gaspar, Victor C., 53
Geiss, Imanuel, 147, 210, 211
Gerber, Julius, 16, 73
Gitlow, Benjamin: as candidate for office, 115; on Huiswoud, Otto, 74, 236; and Lovestone crisis, 170, 173, 175–77; and Negro question, 170; on Socialist Party and Negro question, 47
Golden, Bessie (Jane), 202, 203
Golden, Lily, 268n51
Golden, Oliver John, 143–44, 148, 162–65, 202–3, 234, 268n51
Goldfarb, Max, 156, 159
Gomez, Manuel, 22, 145, 147, 158
Grey, Edgar M., 88
Gross, Theodore L., 130
Gruening, Ernest H., 13
Guillén, Nicolas, 222, 223, 224
Gumede, Josiah, 146, 205
Gusev, Sergei, 176

Hall, Heywood. *See* Haywood, Harry
Hall, Otto, 163–65; as candidate for office, 140; on chauvinism, 161; election to CEC, 171; on factionalism, 236; on Huiswoud, Otto, 115; KUTV student, 143; Lovestone crisis, 173, 175; and Moore, Richard B., 159; on Negro question, 156–59, and TUEL Negro Department, 179
Handy, William C., 125
Harlem, description of, xix, 8–9, 27–30, 124–25, 127
Harlem Community Church. *See* Harlem Unitarian Church
Harlem Educational Forum, 112
Harlem Renaissance, xviii–xix, 125–26, 130–32, 243–45
Harlem Tenants League, 136, 160, 168, 170, 178
Harlem Unitarian Church, 69–70, 125, 266n30. *See also* Brown, Rev. E. Ethelred
Harrison, Hubert Henry, xvii, 25, 32, 126, 129, 146, 231; and ANLC, 140; background, 14, 15; on Caribbean American contributions, 121; *Colored American Review,* review by, 36; death, 140; employment, 16; on Foster, William, 236; *From "Superman" to Man,* review by, 67; and Institute for Social Study, 148; Liberty League of Negro Americans, founder of, 48–49; marriage, 15; and McKay, Claude, 66, 88; migration to United States, 15, 71; Moore, Richard B., on, 19; and *Negro World,* 63; *New Negro* (1919 magazine), editor of, 128; as orator, 10, 43, 58–59; and People's Educational Forum, 53; on race first, 48–49; and Socialist Party, 14–19, 110; *The Voice of the Negro,* founder of, 49
Hathaway, Clarence, 156
Haynes, Samuel, xx
Haywood, Harry: and Huiswoud, Otto, 120, 181, 183–84, 186, 188; KUTV and Lenin School student, 143, 159, 183; and LSNR, 184; and Nasanov, Nikolai, 156, 183; and Negro Bureau, 183–84; and Negro question, 156–59, 239
Haywood, William (Bill), 18
Hendricks, Arthur, 75, 87
Hendrickson, A. Elizabeth, 53, 136
Herndon, Angelo, 232, 244
Hill, Robert, 32, 61, 139, 142, 235
Hillquit, Morris, 46, 51, 73
Ho Chi Minh, 196, 210
Holmes, John Haynes, 69–70
Hoover, J. Edgar, 82–83
Hope, Cecil, 136,
Houston, Marie, 143
Hubert Harrison Memorial Church. *See* Harlem Unitarian Church
Hughes, Langston, xix, 32, 123; *Black and White* (film), 200–201; Central Asia trip, 203; "Goodbye, Christ," 203–4; and International Association of Writers for the Defense of Culture, 223; and Huiswoud, Hermina, 2, 91, 203, 223–24; as LSNR president, 184; "Madrid—1937," 223; Moscow stay, 202–4; and Paris, 222–24; and Scottsboro Boys campaign, 205; and Second International Writers Congress, 222–23; on writer's assistance, 126–28
Huiswoud, Christopher, 10
Huiswoud, Hermina: Amsterdam, residence in, 226, 246–47; arrest in Antwerp, 215; background, 5–7; on *Black and White* (film), 201; on Campbell, Grace, 25; and Crusader News Service, 59, 142; Cuba visit, 226; death, 250; and Dennis, Peggy, 191, 236; description of, 242; employment, 7–8, 227; on Ford, James, 186; on Garvey-Huiswoud debate, 139; on Harlem, 8; on Harlem Tenants League, 136; on housing, 9–10; and Hughes, Langston, 2, 91, 203,

223–24; on Huiswoud, Otto, 10–11, 25–26, 27, 123–24, 153, 226, 246–47, 249–50; and Lenin School, 187, 236; and *Liberator* (Harlem) 59, 153; marriage, 123–24; migration to United States, xiii, xv, 1–2, 4–6; Moscow life, 187, 190–91, 200, 203–4, 214; and *Negro Worker*, 59, 214; on orators, 58–59; on Padmore, 150; Paris life, 220, 222–24; radicalization of, xvii, xviii, 14, 124, 154, 242–43; "Two Epitaphs in an English Graveyard," 112–13, 251–52; vacation in Georgia (USSR), 206; on White, Maude, 143; and women's issues, 153

Huiswoud, Otto: and ABB, 57, 88–89, 93, 99, 111–12; Amsterdam, residence in, 226; ANLC, 117–18, 132, 140, 163–64; arrest in Antwerp, 215; background, 11–14, 23–24, 30, 39, 52; and *Black and White* (film), 202–3; and Bloor, Ella Reeve, 177, 236; and Browder, Earl, 216; and Burroughs, Williana, 148, 203; as candidate for pubic office, 140–41; and Cannon, James, 236; and Caribbean tour, 152; on church policy, 167; on *Cri des Nègres,* 212; Crosswaith, Frank, debate with, 112; and Cuba trip, 226; and Davis, Benjamin, Jr., 216; death, 224, 225, 246; and Debs, Eugene, 46, 79; "De Koerier," editor of, 227; description of, 27, 109, 242; with Domingo, W. A. in produce business, 117; "Dutch Guiana: A Study in Colonial Exploitation," 52; ECCI, elected candidate member, 159; ECCI Negro Bureau opposition to, 186; Fall River Line protest by, 23, 50; and Farmer-Labor Party, 115; and FBI, 84, 240; and Ford, James, 216; and Foster, William Z., 117, 169–70, 177–78, 236; as Fourth Comintern Congress delegate and Negro Commission chairman, 23, 89–90, 95, 99–108, 230; as Fourth Pan-African Congress delegate, 147; and Franke, Genosse, 100; Garvey, Marcus, debate with, 139; and Gitlow, Benjamin, 236; on Golden, Oliver John, 144, 203; Harlem Branch (West Side) of Communist Party organized by, 85–86; Harlem Community Church, 70; Harlem Renaissance participant, 121–22, 152, 244; and Harlem Tenants League, 136; and Harrison, Hubert, 14, 19, 23, 235; and Haywood, Harry, 120, 181, 183–84, 186, 188, 216; and Huiswoud, Hermina Dumont, 10–11, 226; internment and work in Dutch Guiana, 225–26; and ITUC-NW, 177–78, 185, 186–87, 192, 195, 211, 214, 217, 219, 224; and Katayama, Sen, 22–23, 101, 176–77, 214; Lenin, meeting with, 107, 243; and Liberty League, 49; and Lovestone crisis, 172–78; and Lusk Committee, 81; marriage, 123–24; and McKay, Claude, 66, 88, 105, 108–10; and Merlin, Felix, 223; and *Messenger,* 24; migration to United States, xiii, 11–12, 32, 71; and Moon, Henry Lee, 152; Moscow life of, 187, 190–92; "The Negro and the Trade Unions," 141; as Negro Commission (CP), chairman, 163–65; as Negro Department (CP) head, 162–63; and Negro question, 131–32, 159, 162, 181–85, 238–39; "Negro Slave Revolts in Mexico," 224; *Negro Worker*, editor of, 213, 219–20; Ons Suriname, president of, 227; as orator, 44; and Padmore, George, 209, 213; in Paris, 222; and People's Educational Forum, 53; and Profintern (*see* ITUC-NW); and Radek, Karl, 107; radicalization of, xvii–xviii, 32–33; and Rand School of Social Science, 52, 57–58; relationship with Briggs, Domingo, and Moore, 58; reports of, 163, 177–78, 179–80, 188–89, 190, 195–97, 208, 213–14, 215–16, 217–18; and Rutgers, S. J., 23, 235; and Ruthenberg, Charles E., faction ally, 235–56; and Sanhedren, 113; Schuyler, George S., debate with, 112; and Scottsboro Boys campaign, 204, 239; and socialism, 229, 242–43; and Socialist Party, 24, 45, 46, 47; and South Africa, 204, 205, 207–8; Suriname school named for, 246; and Swaback, Arne, 116; on TUEL, 111, 112, 117, 141, 175; on TUUL, 182; and UNIA, 139, 180; "World Aspects of the Negro Question," 205; and women's issues, 177, 231

International Association of Writers for the Defense of Culture, 223
International Congress against Colonial Oppression and Imperialism, 146–47
International Lenin School, 143, 191
International Trade Union Committee of Negro Workers (ITUC-NW), 164, 193–200, 209–19
Industrial Workers of the World (IWW), 18

Jackson, Anselmo, 78
Jackson, T. *See* Nzula, Albert
Jamaica Trades and Labor Union, 153

James, C. L. R., xvii
James, Portia, 16
James, Winston, xv, xviii, 4, 18, 39–40, 131
Johnson, Charles S., 4, 91, 128
Johnson, Fenton, 53
Johnson, James P., 125
Johnson, James Weldon, xix, 30, 54, 61–62, 93–94, 113
Johnson, Manning, 240
Johnstone, Jack, 158
Jones, Claudia, 231

Kanet, Roger, 233
Katayama, Sen, 74, 145; background, 20; death, 214; education, 20; and Fourth Comintern Congress, 101, 102; and Gomez, Manuel, in Mexico, 22; and Huiswoud, Otto, 20, 23, 103, 115; and International Congress against Colonial Oppression and Imperialism, 145; Japanese Social Democratic Party, founder of, 135; Japanese socialists in New York, organizer of, 20–21; and Left Wing, 72–73; and Lovestone crisis, 176–77; migration to and from United States, 20, 22; and Negro Bureau plan, 110; and Negro question, 156–57, 159, 160; and Rutgers, S. J., 21, 22; and Second Comintern Congress, 22; and Sixth Congress of Second International, 20
Katterfeld, Ludwig E., 101, 105
Kellogg, Paul U., 128
Kesteloot, Lilyan, 222
Khanga, Yelena, 268n51
Kipling, Rudyard, 112–13, 251–52
Kirnon, Hodge, 63
Kolarov, Vasil, 105, 111
Kollontai, Alexandra, 73
Kornfeder, Joseph Z., 158, 160, 162
Kornweibel, Theodore, Jr., 81, 241
Kotane, Moses, 208–9
Kotoku, Shusui, 20
Kouyaté, Tiemoko Garan, 195, 198, 199, 209–13
Kublin, Hyman, 20, 21, 40
Kuusinen, Otto, 102, 106, 110, 159, 173, 176

La Guma, James, 146, 205
Lam, Truong Buu, 221
League of Struggle for Negro Rights, 184, 189–90
Lee, Algernon, 45, 85

Lenin, Vladimir I.: Domingo, W. A. on, 76; and Fourth Comintern Congress, 99; Huiswoud, Otto, conversation with, 107, 243; Rutgers, S. J., report to, 72; and Thesis on National and Colonial Question by, 97, 99, 145, 157; and Third International criteria, 96–97
Leve, Anna, 24, 74, 89, 123, 237
Liberator (Harlem), 59, 153, 238
Liberty League of Negro Americans, 48–49, 61–62
Ligue de Défense de la Race Nègre, 210–11
Litvinov, Ivy Low, 191
Locke, Alain, xix, 128–29, 130
London, Mayer, 43
Lore, Ludwig, 73
Lovestone, Jay, 114, 158–60, 170–78
Lozovsky, Solomon, 173–74
Lusk Committee of New York State Senate, 77, 84

Mahoney, Roy, 143, 156, 158, 159
Maran, René, 210, 220, 222, 223, 224
Marcantonio, Vito, 244
Marke, George O., 138
Martins, Carlos Deambrosis, 146
Mason, Edward. *See* Huiswoud, Otto
Maxwell, William, 131
McClellan, Woodford, 144
McKay, Claude, xviii, 79, 203, 210, 222; ABB, 86, 87, 90, 99; *Banjo*, 211, 221; on Briggs, Cyril, 87, 105; and Communist Party, 86, 87, 88; and Communist Party of Great Britain, 88; and Domingo, W. A., 105, 229; description of, 109; education, 63–64; "Exhortation: Summer 1919," 92; and Fourth Comintern Congress, 90, 96, 99–110, 122, 230; on French imperialism, 221; and Harrison, Hubert, meeting, 88; and Huiswoud, Otto, 109; on Huiswoud, Otto, 105; "If We Must Die," 64–65, 91; and Katayama, Sen, 102; and *Liberator*, 88; *A Long Way from Home*, 66, 109; migration to United States, xvii, 71; and Minor, Robert, 88; and Moore, Richard B., visit to, 147; Moscow stay, 108; "Mulatto," 109; *The Negroes in America*, 88, 106; on Negro question, 131; "Pushkin," front matter, 147; on racism, 63, 103–4, 234–35; and Radek, Karl, 107; and Stokes, Rose Pastor, 102; "The White House," 128–29; on women's issues, 231

Merlin, Felix, 223
Messenger, 32, 49–51, 54, 55, 80–91
migration, Caribbean: and Caribbean economies, xiii–xvii; from, xv, 4; to, xiii–xvii; within, xiv–xv, 4
migration: from the South, xviii, 3–4
Miller, Rev. George Frazier, 53
Miller, Kelly, 113
Miller, Loren, 203
Miller, Sally, 50
Minor, Robert, 87, 163–65; and ANLC, 133, 135; on church, 166; on factionalism, 236; and Lovestone crisis, 172, 176, 177, 179–80; and Negro question, 156; and Negro work responsibilities, 162, 165; on racism, 115–17, 234; and Sanhedrin, 113; and UNIA, 138
Mohamed, Duse, 63
Molotov, Viacheslav M., 176
Moon, Henry Lee, 151–52, 204
Mooney, Tom, 232
Moore, Fred R., 53
Moore, Richard B.: and ABB, 56–57, 94; and ANLC, 117–18, 132, 135–36, 140–41, 145, 163–64; background, 33–34, 39; and Barbados independence, 246; on Briggs, Cyril, 168; and Burroughs, Williana, 148; as candidate for public office, 140; and Communist Party, 86, 87, 119–20, 154, 163–69, 228, 232, 237–38; description of, 242; and Domingo, W. A., 35, 66, 78–79; and *Emancipator,* 59, 78–79; and factionalism, 236; and FBI, 82, 83, 84, 240; on Fort-Whiteman, 168; as Fourth Pan-African Congress delegate, 147–48; and Garvey, Marcus, 61; and Golden, Oliver John, 144, 203; and Harlem Community Church, 69, 70, 165–67; and Harlem Renaissance, xix, 121–22, 132; and Harlem Tenants League, 136; and Harrison, Hubert, 34; on Harrison, Hubert, 19; and Huiswoud, Hermina, 124, 227; and Huiswoud, Otto, 25, 124, 227; on Huiswoud, Otto, 167–68; Institute for Social Study director, 148; as International Congress against Colonial Oppression and Imperialism delegate, 145–47, 243; on Liberty League, 49; as LSNR General Secretary, 184; marriage, 34; and McKay, Claude, 66, 88, 90, 108, 147; migration to United States, 33, 71; and National Negro Committee (1928) 162, 180–81; and Negro Commission (CP, 1928), 163–65; and Negro question, 131–32, 158–59, 162, 167–68, 170, 181, 238–39; and Negro Workers Relief Committee, 136; as orator, 44, 235; and Padmore, George, 150, 168, 181; and People's Educational Forum, 53; and Pepper, John, 165–69; radicalization of, xvii–xviii, 32–33; on Rogers, J. A., 68; and Sanhedrin, 113; and Scottsboro Boys campaign, 204, 239; and socialism, 229, 242–43; and Socialist Party, 46, 75, 76, 85, 96; and UNIA, 138; on women's issues, 231
Münzenberg, Willi, 145, 147

Naison, Mark, 87, 233–34
Narcisse, Danaé, 212
Nasanov, Nikolai, 156, 160, 183, 186
National Association for the Advancement of Colored People (NAACP), 31, 40, 93, 127–28
National Urban League, 40, 127–28
Nearing, Scott, 146
Negro Champion, 141
Negro Miners Relief Committee, 136, 160, 168, 177–78
Negro Welfare Association (London), 215
Negro Worker, 194, 195, 214, 216, 219–20
Negro Workers Relief Committee, 136, 169
Negro World, 32, 63, 80–81
Nehru, Jawaharlal, 145
New Negro (edited by Hubert Harrison in 1919), 128
The New Negro, 120, 128–30
Newton, Herbert, 143
New York State Senate Lusk Committee on radicalism. *See* Lusk Committee of New York State Senate
Nguyen Ai Quoc. *See* Ho Chi Minh
Noral, Alex, 172, 177
Nurse, Malcolm. *See* Padmore, George
Nzula, Albert, 207

Ons Suriname, 227, 249
Opportunity, 126, 128
Owen, Chandler, 50–53, 55, 78–79, 83, 96
Owens, Gordon, 116
Owens, John, 140

Padmore, George, xvii, 165, 168; and Communist Party, 150; expulsion, 213; and Ford, James, 193–95; and Huiswoud, Otto, 195, 197, 209, 213; on Huiswoud, Otto, 185, 187–88; and ITUC-NW, 193–200; and Kouyaté, Tiemoko Garan, 210–13; and

Moore, Richard B., 136, 141, 150; as *Negro Worker* editor, 197; on Profintern, 192
Palmer, A. Mitchell, 83
Pan-African Congress, Fourth, 147–48
Pankhurst, Sylvia, 88
Patterson, Louise, 201, 224
Patterson, William, 143, 144, 157, 227, 240
Payton, Philip, 8
People's Educational Forum, 53–54, 83
Pepper, John: Comintern representative, 233; and Communist Party factionalism, 114–15, and Lovestone crisis, 176–77; and Moore, Richard B., 163–69; and Negro Commission (CP, 1928), 163–65; and Negro question, 157, 159–69
Perry, Jeffrey Babcock, 18, 48
Petioni, Charles, xviii
Petrovsky. *See* Goldfarb, Max
Phillips, Charles. *See* Gomez, Manuel
Phillips, Howell V., 143, 158–59
Pickens, William, 63, 65, 128, 146–47
Pogány, József. *See* Pepper, John
Pollitt, Harry, 172, 219
Potter, Thomas A., 53, 69, 78, 110
Powell, Rev. Adam Clayton, Jr., 244
Poyntz, Juliette Stuart, 172, 187
Price-Mars, Jean, 222
Profintern. *See* International Trade Union Committee of Negro Workers
Pushkin, Alexander, 108, 202
"Pushkin" (McKay), front matter, 147

Racamond, Julien, 211
Radek, Karl, 103, 106
Rampersad, Arnold, 131, 223
Randolph, A. Philip: background, 50; as candidate for public office, 51; and *Emancipator,* 78; and FBI, 82, 241; on Garvey, Marcus, 61; and *Messenger,* 49–50, 76; Pullman Porters, organized by, 137; as Rand School lecturer, 52; and Socialist Party, 50–53, 55, 58, 96
Rand School News, 24
Rand School of Social Science, 19–20, 24, 40, 44–45, 76–77
Razaf, Andy, 125–26
Red International of Labor Unions for Latin America, 22
Red Scare, 81–84
Red Summer of 1919, 54, 84
Reed, John, 97, 103
Reid, Ira, 38–39, 151

Reinstein, Boris, 97
Richman, Al, 163–65
Rivera, Diego, 243–44
Robinson, Robert, 148, 227, 264n81
Rogers, J. A.: xvii, 129, 194; background, 66–68; and FBI, 84–85; *From "Superman" to Man,* 66–67; Harlem Renaissance contributor, 68; on Harrison, Hubert, 14; migration to United States, 66, 71; and Moore, Richard B., 228
Romansky, Samuel M., 16
Roosevelt, Franklin D., 204
Rosemond, Henry, 136
Roumain, Jacques, 222, 223, 234
Roumain, Nicolle, 222, 223, 224
Rudd, Wyland, 202
Rutgers, Sebald Justinus: background, 21; and Comintern, 22; and *De Tribune,* 21–22; and First Comintern Congress, 97; and Huiswoud, Otto, 20, 22–23; and International Congress against Colonial Oppression and Imperialism, 145; and Katayama, Sen, 21; New York stay, 21–23; and Socialist Party Left Wing, 21–22, 72–74; and Socialist Propaganda League, 21
Ruthenberg, Charles E., 106–7, 114, 117–18, 134, 137–39

Safarov, Georgii I., 102
S. A. G. Cox's National Club, 34, 39
Sanhedrin, 111–14
Schomburg, Arturo, xvii, 90, 126
Schuyler, George S., 112, 113
Scottsboro Boys campaign, 195, 203, 204, 239
Sechaba, Tsepo, 295
Senghor, Lamine, 146, 210–11
Senghor, Leopold, 222
Shannon, David A., 46–47
Shaw, Matthew A. N., 113
Shiek, Andre, 157, 183
Shipman, Charles. *See* Gomez, Manuel
Sidney, Ioanthe, 7
Sixth World Comintern Congress. *See* Comintern
Smith, Homer, 148, 202, 227, 264n81
soapbox orators, 44
Socialist Party: activities of, 40–48; African American candidates for public office, 51, 53, 77, 86; African American members of, 53; and Comintern, 97; Harlem Branch of, 51–52; and Harrison, Hubert, 14, 16–19, 110; immigrants and, 41; on immigration, 46;

Left Wing of, 72, 73; on Negro question, 47, 76, 85, 110; on World War I, 47–48
Socialist Propaganda League, 21–22, 51–52, 72, 74
Solomon, Mark, 114, 115, 143, 152
South Africa, 205–9
Stachel, Jack, 172, 176
Stalin, Josef, 156, 171–76, 203, 243
Stevens, Hope, 226
Still, William Grant, 125, 222–23
Stokes, Rose Pastor: and Briggs, Cyril, 86–87, 95; Fourth Comintern Congress delegate, 101–5, 107, 111; and Harrison, Hubert, 88; and Huiswoud, Otto, 88, 105; and McKay, Claude, 88; and Negro question, 102, 103, 104
Stokowski, Leopold, 125
Sun Yat-sen, Madame, 145
Survey Graphic, 120, 126, 127–30
Sutton, John, 202
Swaback, Arne, 116

Theses on the National and Colonial Question (1920), 97–98
Theses on the Negro Question (1922), 102–4, 111; (1928), 159–62, 168–70
Third International. *See* Comintern
Thompson, Orlando M., 61
Thorne, A. A., 39
Thurman, Wallace, 28
Trade Union Educational League (TUEL), 111, 112, 114, 117, 141, 163, 175, 177, 178, 179
Trade Union Unity League (TUUL), 177, 182
Triangle Shirtwaist Factory fire, 45–46
Trotter, William Monroe, 113
Trotsky, Leon, 73, 171
Tulsa Riot, 93 96, 103, 104
Turner, W. Burghardt, 66
Tynes, George, 202

Ulianova, Maria, 200
Union des Travailleurs Nègres, 211
Union Intercoloniale, 210
Universal Negro Improvement Association (UNIA), 60–63, 89, 137
University of the Toilers of the East (KUTV), 142–44

van het Reve, Gerard J. M., 100, 107
Van Vecten, Carl, 203
SS *Vestris,* 164, 265n27
Vietnamese protests, 221
Voice of the Negro, 32, 49, 55

Walker, Margaret, 245
Walrond, Eric, 63
Ward, Arnold, 198
Warren, J. *See* Kotane, Moses
Washington, Booker T., 16, 63
Weigand, Kate, 231
Weinstone, William W.: 179; on Huiswoud, Otto, 183–84, 186; Lovestone crisis, 173, 177; and Moore, Richard B., 135; and Negro question, 184
Welcome, E. Touissant, 36
Welsh, Edward, 162; as candidate for public office, 140; elected to CEC, 171; and Harlem Tenants League, 178; and Lovestone crisis, 172, 173, 178
Weston, George A., 138, 139, 146, 228
White, Maude, 143
White, Walter, 53, 93
Whiteman, Olivia, 137
Wicks, Harry M., 173
Wijnkoop, David, 100
Williams, Clarence, 125
Williams, Harold, 163–65; and ANLC, 117–18, 165; and Comintern, 184–85; KUTV student, 143, and Lovestone crisis, 172, 173; and Negro question, 156, 159
Wilson, Woodrow, 55, 76, 83, 98
Wolfe, Bertram D., 158, 168, 173, 177
women's issues. *See* Communist Party USA
Woodson, Charles. *See* Huiswoud, Otto
Workers Party. *See* Communist Party USA
Wright, Ada, 204
Wright, Andrew, 205

Yamanouchi, Akito, 21
Young, George, 126

Zack, Joseph. *See* Kornfeder, Joseph Z.
Zinoviev, Gregori, 118
Zusmanovich, Alexander, 199

JOYCE MOORE TURNER is the coeditor of *Richard B. Moore, Caribbean Militant in Harlem: Collected Writings, 1920–1972.*

W. BURGHARDT TURNER is an emeritus professor of history at State University of New York at Stony Brook, coeditor of the book on Richard B. Moore, and the author of the introduction to the Black Classic Press edition of *The Negro* by W. E. B. Du Bois.

FRANKLIN W. KNIGHT is the Leonard and Helen R. Stulman Professor of History at Johns Hopkins University, past president of the Latin American Studies Association, and the president of the Historical Society (USA).

The University of Illinois Press
is a founding member of the
Association of American University Presses.

Composed in 10.5/13 Minion
with Minion & Meta display
by Celia Shapland
for the University of Illinois Press
Manufactured by Sheridan Books, Inc.

University of Illinois Press
1325 South Oak Street
Champaign, IL 61820-6903
www.press.uillinois.edu